# POSTWAR PLANS OF THE UNITED NATIONS

# POSTWAR PLANS OF THE
# UNITED NATIONS

*By*
LEWIS L. LORWIN

*New York*
THE TWENTIETH CENTURY FUND
1943

*First published November 1943*
*Reprinted February 1944*

MANUFACTURED IN THE UNITED STATES OF AMERICA

# FOREWORD

THE TWENTIETH CENTURY FUND offers this survey of the domestic postwar plans of the United Nations as part of a systematic effort to inform the public about the problems we shall have to face when the war is over, and about the plans which are already being made to solve those problems.

The Fund has already published two editions of a directory of national agencies, both government and private, in the United States which are engaged in research and education in the field of postwar problems (*Postwar Planning in the United States*) and a study and discussion manual entitled *Wartime Facts and Postwar Problems* which briefly states the probable postwar problems in each major field of American economic life in the light of wartime developments in our economy. A major research project to estimate the probable postwar needs and resources of the United States is being carried out under the direction of the Fund's Economist, Dr. J. Frederic Dewhurst. The Fund has also commissioned Stuart Chase to write a series of six popular reports of which three have already been published, to give the public a vivid word picture of profound forces for change which, let loose in the years before the war, are being given new force and directions under the stress of the conflict, and to suggest how their consequences may be dealt with when the war is over.

This volume of Dr. Lorwin's extends the canvas of the Fund's reports beyond our own borders to include the problems and plans of all the United Nations. It is offered to the public, as have been the other Fund publications in this field, with the conviction that the more clearly our goals for the peace are defined, the greater will be the vigor with which we carry on the war—and the more likely we are to avoid the terrible disasters that came upon us in the years that followed World War I.

The Fund is grateful to Dr. Lorwin for the thoroughness and the dispatch with which he has covered this assignment and to those who assisted him in his task.

EVANS CLARK, *Executive Director*
*The Twentieth Century Fund*

330 WEST 42D STREET
NEW YORK 18, NEW YORK
SEPTEMBER 1943

v

# AUTHOR'S PREFACE

MUCH HAS BEEN WRITTEN in the past two or three years on the political and economic aims of the Axis Powers. Many recent books deal with National Socialism, Italian Fascism, Japan's "Co-Prosperity Sphere," and with the "New Order" which they propose to establish in Europe, Africa, Asia, and in other parts of the world. These volumes have clarified for the American people the threat to freedom and peace inherent in totalitarian doctrines and schemes.

On the other hand, writings on the purposes and plans of the United Nations with regard to the postwar world are scanty and spotty. There is no single volume today which gives a general picture of the way in which the members of the United Nations plan to organize their own countries after the war and to co-ordinate their national policies for purposes of international co-operation.

This volume attempts to fill the gap, at least with regard to their domestic plans. It describes the proposals and programs for national or domestic postwar reconstruction which have been formulated by governments and government officials, by organized economic groups —employers' associations, chambers of commerce, trade unions, etc.—and by various social groups in the different countries. So far as possible, it presents the economic and social conditions which influence the making of such plans in each country.

The present volume is a factual and objective survey. The task has been to describe and explain, not to judge or evaluate programs.

The writer has been greatly helped by the co-operation of many organizations and agencies in this country—public and private, American and foreign—which are concerned with postwar planning. These agencies have kindly supplied their publications as well as unpublished material and have freely given information at their disposal. As far as possible, references are made to these materials in the footnotes to the text. The writer is under special obligation to the National Resources Planning Board for permission to use the materials of its reports and to reprint the table in Chapter 7. It is understood, of course, that none of these agencies is responsible for the use made of the data supplied or of their interpretation in the text.

This study could be completed as planned only owing to the co-operative attitude of the National Resources Planning Board which extended to the writer the opportunity of taking leave from his official duties, thus enabling him to find the time necessary for the task. The preparation of this study is, however, entirely independent of the work of the Board itself and of his work for the Board.

A large part of the materials used in this study was collected with the help of Theodore A. Sumberg. It is a pleasure to acknowledge here his good judgment and research capacities and the co-operative spirit in which he rendered assistance.

This study was undertaken in the hope that it would help the cause of the United Nations. This hope is based on the belief that a clearer view of the domestic plans and programs of the members of the United Nations is essential for a postwar settlement on the basis of common aims and ideas. Nothing can be gained by slurring over differences of views, interests, and policies. Frank and open discussion may ruffle the surface for a while, but, in the end, it should smooth the waters for those seeking larger and safer harbors.

LEWIS L. LORWIN

WASHINGTON, D. C.
SEPTEMBER 21, 1943

# CONTENTS

*Chapter 1*

# THE UNITED NATIONS AND POSTWAR PLANNING

THIRTY-TWO NATIONS in all parts of the world stand united today in the struggle against Germany, Italy, and Japan, pledged to employ all their resources, military and economic, until complete victory is achieved. They are the United Nations, forged in the crucible of war against the aggression of the Axis Powers.

The United Nations came into being on January 1, 1942, when twenty-six nations jointly subscribed to the purposes and principles of the Atlantic Charter. These twenty-six nations were the United States of America, Canada, Costa Rica, Cuba, the Dominican Republic, El Salvador, Guatemala, Haiti, Honduras, Nicaragua, and Panama on the American continent; the United Kingdom of Great Britain and Northern Ireland, Belgium, Czechoslovakia, Greece, Luxembourg, the Netherlands, Norway, Poland, and Yugoslavia in western, central, and eastern Europe; the Union of Soviet Socialist Republics, China, India, South Africa, Australia, and New Zealand. Mexico, Brazil, and several other countries gave their adherence somewhat later.

The thirty-two members of the United Nations differ widely in area and population, in economic resources and wealth, as shown in the accompanying table. They differ in social organization, and political status. They speak different languages. They have diverse backgrounds, traditions, and international connections. Some are large and powerful, others are small and weak. Furthermore, they are differently situated with regard to the conduct of the war. The Soviet Union is at war with Germany, but not with Japan. Great Britain has declared war on Finland, while the United States has not. Some of the countries have been overrun and occupied by the German, Italian or Japanese armies. Others are involved in military operations only to a limited degree, if at all. These differences may give rise to difficulties and friction but they need not be an obstacle to unity in so far as they make the different countries supplementary to one another and are subordinated to a common purpose.

Despite differences, the United Nations are bound together by the desire to win the war and by the hope of winning the peace.

| Country | Area in Square Kilometers | Population at End of 1939 | National Income per Head of the Working Population[a] 1925–1934 in dollars of equal purchasing power | Exports 1938, in Old U. S. Gold Dollars | Imports 1938, in Old U. S. Gold Dollars |
|---|---|---|---|---|---|
| | *(In Thousands)* | | | *(In Millions)* | |
| UNITED NATIONS | | | | | |
| Australia............... | 7,704 | 6,997 | $980 | $306.6 | $302.1 |
| Belgium[b]............. | 30 | 8,396 | 600 | 429.2 | 452.8 |
| Bolivia................ | 1,090 | 3,400 | — | 20.3 | 14.7 |
| Brazil................. | 8,511 | 40,900 | 400–500 | 176.0 | 174.8 |
| Canada................ | 9,569 | 11,368 | 1,337 | 561.7 | 398.6 |
| China[c]............... | 11,103 | 450,000 | 100–120 | 191.7 | 355.9 |
| Costa Rica............ | 50 | 639 | — | 6.0 | 7.5 |
| Cuba.................. | 114 | 4,253 | — | 84.2 | 62.6 |
| Czechoslovakia[d]....... | 140 | 15,239 | 455 | 209.0 | 171.9 |
| Dominican Republic..... | 50 | 1,650 | — | 8.5 | 6.6 |
| El Salvador............ | 34 | 1,745 | — | 6.5 | 5.4 |
| Ethiopia............... | 900 | 5,500 | — | — | — |
| Greece................ | 130 | 7,201 | 397 | 53.2 | 78.1 |
| Guatemala............. | 110 | 3,260 | — | 9.7 | 12.4 |
| Haiti.................. | 26 | 2,600 | — | 4.1 | 4.5 |
| Honduras.............. | 154 | 1,090 | — | 4.8 | 6.1 |
| India[e]................ | 4,079 | 382,000 | 200 | 350.4 | 325.1 |
| Iraq.................. | 302 | 3,700 | — | 10.6 | 26.9 |
| Luxembourg............ | 2.6 | 301 | — | — | — |
| Mexico................ | 1,969 | 19,380 | 360 | 110.9 | 64.8 |
| Netherlands............ | 33 | 8,834 | 855 | 337.4 | 459.7 |
| New Zealand........... | 268 | 1,642 | 1,202 | 131.6 | 127.0 |
| Nicaragua............. | 128 | 883 | — | 3.5 | 3.0 |
| Norway............... | 323 | 2,937 | 539 | 112.0 | 171.1 |
| Panama............... | 75 | 570 | — | 2.2 | 10.4 |
| Philippine Islands....... | 296 | 16,300 | 375 | 67.3 | 77.2 |
| Poland[f].............. | 389 | 35,090 | 352 | 132.9 | 145.9 |
| Union of South Africa...... | 1,222 | 10,251 | 276 | 289.0 | 287.4 |
| Union of Soviet Socialist Republics[g]............. | 21,176 | 172,000 | 320 | 148.4 | 158.5 |
| United Kingdom.......... | 244 | 47,735 | 1,069 | 1,358.6 | 2,478.1 |
| United States............ | 7,839 | 131,416 | 1,381 | 1,805.6 | 1,151.4 |
| Yugoslavia.............. | 248 | 15,703 | 330 | 68.6 | 67.4 |

Sources: *Statistical Year Book of the League of Nations*, 1940–1941, and Colin Clark, *The Conditions of Economic Progress*, 1940.

    a. For a few countries, not all the years from 1925 through 1934 were included.

    b. National income and foreign trade include Luxembourg.

    c. Including Manchuria, Outer Mongolia, and Tibet.

    d. Population is for end of 1937.

    e. Population and trade include Indian States; income is for British India alone.

    f. Population is for end of 1938.

    g. Area as of 1938.   The income is for 1934 only.

| Country | Area in Square Kilometers | Population at End of 1939 | National Income per Head of the Working Population[a] 1925–1934 in dollars of equal purchasing power | Exports 1938, in Old U. S. Gold Dollars | Imports 1938, in Old U. S. Gold Dollars |
|---|---|---|---|---|---|
| | (In Thousands) | | | (In Millions) | |
| ASSOCIATED NATIONS | | | | | |
| Chile...................... | 742 | 4,940 | 500–600 | 82.1 | 60.7 |
| Colombia................. | 1,139 | 8,986 | — | 55.7 | 52.6 |
| Ecuador.................. | 455 | 3,000 | — | 7.0 | 6.2 |
| Egypt..................... | 1,000 | 16,680 | 300–350 | 84.6 | 106.0 |
| Iceland................... | 103 | 120 | — | 7.5 | 6.4 |
| Iran...................... | 1,643 | 15,000 | — | 83.1 | 50.1 |
| Liberia................... | 120 | 2,500 | — | — | — |
| Paraguay................. | 397 | 970 | — | 5.3 | 5.7 |
| Peru...................... | 1,249 | 7,000 | — | 44.9 | 35.1 |
| Uruguay.................. | 187 | 2,147 | 650 | 36.6 | 36.4 |
| Venezuela................ | 912 | 3,650 | — | 161.4 | 57.6 |

That is the significance of their adherence to the Atlantic Charter. For the Charter, even if it be regarded as provisional in character, lays down the principles on which the United Nations can develop co-operative action to maintain a lasting peace and to promote economic prosperity throughout the world after the war.

The United Nations are agreed that in the postwar world they must endeavor to secure improved labor standards, economic advancement, and social security for all by the fullest collaboration between nations in the economic field, by guaranteeing all states access on equal terms to the trade and raw materials of the world, and by other means. To the extent to which these goals depend on international co-operation, they can be achieved only if appropriate forms of organization and effective methods of international collaboration are devised and put into effect. Many specific questions arise such as the form and powers of international and regional associations, the maintenance of order by means of an "international police" or otherwise, the conduct of international trade, methods of exchange stability, and so on.

These questions call for much thought and negotiation, and are the subject matter of what may be called "international postwar planning" by members of the United Nations. Many proposals and plans for the solution of these problems are now under discussion. They form an important phase of the preparations by the United Nations for the peace and the postwar world. However, they are outside the scope of the present study.

The goal of the United Nations to achieve "security and economic advancement for all" has another, purely national, aspect. It would obviously be impossible to obtain the objectives of the Atlantic Charter by international means if each country or a number of countries followed policies at home having opposite purposes and aims. The international obligations and promises of the United Nations imply that each nation will pursue *national* policies which have the same objectives of improved labor standards, economic advancement, and social security. Each member is faced with the problem of formulating in advance the economic and social policies which it hopes and intends to pursue within its own borders at the end of the war, in harmony with the common goals of the other United Nations. It is with such national postwar planning that this study is concerned.

This national aspect of postwar planning has been coming into fuller view gradually. Soon after the outbreak of the war, there was some discussion in a few countries of the United Nations concerning the social and economic order which was to emerge after the war. This was stimulated by the very difficulties in which these countries found themselves. It was during the agonizing months of 1940 that the first public discussion of postwar aims and purposes took place in Great Britain. At the time when England stood almost alone against the threat of the Nazi armies, this discussion helped the British people to muster the spiritual energies for the struggle.

As the war proceeded and the outlook became more favorable for the United Nations, the need to prepare for the period following the end of hostilities became increasingly recognized. From being merely an expression of ideas on the part of some groups of the population, postwar planning became a function of governments. Official committees and commissions were set up for the purpose in a number of countries, and technical studies were begun on a large scale. During 1941–1942, postwar planning became part of the conduct of the war and of preparations for the peace to follow.

During the past six months, postwar planning has emerged from the stage of mere discussion into that of practical consideration by the public authorities in all the different countries of the United Nations. In the first half of 1943, general principles and specific proposals and legislative measures were elaborated and debated in the British Parliament, in the Congress of the United States, in the Parliaments of Australia, Canada, and New Zealand, in the provisional consultative bodies of the governments-in-exile, in the government councils of Mexico, Brazil, and other Latin American countries, as well as in the political and legislative bodies of India and China. More than that, legislation has already been passed in some countries dealing with special postwar problems such as demobilization, repatriation, social insurance, and housing.

The separate countries of the United Nations are now shaping the outlines of their postwar national economic and social systems. How far this process is advanced before the end of the war will be an important factor in the transition from war to peace, and will determine the rapidity and surety with which postwar policies may be put into effect.

The postwar planning of the members of the United Nations raises three questions which are of basic importance for the future peace and welfare of the world. (1) To what extent are the separate national plans now under discussion in accord with the social and economic goals for which the war is being fought? (2) Are these plans and policies likely to facilitate international collaboration by the United Nations? (3) How and by what means can the national plans in the separate countries be brought into greater harmony with one another and with policies for international co-operation?

These questions can be answered only on the basis of a more complete knowledge of the facts. It is necessary to have a clear picture of the national plans in the different countries, of the problems which they are expected to meet, and of the factors which determine the choice of policies and measures. It is further necessary to analyze the possible interaction of the proposed national programs and the repercussions which they are likely to have internationally.

This study is designed to supply some of these facts. It describes the postwar plans now under discussion in most countries of the United Nations, in the light of their economic and social backgrounds so as to make clear how each nation or country intends, or would like, to reorganize its social and economic life after the war. In so far as most countries depend on exports, this involves a consideration also of their proposed export, migration and investment policies. But it is not part of this study to examine international policies as such, e.g., proposals for monetary stabilization, international banks, and the like.

The terms "postwar planning" and "postwar plans" are used here rather broadly, in accordance with the different meanings which they have in different countries. In its broadest usage, planning means simply the preparation of policies and programs in advance to meet expected postwar situations and concrete problems.

In the United States and Canada, the term planning is most often used to designate the effort to correlate national economic and social policies in a way consistent with general national purposes. Some of these policies involve public controls and government guidance, but the emphasis is not so much on government intervention as on the need for the co-operative action of all economic groups and government for common aims.

In other countries, such as New Zealand, planning involves the control of the state over certain strategic sectors of the economy, such as the banks and foreign trade. This is combined, however, with the individual initiative and activities of private enterprise. Planning is conceived largely as a method of economic regulation and social control by the government in the interest of integrated national development.

In the Soviet Union, the word "planning" is used to designate the processes of organizing and operating a collectivist economic system on the basis of a unified state budget, under the direction of the government and of its agencies. Planning then involves government management of a completely co-ordinated economy and social system, and is equivalent to "planned economy."

In still other countries, e.g., Czechoslovakia, planning refers to a combination of several types of economic control. Also different meanings are attached to the term in the same country by different groups of the people. These variations will be brought out in the consideration of the national plans of the individual countries of the United Nations.

The ways in which postwar plans are being prepared in the several countries of the United Nations differ widely. In some, the only plans which have practical importance are those advanced by the government. In most countries, however, private social groups and economic organizations are actively engaged in preparing for the postwar world. Planning by unofficial groups is important in so far as it supplements, and often shapes, the plans and policies of the government. It is also significant as an expression of democratic processes of discussion. It is for these reasons that this study is not confined to government proposals.

In most countries of the United Nations, the war has stirred men's minds to a re-examination of all basic values and social institutions.

Whether the war is regarded as a struggle for the preservation of traditional ways of life or as a necessary, if painful, step in a world-wide economic and social revolution, it is accepted as a challenge to rethink and restate the issues. For even those who wish to maintain the status quo after the war must plan to meet the forces which threaten it and must find ways of giving new strength to old forms.

So the postwar plans of the United Nations have a wide range. Not only questions of economic and social policy, but of political organization, education, religion, administrative procedures and the like are being raised. Some of the countries are elaborating proposals which aim to reorganize their entire system of life.

This study is aimed to give as clear a picture as possible of this large and manifold process. It is not necessary, however, to cover all phases of planning in each country or to catalogue all proposals made by government and private groups. On the contrary, both the scope of planning in each country and its individual features can best be brought out by selecting basic issues and plans and at the same time viewing them in the light of the general development of the country.

In looking forward to life after the war, the thirty-two members of the United Nations are moved by national hopes and aspirations. But past experience and the events of the war prove forcibly that the reasonable aspirations of each nation depend for their fulfillment on the capacity of the United Nations to act together. It is also evident that united action can not be entirely spontaneous, but must be planned and organized.

In preparing for this community of purpose and action after the war, the countries of the United Nations must know each other's problems and each other's hopes and plans for the future. This knowledge is essential to smooth out differences in their points of view, to promote mutual tolerance and respect, and to pave the way for better understanding. It is hoped that this study may add to such knowledge and help to clarify and unify the preparations of the United Nations for the world after the war.

## Chapter 2

# PLANS OF ECONOMIC AND SOCIAL GROUPS IN THE UNITED STATES

A SURVEY issued this year[1] lists 137 agencies and groups, private and public, in the United States engaged in "postwar planning." These agencies and groups differ widely in aims, scope, and methods of operating. Postwar planning means different things to them and a listing of their plans gives no picture of an orderly preparation for a well-defined task.

However, an inner logic in this planning may be made clear by a proper method of classification. To begin with, the various planning activities in the United States fall under the two large headings of national and international planning. Many of the private groups and some of the public agencies actively concerned with postwar policy are interested entirely or primarily either in the adjustment of relations among nations, such as the fixing of frontiers, the repatriation of refugees, or in the setting up of international mechanisms, political and economic, for the maintenance of peace. Such agencies pay only incidental attention, if any, to domestic problems or to the relations between domestic and international policies. Their work and plans are outside the scope of this study.

The activities of the groups which deal with national postwar problems can be conveniently considered under five subheadings. First are the plans and proposals, numerous enough, advanced by individuals, either as specific schemes or in the form of general programs and "panaceas." While some of these plans may exercise influence on public policy, they do not come within our purview here.

Second are the plans and programs of organized economic groups. In general, they are formulations of demands and policies which are regarded as essential to the prosecution of the social-economic interests of the respective groups. It is the assumption of such plans that the interests of the group coincide with the general public welfare, but the point of departure is the group interest. The groups whose plans will be considered here include the farmers, business and labor.

Third are the more general plans of mixed social groups which aim to find and express the national point of view and a national program.

1. *Postwar Planning in the United States: An Organization Directory*, 2, The Twentieth Century Fund, New York, 1943.

8

These groups include the churches, political parties, and some private research and educational associations.

Fourth are the specific, and largely technical, plans of government departments and agencies affecting a limited field of economic and social life. Almost all government departments in Washington now have, under one name or another, postwar planning sections which deal with the problems likely to arise at the end of the war. These sections are studying problems of demobilization, reconversion of industry to a peace basis, occupational outlooks, agricultural policies, fiscal problems, housing, social security, etc., and are elaborating specific proposals which may become the basis of public policy and legislation.

Fifth are the studies and research of those government agencies whose function it is to combine special technical proposals into a co-ordinated program which may serve as a basis of a general national policy.

It is impossible, within the limits of the present study, to survey in detail the large amount of work which has been done by the many public and private agencies on the various aspects of postwar reorganization. In this and in the following chapter the most significant parts of that work are summarized so as to indicate its general trend and significance for national postwar development. The studies and proposals of the government departments are considered in Chapter 3. In this chapter, only the programs of the several private groups are examined. But to avoid repetition, the planning work of the United States Department of Agriculture is described in this chapter together with, and in the light of, the programs of the farmers' organizations.

### 1. AGRICULTURAL PLANNING AND FARMERS' PROGRAMS

It was widely recognized, on the eve of the present war, that the condition of large groups of American farmers was unsatisfactory and that American agriculture in general was facing difficult and complex problems. Commercial farmers had large surplus stocks of wheat, feed grains, tobacco and cotton which could not be disposed of in domestic or foreign markets, and which tended to depress prices and farm incomes below what was regarded as a satisfactory level.[2] The "sur-

2. A satisfactory level of prices and incomes has become identified with the idea of a "parity level." Income parity has been defined as "that per capita net income of individuals on farms from farming operations that bears to the per capita net income of individuals not on farms the same relation as prevailed during the period August 1909, to July 1914." Price parity is such a ratio of prices received by farmers and prices paid by them which is equal to the ratio as it was between 1909 and 1914. See Oris V. Wells, "Planning and Agricultural Adjustment," George B. Galloway (editor), *Planning for America*, 1941, p. 234.

pluses" were due to an uneconomic use of land, to low consumption levels of the American people, to shrinking foreign markets, and other causes.

The outlook for enlarging the markets for agricultural products either at home or abroad was not encouraging. Surplus stocks were accompanied by "surplus acres" and "surplus farmers," as millions of acres of good agricultural land and at least one fourth of the agricultural population were underemployed or suffered from "concealed unemployment." On the other hand, in many parts of the country, e.g., the Southern Appalachians, the Great Plains, over large sections of the Cotton Belt, farm population had outrun resources and was being forced to seek a livelihood elsewhere, thus giving rise to the problem of the "migratory worker."

Farm tenancy was everywhere on the increase and was resulting in the steady enlargement of a class of permanently landless agricultural tenants and laborers. The proportion of low-income groups among the farming population was large. Many farm families were in a state of poverty and dependent on some form of direct relief to eke out a meager living. Housing, sanitary and health conditions, and educational opportunities in many farming communities were far below those in the cities and below minimum standards of decency.[3]

By 1939, American agricultural policy, after fifteen years of agitation, had reached the end of a cycle. American farmers were settling down to a definite way of looking at their problems and of adjusting to them. In 1937–1938, legislation was passed which was destined to determine the entire course and conditions of farming in the United States, and agencies were set up to help the farmers in using the new laws to their benefit. The Agricultural Adjustment Act, passed in 1938, provided for soil conservation, good farm management, and balanced output; for storage loans to producers of wheat, corn, cotton, tobacco and rice; for crop insurance; for parity payments to

3. For a summary of the economic position of the 6 million odd farms in the United States as revealed by the Census of 1940, see *Report of the Secretary of Agriculture*, 1941, pp. 160–166. A few striking figures may be cited here: Between 1900 and 1935, the number of large farms of 500 acres or more increased 67 per cent. About 90 per cent of the total commercial farm output was produced by about 50 per cent of all the farms in the United States. Owing to technical and managerial changes, the number of workers required for farm production declined from 12 to 10 million between 1909 and 1939. In 1936, 1.7 million farm families had an average annual income of less than $500, and half of these families had an average annual income of $250. In the period 1930–1940, almost 1.7 million mortgaged farm businesses failed. In 1937, farm migrants aggregated about one million individuals and families. More than one million farm families live in slum houses.

increase the income of producers; and for the diversion of agricultural surpluses into domestic and foreign channels.[4]

While this Act was intended primarily to help commercial farmers, the Bankhead-Jones Farm Tenant Act of 1937 was designed to aid tenant farmers by advancing loans to them to purchase small farms on a long-term mortgage basis. Small-scale and subsistence farmers were helped by special grants and subsidies, by conservation policies, by improvements of technical operations, and by subsidiary rural industries. At the same time, it was proposed to help all farmers by raising nutritional standards, by stabilizing industrial employment, and by regularizing foreign markets for American farm products through international commodity agreements and in other ways.

These aims and policies, endorsed by the farmers' organizations, became the "farmers' program," which gave direction to planning for agriculture. In the fall of 1938, the Bureau of Agricultural Economics in the Department of Agriculture was made the central planning agency for the Department. So that planning might be effective and as democratic as possible, the Department of Agriculture made an agreement with the state agricultural colleges to carry on state and county planning co-operatively. Steps were taken to draw farmers into the process by organizing county and state committees through which the farmers could formulate their ideas and suggestions, discuss proposals, and reach agreement on policy. Within the Department of Agriculture, interbureau co-ordinating committees were set up to consider the recommendations of farmers, experts, and administrators and to make suggestions to the Agricultural Program Board of the Department. This Board was made up of the Secretary of Agriculture and bureau chiefs of the Department.

The effects of the Second World War so far have been to remove or soften some of the problems with which American agriculture struggled before 1939. The needs of the United Nations, the operations of Lend-Lease, and the increasing consumption of the American Armed Forces and of the people since 1939, and especially since December 7, 1941, have diminished surpluses in grains, cotton, and tobacco, and have created shortages in dairy and animal products,

4. The agencies which were to carry out these policies, either as part of the Agricultural Adjustment Administration or in co-operation with it, are the Soil Conservation Service, the Federal Surplus Commodities Corporation, the Federal Crop Insurance Corporation, the Farm Credit Agency, the Farm Security Administration, etc. See *Farmers in a Changing World*, U. S. Department of Agriculture, 1940, pp. 23–24.

fats and oils, vegetables and fruits. Under the "Food for Freedom" drive and the lure of higher prices, American farmers are now engaged in expanding output in products other than grains and cotton. Higher prices have increased cash incomes of farmers, especially of some groups of farmers. Total net farm income in 1942 was over $10 billion, larger than in any previous year. Though there are still many farm families in need of help, the general situation is greatly improved. The problems which vex the farmer today are those of a wartime economy—higher costs, labor shortages, priorities, shipping difficulties, and the like.

American farmers are aware, however, that the war cannot solve the underlying problems with which they have been faced for two decades. They remember the experience of the First World War, when they were catapulted from the height of war prosperity into the abyss of postwar distress. The problems arising out of the Second World War may differ from those of 1919–1920, but they are likely to be difficult in their own way.

Today, in contrast to 1919–1920, the farmers are trying to anticipate these problems and to make some preparations for answering them. They are also relying on the Department of Agriculture to assist them in studying the possible consequences of the war on agriculture and in finding ways for adjusting to the postwar situation. An examination of the proposals of the farmers themselves through their organizations and of the work of the Department of Agriculture indicates the lines along which postwar American agricultural policy is being shaped.

### a. PROGRAMS OF FARMERS' ORGANIZATIONS

There are three outstanding national organizations of farmers in the United States: The National Grange, the American Farm Bureau Federation, and the National Farmers' Union.[5] Together these three organizations have a membership of several million[6] and claim to represent the majority of the farmers of the country.

5. This short name is generally used instead of the rather long full name—National Farmers' Educational and Cooperative Union of America.

6. The Grange—the oldest of the three organizations—claimed in 1939, 800,000 dues-paying members in 8,000 local Granges. Its main strength at present is in New England (known as "the Gibraltar of the Order" with a membership of 150,000), New York, Pennsylvania, New Jersey, and Ohio. Over one third of the membership of the Grange is composed of women and of boys and girls over fourteen years of age. The American Farm Bureau Federation had in 1940 some forty state Farm Bureaus and a membership of 400,000, a majority of whom live in the Corn Belt. In 1939, its total income was over $253,000. The

Some rivalry exists among the three organizations, and also differences of opinion due in part to differences in the economic and social position of their membership. The Grange is dominated by middle-class farmers of the East and Middle West. The Farm Bureau Federation has a strong element of members with larger-sized farms. The Farmers' Union is more under the influence of low-income farmers, share-croppers and tenants. On some points, however, these organizations are agreed. Both the points of agreement and of difference may be brought out by summarizing briefly the postwar programs of the three organizations.

## (1). *Program of the National Grange*

According to its leaders, "the soul of the Grange is its ritualistic side, and its emphasis is on moral and spiritual ideals."[7] These are not seriously affected by the war; neither is the social-economic program of the Grange which is based on these ideals. The Grange claims to stand for self-help and equality of opportunity, for "fair treatment rather than special privilege," and for "economic justice rather than subsidy." On the basis of these principles, it wants to give American agriculture a "fair share of the national income" through more efficient production, higher prices, better distribution based on co-operative marketing methods, low interest rates and credit, new uses for farm products, lower taxes, and agricultural education.

The tenor of Grange declarations is against government centralization, large public expenditures for relief, and government interference in business. It regards the Agricultural Adjustment Act merely as a temporary measure to tide over the farmer until he can secure his proper place in the market by his own efforts. At the same time, the Grange opposes "monopolistic practices" which "rob the people of the fruits of their toil," and favors "more adequate enforcement of the anti-trust laws." While endorsing "the inherent right of labor to strike," it would make labor unions more "responsible" and would give agriculture exemptions under the Wage-Hour Act and similar social legislation.

---

National Farmers' Union claims to represent 100,000 farm families in forty states. Its co-operative associations for buying and selling have a membership of about 300,000 farmers and do a business running into large sums. The Farmers' Union Grain Terminal Association of St. Paul is one of the largest grain marketing co-operatives in the world. For a survey of these organizations see DeWitt C. Wing, "Trends in National Farm Organizations," *Farmers in a Changing World*, pp. 941–979.

7. *Farmers in a Changing World*, p. 950.

Especially important for international economic relations are the demands of the Grange to "give the American farmer the American market to the limit of his ability to supply it," and its disapproval of the Reciprocal Trade Agreements program on the ground that it depresses farm prices "by encouraging imports of competitive products from countries where sub-standard labor conditions prevail." To protect "American interests" and the "system of free enterprise," the Grange favors the levying of excise taxes on all imports on the dutiable list when the landed cost of such goods falls below the American wholesale selling price, provided the commodities are commercially available in the United States. The Grange would create a nonpartisan board, responsible to Congress and representing both producing and consuming interests, with power to regulate imports. "Regulation" in this case means largely restriction. The Grange seemingly has no objections to an expansion of agricultural exports, and is in favor of completing the St. Lawrence Seaway project which has value chiefly for overseas trade.

In the field of wider national policies, the Grange favors continued private ownership and operation of the railroads, more highway construction, rural electrification with government help, a "sound program for the relief of tenancy," voluntary group health insurance as against "state medicine," the registration of all immigrants and the deportation of those who refuse to become naturalized "within a reasonable length of time," and the "taking the profits out of war."

Since December 7, 1941, the Grange has been mainly concerned with wartime problems as affecting the farmer. Its position on agricultural policy after the war is to continue along traditional lines.

## (2). *Program of the Farm Bureau Federation*

The Farm Bureau Federation emphasizes more than the Grange the business interests of farming. It regards the Agricultural Adjustment Act, with its companion measures covering soil conservation and price stabilization by means of commodity loans, as the "incomparable" American national farm program. At the same time, the Federation wants the law to be administered strictly and narrowly, partly because of its opposition to "bureaucracy" and to governmental agencies which presumably compete with the farmers' organizations, partly because it prefers to rely on government aid only when markets are discouraging and to take advantage of market conditions when they are favorable to the farmers. In 1943, the Federation, together with other farm organizations, declared strongly against "the use of subsidies in lieu of a fair return in the market place." According to the Federation, "for the first time in twenty years, normal adjustments in the national economy, if permitted to function, would put the farmer on an equal basis with American labor and industry."[8]

More emphatically than the Grange, the Farm Bureau Federation voices opposition to the Farm Security Administration which the Federation accuses of "experimentation in collective farming and other socialistic land policies" and of "persistent attempts to foster under the guise of supporting the war effort far-reaching social controls over farmers and farm laborers." Similarly, the Federation denounces what it regards as "alarming trends" towards the growth of the powers of the executive branch of the government; the growth of government bureaus and "red tape"; labor "abuses" such as the closed shop, and jurisdictional strikes.

In brief, the Federation sees the farmers' problems after the war as not very different from those before 1939. Its main emphasis in this respect is that the war should not result in inflation and in a tax burden which would affect farmers unfavorably. It also advocates greater participation of Congress in the preparations for the postwar situation. The resolution on "Post-War Planning" adopted at its convention in December 1942,[9] reads as follows:

The end of the present military struggle will bring us to the immediate and pressing question of return to a peacetime economy. The fullest participation of the people should be sought in preparing to meet this problem. Citizens generally are increasingly concerned over the many departments and bureaus in Washington that are giving attention to this matter, and they fear that it will result in conflicting views and recommendations which will retard rather than speed sound decision and action. We recommend that the Congress give immediate review and study of all efforts now being made in this direction and take action for their elimination or coordination under an authority set up by Congress and responsible to the Congress, the representatives of the people.

We recommend that the American Farm Bureau Federation, in cooperation with other farm groups, provide for an independent study, and thus be prepared to make recommendation to such Congressional authority.

8. Press release dated January 28, 1943, by the National Grange, the American Farm Bureau Federation, and the National Council of Farmer Cooperatives. See also American Farm Bureau Federation, *Resolutions Adopted at 24th Annual Convention, December 10, 1942.*

9. American Farm Bureau Federation, *op. cit.*, p. 12 .

## (3). *Program of the National Farmers' Union*

In contrast to the declarations of the Grange and of the Farm Bureau Federation, those of the National Farmers' Union sound a call for social change. The Union's 1943 program starts with a statement which reads:

> The world of yesterday is gone. A new world is being shaped in the course of the present conflict, long predicted as the inevitable end of the cruel and outmoded system based upon unbridled exploitation. That new world, the People's Century, can be born alive or dead. It will be born alive, in victory, freedom, and hope, if we prove ourselves worthy of the new free world we seek.[10]

The "new world" after the war which the Union envisages is to be based, as far as agriculture is concerned, on "the security of farm families operating their own land." The working farmer must be protected, during the war and after, against the encroachments of the industrialized or factory-type farm. There must be full use, now and after the war, of our land and machines to cover rural America with sturdy farm families operating their own family-type farms. The Congress of the United States should declare that "the national policy is to maintain the family-type farm as the pattern of American farming."

The working farmer can be made secure by the maintenance of "a parity floor for farm products," by interest rates which do not exceed the cost of administering credit, by conservation policies which conserve not only natural resources but also human beings, by sound crop insurance,[11] a graduated land tax, a "fair" income tax, and by the extension of co-operative practices in the field of distribution and in the use of costly farm machinery. The farmers should be given full opportunity to organize and to form co-operative associations which are "the engine of economic democracy." The farmers' co-operatives must not be weakened in the war economy so that they may play a significant part after the war. For this reason, the government should refrain from invading, through the Commodity Credit Corporation, the field of warehousing, marketing, or processing of farm products. On the other hand, the Union favors strongly the Farm Security Ad-

---

10. *National Farmers' Union, 1943 Program. Adopted by the Delegates to the 38th Annual Convention at Oklahoma City, November 19, 1942,* p. 3.

11. The Union demands that crop insurance be extended to corn, flaxseed, and other commodities, that the premium structure be rationalized, that the top 75 per cent of loss be covered, and that the expense of administration be carried by the federal government.

ministration, which it wishes "to save" from attacks by "spokesmen for commercialized and factory-type farming."

The Union is friendly towards organized labor. It demands the extension of social security "to every group of our people, including farmers and farm workers." It is in favor of anti-poll-tax laws.

The Union stresses the point that "post-war and wartime planning are inseparable." It demands a place for "working farmers" on all government wartime boards. Likewise, it wants "organized working farmers and organized workers" to have "their responsible representatives at the peace table."

### b. GOVERNMENT PLANNING FOR AGRICULTURE

The farmers' programs have influenced Congressional legislation and the activities of the executive branch of the federal government— in this case the Department of Agriculture. The latter, on the other hand, aims to reconcile the farmers' demands with general national policy. This purpose is the basis of the work of the Department which is usually referred to as "agricultural planning." It has been developed since 1938 under the provisions of the Agricultural Adjustment Act, and since 1941 in response to the war situation.

The Department aims to carry on its postwar planning work in a democratic way and to combine regional decentralization with central guidance. The farmers are drawn into this work through community, county and state agricultural planning committees which meet to discuss local and national farm problems and which pass on their suggestions and proposals to the planning sections of the Department. Some 10,000 community committees are now taking part in this work in about 2,000 counties in forty-seven states. About 140,000 members are on these committees, of whom about 122,000 are farm men and women and 18,000 are representatives of the Department and of local and state government agencies.[12]

These committees are aided in their work by the Committee on Post-War Programs of the Department which supplies the local committees with information and expert assistance and which aims to co-ordinate their activities. To facilitate this postwar phase of planning, the Department has established regional postwar planning committees in nine regions throughout the United States. These regional committees comprise officials of the various agencies of the Depart-

12. *Report of the Secretary of Agriculture*, 1941, pp. 147–148. U. S. Department of Agriculture, *Post-War Plans*, No. 1 (mimeographed).

ment. They are a link between the state, county, and community planning committees on the one hand and the Committee on Post-War Programs of the Department on the other.

In the view of the Department of Agriculture, the task of postwar agricultural planning falls into five main parts: (1) an assessment, in quantitative terms, of the probable productive plant in the decade after the war which will be needed to feed adequately and supply with raw materials an estimated population of 134 million; (2) a program of physical resource conservation and development which will provide employment to the population in the rural areas as needed; (3) a program of rural social services and facilities to improve rural living conditions, namely, health, housing, medical care, electrification, education; (4) a study of agricultural-industrial relations which would indicate the lines along which rural and urban development can be promoted simultaneously; and (5) surveys of various regions and special areas of the country in order to map out regional agricultural land use and development plans.

The Department maintains that it is impossible and undesirable to draw a sharp line between wartime and postwar planning. The problem is one of considering longer-time possibilities while carrying on the war effort and while preparing for the transition to peace. The Department expects to complete the various parts of its postwar program in the course of 1943.

In general, the postwar planning of the Department does not involve any radical changes in agricultural policy as developed during 1936–1938. It is focused more on translating general objectives into concrete and, where possible, quantitative terms. From this point of view, it is interesting to quote here from the statement made recently by an official of the Department on the goals of postwar agricultural planning. The main points of this statement are as follows:

1. (a) Prices of all agricultural commodities for domestic consumption should be maintained at such levels as to yield parity income (either parity income as defined in existing legislation or under some other definition if a better one can be found), without, at the same time, pyramiding and freezing surpluses in storage at high government loan rates, or (b) prices of all agricultural commodities for domestic consumption should be maintained at about current parity levels and that prices for that portion of export crops sold abroad be maintained at one half to two thirds of current parity.

2. Not to exceed 20 per cent of the total national population, or 80 per cent of the population on farms in the period 1935–1939 (whichever is higher) should be maintained in agriculture for the primary or sole purpose of farming.

3. Agricultural production should be maintained at such levels and in such patterns as to permit adequate nutritional diets—adapted to the economic resources and food habits of the different income groups of the population.

4. Agricultural production should be distributed among the different regions, states, and areas so that: (a) production will be maintained on a sustained yield basis, (b) the crops and livestock in each area will be those best adapted to the physical and other conditions existing in the area, and will be grown on units large enough to permit efficient operation and to yield incomes adequate for a decent standard of living.

5. Land not suited for farming (cropping) should be kept in forests (public and private), parks, grazing and game preserves, watersheds, etc., so as to bring about the most effective utilization of all our resources and to assure the nation an adequate supply of forest products, water, and recreational facilities.

6. Facilities and services (housing, hospitalization and medical care, schools, electrification, etc.) should be maintained in rural areas at levels necessary to result in reasonable parity treatment with other groups of the population.

7. The marketing system should be so organized as to (a) process and distribute agricultural products at the lowest possible costs, thus making it possible for farmers to receive a parity income without placing an undue burden upon the consumer; (b) provide an efficient mechanism whereby market prices at all stages can be correctly determined and known; and (c) broaden market outlets so that farmers can dispose of unrestricted output of the farm plant as a whole without having to accept "surplus" prices for the entire volume of production.[13]

One more point should be added. The programs of the farmers' organizations are centered around the needs and interests of the family-type farm. In large measure, this holds also for the agricultural planning of the government. The latter is aware, however, that the problems of the small farmer, of the low-income subsistence farmer and of farm labor call for an answer. The Department of Agriculture would meet these problems by dividing some government lands into family-sized farm units, by using the credit facilities of the government to encourage a better balanced agriculture, by discouraging speculation in land values by basing credit on the normal income returns of farms, by flexible mortgage payments in place of present fixed annual charges, by continuing homestead development and co-operative community services, and by enlarging proper camp facilities for migrant workers and housing accommodations for farm workers. These policies were an important part of the new agricultural policy outlined in 1937–1938, and they form part of the agricultural planning for the years after the war.

13. U. S. Department of Agriculture, Bureau of Agricultural Economics, *Statement by F. F. Elliott, Chief Agricultural Economist, before the 20th Annual Agricultural Outlook Conference, Washington, D. C., Oct. 21, 1942*, pp. 17–18.

## 2. PLANNING BY AND FOR INDUSTRY AND BUSINESS

American industry and business are well organized for a variety of purposes. There are in the United States some 2,000 national and interstate trade associations, which are concerned with the promotion of the technical and business interests of their members. State and local associations number over 6,000. There are about 3,000 local chambers of commerce and other community development groups. About half of these chambers, including the most important ones, are associated in the Chamber of Commerce of the United States.[14] The trade associations have no national organization for common action,[15] and operate on a trade or industry basis only.[16] But a number of manufacturers and industrial corporations, chiefly among the larger establishments, are united in the National Association of Manufacturers.

It cannot be said that any one organization can or does speak for American industry and business as a whole. The division of interests and points of view on many issues is reflected in the declarations and activities of the various trade and national associations. These differences are based on: (1) varying types of business;[17] (2) industrial importance, financial strength, reliance on competitive or monopolistic practices, market interests, and related factors;[18] (3) position in

14. For a complete list of trade and other associations in the United States and detailed information on their activities, see C. J. Judkins, *Trade and Professional Associations of the United States*, Department of Commerce, Washington, 1942.

15. The American Trade Association Executives is a national organization of secretaries of trade associations, for the exchange of information on trade association problems. The ATAE does not represent the trade associations as such, nor does it take a stand on policy.

16. A trade association has been defined as "a voluntary non-profit organization of business competitors (usually in one branch of the manufacturing, distributing, or service fields), the objective of which is to assist its members and its industry in dealing with mutual business problems in several of the following areas: accounting practices, business ethics, commercial research, industrial research, standardization, statistics, trade promotion, and relations with the government, with labor, and with the general public." Judkins, *op. cit.*, p. 2.

17. Of the 1,900 national and interstate trade associations recorded in 1941, 1,100 were composed of manufacturers, 400 of distributors, and 400 of persons in business service.

18. A summary of the position of American business with regard to these features is given by Clair Wilcox in his study *Competition and Monopoly in American Industry*, published in 1940 as Monograph No. 21 by the Temporary National Economic Committee. Some of the main points of his summary are as follows: In the late thirties, there were nearly 11 million entrepreneurs in the United States. Of these, nearly 7 million were in agriculture, nearly 1.5 million in wholesale and retail distribution, and another 1.5 million in the service trades. The 2 million business concerns in fields other than farming, finance, railway transportation and the professions included only 530,000 corporations, and of these only 6 per cent had assets of $1 million or more. Some 1.5 million business units are in agriculture, wholesale and retail distribution, personal service, building construction, and a miscellany of smaller trades, and they are typically small and competitive. Some 500,000 business units are in transportation, public utilities, manufacturing, mining and finance, and they are typically large and given to monopolistic practices at least as much as to competition. The first group employs more than 55 per cent of all persons engaged in public and private enterprise, the second employs more than 35 per cent. See Clair Wilcox, *op. cit.*, pp. 307–308.

foreign markets; and (4) the personal and social backgrounds of owners, leaders and managers, especially of the larger industrial corporations as compared with those of "small business."[19]

Since the middle of 1941, American business and industrial groups have shown increasing interest in planning for the postwar period. Statements to that effect by individual businessmen and by spokesmen of corporations could be quoted in profusion, if space permitted. Some of the leading industrial corporations have established planning divisions to prepare for postwar eventualities. Many trade associations and the larger national business associations have formed "postwar planning" committees. And new organizations have been established to deal with the subject specifically.

While none of the statements of any single organization or group can be taken as expressive of the point of view of American business, there are many common elements in the various statements which may be regarded as the platform of business. These common elements, as well as the differences of opinion, may be brought out by surveying the position taken by the several national business groups. The survey will cover the declarations and activities of the National Association of Manufacturers, the Chamber of Commerce of the United States, of particular leading industrial corporations, and of the recently organized Committee on Economic Development.

### a. THE NATIONAL ASSOCIATION OF MANUFACTURERS

Though it does not include a majority of manufacturing firms, the National Association of Manufacturers designates its annual meetings as The Congress of American Industry. The recent sessions of this Congress have reaffirmed the declarations of principles adopted before the war,[20] as a basis for postwar development. In brief, these are: constitutional representative democracy, private enterprise, civil and religious liberty. The Association stresses the value of the profit motive as "a powerful incentive to productive effort," the need for encouraging the investment of private capital and the preservation

19. The preliminary reports of the Census of Manufactures for 1939 cover 184,230 factories which employed 7,886,000 workers and 909,000 salaried employees. The number of proprietors and firm members was 123,655 while salaried officers of corporations numbered 139,350. Of all manufacturing companies, the hundred largest control about one third of the nation's factory production. See *Census of Manufactures; 1939*, U. S. Department of Commerce, October 1941. Also, *The Structure of the American Economy*, National Resources Planning Board, Washington, 1939.

20. These are formulated in *Industry's Program for American Progress* and in the *Declaration of Principles Relating to the Conduct of American Industry*, adopted in 1938 and in 1939.

of competition as the best assurance of reasonable prices and of greater efficiency.

Neither has the war changed much the attitude of the Association towards labor, social security, or government relations to business. The Association stands today, as in times past, for increasing earnings of workers through more employment and incentive systems rather than higher basic wage rates. It insists on the "freedom of the individual American worker" to join or not to join a labor organization and is, therefore, opposed to the "closed shop" in any form. It wants the government to "protect the right of workers to bargain individually or collectively through representatives of their own choosing." It demands that labor unions "should be held to a responsibility equal to that of business." It is against the extension of the social security laws and wants each state to have "wide latitude in enactment and administration of unemployment compensation laws" and advocates "sound experience rating" in all such state laws. It is opposed to "government interference" in business and to "extravagant and wasteful" government expenditures. To meet "the inevitable international economic competition when peace comes," the Association demands that means should be provided both "to promote our foreign trade" and "at the same time protect American markets for American producers."

The National Association of Manufacturers is lending its support to the planning which is being done by individual establishments and corporations in preparation for the postwar period. It recommends that each firm or company avoid temptations to relax controls over expenditures during the war, that it avoid excessive inventories, establish "rainy day" reserves for the postwar period, keep capital liquid and usable, allow for heavy depreciation charges now, and carry on research and exploration work in order to develop new products after the war and find markets for them.

The Association has a Post-War Problems Committee which is studying questions of demobilization and postwar employment. In March 1943, the Committee published a report entitled, *Jobs, Freedom, Opportunity in the Post-War Years*, which outlines its ideas on the "nature of the post-war problem" and on "the domestic and external requirements for prosperity." The report restates the main general principles of the Association. It also calls for a prompt restoration after the war of fair and flexible prices and of "a healthy and vigorous business competition." It demands further that the government remove restrictions to private investment and that the tax system be overhauled so as to leave sufficient corporate and individual income "to provide an incentive to invest savings in industries which provide jobs." In relation to labor, the Committee suggests that "collective bargaining" implies a desire of "one side to gain an advantage over the other," and that it should be replaced by "collective negotiations" between an employer and his employees or their representatives "with a view to seeking an agreement to their mutual advantage."

The Committee estimates that by the end of 1943, the accumulated demand for consumers' goods will total some $12 billion, including a demand for 10 million automobiles and 20 million radios; that there will be a demand for one million private homes and deferred maintenance costs of $3.5 billion for public and private property, and that some $24 billion of war bonds will be in the hands of the public. Given favorable governmental and labor conditions, the demand for goods, the buying power, productive capacity and the man power accumulated at the end of the war will make possible a "well-rounded and self-sustained prosperity."

The Committee strikes a new note on international economic relations. It suggests that "some framework should be established through which the political and economic relationships between nations of the world can be developed and maintained on an orderly basis." While free enterprise is the rule of our country, the Committee states, it does not follow that free enterprise will necessarily be the rule in the countries where great developments are likely to take place. But whether capital funds for the improvement of undeveloped countries should be made available through private enterprise or governmental action, "adequate agencies should be established to insure that they are administered with due regard for whatever obligations may be incurred in making them available." The best chance for economic progress in the United States, according to the Committee, will be through co-operation with other nations in a real effort to maintain postwar world peace, and to participate in international agencies for that purpose.

b. THE CHAMBER OF COMMERCE OF THE UNITED STATES

The Chamber of Commerce has emphasized the need of immediate planning for the postwar period. In 1942 the Chamber of Commerce set up a Committee on Economic Policy to report on the economic policies under which "post-war progress" can be made. According to this Committee, planning does not contemplate an expansion of government economic functions but the making of decisions in advance as to the conditions under which private enterprise will be allowed to operate. The Committee proposes to tabulate and analyze "all the favorable and unfavorable factors affecting post-war conditions" and to study methods for increasing the assets and diminishing the liabilities on this balance sheet. In addition, the various departments of the Chamber are preparing programs of postwar readjustments on specific problems such as social security and urban development.

The ideas underlying this work are not essentially different from those of the National Association of Manufacturers. The Chamber looks forward, after the war, to a "private financial and economic system" which should be allowed "to develop its full strength." It demands that every form of legitimate private enterprise be relieved from "the repression of government competition." It demands that the government refrain from entering any field of business which can successfully be conducted by private enterprise. It denounces as destructive what it calls "tax-free, rent-free and cost-free competition" of government with the lawful enterprises of private citizens. It is against expanding benefits under the Social Security Act in wartime. In its opinion, housing improvements for the lowest-income families can be best achieved through the enforcement of local sanitary and housing legislation and through "rental aid" to "families suffering hardships" where needed. It wants tariff laws which would "assure reasonable protection" for American industries, including some branches of agriculture.[21]

Like the National Association of Manufacturers, the United States Chamber of Commerce thinks that the backlog of consumer demand and the wartime deterioration of property will stimulate postwar business activities. According to the recent survey of the Chamber of Commerce which covers the period through 1942, if the war should end tomorrow, there would be an immediate demand for about 3 million automobiles at a value of over $2.3 billion; major household electrical appliances (radios, washing machines, refrigerators, etc.) valued at $860 million, and for furniture valued at over $709 million. There would also be a possibility for a building boom of at least $5 billion.

21. *Policies Advocated by the Chamber of Commerce of the United States*, Washington, 1942.

Owing to its mixed and local membership which includes also small manufacturers and businessmen, the Chamber is more concerned than the National Association of Manufacturers with problems of local and community development. The solution of these problems is sought in the operations of the free market, free flow of investment and free operations of business enterprise. The postwar planning of the Chamber is thus carried on in terms of efforts to remove government "interference," to reduce public expenditures and taxes, and to stimulate private investment and activity. The effects of the war are regarded as distortions which should be corrected and which would be corrected if the government restricted its economic activities and controls to a minimum.

The postwar program of the Chamber of Commerce is being shaped by the interaction of its somewhat mixed membership. Some assume that the effects of the war do not call for important changes in principles or programs. On the other hand, a group in the Chamber, under the leadership of its present President, Eric A. Johnston, would modify the program in the direction of more co-operation with labor and the government.

### C. CORPORATE PLANNING OF A PRIVATE WORK RESERVE

While the National Association of Manufacturers and the Chamber of Commerce have restated the principles and some of the specific policies on the basis of which private industry should proceed after the war, a number of large corporations have made a step beyond that and have inaugurated a practical process of planning for the postwar period.[22] The leaders of these corporations feel that despite the demands of the war program and some uncertainty as to the exact economic situation at the end of the war, it is necessary and possible to plan for peacetime industry in a concrete and realistic way.[23]

The central aim of this corporate planning is to prepare in advance what may be called a "private work reserve" which would enable private industry to provide jobs to all those who will be seeking employment when the war ends. This task has four aspects: (1) the demobilization of the armed forces and their placement in productive work; (2) the transfer of some 15 or 20 million workers from war work

22. Many corporations now have planning committees for this purpose. Information on the work of these committees may be obtained from the Trade Association Unit of the U. S. Department of Commerce.
23. See Charles E. Wilson, President, General Electric Company, "Post-War Planning," *Dun's Review*, September 1942.

to peacetime industries and occupations; (3) the reconversion of plants working on war orders to civilian purposes and operations; and (4) the maintenance of production on the high level which enlarged plant capacity and the need for continuous employment make both possible and necessary.

Those who are sponsoring this advance planning do not underestimate the magnitude of the task.[24] But they claim that private industry can meet it since many factors will be favorable.[25] Private industry must meet this task, for upon its ability to do so depends the future of the system of private enterprise in the United States. If private industry fails to provide jobs for the workers on conditions which will assure satisfactory living standards, it will have to accept the alternative of letting the government do, in one way or another, what it cannot do itself.[26]

The specific procedures adopted by the various corporations differ. In a general way, the work of the planning committees may be illustrated by the planning of the General Electric Company, which has taken a leading part in this movement. According to the president of this corporation, the operating departments of the company are instructed to do five things:

1. To draft detailed plans for reconversion of facilities to postwar volumes of manufacture. These plans, with the estimates of money and time required to accomplish them, should be kept continually up to date.
2. To bring redesigns of products, and new developments, up to the point of exploitation by assigning engineers as rapidly as the war effort permits.
3. To establish pilot plants for the development of processes, and to instruct skeleton crews.
4. To study intensively, at the present moment, the problems of sales, distribution, and personnel.
5. To study manufacturing operations comprehensively, taking advantage of the transition period to make major changes. Particular emphasis should

24. A few figures may illustrate some of the problems involved. The most generally accepted estimates are that it will be necessary in the two or three years immediately following the war to find employment for about 57 million persons; that full employment can be provided if the national output of goods and services is maintained at a level of $110–$120 billion; that to uphold living standards some $77 billion of consumer goods must be produced, including about $13 billion of consumers' durable goods.

25. It is estimated that at the end of the war the accumulated demand for civilian goods will be equal to two and one half years of normal business. There will be the job of retooling the factories. There will be a "limitless" market for housing. There will be large capacities for making plastics, synthetic fibers, nitrates, scores of chemicals, aluminum, magnesium, etc., all of which will be used to make new types of cars, planes, refrigerators, houses, furniture, etc., for which the demand both at home and abroad will be enormous. See speech by Dr. Charles M. A. Stine, Vice President of E. I. du Pont de Nemours & Co., Inc., *National City Bank Letter*, October 1942; also, George A. Sloan, *Mechanical Engineering*, March 1943.

26. See Charles E. Wilson, *op. cit.* Also, David C. Prince, *Post-Defense Readjustments*, 1941. Also, Bert H. White, "Sunrise on D. Day—How Business Men Are Planning to Provide Employment When War Ends," *Barron's*, June 29, 1942.

be placed on purchasing and utilizing new buildings, whether private or government-owned.[27]

How far this corporate planning has been carried it is impossible to say, as few details are available. But it is claimed by some that before the end of the war, progress will have been made to meet the postwar situation. It is realized, however, that the success of this planning will largely depend on the policies adopted by the government, especially those relating to demobilization, maintenance of a military establishment, relief abroad, taxation, and foreign trade.

## d. THE COMMITTEE FOR ECONOMIC DEVELOPMENT

Important as business postwar planning may be, many businessmen believe that it has serious limitations at present and that in order to make it more effective, it must be made more general in scope and more co-operative in method. To achieve both these ends, a number of business leaders and corporation officers have organized the Committee for Economic Development, to stimulate and assist private business to plan for the postwar period, by and for itself, on a nationwide scale.[28]

The Committee is not intended "to act as an overall post-war planning group." It has one objective only—"jobs in private industry." Its activities are concerned with helping industry and commerce "to gear themselves for the post-war effort." The Committee urges that the hundreds of thousands of individual enterprises in the United States must prepare now, while the war is on, to develop their own postwar production and marketing programs. By so doing, they will help their own businesses and make "their full contribution to stability and prosperity through high levels of employment and productivity when peace comes."

The problem, as the Committee sees it, is first of all to make the transition from war to peaceful economic activity. When peace comes, the government will no longer be in the market for $85 billion worth of war goods which it is spending in 1943. A minimum of 7 million men in the armed services and most of the 20 million persons now in the war industries will be eager for productive work in peacetime

27. Charles E. Wilson, *op. cit.*
28. The Chairman of the Board of Trustees is Paul G. Hoffman, President of the Studebaker Corporation. For other members of the Board and of the several divisions of the Committee, see *Preparing for High Levels of Employment and Productivity*, Committee for Economic Development, Washington; also Paul G. Hoffman, "Employment and Private Industry," *Survey Graphic*, May 1943.

pursuits. To provide employment to these millions of men and women, it will be necessary to offset quickly the billions of dollars of war production with an equivalent output of peacetime goods and services. Approximately an output of $135 to $150 billion (at 1941 prices) will be required. This output must be reached quickly—at most within two years after peace comes—and employment must be increased by half a million jobs per year in subsequent years to take care of normal increases in available man power.

The Committee has no definite plan as to how this is to be done, nor does it promise to formulate such a plan; but it hopes: (1) to collect information which may be useful to businessmen in making their own postwar plans; (2) to find out what public policies may create a favorable environment for private business for the accomplishment of its postwar tasks; (3) to stimulate the planning activities of individual companies, trade associations and communities; and (4) to serve as a liaison for exchange of information among the individual companies, trade associations, and local communities in such a way as to disseminate information and integrate ideas as effectively as possible.

The Committee has so far formulated a number of suggestions to individual companies as to how to proceed with postwar planning. These are similar to those outlined by the National Association of Manufacturers.

### 3. Labor and the Postwar World

Like agriculture and business, American labor is highly organized and yet not fully united. The 12 to 13 million organized workers are divided between the American Federation of Labor (AF of L), the Congress of Industrial Organizations (CIO), the four Railway Brotherhoods, the United Mine Workers and other unaffiliated unions.[29] There are also several hundred thousand workers in so-called "independent" unions which the AF of L and CIO dub "company unions."

The number of organized workers has grown greatly since 1937, but in view of the large increases in the labor force, the proportion

29. The membership claimed by the American Federation of Labor as of August 31, 1942 was 5,482,581. Since then it has been stated as over 6 million. The CIO does not publish membership figures, but claims that its influence and collective agreements cover over 5 million workers. See *Report of the Proceedings of the Sixty-Second Annual Convention of the American Federation of Labor, 1942*, p. 34; and *Daily Proceedings of the Fifth Constitutional Convention of the Congress of Industrial Organizations, November 9–13, 1942*, Boston, pp. 53–58.

of organized workers to the total number of wage earners is not over 35 per cent. Such figures, however, do not always tell the whole story. In some trades and industries the unions include the majority of workers while in others the unions exercise influence far beyond their membership. The labor organizations, therefore, claim to be the spokesmen of the large mass of American wage earners.

Broadly speaking, organized labor in the United States favors the maintenance of what is called the free enterprise system. Some individual unions both in the AF of L and in the CIO have socialistic leanings and look forward to the development of a socialist society in the somewhat vague "future." Small groups of Communists exist in a number of unions, and a few unions are under the influence of Communist leadership. But the dominant economic outlook of American trade unionism, in contrast to that of Great Britain, Australia and some other countries, is definitely that of a free capitalist system modified by collective bargaining and government controls. American labor maintains that collective bargaining tends to introduce constitutional government into industry, and to transform gradually what was once an oligarchic system of economy into a truly democratic system of free enterprise.

American labor regards the present war largely as a struggle, not to revolutionize the economic system, but to preserve the essential features of free initiative, free unions, and voluntary collective bargaining. The AF of L and the CIO have been in the front ranks of the opponents of Fascism and Nazism partly because the Nazis and Fascists destroyed free trade unions and free contractual relations between employers and workers on an organized basis. Though concerned with the large problems of war and peace and of international relations, American labor stresses what it regards as the supreme issues—individual freedom and the rights of labor to bargain collectively, to have a voice in the determination of working conditions, to improve living standards, and to give the wage earners greater economic and social security.

The postwar programs of American labor are thus free of the revolutionary or radical elements characteristic of labor programs in other countries. Their programs are essentially demands for the reforms which were advocated by labor before 1939. The new element in these programs grows out of the problems created by the war and the transition to peace.

The differences between the AF of L and the CIO are not as fundamental as is often claimed. The differences are largely those of emphasis and tone, of methods of organization and tactics. The CIO represents new and hitherto unorganized groups of workers in mass production industries whose entrance upon the industrial scene cannot but be somewhat explosive. The break between the two organizations is important not so much from the point of view of labor's postwar demands as of its capacity to realize them.

However, since the two organizations differ in the formulation of their demands, it is well to consider their postwar programs separately.

### a. POSTWAR DEMANDS OF THE AF OF L

The AF of L has not formulated any general program for the postwar period. The 1942 annual convention of the Federation held in Toronto was confronted with a number of questions on postwar policy, but it refrained from answering them. All that the convention did was to recommend that a postwar problem committee be set up by the president and executive committee of the Federation. A postwar planning committee has since been appointed, and it has met several times to consider the task assigned to it.[30]

The postwar demands of the Federation are thus largely an extension of its prewar program. The Federation will continue to support the 40-hour week, the Fair Labor Standards Act of 1938,[31] the Walsh-Healy Public Contracts Act,[32] the protection of labor unions against the application of antitrust laws, child labor legislation, public housing projects, the Wagner Labor Act and collective bargaining, better educational facilities for the people, union-management co-

30. Matthew Woll is chairman of the committee. See "Labor Looks Ahead to Peace," *American Federationist*, May 1943.

31. This Act provides for a minimum wage of 30 cents per hour which is to be automatically increased to 40 cents on October 24, 1945. The Wage and Hour Division of the U. S. Department of Labor estimated in August 1942 that about 7.5 million wage earners were paid less than 40 cents an hour. About 1.5 million of these workers were protected by the provisions of the Act and were receiving between 30 and 40 cents an hour. Considerable numbers of workers in retail trade, agriculture, domestic service, fisheries, etc., not covered by the Act were receiving less than 30 cents an hour. See *Proceedings of 1942 AF of L Convention*, p. 85.

32. This Act sets standards of minimum wages, hours of work, child labor, safety and health on all government contracts in excess of $10,000. It forbids, for instance, the employment of boys under sixteen and of girls under eighteen years of age on such contracts. Between July 1936 and July 1938 the provisions of this Act were applied to government contracts valued over $575 million. Between July 1, 1941 and July 1, 1942, the Act was applied to contracts valued over $15 billion. *Ibid.*, pp. 68–69.

operation, fair income taxes,[33] and the right to strike for higher wages as a means of improving the living standards of the workers.[34]

The main point, however, in the postwar program of the Federation is the demand for greater economic and social security. The Federation maintains that social security is "a basic social justice measure by which workers who have successfully demonstrated their ability to be self-supporting are protected against becoming dependent recipients of relief because of emergencies outside of their control."

The three main emergencies in the life of the worker arise as a result of old age, permanent and temporary disability, and unemployment. The competitive system under which we live, according to the Federation, cannot guarantee permanent employment or income to the workers. The instability which results is in the interests of individual businesses and of society. It, therefore, has to be accepted, but it should not be exclusively at the expense of the wage earners and salaried workers. Social security, based on the collective pooling of risks, makes it possible to tide the workers over the emergencies which interfere with the earning of income.

The Federation regards the Social Security Act of August 14, 1935 as "the foundation upon which wage-earners can plan their future." The "first step in Labor's post-war planning" is to strengthen and enlarge the provisions of this Act. The Federation would extend the old-age insurance provisions, which now cover some 32 million persons, also to domestic servants, farmers, agricultural laborers, small-salaried persons, and self-employed persons. It wants to amend the unemployment compensation provisions so as to increase the amount and duration of benefits, do away with merit rating, and federalize its administration. It also asks that compensation benefits be paid to those who are temporarily unemployed because of sickness as well as to those totally disabled. The Federation also demands that the federal government make provisions for maintaining the old-age insurance equities of workers in the armed forces and should finance unemployment benefits to be paid demobilized soldiers while they hunt for jobs.

33. The Federation opposes a general sales tax, a manufacturers' sales tax, or a spending tax.

34. The Federation quotes estimates compiled by the Office of Price Administration showing that 62.5 per cent of all American nonfarm families will have received for 1942 less than $2,500, which is estimated as necessary for a minimum health and efficiency living (for a family of four), and 29 per cent will have received less than $1,500, necessary for a bare subsistence living level. *Ibid.*, p. 120. The Bureau of the Census reports the medium income in the United States in 1939 as $967 for men and $540 for women.

The Federation regards proposals for expanded social security provisions not merely as an aid to the worker but as one of the principal means for facilitating the transition from war to peace. Such expansion now will, in its opinion, enable business to accumulate reserves for meeting future obligations which would otherwise require postwar taxation. It would assure consumer buying power, and enlarge the funds available to the government for current use through investment of the accumulated reserves in federal bonds.

Besides its postwar problems committee, the Federation has appointed a Commission on International Relations to prepare an international peace program for labor. The Federation demands that labor be represented at the peace conference and take part in the making of the future peace. Isolation, in the opinion of the Federation, has been made impossible by technical progress, and some form of international organization is necessary. But ideals must be tempered by facts, and the Federation wants "to make sure that world trade in the future does not profit financially because of substandard labor conditions in any industry or any country." That is one of the reasons for its support of the International Labour Organization, which it expects to play an important part in reconstruction.

### b. THE CIO PROGRAM

The CIO has no general postwar program. At its last convention in November 1942, it decided to establish a committee on postwar requirements composed of union officials, and a department of postwar requirements in the national headquarters. The committee and the department are to prepare a program which is to be presented to the government of the United States and to the governments of all the victorious United Nations.

Pending the preparation of this program, the CIO, like the AF of L, has stressed chiefly the need to provide against unemployment after the war. The CIO forecasts that the reconversion of industry to a peacetime basis will cause many dislocations resulting in unemployment. To carry reconversion forward as swiftly as possible and to protect the workers who might be adversely affected, the CIO would make "advance provision of generous dismissal wages." These funds should be large enough to support all people satisfactorily during the reconversion period.

Reconversion, according to the CIO, is likely to be followed by a boom. But booms come to an end, and this means unemployment on a large scale. The remedy of the CIO for depression unemployment is social security. The program of social security which the CIO advocates is wider than that of the AF of L. It includes the following provisions:

1. A single federal system of old-age insurance with universal coverage for all the aged population, including the presently exempt groups of wage earners, farmers and self-employed. Such a system should assure a guaranteed monthly minimum income that will provide the essentials of a decent standard of living.

2. A single federal system of unemployment compensation, with extended coverage to all workers, adequate benefits, low eligibility standards, provisions for benefits for partial unemployment, and limited disqualification penalties with no employer-experience ratings schemes.

3. Adequate provision for workers who lose their earning ability through total and permanent disability.

4. Adequate provision to workers for loss of earnings due to illness.

5. A national health program which would include insurance for medical care on a federal basis covering all persons and families, with free medical care for those who cannot afford insurance.

6. Increased assistance to state programs of aid for the blind, for dependent children and for maternal and child health care.

7. Adequate provision for protection of the rights of men in the armed forces, particularly with an eye to the situation that may face them on their return.

8. The entire social security system to be financed in the largest measure possible by taxes upon aggregates of excess income and wealth.

The CIO also favors the establishment of industrial councils composed of representatives of management and labor to consider plant and industry problems. Such councils would give labor a share in production management and would, according to the CIO, encourage peaceful and democratic relations in American industry.

## 4. PROGRAMS OF SOCIAL GROUPS

The several functional economic groups—farmers, businessmen, organized labor—aim to fit their plans and programs into a general scheme of national social-economic policy. Nevertheless, they are concerned primarily with their respective group interests, which are in conflict on many points. Presumably such conflicts can be largely adjusted by discussion and compromise, but generally each group proceeds on the assumption that it may obtain better results for itself by using its political and economic power to the full, even if that may result in group struggles.

Social groups proceed on opposite principles. Their purpose is to formulate general national policies within the framework of which group interests may be reasonably met and group conflicts amicably adjusted. Their emphasis is on what they conceive to be the national or public interest to which group and sectional demands must be subordinated.

Postwar plans have been advanced in the past two or three years by a variety of such social groups in the United States. Most of these groups include men and women from all walks of life, but they are preponderantly of a middle-class character. They vary with regard to the aims which they pursue, such as reform of educational institutions, improvement of social conditions, changes in political organization or in the economic system. It is impossible to survey here the numerous plans of these groups for lack of space. Besides, many of these plans are familiar and represent no new attempt to adjust to the postwar period. Such, for instance, are the programs of the technocrats, the Socialist Party, the Communists, the co-operative societies, educational groups, e.g., the Progressive Education Association, research organizations such as the National Planning Association, and of a number of individuals who speak to some extent for larger or smaller groups.

However, among the plans of social groups for the postwar world, two call for some consideration here, because of their relation to changing economic ideas and social policies. One is the composite result of many efforts to develop a basis and program for what may be called neo-capitalism.[35] The other is the attempt of some groups to formulate a workable postwar program on a socialist basis. The neo-capitalist view has been stated by several groups and individuals, but it has found its best and most comprehensive formulation in a report issued under the auspices of the editors of *Fortune* under the title *The Domestic Economy*.[36] The socialist attempt is that made by the League for Industrial Democracy.[37]

### a. THE NEO-CAPITALIST PROGRAM

The essence of the neo-capitalist thesis is that the postwar economy can be consciously reconstructed in such a way as to reconcile freedom

35. For an analysis of the movement towards such a neo-capitalism not only in the United States but in other democratic countries, see Lewis L. Lorwin, *Economic Consequences of the Second World War*, Random House, New York, 1941, pp. 100–108.

36. "The United States in a New World, The Domestic Economy," *Fortune*, December 1942, Supplement.

37. "Economics of Defense and Reconstruction," *Proceedings of the Twenty-Seventh Summer Conference of the League for Industrial Democracy, June 20–22, 1941.*

and security and to initiate an era of "expansive prosperity" on the basis of private enterprise which will do away with poverty and provide a steadily better livelihood for everybody. To obtain this objective, however, it is necessary to break away from the traditional views of laissez faire and the "free market" and to bring into operation the new economic doctrines, fiscal techniques, and social policies which were projected during 1929–1939 in England, the United States, and elsewhere, and which, if properly applied, offer a basis for the reconciliation of group interests in a dynamic national policy.

The neo-capitalist analysis of laissez faire and of the free market has its roots in the work of John Maynard Keynes in England and of his disciples in the United States. According to this analysis, laissez faire can no longer be, under twentieth century conditions, a guarantee either of economic security or of economic freedom. The growing economic and social power of big corporations and of organized economic groups has done away with the "free market" of the nineteenth century and has changed the process of price making. Furthermore, the entrepreneur or businessman can no longer carry alone the responsibility for providing steady jobs to the workers, since he is not in a position to control savings and investment on which the full use of economic resources depends.

The neo-capitalists propose that the government undertake to guarantee reasonably full employment and to police the competitive process in such a way that a new type of "free market" will result. The government has three weapons at its command for guaranteeing employment and thus "underwriting permanent prosperity." The first consists in giving private industry every chance to operate at full capacity and to invest as much of the nation's savings as possible. The second is to implement a full-production policy by an extensive system of social insurance and services, including unemployment insurance, old-age pensions, etc., and public provisions for better housing, nutrition, schools, and health. The third weapon is a "flexible program of public works" which can be "turned on" in times of depression and whenever our resources are going to waste by not being used.

All this implies a new relationship between business and government, and also between business and labor. The businessmen must cease to think of government as an outside force which "interferes" in their affairs and accept it as a vitalizing and co-operating factor. Businessmen must also accept trade unions as a legitimate factor in industry and co-operate with them in improving labor and social conditions. In return, business will be recognized as the main driving force of economic life, the profit motive will be encouraged as the main motivation of enterprise, and the "daring and risk-taking entrepreneur" will become the "darling" of America's economy.

These general objectives have been translated by the editors of *Fortune* into specific measures for the postwar period which together form in some ways the most complete and consistent program of American neo-capitalism. These proposals may be summed up as follows:

1. The government should set a minimum reasonably close to our full capacity below which employment should never be permitted to fall.

2. The system of social security should be extended.

3. A large program of public works should be planned in advance to be applied when and where necessary to compensate a decline in private employment.

4. The government should "police" the free market so as to allow for the proper growth of enterprise and for the most appropriate price policies. This involves different methods of treatment for different types of business. The public utilities must remain monopolies, whether private or public, and the main task of the government is to keep them technologically alert. In agriculture, lumber, textiles, clothing, and in many other industries a "workable competition" can and should be maintained, with the aid of the antitrust laws. Industries in which "monopolistic competition" prevails—i.e., industries dominated by a few large sellers whose products are differentiated by quality, trademarks or advertising and in which there is a total absence of price competition—should be encouraged to lower prices as much as possible, especially during depressions. Where such industries persist in maintaining "administered" prices at what is considered too high a level, their policies should be subject to review by a special quasi-judicial court or commission composed of economists or jurists or both.

5. The Robinson-Patman and the Miller-Tydings Acts should be repealed.[38]

6. The patent laws should be changed so as to prevent them from fostering monopoly.

7. Tariffs should be reduced as soon as and as much as possible. Until world trade becomes freer, the exporting cartels organized under the Webb-Pomerene Act (there are now forty-five such cartels) should be maintained.

8. Federal incorporation of corporations doing an interstate business should be made legally voluntary, and made subject to certain obligations such as no interlocking or dummy directorates, a simple capital structure, a certain degree of management ownership.

9. American farming should be improved by means of diversification, conservation, and especially by providing a rising domestic market. Eventually, such improvement should make farm-market subsidies or "parity" legislation no longer necessary.

38. The Robinson-Patman Act requires that when a large buyer gets a better price than a small buyer, the seller must prove that the discrimination is justified by a difference in costs in filling the order. The Miller-Tydings Act enables state legislation to permit contracts between manufacturers and retail stores fixing the resale price of brand-name merchandise.

10. Labor should exercise the right to organize, and management should learn to respect this right and to live with unionism. The full recognition of this right and the guarantee of full employment will do away with the issue of the closed shop and with such abuses of trade unionism as racketeering, slowing up on the job, etc.

11. The small businessman should be helped to obtain credit through special "equity banks," to get better technical advice through government laboratories, and in other ways.

12. The federal tax system should be completely overhauled. During the immediate postwar years, when inflationary tendencies may prevail, it will be wiser to maintain high taxation of all kinds. But the long-run tax policy should have as its main purpose to stimulate the maximum activity, investment, and progress of which private industry is capable. Such a policy would call for a substantial reduction of all corporate income taxes. Instead, the government should rely on a progressive personal income tax, on an undistributed profits tax to prevent corporate hoarding, and on high inheritance taxes.

According to its proponents, this program is "not socialism, nor fascism, nor a return to laissez faire." It is, in their opinion, "a synthesis of the conflicting elements in our recent past; a new democratic capitalism, which will allow production and consumption to keep on expanding as fast as science and human ingenuity point the way." In any case, it is the most optimistic program so far put forth which seeks to reconcile business leadership with public control.

### b. A MINIMUM SOCIALIST PROGRAM

While the efforts to promote a new capitalism stem from recent economic trends, the attempt to formulate a socialistic program on a basis of minimum and immediate demands is an old story in the socialist movement. The present war has stimulated anew several such attempts. That of the League for Industrial Democracy (LID) is singled out here because the League is nonpolitical in character and its activities reach the youth in American colleges and universities.

The LID has carried on work for over two decades under the slogan "production for use and not for profit." It derives its principles from socialist theory, but is not strictly Marxian. Its postwar program, as formulated in 1941, is a combination of demands for social security and for the gradual and partial application of public ownership. It may be summarized under the following nine points:

1. A public works program in city, state and nation calculated to provide jobs to all men and women able and willing to work, but denied employment in private industry. The WPA and other agencies of the government during the war period should map out a plan toward that end, ready to be put into

operation just as soon as we begin to return to a peace economy. This plan, as former plans worked out by the National Resources Board and other agencies, should include a vast program of conservation reforestation, flood control, soil conservation, hydroelectric power development, etc.; of needed highway construction; of railroad electrification and reorganization; of public housing, of increased recreational, hospital, health and educational facilities in city, state and nation; of necessary research and art projects, etc.

2. A taxation program which would co-ordinate city, state and federal taxation systems, which would be based increasingly on the principle of ability to pay, and which would seek continuously to reduce the national debt and sustain the social services at a high level.

3. The retention in public hands of those industries of a peacetime nature which were taken under public control during the war.

4. Increasing public control and ownership of industry, particularly of natural resources, public utilities, credit and monopolistic industries.

5. The expansion of the social insurance system, including health insurance, and the steady enlargement of public health, public welfare and public housing services.

6. The strengthening of labor laws favoring collective bargaining, minimum wages, maximum hours, elimination of child labor.

7. The extension of voluntary consumer co-operation as a means of social control.

8. A program for education better calculated to fit students to meet the economic needs of the time.

9. Legislation and education to eliminate race discrimination.[39]

This program may be regarded as a trend towards a moderate neo-socialism in opposition to the neo-capitalism outlined above.

## 5. STATEMENTS OF RELIGIOUS GROUPS

For many years now the churches and religious organizations in the United States have shown a growing interest in economic and social problems. The war strengthened this interest greatly. Since 1940, various religious groups in the United States have tried to interpret the present struggle in terms of a conflict of human and spiritual values and as a challenge to religious leadership to help bring about a world in which a repetition of such a tragedy would become impossible. Many conferences have been held during the past three

39. The war has brought to the fore in the United States as elsewhere the problems of the economic position of racial and other minority groups after the war. This is particularly true of the problem of the Negro in the southern states. Of the many statements on the subject, reference may be made here to the "new charter of race relations in the South" issued on December 15, 1942 by a committee of the Conference on Race Relations held at Durham, North Carolina. The statement was signed by leading Negro educators, editors and professional men of the southern states and thus represents the point of view of a large group of the Negro race itself. The statement calls for the "abolition of all forms of discriminatory practices," for opportunities of education at all levels, for measures to improve the position of the Negro share-cropper and tenant by means of written contracts, higher farm wages, etc., and for provision of more adequate social services for the Negro population. See *Bulletin of the Committee on Youth Problems of the American Council on Education*, February 1943, Vol. VI, No. 5.

years by these groups to consider the "bases of a just and durable peace" and to formulate the essential conditions of a peaceful world order.

As a result of these conferences and less formal meetings, proposals for postwar reorganization have been made by the Federal Council of Churches of Christ in America, the Commission on World Peace of the Methodist Church, the Catholic Association for International Peace, the Central Conference of American Rabbis, the American Friends Service Committee, and others. It is impossible to examine here all these statements and proposals.[40] Most of them deal in large part with problems of international organization and policy which are outside the scope of this study.

In so far as the religious proposals deal with issues of postwar national policy, they reveal some differences both of viewpoint and of emphasis. Some Catholic groups, for instance, emphasize the need for "promoting the cause of rural life,"[41] and the dignity of farming. According to the American Friends Service Committee, full employment involves the organization of a "mixed economy" based on three types of production, namely, commercial or private production on a competitive basis, voluntary group or co-operative production, and public production for social needs.[42] Most of the statements, however, have many points in common, especially the demand for full employment and social security.

The most representative statement in many ways is that approved by the National Study Conference held at Ohio Wesleyan University in March 1942.[43] The conference was convened by the Commission to Study the Bases of a Just and Durable Peace of the Federal Council of Churches. The meeting was attended by 377 delegates, some of whom were appointed by twenty-seven Protestant communions while others represented over forty religious bodies allied with various Protestant churches and organizations. The resolutions approved by this Conference may be taken as an expression of the more socially

40. For a summary, see Liston Pope, *Religious Proposals for World Order. An Analysis of Thirty-Four Statements*, December 1941. Most of the documents of the religious associations may be obtained from the World Alliance for International Friendship Through the Churches in New York or from the Commission to Study the Bases of a Just and Durable Peace in New York.

41. See statement of National Catholic Rural Life Conference in *The New York Times*, October 8, 1941.

42. *Looking Toward the Post-War World*—Statement of the Friends Conference on Peace and Reconstruction, held at Wilmington, Ohio, August 31–September 4, 1942.

43. *A Message from the National Study Conference on the Churches and a Just and Durable Peace*, convened at Ohio Wesleyan University, Delaware, Ohio, March 3–5, 1942. This program was reaffirmed by the biennial meeting of the Federal Council of Churches held in Cleveland, Ohio, December 8–11, 1942.

progressive elements and groups of the Protestant churches in the United States.

The special significance of the resolutions lies in their purpose—to formulate a postwar social-economic program in accord with Christian ideas and ethics. The guiding principles underlying these resolutions are that "moral law, no less than physical law, undergirds our world," that the "sickness and suffering" afflicting present society are due to the violations of the moral law, and that inherent in the moral law is the principle of co-operation among nations.

The moral law of the world implies that economic security is no less essential than political security to a just and durable peace, that economic security requires some form of international machinery to give it effect, that all men, of whatever race, color, or creed, have the right to pursue work of their own choosing and to enjoy security from want and oppression. It is the supreme responsibility of the Church and of all Christian citizens to translate these principles into practical realities and "to create a public opinion which will insure that the United States shall play its full and essential part in the creation of a moral way of international living."

On the basis of these principles, the religious groups represented at the conference stressed the need of "Christian motivation" in productive life and in economic matters. The duty of the Church is not "to line up on the side of any economic system" nor "to prescribe details or advocate panaceas," but to demand economic arrangements which promote human welfare and human freedom. On this basis, a specific program was adopted, the main provisions of which are as follows:

1. That every man should have the opportunity to share in the ownership of both personal and productive property, such as a home, a farm and economic enterprise.

2. That every member and family of the human race have a right to steady employment and to earn an income such as may provide the necessities of life and growth, in accordance with the wealth-producing capacity of the day and with the requirements of responsible conservation of natural resources.

3. That in early years every individual has the right to full-time educational opportunities with reasonable consideration of his talents, interests, and probable vocation; that in later years every individual is entitled to economic security in retirement and the continuation of cultural opportunities; that in the whole span of life every individual is entitled to adequate health service and professional medical care; and that in the productive years there is the universal obligation to work in some socially necessary service.

4. That every man has the right to employment of a kind that is consistent with human dignity and self-respect, and to such leisure as is essential for cultural and spiritual development; and that employers of all kinds should recognize and safeguard these rights.

5. That citizens, through their governments or other appropriate agencies,

have not only the right but the duty: (1) to prevent destructive cyclical trends in business by regulatory measures, or, if these prove inadequate, by direct initiative; and (2) to counteract the unemployment resulting from technological change through vocational re-education, through public employment agencies, and, if necessary, through a reorganization of industries and markets.

6. That industrial democracy is fundamental to successful political democracy, and that labor should, therefore, be given an increasing responsibility for, and participation in, industrial management. The principle of democracy in economic relations should be accorded wider expression by the development of stronger *voluntary* producers' associations, farm organizations, labor organizations, professional groups, and consumers' organizations. Such organizations should be integrated into some form of national economic council to plan, in co-operation with government, for maximum production and consumption and for the abolition of unemployment. In each industry, industrial councils should be established, representative of management, labor and consumers, for democratic direction of industries towards these same ends. The effect of maximum production and consumption in each country would be to decrease the pressure of competition for world markets and thus to mitigate one of the major economic causes of war.

7. That the means of preventing social disorder can be found only by doing away with the paradox of poverty in the midst of plenty. A tax program should be formulated in such a way that the burden be placed in proportion to the ability to pay, to the end that wealth may be more equitably distributed.

8. That agriculture has a dual importance, both as a way of making a living and as a basis of family and community life. The economic system must become servant and not master in maintaining the socially significant services of agriculture, such as feeding the world and producing the organic raw materials essential to industry.

9. Restrictions on world trade, such as tariffs and quotas, should be eliminated, through international organization and other appropriate methods.

## 6. Summary

Disregarding details, postwar plans of economic and social organizations in the United States can be arranged in four groups: (1) those which advocate the maintenance of the prewar status quo; (2) those which aim to establish a "new public capitalism" based on the partnership of industry and government; (3) those which advocate a gradual but systematic development of public ownership; and (4) those which would find a compromise in some "mixed economic system."

The groups which advocate gradual economic and social changes have many points in common. That is especially true with regard to their attitudes on the need for social security, public works, the control of monopoly, and collective bargaining. The programs of these groups supply a basis for a common national postwar social-economic policy.

## Chapter 3

# GOVERNMENT PLANNING IN THE UNITED STATES

A LARGE PART of the work carried on by government departments and agencies in Washington[1] is closely related to economic and social planning. Under normal conditions government departments are required by the nature of their duties to look ahead and to prepare data and proposals which may help the Congress and the Administration to formulate policies and to embody them in specific laws. Government departments also prepare data to help private organizations in formulating economic policies.

Some of the guiding ideas of this planning are also not new. They have been developed by government departments in the course of many years and some of them have been embodied in legislation passed by the Congress of the United States during the past ten years. Many of the current plans are merely recommendations to amend or extend existing laws to meet situations which may be expected as a result of the war.

Several features, however, distinguish the work of today from that of prewar days. The government agencies have to deal with many problems which are a direct outcome of the war such as demobilization and the reconversion of wartime industry to a peacetime basis. They have to consider some problems of long standing, e.g., housing or social security, in the light of the effects which the war may have.

Furthermore, some of the work of these agencies is geared to the larger goals inspired by the expectations of a better world after the war. The United States government has declared on more than one occasion since December 7, 1941, that the present war is a struggle for freedom and for a better world to come. The people of the United States have been promised that every effort will be made after this war to ban aggression and to provide security from want and fear. The government departments and agencies are confronted with the task of studying the ways in which these promises can be realized at the end of hostilities. Postwar planning is imposed on the government by the aims for which the war is being fought.

1. A number of states and cities have appointed special committees or commissions to prepare programs of public works and other measures for the postwar period. These commissions are limited to their respective state and municipal problems, but are co-operating with federal agencies. Their work is often of more than local importance, but in view of limitations of space, it cannot be considered here.

## 1. General Aims and Guiding Ideas

The postwar social-economic aims of the government of the United States have been stated most authoritatively and eloquently, both before our entry into the war and since, by President Franklin D. Roosevelt. In his first message to Congress after his re-election in 1940, on January 6, 1941, he stated these aims in terms applying not only to the United States but to the whole world. The relevant passages from this statement are as follows:

In future days which we seek to make secure we look forward to a world founded upon four essential freedoms. The first is freedom of speech and expression—everywhere in the world. The second is freedom of every person to worship God in his own way—everywhere in the world. The third is freedom from want which, translated into world terms, means economic understanding which will secure to every nation a healthy peace-time life for its inhabitants—everywhere in the world. Fourth is freedom from fear which, translated into world terms, means world-wide reduction of armaments to such a point and in such a thorough fashion that no nation will be in a position to commit an act of physical aggression against any neighbor—anywhere in the world.

That is no vision of a distant millenium. It is a definite basis for the kind of a world attainable in our time and generation.

The President stated his views more specifically with regard to the United States in his message to the 78th Congress on January 11, 1943. The passages relating to social-economic problems follow.

The people at home and the people at the front—men and women—are wondering about the Third Freedom—Freedom from Want. To them it means that when they are mustered out, when war production is converted to the economy of peace, they will have the right to expect full employment—for themselves and for all able-bodied men and women in America who want to work.

They expect the opportunity to work, to run their farms, their stores, to earn decent wages. They are eager to face the risks inherent in our system of free enterprise.

They do not want a post-war America which suffers from undernourishment or slums—or the dole. They want no get-rich-quick era of bogus "prosperity" which will end for them in selling apples on a street corner, as happened after the bursting of the boom in 1929.

When you talk with our young men and women, you will find they want to work for themselves and their families; they consider they have the right to work; and they know that after the last war their fathers did not gain that right.

When you talk with our young men and women, you will find that with the opportunity for employment they want assurance against the evils of all major economic hazards—assurance that will extend from the cradle to the grave. This great Government can and must provide this assurance.

## 2. DEPARTMENTAL STUDIES AND PROPOSALS

The President's message to the 78th Congress emphasizes the elements involved in the idea of "freedom from want." They are employment, security, decent living standards, health, adequate educational facilities, and an economic structure which makes these aims possible in accordance with the personal freedom and social ideals of the people.

Practically every department or agency of the federal government is engaged in studies which bear on the solution of these postwar problems. Much of this work is technical and is intended to supply the data on which legislative measures may be based. Some departments and agencies have gone further and have formulated recommendations for legislation. However, not all of these proposals have as yet been made available for public discussion.

Most of the problems of national policy require work on the part of several government departments and agencies. This is not necessarily duplication but the inevitable result of the fact that each problem has different technical aspects. However, in order to avoid repetition, the summary below is made on the basis of problems rather than of the departments concerned. The summary, therefore, covers only part of the postwar planning of each department.[2]

### Demobilization of the Armed Forces

Several departments and agencies are studying the problems connected with the release of men from the armed forces and with their return to peacetime occupations. Some of the questions involved are: (1) the maximum number of men who will be in the armed forces, in war production, and in war agencies of the executive government; (2) the number to be demobilized, assuming that considerable defense requirements will continue after the war and that business activity will be at the 1939 level or above; (3) the probable number of those who will voluntarily retire from gainful occupations, e.g., women, older persons, young persons of school age. These are problems within the sphere of work of the Bureau of Labor Statistics of the United States Department of Labor and of the War Manpower Commission.

On the other hand, it is also necessary to know the educational background and occupational experience of each man in the armed

2. The agricultural planning of the government is described in Chapter 2.

forces, his military record, and the special training received in the service. On the day of demobilization, it will be necessary to know what the physical and mental condition of each man is, what medical care he may need, and what vocational rehabilitation or retraining may be provided for him. The data necessary for answers to these questions and preparations for future action are the concern of the Re-employment Division of the Selective Service and of the Special Services Division of the Army.

### Reconversion of Plant

The re-employment of released men immediately after the war will depend not only on how demobilization is timed and carried out and on the retraining of the labor force, but also on the reconversion of plants to peaceful industrial operations. Reconversion will present problems of differing complexity depending on how far the industry has expanded or contracted during the war, how its machinery and processes have changed, the extent to which markets have been affected by synthetic or substitute products or by changes in consumption. These topics are being studied in their various aspects by the Bureau of Labor Statistics, the Bureau of Foreign and Domestic Commerce and several other agencies. Also, the War Department is making studies of the effects of the cancellation of procurement contracts and of methods for carrying out cancellations in such a way as to ease the transition to peaceful industry.

### Aid to Industry

The reconversion of plant and the re-employment of workers immediately after the war will presumably be the task of private industry and of individual and corporate employers. The government is preparing to be of aid to private industry in a variety of ways. Studies are now being carried on by the Bureau of Foreign and Domestic Commerce and by the Bureau of Labor Statistics of current developments of new products, of changes in distribution methods and of their effects on postwar markets. These studies should help to estimate America's postwar capacity to produce, the postwar private works reserve in important industries, and the expected demand for electric power, steel and railroad transportation in selected industries. The Industrial Section of the National Resources Planning Board has surveyed the changes in the geographic location of industry due to the war, the extent to which such changes may continue after the war, and the factors which should determine the geographical structure of American industry.

The Bureau of Labor Statistics has undertaken a series of studies to describe the wartime changes and to suggest the postwar readjustment problems of selected local areas. The purpose of these studies is described by the Bureau as follows:

Nearly 80 per cent of the Nation's employment in mining and manufacturing is concentrated in 413 counties. These, by and large, are the areas which have felt the heaviest impact of the war effort. The 1940 population of these counties was 77,000,000, or 59 per cent of the national total. Their cities and towns included 80 per cent of the urban population of the United States. It is in these areas that the major problems of industrial adjustment after the war will arise.

An effective program for transition to peace will require a common understanding of the problems to be dealt with, on the part of the people of the local areas, their local and State governments, and the Federal Government. Some phases of readjustment will be accomplished entirely through local enterprise. In other respects local programs may depend heavily on coordinated State and Federal government action. Hence these studies have a twofold purpose. First, they are designed to aid in the development of locally directed programs of economic readjustment. Second, they are intended to indicate the extent to which local readjustment is related to the prospects for high-level economic activity for the Nation as a whole.

The final campaign of the war, the drive for sustained full employment and business prosperity, may well prove to be the most difficult task that lies ahead. Much of the preparation can be made only in the local areas where the readjustments will occur. It is to be hoped that all the forces in each community will mobilize for this last campaign.[3]

*Transportation Development*

Various aspects of transportation as related to postwar industrial needs are being studied by the Department of Commerce, the Interstate Commerce Commission, the Maritime Commission and several other agencies. The Civil Aeronautics Administration of the Department of Commerce is investigating problems of private flying after the war. Such are: the demand of private fliers for safer and more easily maneuverable light-weight planes, radio communications, and other aviation equipment; the need of airways to accommodate the expected increase in air traffic; the co-ordination of airport systems at home and abroad.

The Interregional Highway Committee of the Public Roads Administration is examining the probable costs of an interregional highway

3. U. S. Department of Labor, Bureau of Labor Statistics, *Impact of the War on the Pittsburgh, Pennsylvania Area*, January 1943, Industrial Area Study No. 1 (processed).

system of about 35,000 miles. The Interstate Commerce Commission is studying, among other questions, the possibilities of air freight development as affecting railway traffic. The Maritime Commission is considering problems of the postwar use of vessels constructed during the war, the possibilities of employment in the shipping industry, the relation of overseas air transport development in relation to water transport.

### Social Security

No matter how effectively measures are devised in advance to provide employment, there will remain during and after the transition period, the economic and social risks which are inherent in modern industrial and social life. The Social Security system established by the Congress in 1935, as amended in 1939, provides a method for meeting these risks to a certain extent after the war. Many millions of American workers who may not be able to find jobs quickly will be paid unemployment benefits. Hundreds of thousands of aged workers who will have to retire from work will have built up wage credits on which they can draw. Protection will be available to the dependent survivors of insured men and women in case of death. Assistance will be provided to the needy aged, the needy blind and needy children.

However, the extent to which protection can be afforded under existing laws is regarded by the Social Security Board as far from adequate. Even before the war, the agency repeatedly pointed out defects in the present system and advocated changes which would improve it. The war has complicated the situation in many ways and makes more urgent modifications in the law to enable it to meet postwar conditions.

On the basis of its studies, the Social Security Board recommends certain changes for the postwar period. The Board urges above all the reorganization of the financial basis of the unemployment compensation system on a federal basis. At present the funds of each state are held separately for benefit payments to workers under the law of that state. This raises doubts, in the opinion of the Social Security Board, as to the ability of some state funds to finance benefits under postwar emergency conditions.

Furthermore, variations in state laws with regard to eligibility, benefit amounts and duration, disqualifications, etc., result in marked inequalities in the proportion of workers protected in the different states and in the degree of protection afforded. In many states, for instance, the law does not cover workers in very small firms. In 1940, half of the beneficiaries under state laws were still without a job when they exhausted their benefit rights. A worker whose high-quarter earnings and annual earnings are respectively $400 and $1,000, would get a weekly payment varying from $11 to $17 and total benefits varying from $100 to $400, depending on the state in which he earned his wage credits.[4]

The Board proposes to federalize the system of unemployment compensation to remove these disparities. A federal system would also do away with the present condition under which some states have funds far in excess of immediate and future needs, while others may be hard pressed to meet their liabilities. By pooling all funds, the Social Security Board claims, it would be possible to ensure payment of adequate benefits to all eligible unemployed workers, regardless of the states in which they are now covered, during the postwar readjustment period. A federal program would further equalize the cost of unemployment compensation among employers in the different states.

The Social Security Board also believes that more adequate benefit payments than now prevail are necessary. In its opinion, "in unemployment insurance, as in the present federal system of old-age and survivors insurance, benefits for dependents could afford a means of providing compensation more nearly adequate for family needs." Such a system "is needed to underwrite the Nation's future security."[5]

In contrast to that of unemployment insurance, the federal old-age and survivors' insurance system, in the opinion of the Board, is sound. About 41.6 million workers earned old-age and survivors' insurance wage credits in 1941, and their total taxable wages were $41.9 billion. What is needed now, according to the Board, is to extend the benefits of the system to agricultural labor, domestic service, public employment, service for nonprofit institutions, and to self-employed persons. The Board recommends that provisions be made under the law for workers who become chronically disabled and for those suffering temporary disability. The risk of hospital costs should also be insured to offset the heavy burden of hospital bills on family income in cases of major or prolonged illness. The Board would also change the public assistance laws so as to provide for more persons in need, equalize benefits in the different states, increase the amount of payments for aid to dependent children, and extend

4. Federal Security Agency, *7th Annual Report, Social Security Board, 1942*, Washington, pp. 15–16.
    5. *Ibid.*, p. 17.

federal aid to the states to finance medical care for recipients of public assistance.

These proposals are regarded by the Social Security Board as steps towards a unified social security program which would "give full recognition to needs at all ages from infancy to ages when earnings dwindle or cease." The Board urges the need to begin now preparations for "the sweeping readjustments which will be inevitable at the end of the war and for the continuing advance toward economic security" which is one of the main objectives of the United States.

## Social Services

Several agencies are considering the need and methods of extending existing social services such as that for mothers and children, public health, nutrition and health. A Committee on Post-War Planning in the Children's Bureau is studying measures for putting into effect the standards laid down in the White House Conference on Children. A Committee on Post-War Planning of the U. S. Public Health Service is studying the health needs of the country and the ways in which the public health services and medical care and hospitalization may be improved. The Veterans Administration is preparing plans for the insurance, hospitalization and rehabilitation of the veterans of the present war. Some of the problems are the prompt adjudication of claims for insurance by beneficiaries, as a result of the present conflict, and the maintenance of this insurance after hostilities end by those who may wish to do so.

## Urban and Rural Housing

Problems of urban and rural housing are under investigation by the National Housing Agency and by its constituent subdivisions and by the Department of Agriculture. Estimates are being prepared of the volume of annual housing construction which will be needed and possible after the war. Studies are being made of housing standards, of prefabricated housing, of the use of new materials and construction methods, and of the federal and state legislative measures, needed to promote postwar urban and rural housing development. Specific proposals on the subject have not as yet been made public.

## 3. RECOMMENDATIONS OF THE NATIONAL RESOURCES PLANNING BOARD

The studies, proposals and plans of the several government departments and agencies are limited to special problems, and they result in particular suggestions of policy which may or may not be consistent with one another. The need of co-ordination has long been recognized. The need has been felt even more keenly since 1939, as a result of the expanded activities of the regular government departments and of the establishment of many new defense and war agencies.

Early in 1941, the President requested the National Resources Planning Board to correlate the plans and programs under consideration in many federal, state, and private organizations for postwar full employment, security, and building America.[6] The Board concentrated its activities during 1941–1943 on carrying out these instructions. In performing this task, the Board[7] has conducted a number of special studies by its own staff, has enlisted the services of outside consultants and collaborators, and has organized committees and conferences composed of members from various government agencies to deal with special problems.

The studies of the Board on special aspects of postwar planning have been published during the past two years in a series of reports, technical papers and pamphlets. The general views of the Board on the nature and problems of postwar planning are presented in its report

6. National Resources Planning Board, *National Resources Development, Report for 1942*, Washington, p. 8.

7. The National Resources Planning Board was the outgrowth of legislative efforts to establish a government central planning agency which go back at least ten years. On July 20, 1933, a National Planning Board, consisting of Frederic A. Delano, chairman, Charles E. Merriam and Wesley C. Mitchell, was established by the Administrator of Public Works at the direction of the President. This first Board was superseded by the National Resources Board (an interdepartmental group under the chairmanship of Secretary Ickes) which was established by executive order on June 30, 1934. The second Board was in its turn superseded by the National Resources Committee which was established by executive order on June 7, 1935 and which continued in existence until April 1939. On April 25, 1939, the President submitted to the Congress Reorganization Plan No. 1 which was approved by Congress on June 7, 1939 and made effective as of July 1, 1939. Under this plan the National Resources Committee and the Federal Employment Stabilization Office (organized in 1931) were abolished, and their affairs and functions were transferred to the newly established National Resources Planning Board. The Board became part of the Executive Office of the President. The main functions assigned to the Board were to survey data and analyze problems affecting natural and human resources, to inform the President of the general trend of economic conditions and to recommend measures for their stabilization, to consult with other federal, state and local agencies in developing public works programs, to recommend to the President and to the Congress long-term plans and programs for the wise use and fullest development of natural and human resources, and to act as a clearinghouse and co-ordinating agency for all planning activities. The members of the Board were appointed by the President with the approval of the Senate, and served without pay, being compensated only for time spent in exercising their duties. The members of the Board from July 1939 to 1943 remained the same: Frederic A. Delano (chairman), Charles E. Merriam, and George F. Yantis. Beardsley Ruml and Henry S. Dennison served as advisers. The Director of the Board was Charles W. Eliot who headed the staff from 1933 on. The 78th Congress did not appropriate funds for the Board, and it ceased operations after July 1, 1943. The reports and plans of the Board have, however, a practical interest as an important current in American postwar planning. For details, see *National Resources Committee Progress Report, 1939*, Washington, pp. 161–168.

for 1943.[8] This report is of especial interest in so far as it brings together data which give a comprehensive survey of the problems of physical and social-economic reconstruction in the United States not easily available elsewhere.

### a. ASSUMPTIONS AND PRINCIPLES

The National Resources Planning Board emphasizes the need of planning now for the postwar period for two reasons. In the first place, peace aims are in themselves weapons of war. A clearer vision of the kind of world toward which we are headed is a powerful means of strengthening the fighting spirit of the armed forces and the ardor of the industrial workers. Second, the war may end suddenly or at different times in different parts of the world, and there will not be time at the end of fighting to consider calmly and fully the policies, or to create the machinery, necessary for an orderly reorganization to a peacetime basis.

Planning, however, can be effective only if it is related to clearly defined principles and objectives. The National Resources Planning Board believes that postwar planning in the United States must have three general aims. First, to obtain the fullest development of the human personality compatible with justice, liberty, and democratic order. Second, to develop fully all our productive resources, material and human, in such manner as to provide full employment, continuity of income, and "equal access to minimum security and living standards," and so as to maintain a balance between economic stability and social advancement. And third, to establish an effective "jural order of the world outlawing violence and imperialism" to insure international peace essential for the highest development of resources and rights.

The Board has stated these general aims in a "New Bill of Rights." The nine points of this "Bill of Rights" are as follows:

1. The right to work, usefully and creatively through the productive years;
2. The right to fair pay, adequate to command the necessities and amenities of life in exchange for work, ideas, thrift, and other socially valuable service;
3. The right to adequate food, clothing, shelter, and medical care;
4. The right to security, with freedom from fear of old age, want, dependency, sickness, unemployment, and accident;

8. National Resources Planning Board, *National Resources Development, Report for 1943*, Washington.

5. The right to live in a system of free enterprise, free from compulsory labor, irresponsible private power, arbitrary public authority, and unregulated monopolies;
6. The right to come and go, to speak or be silent, free from the spyings of secret political police;
7. The right to equality before the law, with equal access to justice in fact;
8. The right to education for work, for citizenship, and for personal growth and happiness; and
9. The right to rest, recreation, and adventure, the opportunity to enjoy life and take part in an advancing civilization.

The realization of these rights, according to the Board, depends on our capacity to weld together democracy, peace and a dynamic economy—a feat which has never been achieved in history before. It has become possible today because we have today all that is needed for a dynamic expanding economy. Not only do all necessary physical things—plant, labor, capital, and raw materials—exist to supply the reasonable wants of the people of the civilized world, and especially of the United States. We have also learned in the past decade, according to the Board, how to direct these physical things so as to make the economy serve social aims. We know now that there are no automatic devices in our economic system that will insure an equitable distribution of income between various kinds of goods and services or guarantee full use of resources. But the Board believes that there are "tools of resource management"—such as fiscal and monetary policy and methods of improving industrial organization and of stimulating consumer demand—which would enable us to operate a dynamic economy on a high level of production and consumption, given the will to do so.

For the immediate postwar years, the National Resources Planning Board sees the possibility of an economy on the order of $100 to $125 billion national income (in 1940 prices). The national income of the United States, according to the Board, is capable of far larger expansion, in view of the large opportunities for technical progress, invention and organizational improvements in the use of our resources. Indeed, the Board believes that the United States is on the threshold of "an economy of abundance," and that the present generation has it within its power not only to produce in plenty but to distribute that plenty in fairness and in justice to all.

To turn these possibilities into realities some changes in ideas, in methods, and in social-economic organization are obviously necessary. These changes, the Board emphasizes, are of an evolutionary character. They can be made in a planful way by democratic methods.

The National Resources Planning Board does not claim to have a complete and finished program. But it makes a series of recommendations which come close to such a program. The main recommendations deal with the transition from war to peace, with the maintenance of an expanding economy, with the improvement of the physical facilities of the United States, and with provisions for social security.

### b. THE TRANSITION FROM WAR TO PEACE

The transition from war to peace, according to the National Resources Planning Board, involves three steps which may overlap in time—namely, the demobilization of men from the armed forces and war industries, the demobilization of machines and war contracts, and the demobilization of war economic controls. The Board suggests that measures be prepared now for making the transition as easily as possible. For the ability to meet the immediate postwar situation wisely, declares the Board, will determine whether we shall have the opportunity to pursue an orderly progress towards long-range goals.

### (1). *The Demobilization of Men*

The Selective Service Act of 1940 requires that arrangements should be made for the return to previous employment of all those called for service with the armed forces of the government. The National Resources Planning Board has sponsored an informal conference on postwar personnel adjustment which has been meeting for over six months to suggest definite measures for this purpose. The report of this conference follows suggestions outlined by the Board for meeting the situation.

The recommendations of the Board include proposals that men and women from the armed forces be released as rapidly as military requirements and transportation facilities will permit, with "dismissal pay" in bi-weekly or weekly payments for three months' compensation. In addition, they may choose:

(1) A voluntary three or six months' "retraining course" in camp any time within six months of release; or
(2) a voluntary six months' enlistment in Civilian Work Corps; or
(3) voluntary "retraining" in service in countries of the United Nations in or near which stationed at the close of hostilities.

For all employees in war production plants or services provision should be made for comparable "dismissal pay," in weekly payments equal to six weeks' wages at the average for the previous six months; and thereafter unemployment compensation as now provided by law.

Further, provisions should be made for the rehabilitation of men and women of the civilian or armed forces, of wounded, sick, or otherwise incapacitated by war service for customary prewar occupations, through hospitalization, medical care, retraining and education to fit them for useful roles in the national life and to make them as independent as possible of further public or private aid.

### (2). *The Demobilization of War Plants and War Contracts*

The demobilization of men depends on the demobilization of war plants and on their conversion to peacetime uses. The National Resources Planning Board suggests the following interrelated policies for this purpose:

1. War plants which are to be maintained in operation should be selected before the end of the war so that local communities and industries can adjust their plans accordingly.
2. War contracts which are to be continued should be allotted to areas where the replacement of war production by peacetime activities is likely to be slow and difficult.
3. All other war contracts should be liquidated as speedily as possible with due regard to employment conditions and liabilities of contract holders.
4. Government-owned war plants should be disposed of to private operators who are willing and able to use them productively and speedily. The government should distribute these plants to numerous operators in many areas so as to prevent monopoly control and to promote a desirable regional distribution of manufacturing industries.
5. The government should facilitate the reconversion of war plants by means of plant rehabilitation grants, by low interest rates, by establishing now in the federal tax laws a "Post-War Conversion Reserve," by placing new government orders for public projects, and by supplying information to industries on consumer demand, on technical improvements, and on opportunities for new processes and products.

### (3). *The Demobilization of Wartime Economic Controls*

The National Resources Planning Board believes that conditions at the end of the war will necessitate the retention of many wartime economic controls; but that it will be possible to relax or modify some controls.

In general, the Board recommends that consumer rationing and price controls be maintained wherever the demand for goods is likely to exceed supply so as to threaten inflation. That may be especially necessary, according to the Board, in the case of consumer durable goods. It will also be necessary to continue for some time priorities for strategic raw materials and for producers' goods.

On the other hand, the Board believes that the supply of labor will be so great as to threaten labor standards built up over the years, and that vigorous enforcement of labor standards will be necessary. The Board further recommends that the government maintain control over industries which are of special importance for national defense and public welfare, such as those based on scarce raw materials, those with rapidly diminishing reserves, those supplying power and fuels, and the transportation and other public service industries. The government should also, according to the Board, retain control over patents and properties seized from enemy aliens and operate them directly or license their use in such a way as to encourage competitive development by private operators.

### C. EXPANDING ECONOMY AND FREE ENTERPRISE

For the long run, the National Resources Planning Board posits as the national economic aim the maintenance of high living standards combined with personal freedom. This can be achieved, according to the Board, only in a dynamic and expanding economy which steadily enlarges national output and income by using new scientific discoveries and better methods of organization.

The Board takes for granted that the main impulse for a dynamic economy after the war must come from private initiative and private enterprise. But it is concerned with the fact that private enterprise needs the co-operation of government in order to develop its capacities to the full and to serve social ends. Private enterprise after the war will call for government assistance to free it from the uncertainties and breakdowns from which it has suffered in the past.

The program of the Board for the development of a dynamic economy centers around the problem of the methods by which government and private enterprise can co-operate to achieve common national aims. The policies outlined by the Board deal (1) with government measures to assist and promote private enterprise directly, and (2) with economic and social activities—especially, the improvement of physical facilities—which belong properly in the domain of government and which supplement and reinforce those of the private sector of the economy.

## (1). *The Promotion of Free Enterprise*

If private enterprise is to be free and democratic after the war, it must be assisted by the government, according to the National Resources Planning Board, in three ways. First, the government should help private business to develop new processes and improved products, to stimulate initiative so as to open the channels of investment opportunity, large and small. For this purpose, the government should undertake and foster a large program of technological research, provide industry and agriculture with scientific and technical information, enlarge its scientific agencies such as the National Bureau of Standards, and provide funds to support technical workers and research in industry and in educational institutions.

Second, the government must take measures, in the opinion of the Board, to prevent excessive concentration and abuse of economic power, or monopolistic privilege, and to check the wasteful exploitation of the nation's resources. Where the productive capacity of industry becomes concentrated in the hands of a few large corporations which use their power not to improve efficiency but to increase profits through financial and market controls, the Board recommends more vigorous and discriminating prosecution of the antitrust laws. The war production program has led to the concentration of contracts in large concerns and has tended to strengthen the large business concerns. About 70 per cent of the value of all war contracts to July 1, 1942, was concentrated in one hundred corporations. The concentration of production after the war will, therefore, be greater than before, especially in many basic industries. The government, according to the Board, should use the antitrust laws to prevent these large corporations from exercising their powers for monopolistic ends.

Where large production units exist because they are economically more efficient, it is not desirable to break them up into smaller units. To prevent such corporations from achieving monopolistic control, the Board recommends that they be subject to effective public restraint. The federal incorporation of all business operating in interstate commerce, in the opinion of the Board, would facilitate government control over such concerns.

While antitrust laws and public control may help to limit the activities of large business units, the government must take measures after the war to provide opportunities for independent and small newcomers in industry. It is desirable in a democracy, according to the

Board, that government assist small business units wherever they are economically efficient. As many small businesses will be in a weakened position after the war, the Board recommends that the government help such small businesses by providing technical engineering advice, easier access to raw materials, and favorable terms of financing and marketing. The Board also suggests that greater economic freedom might also be promoted through government encouragement of producers' co-operatives and of other forms of co-operative enterprise.

Finally, in those industries in which the government has already made large investments or which have special importance for national defense and the general welfare, the Board believes that the public interest might best be served either by the use of "mixed corporations" (in which the government and private interests are represented) or by government ownership and operation. The Board recommends the establishment of mixed corporations in the aluminum, magnesium, synthetic rubber, aircraft and similar industries. Such corporations should be given special powers such as the right of eminent domain, the right to assemble existing plants for reorganization, the right to use patents, etc., in order to protect the public interest and to be able to undertake large development programs where possible.

To prevent the rise of new industrial oligarchies and to maintain a democratic system of free enterprise, it is necessary also to secure the rights of the farmers, labor and consumers. The Board recommends measures to maintain the share of the farmers in the benefits of an expanding economy, and the right of labor to collective bargaining, fair wages and hours, healthy working conditions, responsibility in organization and sharing in management.

### (2). *The Improvement of Physical Facilities*

Private enterprise will be incapable after the war, in the opinion of the National Resources Board, of developing the physical environment on which a healthy and expanding social economy must rest. The physical environment of America has deteriorated in many ways over the years and is in need of large improvements and reconstruction. This applies to urban communities, rural areas, transportation, energy resources, etc.

The improvement of physical facilities has both economic and social importance. In the economic sphere, it supplies a large outlet for investment and can thus help to stabilize employment. Socially, it is a necessary part of advancing living standards and of a progressive civilization. In a general postwar program, the improvement of physical facilities can play a central part, through stimulation and direction in the expanding activities of private industry and of public enterprise.

In its report for 1943, as well as in those for previous years and in special publications, the National Resources Planning Board has outlined a large program for the improvement and development of the physical resources and physical facilities of the United States. It is impossible here to do more than to summarize briefly the main points of this program. This program offers opportunities for private enterprise, but in almost every part it requires some governmental authority or assistance to open the way to action.

*Urban Redevelopment*

The Board points out that nearly 75 million of the American people live in 3,464 towns and cities, some of which are mushroom communities, while others are decaying in whole or in part. Many of the communities are bankrupt or are having great difficulty to carry on under accumulated debt and shrinking revenues, despite rising tax rates. The war has aggravated the situation by developing huge war industries on the peripheries of cities and in areas formerly exclusively rural. After the war a new pattern of industry and settlement will develop in the United States, as a result of new technical, transport and other conditions. The problem of urban rebuilding will thus be one of paramount national concern.

There is no one formula or pattern, according to the Board, which would fit all cities and localities in their effort to improve and rebuild themselves. It is clear, however, in the opinion of the Board, that our cities can not continue after the war in the way in which they proceeded in the past, as "the unplanned products of virtually uncontrolled competition." They can be rebuilt only by planful methods which would take into account the new economic and social objectives of a better America and which would put to use the new tools which are now at hand.

Specifically, the Board recommends that cities and metropolitan areas establish planning agencies on a broad enough basis to deal with urban problems in their widest scope. New agencies or "mixed corporations" should be given authority to acquire land by all constitutional means, including condemnation, to issue revenue bonds for the purpose, and to construct, lease, sell or manage housing, commercial and industrial structures, transportation terminals, etc. The federal government, as well as the states, should provide technical assistance and grants-in-aid to the cities for these long-term purposes.

### Rural Land Improvements

There will be, according to the National Resources Planning Board, a great need after the war for public and private improvements to develop agricultural lands. Even on the basis of conservative estimates, the United States will have a population of some 149 million by 1960, or some 16 million more than today. To provide food at present levels of diet for such an additional population, to improve the diet of a large proportion of the population whose diet is now inadequate, and to maintain agricultural exports, some 40 million more crop acres will be needed by 1960. In addition, some 40 million acres of land will have to be retired by 1960 owing to erosion and to other destructive causes, and new areas must be found to take their place in agricultural production.

These additional crop areas may be obtained in various ways such as bringing into use idle and pasture land, irrigation, drainage, land clearing, etc.[9] The Board recommends a series of specific projects for irrigation and drainage, land clearance and settlement, and land conservation, through purchase or retirement of submarginal areas, and expansion of soil conservation activities.

### Range and Forest Conservation

The Board outlines also specific measures for the conservation and improvement of the western range and forest lands[10] through reseeding, reforestation, restocking, fire control, noxious plant and rodent control, better transportation and administration facilities. The pro-

9. In 1938, the Soil Conservation Service estimated that there were 53 million acres of plowable pasture on farms, of which 22 million could be cultivated without special practices to prevent serious erosion. Over 20 million acres of crop lands are now irrigated, largely in the seventeen western states. The Bureau of Reclamation estimates that unused water in these states can be conserved to give a full supply to all lands now irrigated and to reclaim 22 million additional acres. According to estimates of the Department of Agriculture, there are within existing drainage districts about 25 million acres already under cultivation, whose productivity could be increased through additional drainage, and 4 million acres of undeveloped land could be brought into cultivation through improvement in drainage works. There are still today about 42 million acres of woodland and brushland on farms, and 170 million acres of land outside of farms, which might be physically suitable for crops after clearing, *National Resources Development, Report for 1943*, pp. 28–30.

10. Almost two fifths of the 970 million acres of range lands in the United States are publicly owned.

gram of improvements on the range outlined by the Board would cost, at 1940 wage and price levels, over $1 billion a year and would require about a million man-years of labor.[11]

## Water Resources and Valley Development

The Board's program assigns an important place to the need for better control and development of the nation's water resources. In the northeastern states, the dominant need is for the control of floods, the abatement of pollution, and the production of adequate water supplies. In the Great Plains and in the Pacific Coast regions, full economic growth can come only with the proper development of their water resources. It has been estimated that if runoff now uncontrolled in the seventeen western states were to be conserved, it would be enough to supplement the water supplies for 12 million acres of land now inadequately irrigated, and to bring under irrigation 22 million acres of new land. Large increases would also become feasible in hydroelectric power, and public water supply systems.

The Board's recommendations include specific projects for the development of the water resources of the Arkansas Valley region, the Pacific Northwest, the Missouri River Basin, the St. Lawrence, etc. The Board also emphasizes the need for a unified national policy instead of the divergent and contradictory procedures carried on by some thirty federal agencies which now deal with some phase of water control. The Board reports that estimates of "the total investment necessary fully to develop and control the water resources of the nation have ranged up to 50 billion dollars."[12]

## Electric Power and Other Energy Resources Development

An expanding economy will need increasing supplies of mechanical and electrical power. The war is also showing the need and wisdom of a national policy which would aim to conserve the high-grade and scarce resources, and to develop low-grade energy, and which would

11. *National Resources Development, Report for 1943*, p. 44. If carried out to the maximum extent indicated as physically feasible by agencies in the Departments of Agriculture and the Interior, such a rural conservation and improvement program would require, over a period of from twenty to twenty-five years, about 20 million man-years of labor, and cost perhaps as much as $25 billion. The program probably will not be economically justified on this scale during the next two decades; however, much of the work is of such a nature that it can be expanded or contracted quickly and conducted on a large or small scale, to conform to the needs for public works to maintain employment. Costs should be divided among the various levels of government and among individuals according to the distribution of benefits derived from the work.

12. *Ibid.*, p. 46.

integrate the energy resources of the different regions of the country in order to increase their total potential.

In applying these ideas to electric power, the Board proposes that the national power supply be planned for the postwar decade on the basis of estimates of production requirements and utilizing to the full the possibilities of multiple-purpose water development. The Board recommends a national power gridiron consisting of a comprehensive system of low-cost generating stations and of an interconnected system of common carrier transmission lines which would provide a low-cost supply of power in the public interest.

The development of electric power, according to the Board, should be in the hands of a national public agency, while the control of distribution should remain in the hands of local groups. Independent distributing organizations—public, private, or co-operative—would purchase their wholesale supply from wholesale agencies operating as part of, or in co-operation with, publicly owned supply systems, but they would remain free to purchase from better sources, if available, or generate their own supply.

The Board favors an expanded program of electrification in rural areas along the lines suggested by the Rural Electrification Administration. The Board also makes a number of suggestions with regard to the conservation and better use of petroleum, natural gas and coal.

### The Modernization of Transportation

To provide postwar America with the transport facilities which will be needed and which would be in accord with new technical possibilities, the Board recommends the creation of a national transportation agency. The functions of the agency would be to co-ordinate all federal activities in the field of transportation and to take the leadership in the consolidation and reconstruction of transportation facilities and operations.

The Board makes special recommendations for each form of transportation. It suggests: the consolidation of the railroads into a limited number of regional systems, grade and curvature revision, construction of cutoffs and unification of important through railroad routes, application of modern signal and dispatch devices, and revision of trackage facilities to provide adequately for high-class postwar traffic.

For highway transport, the Board suggests the provision of express highways and off-street parking in urban areas. For the expansion of air transport, it recommends the development of an expanded and integrated system of airports and airways designed for both passenger and freight services; and a rational program for co-ordinating the air transport system with other types of transport.

The Board also recommends new river and harbor developments for internal and foreign trade, where required to round out existing systems and where existing or prospective traffic may thereby be handled more economically.

### (3). *Physical Reconstruction and Public Works*

In accordance with its general principles, the National Resources Planning Board finds that a large part of the postwar developmental program can best be carried out through the co-operation of public and private agencies. The Board suggests setting up one or more federal development corporations and subsidiaries in which private individuals or business groups and the government would participate in providing investment funds and in the management of which they would be represented. Such corporations could further co-ordinate their activities with existing government agencies or with new public agencies that might be established, such as the proposed national transportation agency.

However, a large part of the program for the improvement of physical facilities, according to the Board, lies entirely in the domain of public construction. Public sanitation, port and harbor improvements, highways, rural land improvements and afforestation are public works, even in the limited sense of the term. The government has always engaged in building such public works, and, according to the Board, it must do so on an even larger scale after the war.

The Board makes no forecast as to how large the public works program after the war may be. That will depend on how quickly the transition to peace is made and how effectively the postwar private economy is organized. The Board emphasizes the point that public works should be planned now and that a "shelf" or "reservoir" of public construction projects of tested value should be prepared in advance. In order to provide such a "shelf," the Board recommends:

1. The preparation of six-year programs or capital budgets by federal agencies, state governments, local governments, and other agencies, public and private.

2. Development of alternative lists of projects included in six-year programs according to size of the project, types and locations of skilled and unskilled labor involved, materials needed, rapidity of beginning, and flexibility of termination.

3. Immediate inauguration of surveys, investigations and preparation of engineering plans and specifications for selected projects through allocation of aids to federal and non-federal agencies from a fund to be administered by the President through his Executive Office; and reimbursed to the fund as part of the cost of construction of the project.

4. Advance authorization by the Congress of procedures for grants, loans, guarantees of loans, to state and local governments to be used for non-federal projects; such procedures to become effective upon appropriation of funds by the Congress.

5. Advance authorization by the Congress of construction of federal projects in six-year programs of "A" priorities. Such authorization should be effective upon appropriation of funds by the Congress, and not in itself involve any commitment for the immediate construction of the project.[13]

6. Appropriation for advance purchase of sites of projects by appropriate governmental agencies.

The Board points out that public works can not be large enough to assure an expanding national output. But the Board maintains that public works can be so planned and timed as to minimize the fluctuations of private business and thus help stabilize production and employment. The Board gives equal, if not greater, importance to the assertion that public works are essential in maintaining and developing the physical equipment of the country—its land, roads, waters, minerals, forests, harbors, on which economic growth and social advancement depend.

### d. FULL EMPLOYMENT AND SOCIAL SECURITY

The measures proposed by the National Resources Planning Board aim to stimulate private and public activities in the hope of achieving

13. The total "shelf" of federal construction projects on January 1, 1943 was $7.7 billion. Of this total, $1.35 billion was represented by projects which had not been completely surveyed and on which no definite recommendation had been made by the government department concerned. The projects recommended for construction by the appropriate federal departments thus totaled $6.35 billion. Of the latter amount, $3.35 billion will require Congressional authorization before detailed planning can be undertaken. Of the remaining $3 billion, only $1.5 billion are for projects which have been prepared with plans and specifications to the point where they can be put under construction. But many of these projects are of relatively large size and of such a nature that their construction will extend over several years. It is estimated that projects which could be put under way at once represent only about $600 million during the first twelve months of the postwar period. The projects of state and local governments which are now well enough prepared for construction are estimated at $900 million. The total of projects thus ready for immediate postwar operations is about $1.5 billion.

reasonably "full employment." But even if full employment were to be achieved, it would not do away with the need to provide for those who are unable to earn or whose income is stopped because of age, disability, sickness and the other hazards of life.

The Board thus finds that an integrated postwar economic and social program must make provisions for strengthening the social security and public aid systems of the country. The Board's emphasis, however, is on work, and its proposals deal not only with social insurance but also with the "right to work" and with special programs for youth.

### (1). *Implementing the Right to Work*

The Board asserts that "the only satisfactory way to meet the needs created by unemployment is the provision of work." Yet the Board finds that, despite the unprecedented development of public work programs since 1935 in the United States work has never been provided for more than half of the unemployed. In fact, work was not provided even for those in need. Moreover, all work programs, of the WPA and other agencies, failed in their social objectives in so far as they were limited by finances and administered on the basis of need tests in connection with local relief agencies.

To prevent such a situation in the future, the Board recommends that it should be the declared policy of the United States government "to underwrite full employment for the employables." In other words the federal government should assume responsibility for ensuring jobs at decent pay to all those who have exhausted, or are not eligible for, unemployment compensation benefits and who are willing and able to work, regardless of whether or not they can pass a test of need.

To enable the government to carry out such a policy after the war, the Board recommends that plans for socially useful work be made now, that inventories of locally and nationally needed public works and services be prepared, and that the financial resources of the local, state, and federal governments be explored immediately so as to ensure adequate appropriations to implement the guarantee of work. The Employment Service is to be extended so as to serve as the key mechanism for referring unemployed workers to available jobs, public and private. The public works programs advocated by the Board would in this way become an integral factor in guaranteeing the "right to work" and in providing "full employment."

## (2). *Special Programs for Youth*

A special problem is presented, according to the Board, by the young people of the country between school-leaving age and adulthood. The natural desire of young people is to participate fully in opportunities for productive work and economic advancement, and the tragic consequences of thwarting this desire have become all too evident in the past decade or so.

The youth work programs in operation since 1935, the Board claims, have been inadequate both in scope and content to meet the needs of youth. The Board wants a program which would improve the physical health of young people, develop a balanced combination of work experience and education, and provide guidance in planning their future occupational activities.

The Board makes several recommendations of which two are of special importance: (1) to develop adequate counseling and guidance facilities for young people in all parts of the country, utilizing the employment offices as the local co-ordinating bodies; (2) to establish a permanent government agency which would plan youth programs with emphasis on education, on teaching the use of tools and on inculcating good work habits.

## (3). *Social Insurance and Public Assistance*

To meet the problems which arise from permanent or temporary loss of earning power, or from the distressed condition of special substandard groups such as the blind and dependent children, the National Resources Planning Board recommends the use of social insurance principles where applicable, and the strengthening of public assistance schemes. In both cases, the Board's recommendations aim at extending principles and practices already recognized and approved in the legislation of the United States.

*Extension of Social Insurance*

The Board believes that social insurance should be applied as fully as possible because it offers a means of satisfying the desire for security as a right, while setting a limit to the economic and financial risks of society as a whole.

The concrete recommendations of the Board include: (1) the immediate enactment of social insurance against temporary and permanent disability; (2) revision of the old-age and survivors' insurance system so as to increase the benefits payable to low-income groups, extend the coverage of the law to agricultural and domestic workers, and to provide that part of the costs of the program be drawn from general tax revenues; (3) revision of the unemployment compensation laws so as (a) to provide more adequate minimum basic benefits; (b) to allow benefits to dependents; (c) to extend the coverage of the law to include employees of small firms employing one or more workers, of nonprofit corporations, and agricultural workers; (d) to extend the duration of benefits to a flat period of twenty-six weeks, uniform for all beneficiaries; (e) to provide for a sharing of the costs between employers, workers and the general taxpayer, and to pool all reserves in a single national fund; (f) to abolish experience rating, and (g) to replace the present federal-state system of unemployment compensation by a wholly federal system.[14]

### Special and General Public Assistances

To provide for special groups and for those who are not eligible for benefits under the social insurance system, the Board recommends more liberal provisions and wider application of procedures already in use.

The Board points out that a widespread tendency exists in the United States to deny public aid to certain groups of people regardless of the extent of their need. Single men, employable persons, farmers, the self-employed, and, above all, migrants and other persons without legal settlement or resident status are penalized in many parts of the country. Where relief is available, the level of living afforded recipients is meager. It is seldom sufficient to provide even the modest budgets necessary to maintain an emergency standard of living, and in many areas and cities the amount of relief is "disgracefully low." The Board points out further that general relief is today the only public aid measure, other than workmen's compensation, which receives no federal financial aid.

To remedy this situation, the Board recommends (1) that there should be a federal grant-in-aid for general public assistance; (2) that it should be distributed between the states on the basis of need and capacity; and (3) that general, as well as special, public assistance should not be denied any person on the basis of race, sex, marital or

14. Compare with recommendations of the Social Security Board, p. 47.

employment status or residence, such assistance to meet federal standards relating to adequacy of aid and methods of payment.

The Board also recommends special measures for the security of those serving in the armed forces and their families. Finally, the Board suggests that all related security programs should be administered by a single federal agency.

### e. EQUAL ACCESS TO HEALTH AND EDUCATION

The capacity of the individual to work effectively, to be a useful member of the community and to advance his or her social and economic status depends upon health, education, and training. Under present-day conditions, the opportunities in all these respects are very unequal for reasons which are beyond the control of the individual or of the family. In so far as geographic, industrial, and economic conditions result in great inequalities of opportunity, it should be the declared policy of the government, according to the National Resources Planning Board, to guarantee to all the people of the United States "equal access" to health and education.

### Equal Access to Health

In surveying the situation, the Board finds that the loss to the nation from all types of illness and disabilities is very large,[15] that many widespread diseases are preventable,[16] and that the provisions for medical care are distributed very unevenly.[17]

To conserve and improve the health of the people, the Board recom-

15. Estimates by the United States Public Health Service indicate that on the basis of a peacetime labor force, some 400 million man-days are lost annually from all types of disabilities. The economic cost amounts to $10 billion. In 1940 this loss of working time was fifty times greater than that due to strikes and lockouts.

The Technical Committee on Medical Care estimated that in 1938 over 4 million persons were disabled by illness on an average day.

16. Great differences now exist between the mortality and morbidity records of the different states. The death rate of infants during the first year of life for the country as a whole was 47 per 1,000 live births in 1940; Oregon and Minnesota had succeeded in bringing the rate down to 33, but in another state it was as high as 99.6.

17. In 1941, there were in the United States 1,324,381 beds in 6,358 registered hospitals. Of these, 600,000 beds were for general medical care and represent a ratio of 4.6 beds per 1,000 population, a figure slightly above the generally accepted standard for adequacy, which is 4.5 beds per 1,000 population. However, in certain states the ratio is nearly 6 beds per 1,000 people, in others as low as 2. On the basis of a ratio of only 2 beds per 1,000 population, the United States Public Health Service estimated in 1940 that at least 270 new hospitals with a combined capacity of 15,500 beds would be required to provide minimal general hospital facilities for rural areas. There are also great disparities in the availability of medical personnel in various parts of the country. Before the rapid changes resulting from the war, the national ratio of physicians to population was about one to 800, ranging in individual states from one to 500, to one to 1,400.

mends both preventive and operational measures. The preventive health measures include: (1) the development of adequate public health services and facilities in every county within the country through additional appropriations under Title VI of the Social Security Act; (2) the development of a health program for mothers and children ensuring remedial treatment as well as diagnosis and advisory services; adequately staffed maternal and child health clinics, and an expansion of health services in the schools; (3) protection of workers whether in the factory or on the farm from unnecessary accidents, controllable occupational diseases, and undue fatigue.

To assure more adequate medical and health care for all, regardless of place of residence or income status and on a basis that is consistent with the self-respect of the recipient, the Board recommends: (1) federal appropriations to aid states and localities in developing a system of regional and local hospitals and health centers covering all parts of the country; (2) assurance of an adequate and well distributed supply of physicians, dentists, nurses, and other medical personnel; (3) expansion and improvement of public medical care for needy persons through larger appropriations and through increased co-operation by and with the medical and dental professions; (4) immediate action by government in co-operation with the medical profession to formulate plans which may enable the patient to budget expenses over a reasonable period and to contribute toward the costs of care according to his ability, and which at the same time will assure to the medical personnel a decent livelihood commensurate with the high costs of their professional training; and (5) a more economic and efficient organization of the health services through the increased use of clinics, health centers, group practice and through better use of all facilities and of the time of professional workers.

### Proper Nutrition and Wholesome Housing for All

As part of its health and social program, the Board advocates government aid in improving conditions of nutrition and housing. In the case of nutrition the Board recommends continued support for public and private agencies engaged in the dissemination of knowledge of sound nutritional principles and practices, with special attention to demonstration work in the schools, factories, and farming areas; and the extension of the food stamp plan to *all* low-income groups.

The need of government aid in providing wholesome housing is emphasized in various reports of the National Resources Planning Board.[18]

*Equal Access to Education*

The National Resources Planning Board brings together facts showing the unequal distribution of educational facilities, the inadequate provisions for schoolrooms and equipment, and the failure to use the new and improved tools of teaching to prepare the young generation for the tasks of productive work and healthful living.[19] The Board asserts that the United States is now spending less than 50 per cent of the amount needed to provide a justifiable minimum educational program.

To improve these conditions after the war, the Board recommends: (1) that equal access to elementary and high school education be assured all children and youth; (2) that services for young children, such as nursery schools and kindergartens, be made generally available in urban areas and in so far as possible in rural areas where the need is greatest; (3) that equal access to general and specialized education be made available to all youth of college and university age, according to their abilities and the needs of society; (4) that adequate provision be made for the part-time education of adults through expansion of services such as correspondence and class study, forums, educational broadcasting, and libraries and museums; (5) that the *quality of education* at all levels and for all persons be made adequate to meet the needs of a democratic nation; (6) that meals at school,

18. It is estimated that there are over 7 million deteriorated and outmoded dwellings in the United States, or about one fifth of the total, and that the country could absorb from 900,000 to 1.2 million new dwellings a year for ten years besides a large volume of repairs. To meet this need, many changes must be made in the housebuilding industry, in methods of financing, and in adjusting the supply of housing to the demand of the different groups of the population. With respect to building, it is necessary to standardize and simplify parts of the house and develop prefabricating processes on a mass-production basis. Financing involves easier long-term credit arrangements, lower prices for suitable land, reform of property taxation, etc. More houses must be built at lower costs and on such terms as to be available to middle- and low-income groups in metropolitan areas, small towns and on farms. See Miles L. Colean, *The Role of the Housebuilding Industry*, National Resources Planning Board, July 1942.

19. Some of the facts quoted in the Report of the Board for 1943 may be summarized as follows: In 1940, about three quarters of a million children of elementary school age were not in school; the high school enrollment in 1940 was a little over 7 million out of a potential total of about 8.75 million. Many children cannot attend school because of low family incomes. Of the 115,000 local school districts, most of the rural school districts are so small and have such meager taxable resources that it is impossible for them to maintain a high school. In 1940, nine states spent for education less than $50 per pupil enrolled in their schools, while nine other states spent $100 or more per pupil. The value of school property per pupil enrolled, ranged from $80 in Tennessee to $525 in New York. See Report, pp. 69–73.

and supervised work and play projects and other services before and after school hours, be made available to all children who need them; and (7) that dormitories and transportation services for pupils in rural areas be expanded.

The Board recommends further that camp facilities be made available for all youth above the lower elementary grades, with work experience provided as a part of camp life; and that men and women demobilized from the armed forces and war industries be given opportunity to secure necessary retraining for civilian activities, or to continue their education in cases where it was interrupted by the war. The Board also calls for enlarged school repair and building programs and for adequate funds to be made available by the local and state governments and underwritten by the federal government, to carry out its recommendations.

### f. PLANS FOR REGIONAL DEVELOPMENT

In its work during the past decade, the National Resources Planning Board has emphasized the idea that national growth should as much as possible be based on the development of local and regional resources, and that programs should be decentralized as far as possible so as to assure the co-operation of federal, state, regional and local agencies.

Since 1941, the Board has carried on a number of regional studies, in co-operation with state and local governments and private groups, in preparation for dealing with the problems which have arisen out of the war. These problems vary from region to region, but in general they are due to the rapid growth of war industries, migration of large numbers of people, inability of regional authorities to develop public facilities rapidly enough. No less difficult local problems loom ahead at the end of the war in connection with the demobilization of war industries, the return of soldiers to their homes, and the search of war workers for new jobs.

The Board recommends that every effort be made now, and at the end of the war, to co-ordinate the field services of the various agencies of the federal government. The various departments and agencies of the federal government could organize closer co-operation on a regional basis by establishing common regional centers. They could pool their resources to make a more concerted attack on the problems of each region.

## g. FINANCIAL AND FISCAL POLICIES

The postwar program outlined by the National Resources Planning Board, to be realized, involves large outlays of money. Considering only the projects which are primarily of a public character, the federal, state and local expenditures specified in the 1943 Report of the Board mount up to about $18 billion.[20] If projects for urban redevelopment, housing, health, and social security are added—the total would be billions more. The annual amounts required would, of course, depend on the spacing and timing of the separate elements of the program.

The National Resources Planning Board stresses the need of adjusting financial and fiscal policies to this large program of national economic and social development. As a general principle it urges that the fiscal and monetary policies of the federal government be so conceived and administered as to supplement the activities of private enterprise in the maintenance of adequate effective demand.

The Board recommends that the several branches of the federal government dealing with fiscal and monetary policies should work within the framework of a common national policy. For this purpose, the Board suggests an office of economic stabilization on a permanent basis. This office should assure consistent national policy in the fields of taxation, expenditure, federal borrowing, federal lending, and monetary policy, and should co-ordinate the fiscal policies of state and local governments with those of the federal government.

The Board makes only a few suggestions with regard to the specific policies which it regards possible and desirable. It suggests, for the postwar period, the retention of a progressive (graduated) tax structure and a broadened tax base, major emphasis on individual income taxes, less reliance on the corporate income tax; and sharp reductions in consumption taxes.

## h. PUBLIC REACTIONS TO THE BOARD'S PROPOSALS

The two reports of the National Resources Planning Board submitted to the Congress by the President on March 10, 1943[21] aroused

20. For the control of soil erosion—$4.5 billion; flood control structures—$500 million; irrigation projects—$3 billion; drainage—$1 billion; range improvements—$1 billion; watershed developments—$3 billion; recreational land improvements—$4.5 billion; repair and building of schools—$750 million to $1,250 million a year, depending upon period of construction.

21. The two reports are: (1) *National Resources Development, Report for 1943; Part I. Post-War Plan and Program;* and (2) *Security, Work and Relief Policies, 1942.*

widespread comments from the press, the Congress, labor and employers' organizations and from other organized social groups. Though some of these comments seem to have been based on a rather hasty examination of the reports, they are important in so far as they reveal conflicting attitudes towards the proposals of the Board.

The strongest opposition to the Board's recommendations was voiced by the large newspapers and by employers' organizations. The Board's proposals were criticized on various grounds, the chief of which are: (1) that they are contrary to the "American tradition of free enterprise and private initiative"; (2) that they extend government control and increase bureaucracy; (3) that the costs of the program would be "staggering"; and (4) that the program is an embodiment of "New Dealism" and is thus in the nature of a political platform.

On the other hand, the Board's proposals, especially those relating to social security, were endorsed by the American Federation of Labor and by the Congress of Industrial Organizations. The report as a whole was endorsed by what is usually referred to as the "liberal weeklies," and declared by some to be a "charter for America."[22]

### 4. THE CONGRESS AND POSTWAR PROBLEMS

Some of the plans of the National Resources Planning Board and of other government agencies may be realized on the basis of powers already available to the government or through the action of private economic and social organizations. The larger part of these plans, however, require approval of, and appropriations by, Congress.

Even while the United States was still in a state of national defense and emergency, before December 7, 1941, several resolutions were introduced in the Senate and in the House of Representatives to establish a "Post-Emergency Economic Advisory Commission,"[23] or a similar body, to study in advance problems arising out of national defense activities. After December 7, 1941, resolutions were offered for the same purpose in the Senate and in the House by members of the 77th Congress. None of these was reported out of committee.

In the 78th Congress, two types of measures in preparation for the postwar period have been so far considered. One is represented by bills

22. *The New Republic*, April 19, 1943.
23. This was proposed by Senator Robert F. Wagner of New York and by Representative Ramsay in January 1941; also by Senator Claude Pepper of Florida.

introduced in the Senate and House dealing with specific issues. Such are (1) the bills for the rehabilitation and retraining of persons disabled while members of the armed forces or in war industries, and (2) bills for the enlargement of the social security system, introduced in the Senate by Senator Robert F. Wagner of New York and Senator Murray of Montana and by Representative Dingell in the House.

The Wagner Bill is intended to put into law the recommendations of the Social Security Board and of the National Resources Planning Board. It would extend the social security program to 15 million now excluded, including farm and domestic help. It would include all soldiers after the war under unemployment insurance, with benefits generally ranging from $12 to $30 a week depending on the size of family, costs to be met by the government in lieu of pay-roll payments from civilian workers.

It would set up a unified federal insurance system to replace the existing forty-eight different state systems. Unemployment benefits would be increased and reorganized. It would establish a national health insurance system under plans which, Senator Wagner declares, would not include "socialized medicine."

It would establish a national system of employment offices to aid demobilization.

The more important provisions of the Bill are as follows:

1. *Unemployment insurance*: Benefits payable for twenty-six weeks, to maximum of fifty-two weeks if funds are available; rates set at 50 per cent of the first $12 a week wage, plus 25 per cent of the wage exceeding $12 and one half of the basic weekly benefit added for dependents—the total not to be more than 80 per cent of the weekly wages or $30, whichever is the lesser. Domestic and agricultural workers, as well as seamen and employees of nonprofit establishments are included.

Former members of the armed services would get benefits of $12 a week, with dependents' allowances up to $30.

2. *Old-age and survivors' benefits*: Increased from present $10 a month to $20 minimum, from $85 to $120 maximum. Coverage also extended to workers previously left out, with government employees' coverage provided under voluntary agreement.

3. *Sickness and disability*: Federal system of medical and hospital insurance set up; temporary disability and maternity care put under unemployment insurance, permanent disability under old-age and survivors system.

Health insurance would be given to every insured worker, with wife and family. Under the arrangement the individual would be entitled to selection of physician, among those who had voluntarily agreed to come under the system.

Doctors would be free to enter or stay out of the system, and those who entered would be allowed to select patients.

Insured hospital care, under the plan, would be for thirty days, although this might be increased depending on the financial experience. Various limitations are put on the proposed medical care expenses.

4. *Aid to needy*: Federal grants to states under a unified system of public assistance would broaden coverage and raise the limits on benefits.

5. *Financing the program*: Contributions by workers and employers raised to 6 per cent of wages of $3,000 a year and less. Self-employed people shall pay 7 per cent of the market value of their services up to $3,000 a year.

The second type of proposals are in the form of resolutions to deal with postwar planning in a general and comprehensive way. These resolutions differ in scope, in procedure to be used, and in powers asked for. Most of the resolutions would set up committees either in the Senate or in the House, or jointly, to study postwar problems.

One of the more elaborate proposals is that of Representative Everett M. Dirksen of Illinois for a joint committee on planning and reconstruction. Mr. Dirksen's proposed joint committee is to be composed of eleven members of the Senate (six from the majority and five from the minority parties) to be appointed by the President of the Senate, and eleven members of the House of Representatives (six from the majority and five from the minority parties) to be appointed by the Speaker of the House. A Congressional planning and reconstruction service would be created to "more effectively plan and prepare for the problems of demobilization, full employment after the termination of the present conflict, the reconversion of private industry, the maximum utilization of new industrial and agricultural processes and techniques, the cataloging of Federal, State, and local relief and work-relief projects, the evaluation of the usefulness and propriety of such projects, and the utilization of our national resources, and to better survey and supervise the appropriations and the expenditures made in pursuance of such appropriations that are made by the Congress for the above purposes, and to more effectively carry out any plan, plans, or programs of post-war reconstruction." The appropriations for the committee are not to exceed $1,000,000 for each fiscal year.

The bill introduced by Representative Jerry Voorhis of California proposes to bring into the process of planning for the postwar period not only the Congress and administrative agencies but also private groups and organizations. Representative Voorhis proposes to establish a national commission for postwar reconstruction, to be composed of thirty-nine members, ten Congressional members and twenty-nine associate members. The Congressional members shall consist of five members of the House of Representatives, to be appointed by the Speaker of the House, and five members of the Senate, to be appointed by the President of the Senate. The associate members shall consist of twenty-nine to be appointed by the President as follows: three from the executive branch of the government; three from organizations of farmers; three from organizations of labor; three from organizations of business and industry (at least one of whom shall be from an organization of small business); one from organizations of banks and financial institutions; three from church organizations; three from organizations of American war veterans (at least one of whom shall be a combat veteran of the Second World War); two from educational associations; two from organizations of consumers; three from co-operatives—one from consumer co-operatives, one from producer co-operatives, and one from credit unions; one from public health and welfare associations; one outstanding economist; and one outstanding industrial engineer. In the case of appointments to be made by the President any nationally recognized organization of any group from which appointment is to be made may submit to the President for his consideration a list of not less than three persons as nominees for appointment, and the President shall be guided by such nominations in making appointments to the commission.

The aim of the commission's work shall be the development of a practical program for the continuous full employment of all Americans able and willing to work, the achievement and maintenance of a condition of economic health and welfare, for all groups in the population, and the preservation of opportunity for free enterprise. Such a program shall not be limited to legislative proposals but may also include plans for action by business, finance, labor, agriculture, consumers, or any other groups, organizations, or citizens which would, in the opinion of the commission, contribute to the objectives set forth in this section.

The commission shall continue until such time as its work is completed. It shall report to Congress and the President from time to time upon the progress of its work. Within one year from the date of its creation, the commission shall make a preliminary report.

The bill would appropriate $500,000 to carry out its provisions and would focus more directly on the domestic aspects of postwar reconstruction.

Partly as a result of the discussion aroused by the reports of the National Resources Planning Board submitted to the President and to

Congress on March 11, 1943, the Senate passed on March 12 the resolution on postwar planning which had been introduced some time before by Senator George of Georgia. In accordance with this resolution, a Special Committee on Post-War Economic Policy and Planning was set up.[24] The Committee has full authority to investigate all matters relating to postwar economic policy and problems; to gather information, plans and suggestions from all informed sources, to study them and to report findings and conclusions to the Congress from time to time. The Committee as a whole, or through subcommittees, is clothed with full investigatory powers, including authority to subpoena witnesses and documents.

The role of the Congressional committees in postwar planning can be important in three ways. The committees, in the first place, may bring together and study current plans and proposals by private groups and governmental agencies. This should help clarify the alternatives which such plans offer. Second, they can translate some of these proposals into legislative terms and thus enable the Congress to prepare in advance for action on measures which may be necessary at the end of the war. Third, they can serve as a forum through which the American people may be informed on the underlying issues and on the changes which the war may leave in its trail.

24. Senator Walter F. George is Chairman. The other members are Senators Barkley of Kentucky, the majority leader, Hayden of Arizona, O'Mahoney of Wyoming, Lucas of Illinois and Pepper of Florida, Democrats; and McNary of Oregon, the minority leader, Vandenberg of Michigan, Austin of Vermont and Taft of Ohio, Republicans.

The Senate Post-war Committee invited The Brookings Institution to aid the Committee in planning and conducting its inquiry. As part of its collaboration, The Brookings Institution will make several special studies in which the Committee has expressed a definite interest. The Brookings Institution will also make available to the Committee the results of investigations upon which The Institution has been engaged for some time, bearing on the postwar period. Two studies have already been presented to the Committee and the titles of these are, *Post-War Tax Policy and Business Expansion*, and *Post-War Re-employment*.

## Chapter 4

# GOVERNMENT PLANS FOR THE RECONSTRUCTION OF GREAT BRITAIN

SINCE THE BEGINNING of the war, there has been a strong and deep feeling among the British people that England will never be the same after the war and that the war effort must be followed by a peace effort to create a new and better Britain. Out of the evils and suffering of the war must come a greater and richer life which will not be marred by the dread of periodic unemployment, by the discomforts of chronic overcrowding, by the disabilities of inadequate education, and by the frustrations of poverty and social insecurity.

Despite the supreme need for devoting all energy and time to the tasks of winning the war, the British government has given considerable attention to the economic and social problems with which the country will be faced after the war is won. The main social-economic groups organized in trade unions, trade associations and otherwise have come forward, in some cases at the request of the government, with specific proposals for postwar policy or with general schemes of reconstruction. Private research groups have made studies of special problems which will call for action at the end of hostilities. And the major political parties have either indicated the lines of postwar action which they favor or have sketched general programs on which they expect to take their stand.

It is characteristic of the British outlook that a large part of this preparation for postwar reconstruction goes under the name of "planning." The term is used in England not merely in the general sense of advance study and preparation but in a more special meaning. Planning is being more widely accepted as a new principle of social-economic organization and policy in contrast to that of laissez faire and of unorganized individual action. It has become almost general in England to identify postwar reconstruction with physical, economic and social planning in this sense of the word.

This trend can be understood in the light of the changes in British life between 1919 and 1939. During these two decades, and especially in the ten years before the outbreak of the present war, England was gradually drifting away from its traditional policies of unregulated

77

private enterprise, individual responsibility and free trade. Their place was being taken by state aid, government provisions for social security and by protectionist and preferential imperial trade policies. After 1931, England also departed from its traditional adherence to the gold standard and laid increasing emphasis on "monetary management" and on "easy credit" as a means of stimulating business activity and of providing "full employment."

Back of these trends in economic policy and social thought are certain basic changes in the industrial structure and in the economic position of England. In the decade before 1939, Great Britain was losing her hold on a large part of her former world markets for coal, textiles and machinery. As her export trade decreased in volume and value more than her imports of food and raw materials, England found it impossible to pay for the balance out of income from services and was forced to liquidate some of her overseas investments. While export trade was decreasing, an expansion of new industries geared largely to the domestic market and to home consumption took place. In the light of these changes, there was a growing uncertainty as to whether the economic and social future of England might not lie in this new development of the home market rather than in markets abroad.

The nearly four years of war have rather accentuated the economic and social trends of the 1930's. The needs of war production have eliminated many small and inefficient plants and stimulated the "concentration" of production in the so-called "nuclei" plants of larger size and greater productive capacity. The intervention of the government in industrial organization and management has been extended in various ways. Export trade has fallen off considerably and many markets have been lost to British goods as a result of military operations, the submarine menace, lack of materials and shipping, and other factors. On the other hand, the government has had to assume responsibility for feeding the people and for providing minimum standards of nutrition for large elements of the population.[1]

Both the pre-1939 trends and the effects of the war have affected the outlook for the future. The questions which loom particularly large in British economic thinking are: the extent and character of postwar foreign trade, the place of agriculture in the British economy, and

1. For further discussion of these changes, see Lewis L. Lorwin, *Economic Consequences of the Second World War*, Chapter XVIII. Also, Mary E. Murphy, *The British War Economy, 1939–1943*, Professional and Technical Press, New York, 1943.

the relocation of industry. The answers to these questions, it is felt, will determine the structure of the British economy and the standard of living which it may provide for the British people. If satisfactory answers can be found for these questions, it will be possible, so it is thought, to evolve policies and measures which will provide employment and economic security and improve the health and education of the people.

There is a certain division of labor in the British postwar planning which is partly designed and partly accidental. The government is carrying on its planning work through the regular departments and special committees and is evolving machinery which may be used for national planning in a systematic way. The private economic organizations and groups are aiding the government in many ways, but are also outlining their own general programs to influence public opinion on the subject.

To get a clear picture of the plans which are now being made for the reconstruction of Britain after the war it is well to survey first the activities of the principal government committees and agencies, then those of the main organized groups and unofficial associations.

## 1. GOVERNMENT PLANNING AGENCIES

For several years before the beginning of the present war the British government had been concerned about certain aspects of the "physical" development of England. According to widespread opinion in government circles (as well as outside the government) there had been an overdevelopment of industrial areas. It was thought that industry had encroached upon some of the best lands of England which could be put to better agricultural and other uses, and that England was "over-urbanized" to an extent which created serious problems for transportation, housing and public health.[2] As far back as 1932, Parliament tried to deal with these problems by enacting the Town and Country Planning Act which authorized local planning authorities to promote the development of local areas in accordance with town or country plans formulated locally.

Little progress was made under the 1932 Act, owing to administrative and financial difficulties, and a growing opinion developed in favor of national guidance and central planning. This opinion was

2. See Royal Commission on the Distribution of the Industrial Population, *Report presented to Parliament by Command of His Majesty, January 1940*, London. This Commission is usually referred to as the Barlow Commission, as its chairman was Sir Montague Barlow.

strengthened by the war. Owing to the need for producing large supplies of foodstuffs, the government took steps to prevent the further use of agricultural land for other than agricultural purposes. The large-scale destruction of cities and houses as a result of bombings and the relocation of industries in response to war needs suggested that the physical rebuilding of the country should be carried out in accordance with some general plan in the national interest.

## Ministry of Works and Buildings

In October 1940, the British government established the new Ministry of Works and Buildings to study the problem. Lord Reith, an engineer and well-known as organizer of the British Broadcasting Company, was made Minister of Works and Buildings. Lord Reith, long an advocate of planned development, gathered around him engineers, architects, economists and town planners and engaged the services of some of the universities and private planning societies to lay the plans for a new Britain after the war. A consultative panel, established by Lord Reith, began drawing up maps showing the physical features of the land, land uses, population distribution, location of industry and communications, and drafted base maps for the whole country in order to facilitate the co-ordination of the activities of local planning authorities.

On February 26, 1941, Lord Reith stated in the House of Lords, as Minister of Works and Buildings, that the government had authorized him to proceed in his preparatory work on the assumptions that (1) the principle of planning would be accepted as national policy and that some central planning authority would be required; and that (2) this authority would proceed on a positive policy involving agriculture, industrial development and transport.

The British public had clearly realized for some time that the key to planned development lay in the control of the use of land, that such control was bound up with the problem of property rights, and that this problem must be solved before a planning program could be worked out or applied. In January 1941, Lord Reith appointed an Expert Committee on Compensation and Betterment with Justice A. A. Uthwatt as chairman to study the problem.

In July 1941, the Committee submitted an interim report in which it made three important recommendations. (1) The government should forthwith declare, as a general principle, that payment of compensation in respect of the public acquisition or public control of land will not exceed sums based on the standard of "prewar values," that is values as of March 31, 1939. (2) A central planning authority should be established to control building and all other developments throughout the country so that work should not be undertaken which might prejudice national reconstruction. (3) "Reconstruction areas" should be defined as soon as possible and no work in such areas should be permitted except with the license of the central planning authority. These recommendations were intended to prevent speculation in land and to provide national directives for reconstruction.

On July 17, 1941, Lord Reith announced in the House of Lords that the government was ready to accept these recommendations, with some minor qualifications. The Committee continued its work until September 1942, when it published its final report (known as the *Uthwatt Report*).

As the Uthwatt Committee was concerned primarily with urban land, Lord Reith appointed in October 1941, another committee under the chairmanship of Lord Justice Scott to study the problem of agricultural land. In the fall of 1942, this committee, known as the Committee on Land Utilization in Rural Areas, submitted a report which stirred up a good deal of controversy.

*Ministry of Works and Planning*

On February 11, 1942, Lord Reith announced in the House of Lords the conclusion reached by the government that the best means of carrying out its pledge to establish a central planning authority was to establish a "Ministry of Works and Planning." Ten days later Lord Reith was succeeded in his office by Lord Portal.

In April 1942, Lord Portal announced that his ministry would be renamed Ministry of Works and Planning and that legislation to that effect was being introduced. On June 2, 1942, the House of Commons passed the bill to establish a Ministry of Works and Planning. The Planning Act of June 1942, provided for the transfer to the Minister of Works and Planning the existing functions and rights of different departments relating to town and country planning. The new Minister was to co-operate with other departments and with local authorities in order to insure as much as possible that the national policy of urban and rural development was carried out as a single and consistent whole. For purposes of co-ordination, an interdepartmental committee was set up, and questions which it could not settle were to be referred to a committee of ministers.

The Ministry of Works and Planning was thus limited in scope and functions. The government declared its intention, however, to give the new Ministry additional powers necessary for enforcing town and country planning from a national point of view. The government also stated its intention to weld into a single and consistent policy the activities of the various departments concerned in postwar reconstruction.[3]

### Ministry of Town and Country Planning

The Planning Act of June 1942, was regarded by some as a halfway measure and by others as a first step. After much public discussion and a debate on the subject in both Houses of Parliament during the latter part of 1942 and the early months of 1943, the government introduced a bill for the establishment of a Ministry of Town and Country Planning. This bill became law in February 1943, and W. S. Morrison[4] was appointed Minister of Town and Country Planning.

The functions of the new Ministry are defined in general terms. It is to secure "consistency and continuity in the framing and execution of a national policy with regard to the use and development of land." What the "national policy" is to be was left unspecified.[5] The new Ministry thus takes over the functions of the Ministry of Works and Planning and of the Ministry of Health relating to town and country development.

### Minister of Reconstruction

Even before the Ministry of Works and Planning was set up, Arthur Greenwood had been appointed Minister without Portfolio to study proposals for social and economic reconstruction. He was replaced in February 1942 by Sir William Jowitt. Late in 1943 Lord Woolton was appointed Minister of Reconstruction to preside over a ministerial committee which "predigests" material on postwar planning for the consideration of the War Cabinet. The plans are prepared in different departments. The Ministry of Health, for instance, is in charge of the social and financial aspects of housing.

3. See Montell Ogdon, "Britain Creates Central Planning Authority," *Foreign Agriculture*, October 1943.

4. Not to be confused with Herbert Morrison, a leader of the Labour Party and Home Secretary in the present government.

5. *The Times*, London, January 28, 1943; February 6, 1943.

The Ministry of Labour deals with plans affecting the labour situation. It is the task of the Minister of Reconstruction to harmonize these plans when they conflict, and to see that the entire field of economic and social life is adequately covered. He may call the attention of departmental ministers to gaps in their plans. It is emphasized in official statements that Lord Woolton is not the head of a Ministry of Reconstruction but the Minister, i.e., "he relies on various Departments to do work appropriate to them while he, himself, is organizing to see that the plans are presented as a comprehensive whole." Sir William Jowitt works under and with the Minister of Reconstruction and represents his policy in the House of Commons.

## 2. The Physical Reconstruction of Britain

The war is giving the British people a new chance to improve the physical structure of the country: repairing the damage done by bombs, in itself a tremendous task; rebuilding as a result of the changes which have taken place in the location of industry; and new building of houses, schools and other structures which had to be stopped during the war.

### a. URBAN REDEVELOPMENT AND INDUSTRIAL RELOCATION

The new Ministry of Town and Country Planning and the Ministry of Works and Planning are charged with the task of total physical reconstruction. This involves the preparation of plans for town and country development which would take account of the changes in the distribution of the population, of the new needs for transportation, and of the possibilities for more decentralized and diversified industries, and which would make possible a larger enjoyment of the amenities of life. Nineteenth century England, it has been said, built the ugliest towns the world has ever known. It must make up for the errors of the past and lay the foundations of a better civilization in new and better cities and buildings. [6]

One of the basic tasks in this process of rebuilding is to decentralize industry and to distribute the industrial population more evenly. The opinion is widespread in England that the concentration of industry and population has been carried too far. Professor Patrick

6. In addition to the official reports quoted later in this chapter, see "Plans for Physical Reconstruction," *Planning*, Broadsheet No. 198, PEP (Political and Economic Planning), London, December 22, 1942.

Geddes some years ago decried the fact that two fifths of the British population were huddled together in some seven "town-aggregates" with over a million people each, which he called "conurbations" and which, in his opinion, had unhealthy economic and social effects. Such are the conurbations of London, Birmingham, Sheffield, Manchester and several others. To achieve a better economic and social balance, it is thought necessary to break up these conurbations and to spread industrial activities more evenly throughout the country.

The task of such planning is still in the initial stages of fulfillment. Studies are being made of the factors involved in the localization of industry, such as sources of raw materials, power, labor supply, transportation, and markets. The Royal Institute of British Architects has prepared general statements on the subject and some architects have worked out a plan for the rebuilding of London.[7] Several private research associations[8] are engaged, with the aid of the government, in regional surveys to determine the best possible industrial program for the several districts of England.

Some general features of the remedies proposed, however, are already clear. It is proposed, in the first place, to halt the expansion of London and, if possible, to reduce its size by requiring permits for the establishment of new plants and by giving special inducements to manufacturers and other businessmen to locate elsewhere. Second, it is proposed to disperse industries to smaller towns and country places. It is also hoped that the reconversion of industry and the demobilization of the armed forces at the end of the war will offer an opportunity to put such a program into effect.

## b. THE HOUSING PROGRAM

More specific are the plans with regard to postwar housing. The technical aspects of housing are being studied in a special division of the Ministry of Works and Planning[9] while the social and financial aspects, as pointed out above, are within the province of the Ministry of Health.

7. Royal Institute of British Architects Reconstruction Committee, *First General Statement of Conclusions*, August 1942.

8. Among these are: Town and Country Planning, the Nuffield College Social Reconstruction Survey, and the West Midland Group for Post-War Reconstruction.

9. This division, known as the Directorate of Post-War Building, is directed by Sir Ernest Simon, an engineer and formerly Lord Mayor of Manchester. This division has three main committees dealing respectively with the design of houses and flats; a structures policy committee, and an installations policy committee, which deals with heating, ventilating, etc. See *Industrial Standardization*, New York, October 1942.

The estimates of postwar housing needs in Great Britain run into large figures. The destruction due to bombings is likely to create a need for repairing and rebuilding from 1.5 million to 2 million dwellings. The replacement need due to the war is large, and so are the arrears in slum clearance and abatement of overcrowding. The total number of dwellings needed to give the British people more adequate housing facilities is placed between 3 million and 4 million new dwellings to be built over a period of several decades.[10]

After the First World War there was a grave shortage of houses and Lloyd George launched his famous campaign for "Homes for Heroes." Building, however, was slow in getting under way. Speculation in land, high cost of building materials, inefficient organization of the building industry, restrictive trade union practices and high interest rates raised the cost of housing and slowed up the provision of decent homes for the low-income groups. It took nearly a decade of constant and steady pressure from the public and the organized workers to overcome these difficulties. The result was a steady increase in the rate of building, especially after 1929, with the result that during the last years before the war over 300,000 houses were built each year. In the twenty years between 1919 and 1939, nearly 4 million new houses were completed in England, a large part of which were fairly well built.

There is not much interest in Great Britain in prefabricated houses. The type of dwelling which is planned is much the same as that of prewar days—a modest brick one-story, four- to five-room house with modern appurtenances. The cost of such a house is estimated at between £250 and £350 at relatively low rates of interest which would make it accessible to the lower-paid working groups. Brick is preferred in view of England's lack of lumber and large brick and cement industry.

Profiting by the experience of 1919–1939, it is planned to prepare a housing program which would avoid the difficulties of the years after 1919. The housing program is to be scheduled for a period of thirty years, beginning with accelerated building during the first three or four years after the war,[11] maintenance at the peak for another

---

10. The data on British housing are taken in part from the report prepared by PEP (Political and Economic Planning) under the title, *Housing England*, London, 1934, and from the broadsheet published by PEP, October 5, 1937. See also, *Urban and Rural Housing*, League of Nations, Geneva, 1939.

11. It is estimated that during the first year after the war it would be possible to build about 200,000 houses; the number could be increased to 400,000 during the second year.

six or seven years, and then tapering off gradually. In order to carry out such a program, it is proposed to increase the number of workers in the building industry by special training and to rationalize at the same time building operations.[12] During the first ten years of maximum building, a force of some two million workers in the building and civil engineering industries might be maintained. After that, entry to the trade would be closed so that by the end of the thirty-year period the force might again be reduced to the level of one million or less if necessary.

In preparation for this housing program, the Ministry of Works and Planning is studying the problems of mobilizing materials and labor. A report released by the Ministry in March 1943[13] proposes to build up a labor force of 1.4 million men in the building industry within three years after the war. Half of these men would be craftsmen. To achieve this, it will be necessary to train 50,000 workers every six months after the war for three years. This will require 70,000 training places and 6,000 instructors. The productivity of labor is to be increased also by better methods of industrial organization. The building industry in Great Britain is a small-scale industry and much waste results from the dispersion of materials and labor among many contractors and subcontractors.[14]

To carry out the housing program, the Ministry of Works and Planning and other agencies are to have wide powers of control over the building industry after the war. These agencies are to consult, however, with employers and with the trade unions in matters of technical proficiency, training of workers, letting of contracts, and the best utilization of resources in general. The consultative bodies which were set up in the summer of 1941 for war purposes, namely, the Central Council for Works and Buildings and the Builders' Emergency Organizations may serve in such capacity after the war.[15]

12. There were in 1938 about 886,000 insured employees in the building industry.

13. Ministry of Works and Planning, *Report on Training for the Building Industry*, London, 1942.

14. In 1939, there were in England 60,000 contractors, 12,000 architects and trainees, 1,000 surveyors and trainees as well as a large number of consulting engineers and specialist subcontractors. There was little co-ordination or organization among them. The two main employers' organizations are the Building Trades Contractors Federation and the Civil Engineering Contractors Federation. About 8,000 firms belong to the former and some 600 to the latter. The other builders, mainly small, are outside either.

15. The Council consists of employers, workers and some professional people. The members are selected by the Minister of Works and Planning and act as his advisory committee. The Council has thirteen voting members—five builders or contractors, five trade union leaders and three professional men. The Builders Emergency Organizations (BEO) were set up in the fall of 1941 on a regional basis to help control construction operations in the eleven areas into which England was divided for defense purposes. Each regional section of the

The financing of the housing program is obviously of crucial importance. In general, it is expected that most of the houses will be built by private builders with aid from the local authorities and from the central government and under general government guidance with regard to location, design, patterns, and standards of health.

### C. THE USE OF THE LAND

The British public clearly realizes that the housing program and the physical reconstruction of towns and cities will require national control over building operations for some time after the war. Even greater importance is attached to the control over the use and price of land.

The problem of land use in England is being considered from two main angles: (1) how to stabilize the value of land required for developmental purposes and how such land may be acquired by the public authorities on an equitable basis; and (2) how to stop the encroachment of urban growth and industry on land which would be better used for agricultural development. The first question is considered in the report of the Uthwatt Committee, and the second in that of the Scott Committee.

Some sentiment exists in England today, even outside socialist circles, in favor of land nationalization. Many otherwise conservative men claim that acquisition by the state of the freehold of the land is necessary to carry out the large public works of drainage, reclamation, etc., which are necessary to put British agriculture on an efficient basis, and to prevent private interest in land from hampering reconstruction in the national interest.

The report of the Uthwatt Committee[16] rejects immediate and general land nationalization on the grounds that it would interfere unnecessarily with the economic life of the country and with individual enterprise. But it goes far in the direction of nationalization. The Committee recommends that all *rights of development* in land in the vicinity of towns and cities which may be needed for further urban planning should be acquired by the state on payment of fair compensation. Compensation is to be fixed as a single sum for the whole

---

BEO has a management committee at the top composed of six representatives of builders and of workers and an executive board which carries out the decisions of the management committee.

16. Ministry of Works and Planning, Expert Committee on Compensation and Betterment, *Final Report, Presented by the Minister of Works and Planning to Parliament by Command of His Majesty, September 1942*, London, 1942.

country and is to be divided among owners whose land has a development value in proportion to the values which their land had on March 31, 1939. Each owner would continue, under this scheme, to enjoy the ownership and use of his land, but he would give up the right to develop it or to profit from an uncontrolled rise in its value. The state is also to have the power to acquire the land when it is wanted for public purposes or for approved private development.

Control of land development would thus pass from the individual to the state. No scheme for land development could be undertaken unless first approved by a central planning authority. After approval, the land would be purchased by the state at its then fair value, excluding of course, the development value already paid for. The state might then carry out the development project as a public enterprise or, more likely, it might lease the land to a private person or group who undertook the approved project. As development projects are approved, more and more land would come into the hands of the state and would be leased to private developers.

With regard to built-up areas, the Uthwatt Committee recommends that the planning authority be given power of compulsory purchase of (1) war-damaged areas and of obsolete areas in need of reconstruction, and (2) of land which is not being developed in accordance with national plans and interests. The planning authority would develop such areas itself or dispose of them to private development groups, not by way of sale but only of lease. The Committee also urges that, where development rights are not to be bought by the state, a tax should be imposed on increases in annual site values, so that the community may obtain part of the increment in the value of built-up areas due to community growth.

The Uthwatt Committee suggests that there should be a minister for national development who would take over the planning functions involved in its recommendations. This minister would issue directions to a commission composed of specially trained persons who would administer the "development rights scheme" as proposed and in accordance with general national plans.

In one section of its report, the Uthwatt Committee seems to take a favorable attitude towards the proposal of converting all land into leasehold interests. But approval is confined to the plan to give the state unconditional control only of development in areas outside of towns and of the reconstruction of the cities.[17]

17. The Committee devotes a large part of its report to a discussion of the technical details of classifying and valuing land which cannot be considered here.

### d. RURAL HOUSING AND THE IMPROVEMENT OF COUNTRY LIFE

While rebuilding the cities and rehousing the industrial population are regarded as major postwar tasks in England, the need for improving housing and living conditions in the country areas, especially for farm workers, is also recognized. The steady decline in the area under cultivation in England before 1939 and in the number of people engaged in farming[18] is due not only to economic factors but to social conditions which make life on the farm and in the villages less attractive and comfortable than in urban areas.

Between 1931 and 1939, the British government took various measures to improve the economic and social position of farmers and farm workers. As the farmers were suffering largely from low prices and foreign competition, the government tried to assist them by means of subsidies, by the promotion of marketing schemes which were intended to raise prices and by imposing quotas on the imports of such products as wheat, bacon, etc. While these measures had some success, they did not stop the decline of agriculture and did not solve the problems of the farmers whose difficulties were aggravated by high rents, high taxes and the peculiar conditions of British tenant farming.[19] The effects of these economic difficulties were evident in the backward state of housing and especially of public services on many farms and in the villages and towns dependent upon the adjacent farming country.

The condition of farm labor was especially unsatisfactory.[20] Wages were low as compared with the wages of industrial workers and often

18. The arable acreage in England and Wales decreased from 12,217,000 acres in 1900, to 11,320,000 in 1910, to 10,682,000 in 1925, and to 8,877,000 acres in 1938. The number of agricultural workers decreased from an average of 816,000 during 1921–1924 to 593,000 in 1938.

19. British farming since the early nineteenth century has been characterized by the existence of large estates whose owners let the land to tenants who in turn put capital into the business and employ hired labor. The prosperity created for agriculture by the First World War resulted in high land values, and many landowners found it more profitable after the war to sell their land. Between 1918–1921, some 12 per cent of the farming area of the country changed hands with the result that a substantial owner-occupier class of farmers came into being. These farmer-owners bought the land at high prices and often with borrowed capital at high interest rates, and fell into serious difficulties, especially after 1926.

On the eve of the present war, British farming was conducted largely as a small- and medium-sized business by capitalist farmers employing paid laborers, modified, however, by the continued existence of some large estates using tenant farmers. In 1938, there were in England and Wales 365,972 holdings of which 61,685 were between 50 and 100 acres and 226,360 holdings (62 per cent) were under 50 acres. That is, 288,045 holdings (or 79 per cent of all holdings) were under 100 acres. In 1927, about 66 per cent of all land was occupied by tenants. Over 12,000 holdings of 300 acres and over contained about 6,000,000 acres or nearly 25 per cent of the total acreage.

20. The figures cited here are taken largely from Ministry of Works and Planning, *Report of the Committee on Land Utilization in Rural Areas, presented . . . to Parliament by Command of His Majesty, August 1942.* London, 1942.

barely sufficient for the laborer to live on. There was little prospect for the farm worker to become a farmer on his own account, as he could hardly hope to accumulate the capital needed to buy land. The cottages in which the rural worker lived were generally far below the standards of housing for city workers, and many of these cottages were not fit to live in.[21]

The lack of modern facilities in rural areas affected both farmers and farm workers. In 1938 only some 30,000 agricultural holdings out of the total of 365,972 (or less than 10 per cent) were served with electricity. Gas for heating and cooking was restricted to small towns and larger villages, owing to the cost of laying mains and supply pipes. In June 1939, some 3,432 parishes in England and Wales (out of a total of 11,186) and at least one million people living in rural districts were without piped water. At least 5,186 parishes had no sewerage systems in 1939.

The high costs involved and the low returns that could be expected gave no pecuniary inducement to private capital to improve these conditions in the rural areas. The financial assistance by the government under various housing acts passed between 1923 and 1938 was inadequate to do more than scratch the surface of the problem.

While these economic and social trends led to a decline of agriculture, the outward spread of manufacturing industries was an added menace to farm and village life. Industrial plants and settlements encroached upon good agricultural land, brought in economic and social influences which were often detrimental to farm life and destructive of the charm and beauties of the countryside.

To meet these problems the Scott Committee makes a number of specific and detailed recommendations.[22] The Committee urges the building of better and more spacious rural houses (including a larger number of "untied" cottages), ready-wired for electricity and appropriately constructed to receive gas and water supplies even if such services are not immediately available. It recommends the standardization of charges for electricity and gas so as to supply the countryside as cheaply as the cities, the laying of service lines in the larger villages free of charge, and the provision of a water supply to all towns and larger villages not at present supplied.

21. A large number of farm workers in England live in so-called "tied" cottages. A "tied" cottage is a cottage which a farm worker occupies only as long as he is employed on the farm, usually at a low rent, and which he must vacate when he leaves his job.
22. Ministry of Works and Planning, *Report of the Committee on Land Utilization in Rural Areas.*

The Committee favors the development of rural industries and handicrafts which can be carried on in connection with agriculture and which would not disturb the physical and moral life of the village. It sketches a series of measures to keep good agricultural land out of industrial use, to protect the forests and parks for the use of the nation, and to conserve the beauties of the English countryside. It urges the development of "village institutions" and community centers which would make life on the farm and in rural areas more attractive and stimulate social and recreational opportunities.

The Committee emphasizes the need for local and central planning. Local planning, in its opinion, should be made compulsory and local planning bodies should have the assistance of expert technical staffs. A central planning authority is to be set up which is to guide and control rural development in line with the recommendations of the Uthwatt Committee.

The governmental machinery which the Scott Committee would establish for the formulation and execution of national planning includes four parts, namely: (1) a standing committee of the ministers concerned (such as the Ministers of Health, Agriculture, etc.) under the chairmanship of a nondepartmental minister of Cabinet rank; (2) government departments concerned with development; (3) a central planning commission; and (4) such ad hoc bodies as may be needed to carry out functions not already covered by existing ministries or other authorities or bodies. The nondepartmental minister is to be known as Minister of National Planning or Minister of National Organization.

The Scott Committee assumes that the improvement of rural life is important to maintain and develop a "healthy and well-balanced" agriculture after the war. The Committee does not, however, clearly define these aims or the policies involved. Neither does the Committee examine property rights in land or land tenure. It argues that no matter what the system of property may be, the problems of improvement would be the same. It is in favor, however, of giving the state the right to the compulsory purchase of land if that is required for developmental purposes.

The Scott Committee stresses the ideas of control and planning and emphasizes its conception of planning as "a continuous and evolutionary process in national development." It also cites a series of successive steps by which its proposals could be carried out in a period of five years: a "Five-Year Plan for Britain."

## 3. Social Security and the National Minimum

Better cities and towns and better housing are subjects of wide interest in Great Britain, but continuity of income and security from want are even more so. For twenty years before the present war Great Britain had been plagued with chronic mass unemployment. A large proportion of the population lived on the edge of poverty and in fear of slipping off into destitution. To the mass of the people—workers, clerks, small farmers and businessmen, and other groups—the supreme test of a better Britain after the war will be the degree to which the fear of economic insecurity can be removed.

While the Ministry of Works and Planning set up committees to study land use and the rebuilding of towns, the preparation of a plan for social security was stimulated by the office of reconstruction studies. When he was Minister without Portfolio, the Rt. Hon. Arthur Greenwood, created an Inter-Departmental Committee on Social Insurance and Allied Services, under the chairmanship of Sir William Beveridge, to make a survey of existing national schemes of social insurance and to recommend further action. On November 20, 1942, Sir William submitted a report on the subject to Sir William Jowitt, who transmitted it to Parliament. The report put forward a sweeping plan of a universal national system of social security which embraced every group of the population and provided state insurance against the insecurities due to unemployment, occupational hazards, illness, old age, invalidism and the death of the breadwinner.

It is now forty years or so since England began a series of measures breaking with the traditions of the common law of accidents and of the Poor Law of 1834, which led to the passage of the National Insurance Act in 1911.[23] Between 1919 and 1939, the social insurance system was extended to include the majority of workers under both health and unemployment insurance, to pay outdoor relief to unemployed workers not entitled to insurance benefits,[24] and to provide a number of other social services such as aid and pensions to blind persons, and special assistance to widows.[25]

23. The first Workmen's Compensation Act was passed in 1897; in 1908, state pensions for persons aged seventy or over were introduced; the National Insurance Act of 1911 provided a system of health insurance for groups of people below a certain income and a scheme of unemployment insurance for limited groups of workers.
24. An Unemployment Assistance Board was set up in 1934.
25. The background material of this section is based in large part on "Planning for Social Security," *Planning*, Broadsheet No. 190, PEP, London, July 14, 1942.

In spite of the great advance made in British social services in England in the thirty years after 1911, there was a growing feeling that the results were far from adequate. Criticism of the British social insurance system centered around five main charges.

In the first place, the coverage was incomplete both with regard to persons and services. Large groups of the population in the lower income groups—farm laborers, domestic workers, salaried persons—were not included in one or another of the insurance schemes provided by the government, while there were important gaps in the system as a whole such as lack of protection to survivors in case of the death of the breadwinner.

The incompleteness of the provisions was revealed by the extent to which workers had recourse to additional voluntary insurance. The studies of working-class family budgets for 1937–1938 made by the Ministry of Labour showed that the average industrial worker's family was spending a little over two shillings a week on compulsory state insurance, as compared with over three shillings sixpence a week on voluntary social security schemes such as Sick Clubs, doctors, midwifery and nursing, hospital contributory plans, superannuation, and life and burial insurance. It was also found that the poorer families spent relatively more on such voluntary insurance, especially on life and burial insurance.

Secondly, the total costs of administering the services were said to be excessive owing to the many agencies involved. For the period 1934–1937, it cost the Ministry of Pensions about £750,000 to distribute cash and medical benefits of an average annual value of £42 million. It cost about £2.5 million a year to administer contributory and noncontributory widows', orphans' and old-age pensions worth £87 million annually; and it cost £7.5 million a year to administer £79 million worth of unemployment benefits and allowances. It cost about £4 million to administer about £9 million worth of workmen's compensation payments. Most expensive of all was industrial insurance. Private companies and collecting societies collected about £65 million a year in premiums and distributed about £33.5 million in benefits—at a management cost of £22 million, plus a "shareholders' surplus" of about £2 million a year for the companies.[26]

Thirdly, the adequacy of payments and of health, medical and other services was criticized. Not enough was done, it was said, to prevent

26. See "Planning for Social Security," p. 6.

disease and disability or to rehabilitate those who had suffered loss of earning power as a result of accident or illness.

The fourth defect charged to the system was its confused and ill-assorted administrative setup. The social services were scattered among a number of unrelated government departments. Besides, the National Health Act of 1911 had incorporated into the system the various Sick Clubs, Friendly Societies and fraternal orders and commercial insurance companies which had reached a high development in England before that time and which were expected to facilitate the administration of the new law. It was claimed that these societies, to which the majority of insured belonged, did nothing for the welfare of the members beyond their statutory duties of making or withholding cash payments, and that the commercial companies made no pretense of being interested in anything but benefit claims. On the other hand, the participation of those societies and corporations increased the costs of the administration and made it more cumbersome.

The fifth charge involved the principles underlying the whole system. Compulsory social insurance, it was claimed, was a compromise between commercial insurance and social responsibility for uninsurable risks, and was therefore neither genuinely "social" nor genuinely "insurance." The system favored the stronger and higher income groups of the working population and so failed to achieve some of the purposes for which it was intended.

Some groups in England would meet these criticisms by applying the principle of the national minimum on a broad basis. The state should accept as its aim the provision of a "decent" minimum standard of living for all, both as to normal incomes, earned by regular work, and the social service incomes. A "decent" national minimum should be fixed, it is claimed, on the basis of "A Human Needs Family Budget" derived from an analysis of the actual spending habits of working-class families, and revised every five years.

The provision of the national minimum would require appropriate minimum wage legislation, family endowment for dependent children in the form of free goods and services for children, and adequate income-maintenance allowances in the form of social services at sufficient rates and covering all contingencies. Such a system would abandon all traces of commercial insurance and would be based on the idea of a national pool of all insecurity burdens, to be financed by taxation of each citizen according to his means. It would be administered by a single social security commission which would unify and simplify payments, benefits and control.[27]

The Beveridge proposal goes a long way, but not all the way, toward these goals.[28] It does not deal with normal incomes, and is confined entirely to the provision of social insurance. But it extends the social insurance system to cover "all citizens without upper income limit" and is "all-embracing in scope of persons and needs." Also it recommends payments and standards which would maintain social service income in times when normal income is cut off, at a subsistence level which is as close to a national minimum as possible.

The British people are arranged by the Beveridge plan into six classes: (1) workers; (2) others gainfully occupied such as employers, traders, etc.; (3) housewives of working age; (4) others of working age not gainfully occupied; (5) those below working age; and (6) those above working age who are retired. Some of the social services in the plan cover all six classes, while others apply only to some of the classes. But the entire scheme is so conceived that it makes the system a truly national one without distinction of status or economic condition.

The benefits in the Beveridge plan, which carry it far beyond the present system of social insurance, may be summed up under six headings, relating to the six classes into which the population is divided.

1. Persons in class 6, those above working age, are to be entitled to retirement pensions. These are to be paid to all men reaching the age of 65 and to all women of 60 years and over. The old-age benefit, which at present is 20s. a week for man and wife, is to be raised to 40s. a week on retirement from work plus 2s. a week increase for each year that retirement is postponed.

2. Persons in class 5, those under working age, are to be entitled to an allowance, which is entirely apart from the benefits received from the Social Insurance Fund. The children's allowance is to be paid from the national treasury to each married couple for each child after the first. Parents and the government are thus to share in the responsibility for the costs of children. The allowance would be the same for each child, after the first, and would increase as the child grows older, continuing up to the age of sixteen. The allowances would be given in all cases, whether the parents are rich or poor, and where the breadwinner is employed or unemployed or disabled.

3. Housewives of working age in class 3 are considered, not as dependents, but as doing "vital though unpaid" work and as partners of their husbands. According to the Report, "all women by marriage acquire a new economic

27. See "Planning for Social Security."
28. Sir William Beveridge, *Social Insurance and Allied Services*, Report ... Presented to Parliament by Command of His Majesty, November 1942, London, 1942. American Edition: Macmillan, New York, 1942.

and social status, with risks and rights different from the unmarried."
Women on marrying are to be given a grant ranging from £1 to £10 to compensate them for a changed benefit status.

Housewives are entitled to a maternity grant, consisting of a lump sum at
the birth of each child, and to widowhood or separation provisions. Widows
of working age are to receive a widow's benefit for thirteen weeks after the
death of the husband, and a "guardian benefit" so long as they have dependent children to look after.

Housewives not working for pay outside the home are not eligible for
unemployment insurance or disability benefits. But the husband's contribution is considered to be for both and the unemployed benefits to a married
couple are greater than those to a single person.

Housewives working for pay outside the home, may choose whether or not
they wish to be classified as employed workers and to contribute to the Social
Insurance Fund. If they do, they will be eligible for unemployment and disability benefits. In addition to the maternity grant mentioned above, they
would be eligible for a maternity benefit lasting thirteen weeks, to enable
them to take this time off from work during the period before and after childbirth. These grants are to range from £2 to £4 a week.

4. Those in class 2—employers, merchants, or self-employed persons—are
not entitled to unemployment benefits. Instead, they are to receive a "training
benefit" to assist them in finding a new occupation and a new livelihood if
their present one fails. They are also not eligible for the short-time "disability benefits," but if, because of injury or sickness, they should be unable to
make a living after a period of thirteen weeks, they would be eligible for
disability benefits.

5. Persons in class 1, employees in paid jobs, are to be eligible for unemployment benefits, if they are unemployed. Benefits start after three days of
unemployment and are to be paid at the same rate without a means test as
long as unemployment lasts. The unemployed must, however, be willing to
accept work when offered or attend a training center to learn a new trade.
The unemployment benefits continue during the period of retraining. The
plan raises the unemployment benefit from the present rate of 38s. a week for
twenty-six weeks to 56s. a week unlimited in time without a means test.

Persons in class 1 are also to be paid disability benefits in case of disability
due to industrial accident or disease, for a period of thirteen weeks. Payments are to be at a flat rate, regardless of previous earnings. If the disability
continues, thereafter, the disabled individual will be entitled to an industrial
pension in proportion to his or her earnings with a minimum and maximum
limit.

6. In addition to all these benefits, comprehensive medical treatment and
rehabilitation and funeral expenses are provided for all six classes, that is, for
all the people of Britain. The medical benefits under the proposed National
Health Service are to include home and office medical care, hospital, dental,
and ophthalmic treatment, postmedical care, convalescent homes, and the
cost of medical rehabilitation. At the death of the insured, surviving relatives
are to receive a lump sum for funeral expenses running up to £20.

The funds to pay these benefits are to be obtained from contributions
by the insured employees, by employers and by the state. All persons
in classes 1, 2, and 3 are to pay a single security contribution by stamp

on a single insurance document each week or combination of weeks. The contributions are at a flat rate, but they differ for men and women and for the different classes. An insured worker in class 1 is to pay 4s. 3d, a week to cover all benefits and services provided, regardless of what his earnings are. The employer is to contribute 3s. 3d. a week for the insurance of the worker and an additional sum of 4s. 3d. to cover his own benefits under the scheme. Young workers between 16 and 18 years of age and women pay less. Insured women are to pay 3s. 6d. a week, and the employer is to pay 2s. 6d. for each woman worker. The state is to contribute part of the social insurance funds.

The total cost of the scheme to the government is estimated at £350 million in 1945—£85 million more than the commitments of the government under existing social insurance provisions. The cost to insured persons is estimated at £194 million in 1945 compared with present costs of £69 million, and the cost to employers in 1945 is estimated at £137 million as against present costs of £83 million. Total estimated costs for 1945 would thus be £681 million as compared with £417 million now being spent.

The whole system would be managed by a ministry of social security to simplify and unify administrative procedures. The new ministry would be responsible: (1) for social insurance; (2) for the national assistance which would be needed for a limited number of cases not covered by social insurance; and (3) for the encouragement and supervision of voluntary insurance which would be continued by different groups of the population in their present or in some modified form.

In brief, the Beveridge plan provides for over-all compulsory insurance, to which all citizens would contribute and all receive benefits during emergency periods in their lives: unemployment, disability or sickness, marriage, maternity, retirement and death. In addition, two kinds of assistance are to be given outright to the citizen by the national government because they are essential to the well-being of the nation—namely medical and health services, and allowances for children.

While this minimum security would be provided for all and would be compulsory, there is nothing to prevent any person from joining with others in a voluntary plan for greater security for himself. Through trade unions, Friendly Societies or other nonprofit groups, members could still arrange for themselves sickness or other supplementary insurance.

Sir William Beveridge states that careful study shows that Great Britain could afford to put the plan into effect, using the actual contributions and benefits suggested in the Report. The total cost of the social security budget, as planned in the Report, would be £697 million in 1945, and £858 million in 1965, which has been estimated to be about 11 per cent of the national income of Great Britain. While these actual amounts have been worked out with great care in terms of the costs of living in Great Britain adjusted to probable postwar conditions, the Report suggests that they be considered as tentative, to be modified upward or downward according to changes in conditions or in public attitudes when the plan is put into effect.

The Beveridge plan proposes that steps to carry it out be started right away, the necessary legislation passed, and government offices established, so that in the year 1945 the plan could be put into effect, whether or not the war is over by then. It would take a long time for an insurance plan, based on contributions coming in over a period of time, to stand on its own feet and be really self-supporting. This transitional period is figured as twenty years. During this time, direct contributions from the national government would have to supplement the actual insurance funds. These contributions would of course become less during the twenty years, and would finally be unnecessary. Social insurance, together with medical and other services to citizens, would then be on a self-sustaining basis.

The publication of the Beveridge Report aroused wide popular interest and stirred up demands that its recommendations be adopted by the government immediately. The main support for the plan came from the British Labour Party, and the trade unions, but many Liberals and Conservatives expressed approval of its main provisions.

On the other hand, the Report also gave rise to much criticism. The main objections to it are: (1) that the guarantee of a national minimum would destroy the incentive to work; (2) that this guarantee is not sufficient for a decent living;[29] (3) that many persons are better off under existing pension schemes; (4) that the costs would be too high and would be a burden which British industry could not carry; and (5) that the scheme would increase costs of production so much

29. Mr. S. Seebohm Rowntree who favors the Beveridge plan, points out that the Beveridge plan would reduce poverty considerably but would not do away with the poverty which is due to low wages. ". . . those in poverty due to inadequate wages or inadequate earnings," he writes, "are not affected by the social security benefits as long as they are working; the only advantage they receive from the Beveridge Plan is that which arises from the children's allowances. The poverty due to inadequate wages can only be cured by raising wages." *The Times*, London, December 15, 1942, p. 5.

as to make it impossible for British producers to compete in foreign markets.[30] Strong objections to the plan were raised especially by the industrial insurance companies whose business under the plan would be taken over by the government.

The debate on the Beveridge Report in the House of Commons in February 1943 was heated and threatened for a while to break up the present government coalition of the Labour Party with the Conservatives. However, the government won the day and avoided a split in its ranks. The government "welcomed" the basic principles of the Report and many of its specific recommendations, but refused to commit itself definitely on the subject or to establish immediately a ministry of social security.

## 4. "FULL EMPLOYMENT" AND EXPORT POLICIES

In submitting his plan for a new social security system, Sir William Beveridge cited facts which indicated that "abolition of want just before the war was easily within the economic resources of the community." In Sir William's words, "want was a needless scandal due to no one taking the trouble to prevent it." Sir William also argued that despite the destructiveness of the present war England will have the resources needed for carrying out his program.

Social insurance against emergencies, however, is only one part of the battle against want: the biggest part of the battle must be won through working out an economic system that will keep production going, and keep employment at a high level. The provisions for unemployment insurance assume that there will continue to be a certain minimum of "frictional" and "seasonal" unemployment. The average number of unemployed to be provided for is estimated at 1.5 million. But the social insurance scheme will not work if mass unemployment is allowed to sweep over the country.

Planning for a better Britain after the war obviously calls for measures which would reduce business fluctuations, provide full employ-

30. Nicholas Kaldor points out that this criticism is untenable. Even if the employers' entire contribution, which is 3s. 3d. per worker per week, be added to selling prices, it might raise export prices, in terms of sterling, by 2 to 3 per cent. "Any conceivable effect of the Beveridge plan on export prices," he writes, "could be offset if the exchange value (of the pound sterling) were fixed from 2 to 3 per cent lower than would otherwise have been the case." A revaluation of the pound sterling after the war is most likely in view of the great changes in prices due to the war. Mr. Kaldor further argues that the extent of the additional redistribution of income involved in the plan is in fact very small (some 4 per cent of British prewar income), so that it does not involve a heavy burden, even if British postwar income were less than before the war—which is very unlikely. See The Times, London, December 19, 1942, p. 5.

ment and increase national output. It is almost an axiom today in Great Britain that to attain these ends the British must expand greatly their postwar exports of manufactured goods. Lord Keynes has expressed the belief that the British could recover from the effects of the war and return to the export level of 1929 in three years. This would involve an increase in British exports of about 50 per cent[31] and could be accomplished only by a better organization of industry, lower costs, possibly lower wages and profits, and a certain self-denial by consumers. Such "discipline" is necessary for Great Britain to compete successfully in world markets.

Many British businessmen and economists think that the war is creating a situation in world markets which may not be altogether favorable for British postwar foreign trade. Heavy industry has been expanded in Canada, Australia, India, Brazil and elsewhere, and these countries will seek markets for their manufactured goods. Great Britain may have to face a loss of some markets though there is optimism in some sections of the business community that the defeat of Germany will open up larger trade opportunities for British goods in Europe, in Latin America and in the Near East.[32]

The British public also realizes that the formerly important British export industries, such as cotton cloth, coal, and machinery, can no longer rely on the initial advantages which gave them a dominant place in world markets in the past. Some of these industries have no chance of recovering their markets, others can do so only by developing new and more specialized products. A larger portion of British exports will have to be in specialized goods and in the products of the newer chemical and electrical industries.

Plans for meeting such a postwar situation are being made by the Board of Trade. The Board is working in co-operation with the various trade associations to study probable obstacles to full employment in the six to twelve months following the end of hostilities, and methods for overcoming them. The Board is also co-operating with over fifty export industries in studying the possibilities of expanding foreign trade after the war.[33] No specific proposals have been made public. The problem is intimately connected with commitments

31. This percentage is clear from the figures of exports of merchandise from the United Kingdom which are as follows: 1929—£729,349,000; 1932—£365,024,000; 1937—£521,391,000; 1938—£470,755,000; 1939—£438,806,000; 1940—£413,084,000. In 1941–1942, exports were further reduced and are at present most likely below £400,000,000.

32. See, for instance, *Trade Journal*, April 1942, pp. 101–102.

33. See statement of Hugh Dalton, President of Board of Trade, as reported in *The Times*, London, February 4, 1943.

under the Atlantic Charter and the Master Lend-Lease Agreement with the United States, and merges into the questions of international trade and monetary policy.

## 5. THE FUTURE OF AGRICULTURE

British plans for expanding export trade and for raising living standards after the war emphasize the need of maintaining a balance between industry and agriculture. The report of Lord Justice Scott's Committee assumes that the British government will maintain a "healthy" and well-balanced agriculture after the war without saying what that implies.

The subject stirred a lively controversy—and no definite policy is as yet in sight. Some would maintain British agriculture on the expanded scale which it has attained as a result of the war,[34] with a minimum dependence upon imports of foreign foodstuffs. Others would again reduce the size of the agricultural industry and return to dependence on low-priced imported foodstuffs. They argue that the prosperity of Britain and the high living standards of its workers depend on cheap food which can be obtained only by importing it from countries where it is produced more cheaply. Such imports, they claim, are especially necessary if the nutrition standards and the health of the British people are to be improved. Furthermore, Britain cannot expect to dispose of industrial exports in agricultural countries unless it buys their foodstuffs and raw materials in exchange.

The answer to the issue is still in the making. Meanwhile, the Minister of Agriculture has informed the British farmers that they will have an assured market for their products until 1945. With regard to postwar policy, he made the following statement:

We feel now that we require a more extensive survey on which to base our long-range policy as well as our policy for immediate problems. We must collect the information necessary for the formation of a sound post-war agricultural policy. The survey now being carried out will include the preparation of a map of every farm. The information about each farm will include its natural potentialities, the characteristics of the soil, its present state of culti-

34. Owing to special stimulation, government subsidies, fixed prices and guaranteed markets, the British farmers have shown a remarkable performance in increasing production. The arable acreage has been increased from some 13 million acres before the war to about 18 million. The output of the eight principal crops (wheat, barley, oats, potatoes, beets, etc.) increased from 27 million tons before the war to about 35 million in 1941. This has been accomplished owing to the use of larger fertilizer supplies, more tractors, and better organization.

vation, acreage of the various crops, the animal population, and the condition of farm buildings.

On the basis of such information, a policy will be formulated. The Minister thinks that "the cry of cheap food" has depressed agriculture in the past and that it would help British exports if the agricultural countries which buy British goods were paid a "decent price" for the food they produce and so could maintain themselves and their industries on an efficient and prosperous basis.[35]

## 6. Government Planning and Government Policy

It is clear that the plans prepared under government auspices cover a wide range of problems, from town planning to social security and export trade. But so far they have not resulted in any important legislative measures or action.[36]

Moreover, the government has persistently refused to make any promises as to how far it intends to implement the plans submitted. It has put off indefinitely the two main proposals so far advanced, namely, to set up a central planning authority, and to establish a ministry of social security.

The government has been criticized for its "procrastination," "indecision" and "lack of policy" in the face of the recommendations of its own committees and agencies. The government justifies its position on the grounds that it is necessary to win the war first, and to get a clearer view of what the postwar situation may be. Some of the government spokesmen have also warned the British people that conditions after the war will be difficult and that immediate postwar plans for a better life may not be possible, either financially or economically.[37] The government thus takes the position that while it is necessary to plan and to make preparations now, action may not be practicable until after the war.

35. *Hansard*, November 19, 1941, Column 418.

36. The House of Commons passed in the latter part of May a bill introduced by the Minister of Town and Country Planning which provides that land not already covered by plans under existing Town and Country Planning acts shall be deemed to be subject to these acts. Presumably, this bill is a step in the direction of what the Uthwatt Committee recommended, but it is a very small step. The bill has been described as a "minor measure." *The Economist*, May 1, 1943; *Christian Science Monitor*, May 13 and 28, 1943.

37. See speech of Sir Kingsley Wood, Secretary of the Exchequer, in the House of Commons as reported in *The Times*, London, February 3, 1943.

*Chapter 5*

# PLANS OF SOCIAL-ECONOMIC GROUPS IN GREAT BRITAIN

GOVERNMENT POSTWAR PLANS and policies in Great Britain are still in a fluid state. Their final form will depend on their interaction with the ideas and programs of unofficial groups and economic associations. As in the United States, economic groups are highly organized in England, and some of them have gone further than their American counterparts in formulating their views of the postwar social-economic order.

## 1. PROGRAMS OF INDUSTRIALISTS AND TRADERS

Early in 1942, the Board of Trade requested the principal employers' and commercial organizations of England to submit their ideas and proposals on postwar economic policy. In response, reports were submitted, during May and June 1942, by the four principal employers' associations—namely, the Federation of British Industries, the Association of British Chambers of Commerce, the London Chamber of Commerce, and the British Employers' Federation (or National Union of Manufacturers). As these four associations represent in a broad way British business and industry, their reports may be regarded as more or less official statements of the position of British industrialists and businessmen.

Agreement on all points among British manufacturers and merchants could hardly be expected. There are important differences of opinion which spring from differences in the economic position of the several industries, e.g., their dependence on export and domestic markets, their degree of concentration, relations to financial institutions, and other factors.

The Federation of British Industries is composed of over 180 trade associations covering most of the industries of Great Britain. Some of the largest plants and corporations are affiliated with the Federation, but it also has a number of the small and medium-sized plants still prevalent in British industry. The Federation has for years been instrumental in helping to regulate competitive practices among its

members in order to maintain "reasonable" trade practices and profitable margins.[1]

The Association of British Chambers of Commerce, which represents over a hundred local chambers of commerce, speaks largely
for the distributive trades and for the small businessmen, including
the manufacturers who are also the merchants for their own goods.
In view of the importance of export trade in the British economy,
the chambers of commerce have a large sprinkling of brokers, agents
and commission men whose primary interest is in marketing at home
and abroad. Because of its composition, the Association is more concerned with problems of "fair competition" and of opportunities in
the field of domestic and foreign trade.[2]

The London Chamber of Commerce, formed in 1881, is the single
largest organization of its kind in England. It has a membership of
9,000 firms and companies; 39 industrial and commercial associations
with an approximate membership of 50,000 are affiliated with it and
are represented on its council.[3] Even more than other chambers of
commerce, it deals with matters of economic policy from the point
of view of the merchant and broker.

The British Employers' Federation is concerned with employment
and labor problems. Its membership consists of employers' associations whose aim is to establish a unified policy among employers
in their respective industries with regard to wages, hours and working
conditions. Its composition overlaps in some measure that of the
Federation of British Industries, but the functions of the two federations are distinct.[4]

Though differing on many points, the declarations of these four
employers' associations show a degree of agreement which is in itself

1. Trade associations have had a long history in Great Britain. Before the present war,
practically every industry had set up its own national trade association. Some of these trade
associations are well known even outside of England and have played an important part in
shaping the destinies of their respective industries. Such are, for instance, the Cotton Spinners'
and Manufacturers' Association. Some trade associations are concerned solely with interchange of information and supply their members with statistical data, credit information,
and with the results of technical research. Many, if not most, trade associations are active
in regulating prices and output and in allocating markets with the avowed object of
promoting "remunerative prices, steady trade and a reduction of overlapping and waste."
In this respect, they are somewhat analogous to German cartels and to American "trusts."
British law does not specifically prohibit such activities "in restraint of trade" if carried on
by legal means. The trade associations, as a rule, do not deal with labor relations.
2. The first chambers of commerce were formed in England towards the end of the 18th
century. The Association of British Chambers of Commerce was organized in 1860 and has
steadily gained in membership.
3. In 1928, its membership included 3,264 merchants, 376 brokers and agents, 2,906 manufacturers, 214 bankers, 170 insurance men, 144 persons engaged in the transport business.
4. There are about 2,500 employers' associations in Great Britain.

significant. Both the points of agreement and disagreement may best be brought out by examining the statements of the associations on the main problems in which they are interested. These are: industrial organization and government control, public works and employment, and international economic relations.[5]

## a. INDUSTRIAL SELF-GOVERNMENT AND GOVERNMENT CONTROLS

All four employers' organizations are agreed that some government control over industry will be necessary in the immediate postwar period. The government will have to supervise and guide the relocation of industries, will have to aid industry in obtaining the financial resources needed for reconversion to a peacetime basis, and to maintain a relationship between prices and purchasing power conducive to business stability.

But even beyond the immediate postwar years, British businessmen see the need of a new and closer relationship between business and government. All four associations declare strongly and unequivocally in favor of private enterprise and private initiative and emphasize the danger of too much "bureaucratic influence." A system of private enterprise, in their opinion, provides "a greater motive power to secure progress and prosperity in industry and commerce than any other form of industrial direction." But they feel that the traditional forms of private enterprise are no longer effective, that "we are on the threshold of a new world and the theories and practices of the past cannot be taken for granted in the future."

The proposals for industrial reorganization differ in detail but all feature what is referred to as economic or industrial "planning." The Federation of British Industries is the least specific on the subject. It emphasizes its adherence to "voluntary association" and its belief that the "organization of industry should be decided by the industrialists, always subject to the underlying principles that it must be in the national interest." Its most concrete suggestion is that "each industry or, where necessary, section of industry, should possess a trade association with clearly defined functions to suit its needs, and so

---

5. The exposition here is based on the following documents: *Report of the Special Committee on Post-War Industrial Reconstruction* adopted by the Executive Council of the Association of Chambers of Commerce on May 6, 1942; *Report of the London Chamber of Commerce on General Principles of a Post-War Economy,* adopted on May 12, 1942; *Reconstruction: Report by the Federation of British Industries,* adopted by the Grand Council of the Federation on April 15, 1942. These reports are reprinted in the *Bulletin of the Commission to Study the Organization of Peace,* New York, December 1942.

organized as to be capable of their efficient performance." The goal involves a system of "industrial self-government" through trade associations having public recognition and status.

The Association of British Chambers of Commerce makes the most far-reaching proposal. The report of the Association says: "Each industry should be responsible for the planning of its own policy, and, to insure that the policy of each industry fits into the postwar scheme of reconstruction as a whole, it should be agreed by a council consisting of representatives of industry, commerce and labor, to be approved by the Board of Trade and to be known as the Council of Industry." The council would insure co-operation between the government and private enterprise and enable the government, with the approval of Parliament, to give general directions on industrial policy. [6]

## b. PUBLIC WORKS AND THE MAINTENANCE OF PURCHASING POWER

By reorganizing on a new basis, it is hoped British industry may serve more effectively its main object: to provide the 46 million people in the British Isles with "a maximum means of employment and with subsistence at as high a degree as the community can achieve." British industrialists seem agreed that "owing to the development of modern technique, the age-old problem of producing enough to go around has been largely solved."

The problem is to reorganize the process of distribution so as to release to the full all productive energies. As the London Chamber of Commerce puts it: "The system of distributing purchasing power was evolved during an age of scarcity when there were not enough goods to go around. This system aimed, therefore, at insuring maximum production with minimum consumption." It is no longer workable. "Mass production implies mass consumption," and that implies

6. Some individual employers, especially in the newer industries, would go much further. Thus, Mr. Samuel Courtauld, in a pamphlet entitled *Government and Industry*, published in 1942, with a foreword by Lord Keynes, speaks of the growing sense among industrialists of "the inevitability of change" which they accept without bitterness. Mr. Courtauld finds that the industrialists of England are developing a "truer patriotic fervor" and a "real fellow feeling with the lower ranks in industry." He is ready to accept government control of industry, and government planning, on condition that employers and businessmen continue to manage industry through their own associations without interference from outside.

On the other hand, some liberals condemn the new interest of business in "self-government." Thus, *The Economist* finds the reports of the employers' associations paradoxical and depressing. "On the one hand, these documents make a notable plea for freedom and expansion. On the other hand, they paint a picture of national and industrial autarchy and of self-rule by vested interests. They ask for a brave new world, and they advise the retention of a corporative and monopolistic system." *The Economist*, June 6, 1942, p. 781.

a better mechanism for providing purchasing power for consumers to buy the potential output of industry.

None of the associations indicates specifically how this "new mechanism" is to be created and what policies with regard to prices, wages, or social services it implies. In general terms, however, reference is made to the need for balanced production, price stability, and higher consumption standards. It is also assumed that the physical reconstruction of the country, the housing program, and the enlarged social services will provide a basis for employment and mass purchasing power. The Federation of British Industries is less optimistic than the Chambers of Commerce. It believes that there may be a shortage of productive capacity after the war and a need, therefore, to ration many commodities. On the other hand, the Association of British Chambers of Commerce stresses the danger of monopolies and the necessity of preventing their growth in the future.

Despite their emphasis on private enterprise, the employers' associations agree that maximum production and high consumption may need the help and stimulation of government. According to the report of the Federation of British Industries, the government "will have to consider the need of expenditure upon public works in the national interest" in order to provide an outlet for the capital goods industries after the immediate postwar activity begins to slacken and "before the world has really got going again." The Association of Chambers of Commerce advocates, in addition to "easy credit," also a "reservoir of public works" for the absorption of unemployment, should the need arise. The London Chamber of Commerce declares that the unemployment problem cannot be solved by increasing exports, and that it would be better to meet the same problem by distributing goods to the underfed and ill-housed population of England.

### C. A DIRECTED INTERNATIONAL TRADING SYSTEM

The statements of the British employers' and commercial associations reflect the fact that the British business community is no longer wedded to free trade doctrines of the past and that its chief aim is to find methods, in accordance with its new faith in government guidance, which will make possible an increase in British exports.[7]

7. The change in British public opinion on this subject may be gauged by the position of even such exponents of liberalism as *The Economist*. In its issue of February 28, 1942, *The Economist* sums up the effects of ten years of British protectionism unfavorably, but concludes that a return to free trade is out of the question. The following extracts from the article are of interest in this connection: "The traceable direct effects of the Import Duties Act have

In considering the postwar trade policy, British businessmen proceed from assumptions on which there is general agreement. The most important of these is that as a result of the war Great Britain will have lost a very large portion of her overseas investments[8] and that her ability to balance her payments will be seriously affected. As early as the 1930's, the annual gap between the "visible" (merchandise) imports and exports of Great Britain rose to over £400 million. This gap was filled by income from "invisible" items such as payments for shipping and other services and by income from overseas investments. These "invisible" items were large, but not large enough, and Great Britain had to make up the difference by the sale of some £50 million of foreign investments a year. As British income from shipping and other services after the war is expected to decrease further and as the further sale of assets may be difficult, Great Britain faces the problem of finding other ways to fill the gap between commodity imports and exports.

The second assumption is that Great Britain cannot solve her problem by reducing imports. From 40 to 50 per cent of British imports consist of foodstuffs and another 25–30 per cent are industrial raw materials. A reduction in imports would mean a lowering of living standards and a reduction in capacity to expand industry.[9] The conclusion drawn is that England must expand her merchandise exports after the war.[10]

---

thus been small. But the indirect consequences have been more important. . . . The Import Duties Act was the first of a string of British acts which destroyed that possibility [of a gradual lifting of world trade barriers]. . . . The verdict on the Import Duties Act after its first decade must, then, be that it has done little good and substantial, if indirect, harm. *The days have gone when a return to uncontrolled trade can be seriously advocated*—[italics mine]—at least without a long period of adjustment and preparation. But the past ten years . . . should have shown that the control of trade and the protection of industry can only be permitted if the most elaborate precautions are taken to protect the public interest." According to *The Economist*, controlled trade must be accompanied by antitrust legislation to enforce competition and prevent restriction.

8. The extent of this loss is exaggerated by some. The most authoritative estimate, made by Lord Kindersley, president of the National Savings Committee, is that by November 1942, Great Britain's foreign investments had been reduced by one billion pounds sterling. That would still leave the total foreign investments of Great Britain at £2,600 million. See *The New York Times*, November 30, 1942, p. 31.

9. The total of retained imports of the United Kingdom was over £1,111,000,000 in 1929; £625,935,000 in 1933; and £952,690,000 in 1937; it amounted to £919,508,000 in 1938. While the value of food imports declined from £512 million to £327 million between 1927 and 1933, the volume imported was more steady, owing to the fall in agricultural prices after 1929. The imports of raw materials have fluctuated much more than foods both in value and volume.

10. In 1929, exports of United Kingdom merchandise amounted to over £729,349,000; they fell to £365,024,000 in 1932 and rose again to £521,391,000 in 1937. In 1938, total exports were valued at £470,755,000. By 1940, they had fallen to about £400 million. To attain again the level of 1929, British exports must thus be almost doubled, and to reach the level of 1937, they must be increased by about 50 per cent.

In the third place it is agreed that wartime industrial developments will create a new situation in world markets which is not altogether favorable for British foreign trade. Heavy industry has been expanded in Canada, Australia, India, Brazil and elsewhere, and these countries will seek markets for their manufactured goods. Great Britain may have to face a loss of some markets. Some sections of the business community believe, however, that the defeat of Germany will open up larger trade opportunities for British goods in many countries.[11]

Fourth, it is generally agreed that the formerly important British export industries such as cotton cloth, coal, and machinery can no longer rely on the initial advantages which gave them a dominant place in world markets in the past. Some of these industries will have no chance to recover their markets, others can do so only by developing new and more specialized products. A larger portion of British exports must be supplied by the newer industries such as motor cars, aircraft, chemicals, and rayon, in which skill and ingenuity and inventiveness play a large part.

The British employers' associations draw the conclusion that the postwar international trading system must be organized on a new basis. It must be a directed system in the sense that the exporters themselves must be organized to carry on trade co-operatively and that they must have the aid and guidance of the government.

The Federation of the British Industries wants to develop and strengthen the export groups which have developed during the war.[12] It would also "direct" imports, so that Great Britain would import from overseas countries only essential commodities for which those countries are prepared to accept payment in British goods and services. To accomplish this the Association of Chambers of Commerce favors the establishment of an export and import council to work in co-operation with the council of industry.

The details of this directed system of international trade are not stated but some of its general features are clear. It is not to be a mere replica of pre-1939 protectionism. It will have to use to some extent some of the well-known pre-1939 methods such as exchange control, imperial preference, and bilateral trade agreements. Exchange controls will be particularly necessary in the immediate period after the war in view of Britain's expected difficult exchange position and of a

11. See, for instance, *Trade Journal*, April 1942, pp. 101–102.
12. Some 300 export groups have been set up in England for the consideration and regulation of export trade in the different industries. These groups are expected to give information and advice to individual exporters on markets, methods of sale, credit facilities, etc.

shortage of dollar exchange in the entire "sterling area."[13] But the new features will be the organized effort and the "economic planning" by which export trade will be interwoven with efforts to raise standards of living at home and abroad and to increase world purchasing power as a means of creating mass markets for the products of British industry.

The more specific recommendations of the Association of Chambers of Commerce are as follows: (1) international agreements should be entered into to prevent illegitimate speculation in foodstuffs and raw materials such as wheat, cotton, rubber, metals; (2) exchange stabilization should be effected; (3) international production and marketing agreements should be negotiated. Such agreements should be used to establish a better balance between the purchasing power of countries producing raw materials and those producing manufactured goods—a point which all employers' associations stress.

It is generally acknowledged that the United Kingdom after the war will be dependent to a large degree upon the commercial and financial policy of the United States. Some, e.g., the Federation of British Industries, are somewhat apprehensive of what this may mean in practice. But two policies to stabilize postwar world trade are suggested. One is to form larger economic units of agreement, specifically to link the trade of Great Britain with that of Soviet Russia, China and the United States. Another is to apply in some form the principle of lend-lease so as to supply, free of charge, goods and services which would help to reconstruct the devastated areas and to develop the newer countries. This would create a stimulus for economic activity in the advanced industrial countries including Great Britain.

### d. A NATIONAL POLICY FOR INDUSTRY

Though the reports of the British industrial and commercial associations represent a marked departure from the past, a number of employ-

13. The "sterling area" includes the United Kingdom, the Dominions (except Canada and Newfoundland), the British colonies and those countries which tie their currencies to the pound sterling. The demand for dollars will be high because these countries will require American foodstuffs, raw materials and finished products for reconstruction. The supply of dollars will be relatively less because these countries will not be prepared to export goods quickly, because their shipping and other services will be less needed, and because they will be unable to liquidate capital assets in the United States. The United Kingdom, and especially the Union of South Africa, may be able to obtain dollars on a large scale by the sale of gold in the United States, and South African gold production is expected to be on a high level at the end of the war. To safeguard the British currency and the position of the pound sterling in general, Great Britain may have recourse to loans in the United States and to Lend-Lease, but in any case some control of the exchanges will be needed.

ers and businessmen in England find them inadequate to meet conditions and problems after the war. In November 1942, some 120 such industrialists issued a statement of their own "as to the place which industry should occupy in the framework of society." It goes much further than the reports of the four employers' organizations in its recommendations for a reorganization of the British industrial structure.[14]

The statement lauds the past achievements of British manufacturing industry under a system of private enterprise and urges its continuance. But it finds that the structure of industry must change with new technical and economic conditions. If industry is to perform its functions of giving the British people employment and a high standard of living after the war, it must recognize its new position and assume new attitudes on all essential questions of industrial organization and policy.

To begin with, the 120 industrialists want new relations with the workers and the trade unions. They desire to see "the authority of the trade unions strengthened within their own ranks" and closer collaboration between them and management. The trade unions should co-operate with management in examining problems affecting industry in relation to the community as a whole. They should be supplemented by works councils and production committees which would be advisory in character and aid in maintaining plant efficiency and industrial morale.

The 120 industrialists want also to establish a "code of duty" towards their workers which would help in maintaining a decent standard of living. Specifically, they advocate a "basic minimum wage," reasonable working hours, unemployment insurance, provision of work to the unemployed by the state through public works and through financial subsidies to private industry, national health insurance, family allowances, holidays with pay, old-age pensions by private firms and by the state. Adequate housing should be provided as a form of public works, but it is "the ultimate duty of Industry" to house its employees on reasonable terms. All these social provisions for the workers are to be a first charge on industry.

With regard to the consumers, industry, according to the 120 industrialists, is to provide goods of good quality at reasonable prices. Industry is to maintain contacts with "bodies representative of the

14. "A National Policy for Industry," reprinted in the *Bulletin of the Commission to Study the Organization of Peace*, December 1942.

consuming public" or any sections of it in order to know what consumers think and how their wants can be more fully met.

To achieve these aims, the 120 industrialists find that industry must be organized and have powers to carry out policies collectively agreed upon. Their proposal is that "the relations between firms, between different industries and between industry as a whole and government should be more fully and comprehensively organized in some form of permanent association." That is necessary to avoid "wasteful and uneconomic" competition and to enforce decisions.

The proposed scheme is to divide industry into sections and groups and to set up sectional associations and subassociations to secure the co-operation of all producers in their respective sections. Sectional associations would be combined in larger industrial and export groups. Finally, there would be established a central council of industry, representative of the whole of industry. The central council would be elected at fixed intervals by the councils of the sectional and industrial associations. It would deal with questions of a general industrial and national character, conduct negotiations with the Trades Union Congress, and would further the expansion of foreign trade.

The scheme outlined in this "National Policy for Industry" has been criticized as a proposal to organize British industry on a "corporative" and monopolistic basis. It is pointed out by its critics that the 120 industrialists sponsoring the "National Policy" include representatives of the large business and manufacturing firms in England such as Unilever, Vickers, Imperial Chemicals and others. The small and medium-sized employers fear that the proposed scheme would either destroy their businesses or make them completely dependent on "big business." The advocates of the "National Policy," however, deny that such are the intentions or likely consequences of their proposal and describe it as "a reasonable middle way" between socialism and laissez faire.

## 2. LABOR AND A "PLANNED DEMOCRACY"

Like the British employers, the workers of England have been stimulated by the war to restate their general economic and social aims and to reformulate them in terms of policies for the postwar period. British labor is far more unified than the employers. Its economic organizations are the craft and industrial unions combined nationally in the Trades Union Congress. Politically, the labor unions are represented by the British Labour Party.

The labor unions have grown greatly in numbers and influence as a result of the war. At the end of 1941, the total membership of the trade unions in Great Britain and Northern Ireland was 7,090,000. This was an increase of 860,000 as compared with the end of 1939. Since then membership has increased steadily, and is now about 8 million—the peak figure which the unions reached once before, namely in 1920.[15]

The war has also changed in several ways the composition of the unions tending to affect their outlook. The increase in membership has come largely from the ranks of new entrants into industry—unskilled and semiskilled workers and women. The largest increases in membership have occurred in such unions as the Amalgamated Engineering Union which are industrial in structure and radical in character. The number of women members in the trade unions has passed the million mark, and is rapidly increasing.[16]

The Trades Union Congress is more concerned with industrial problems and economic policies than with general principles of social and economic organization. Its tendency is to hew to lines of immediate action rather than to deal with long-range ideals. Also, the methods of representation at the annual meetings of the Congress are such as to give a larger share in the making of policies to unions of more moderate views.[17]

These facts are reflected in the proposals for postwar reconstruction which have been formulated by the Trades Union Congress. They deal with social security, education, relations with management, and similar issues. The reports submitted to and approved by the Trades Union Congress held at Blackpool in September 1942, and the resolutions passed by this Congress, are the most recent expressions of the labor unions on these subjects.

The social insurance program of the Congress demands an extension

15. *The Economist*, January 9, 1943, pp. 41–42.

16. In recognition of this fact, the Trades Union Congress at its annual meeting held in Blackpool in September 1942, elected Miss Anne Loughlin as its president for 1942–1943. See *The Economist*, September 19, 1942.

17. In 1941, there were in Great Britain over 900 separate labor unions. Of these 14 had a membership of over 100,000 each while 661 unions had a membership of less than 1,000 each. At the Blackpool Congress some 230 unions which were represented had 1,000 members or less each. While representation is in proportion to membership, it does not allow fully for the differences in the size and strength of the constituent unions. Thus, the Amalgamated Engineering Union with 600 thousand members elects one representative, while the several general workers' unions with about twice the number of members elect 6 delegates.

of the coverage of the existing system, the removal of the National Health Insurance business from commercial interests, and the introduction of survivors' benefits. The Congress also approved the principle of family allowances on a noncontributory basis. This program anticipated the Beveridge proposals from which it differs only in detail. The Congress, for instance, recommended a flat rate of benefits beginning with £2 per week plus dependents' allowances.[18]

Of the other resolutions adopted by the Blackpool Congress the most significant are those which deal with labor's part in production. These resolutions stem from the unions which have been most directly concerned in war production—engineers, miners, railway workers and electricians. The resolutions passed by the Trades Union Congress call for: increased participation of labor in management; compulsory joint production committees with representatives of technical staffs; and the establishment of a Central Planning Board to co-ordinate scientific and technical research.

The Congress has outlined a large program for the reorganization of the educational system of England with special reference to its effects on the workers.[19] The program demands that the school-leaving age be raised to over fifteen and that a definite date be set for raising it over sixteen. It calls for maintenance allowances to children in secondary schools. It advocates day continuation schools for the sixteen to eighteen age group, vocational training and a "youth service" for young people who have reached the age of eighteen. It demands larger general and technical educational facilities for adults through evening institutes. It demands the extension of the scholarship system to be supported by the state so as to open wider "the avenue to the Universities." It outlines the methods by which these educational reforms could be financed.

The Trades Union Congress is affiliated with the International Federation of Trade Unions,[20] but has recently established closer relations

18. *Report of the Proceedings at the 74th Annual Trades Union Congress, held at Blackpool September 7th to 11th, 1942.* Published by the Authority of the Congress and the General Council, London, pp. 39–40.

19. *T.U.C. Memorandum on Education After the War*, Approved by Congress, September 1942, published by the Trades Union Congress, London.

20. The International Federation of Trade Unions traces its beginnings back to 1900, but was reorganized after the First World War in 1919. Its membership is composed of the central trade union organizations of different countries and of the so-called International Trade Secretariats, e.g., the International Miners' Federation. Since 1939, the International Federation of Trade Unions has had its headquarters in London and has derived its chief support from the British trade unions and from the American Federation of Labor. Its function is to unite labor organizations in different countries as much as possible on questions of interna-

with the Russian trade unions. In matters of international economic policy it stresses particularly the improvement of labor standards in all countries in accordance with the principles and practices of the International Labour Organization.

The larger aspects of the postwar program of British labor are dealt with by the British Labour Party. Early in 1942, the National Executive Committee of the Labour Party prepared a report on the War and Peace Problems of Reconstruction which was circulated for discussion by its affiliated local and regional organizations. This report was approved by the Annual Conference of the Party, held in London, May 25, 1942, and so became the official program of the Party.[21]

The reconstruction program of the British Labour Party is an application of the principles of a moderate socialism to postwar problems. It is rather general in character. The Labour Party declares that there must be no return after the war to the unplanned competitive world of the 1919–1938 years, in which "a privileged few were maintained at the expense of the common good." The Labour Party wants a replacement of the old competitive society by a "planned democracy" in which production will be planned for community use, the workers will be given "the opportunity to develop their capacities, and to share in the making of the rules under which they work."

To promote such a reorganization of society, and "to avoid the scramble for profits" which followed the First World War, the Labour Party demands that the main wartime controls in industry and agriculture be maintained after the present war. It asks that plans be prepared now to transfer workers from war to peace industries, to extend the social services, to retire older workers on the basis of adequate pensions, and to raise the school-leaving age to fifteen immediately after the war and to sixteen within three years thereafter.

Influential leaders of the Labour Party stress the necessity of gradual procedure in reorganizing the economic life of the country. They also point out that social control over industry may take many different forms, that private enterprise in many industries has "a lot of value," and that even the monopolistic industries may be controlled through

---

tional economic and social policy. It works in close co-operation with the International Labour Organization with headquarters in Geneva, Switzerland, but which since 1940 has been located in Montreal, Canada. For the history of the International Federation of Trade Unions see Lewis L. Lorwin, *Labor and Internationalism*, Brookings Institution, Washington, 1929.

21. *The Old World and the New Society*, The Labour Party, London, 1942. Reprinted in the United States in a pamphlet of the League for Industrial Democracy under the title, *British Labor on Reconstruction in War and Peace*, New York, January 1943.

various agencies "from a public corporation to some form of management under a board of directors with a nationally nominated chairman."[22]

The international program of the Labour Party favors an association of nations, disarmament, and co-operation between Great Britain, the United States and the Soviet Union. One of the points in its international program is of particular interest. It calls for the "rapid socialization in each country of the main instruments of production, with their co-ordinated planning for common ends," as a means to maintain world peace. No indication is given, however, of what is meant by "rapid" either in relation to each country's pace of development or relatively to the progress of socialization in England itself.

### 3. Postwar Social Aims of the Churches

Among the many voices for a new postwar Britain, perhaps the most striking is the new and vigorous preaching in the Church of England and other churches of Great Britain which would involve profound economic and social changes. Small groups in the churches have for many years been interested in improving industrial conditions and in "social betterment."[23] It has only been since the outbreak of the present war that their highest spokesmen and large numbers of their following have attempted to view the economic situation as a whole and to present what may be regarded as an integrated program of reconstruction.

Early in January 1941, the Archbishop of York called a conference of members of the Church of England at Malvern, under the auspices of the Industrial Christian Fellowship, which adopted a series of resolutions on the meaning of the present war and on the principles of the "order of society" to be followed after the war.

These are generally referred to as "The Malvern Report."[24] Some of the proposals of the Malvern Conference dealt with somewhat techni-

22. Herbert Morrison, *First Things First*, Speech given at Swindon, England, December 20, 1942.
23. As far back as 1908, the Lambeth Conference, organized by bishops of the Church of England, endorsed the social views of Carlyle, Ruskin, and of other social reformers. Some years later a Church Socialist League was organized but it ceased to exist in 1923. The Industrial Christian Fellowship has had the longest history, going back to 1920, but until the present war it was almost entirely concerned with promoting "cooperation in service for the common good" as a principle of industrial relations to take the place of "unrestrained competition."
24. The Archbishop of York's Conference, Malvern, *The Life of the Church and the Order of Society*, published by the Industrial Christian Fellowship, London, 1941.

cal economic questions such as the profit motive, unemployment, the monetary system, and the trade balance. For the study of these, a committee containing economists, industrialists, and representatives of labor was set up. In January 1942, this committee submitted a report in harmony with the general principles of the Malvern Conference which has since been added as part of the general "Malvern Report."[25]

At the same time efforts were made to unite all the Protestant churches of Great Britain on a common platform of social principles. In January 1941, the Commission of the Churches for International Friendship and Social Responsibility, which consists of delegates officially appointed by the Protestant churches of Great Britain, issued a report entitled *Social Justice and Economic Reconstruction*. It outlined proposals for a radically transformed postwar social order.[26]

In September 1942, a new British Council of Churches was set up which included all the main churches of Great Britain, with the exception of the Roman Catholic Church. The Council, of which the Archbishop of Canterbury is president, held its first public meeting in London on September 23–24, 1942, at which the social aims of the churches were restated by the Archbishop of Canterbury and by dignitaries of the several churches.

The public has been particularly aroused by the stirring statements of Dr. William Temple, Archbishop of Canterbury. He relegates the profit motive to a second place in economic life after that of the general interest, and supports such far-reaching proposals as the nationalization of land and government control of credit. In so doing, however, he voices the conclusions approved by the large body of church members as formulated in the Malvern Report and other documents.

These conclusions rest on assumptions similar in their social aspects to those on which the programs of labor and other social groups are based, although they are woven into general Christian doctrine. The present war is regarded as "one symptom of a widespread disease and maladjustment resulting from loss of conviction concerning the reality and character of God, and the true nature and destiny of man." The Christian doctrine of man, it is stated, supplies the only sure

25. *Malvern and After, Report of the Committee of Industrialists and Economists with Theologians, Introduction by the Archbishop of York*, London, January 1942.
26. *International Labour Review*, November 29, 1941, pp. 536–537.

foundation of freedom and of justice, and this in our own time involves "such an adjustment of machine production as to secure that the use and service of machinery may be a true vocation."

The Church, it is claimed, has a special duty to give its testimony on social and economic matters. While personal religion has "crucial significance," the social problem cannot be solved by trying to change the individual, but calls for specific changes in collective action and organization.[27] True, the church as such can never commit itself to any proposed change in the structure of society as being a self-sufficient means of salvation. It can, however, point to those features of our existing society which can never prevent individual men and women from becoming Christian, but which are contrary to divine justice, and act as stumbling blocks, making it harder for men to live Christian lives.

Among the stumbling blocks to a Christian life, according to the Malvern Report, are "the supremacy of the economic motive," the use of property rights for exclusive personal interests, the "acquisitive temper" which tends to recklessness in the treatment of natural resources, the carrying on of production for profits rather than for the satisfaction of the consumer, the lack of recognition of the rights of labor as being "in principle equal to those of capital in the control of industry," and "the struggle for a so-called favorable balance" in international trade.

The recommendations of the churches center around what may be called the Charter for the Individual, the Charter for Industry and the Charter for World Economy. Every individual should have the opportunity of a decent home, a healthy childhood, and education suited to his abilities, a secure position in industry for which he is fitted, regular employment which would assure his standard of life, and an effective share in determining the policy of his industry. Industry should be protected against unfair competition, should be enabled to maintain fair prices and fair labor conditions, and should have access to the nation's credit. All nations should have access to raw materials, should be safeguarded against economic exploitation, and should co-operate in the development of the world's resources.

27. The following declaration approved by the Malvern Conference may be quoted in full: "It is not enough to say that if we change the individual we will of necessity change the social order. This is a half truth. For the social order is not entirely made up of individuals now living. It is made up of inherited attitudes which have come down from generation to generation, through customs, laws, institutions, and these exist in large measure independently of individuals now living. Change those individuals and you do not necessarily change the social order unless you organize those changed individuals into collective action in a wide-scale frontal attack upon those corporate evils."

The churches favor the housing, rebuilding and land policies recommended by the Uthwatt and Scott committees. They support the social security proposals of the Beveridge Report. They would raise the school-leaving age to sixteen and would expand the large educational opportunities for adults. They are in favor of a tax on the value of sites to discourage speculation in land, and they would establish government control over "the issue and cancellation of money or credit used as money" in order to make money "functional to man in his economic activity."

As may be seen by a comparison with the other British programs examined above, the proposals of the churches support some of the most important demands of the labor group and of official government committees. They reinforce the movement to do away with the excessive features of competitive enterprise and with extreme inequality in wealth and possessions.

The Roman Catholic Church in England has not made as far-reaching statements on postwar issues as have the Protestant churches. The general principles of peace were formulated by Pope Pius XII in his "Five Peace Points." The general social principles were formulated nearly half a century ago by Pope Leo XIII in his Encyclical, *Rerum Novarum*.

A concrete application of these principles to present-day conditions in England was made in a pastoral letter, prepared by the Archbishops of Westminster, Liverpool, Birmingham, and Cardiff which was read in all Roman Catholic Churches in England and Wales in June 1942. It enumerates the "minimum conditions of a Christian way of life."

1. Workers should get a living wage based on sufficiency for comfort and for saving.
2. This should be the first charge on industry.
3. Determining factors would be an agreed standard of work, the capacity of industry to pay, and an agreed minimum for an average family.
4. When the employer could not pay the minimum, the difference should be made up by a share out of a wage percentage pool or by the state.
5. The wife should not have to work to insure a minimum living income.
6. No one should have to sleep in a living room; there should be satisfactory sanitation and a bathroom for each family; slums should be abolished.
7. The enormous inequality in the distribution of wealth and control of the lives of the masses by a comparatively few rich people is contrary to social justice.[28]

28. *The New York Times*, June 22, 1942.

## 4. THE POLITICAL PARTIES AND POSTWAR POLICY

The political complexion of England at the end of the war and the political party which is elected to power will determine how much planning will be done in Great Britain after the war, which of the government committee proposals for physical reconstruction and social security will be put into effect, and what part the programs of the several social-economic groups may play in shaping public policies. The end of hostilities in Europe will mean an end to the present electoral and political truce; out of the new general elections to Parliament will emerge the first postwar British government.

The plans and proposals of all the British groups are now influencing the principal issues of that postwar campaign. All the political parties realize it, and have been working out their policies accordingly. Not only the three principal parties of England—the Conservative Party, the Labour Party, and the Liberal Party—but some of the smaller political groups[29] have made declarations on general and special problems of postwar policy within the past year.

The Labour Party, now the opposition party, was in power twice between 1919 and 1939—in 1924 and again in 1931. It aims and hopes to form a Labour government again after the war on the platform already described—stressing social security along the lines of the Beveridge Report, labor legislation, public control over the basic industries and monopolies, and international co-operation along the lines of the Atlantic Charter.

Besides the Labour Party, two other political organizations make

29. Ten different political parties and groups took part in the 1935 elections to Parliament. The names of the parties, votes received and seats gained in the House of Commons are shown in the following table:

| Party | Number of Votes | Number of Seats |
|---|---|---|
| Conservative | 10,488,626 | 387 |
| National Labour | 339,811 | 8 |
| Liberal National | 866,624 | 33 |
| National | 97,271 | 3 |
| Total | 11,792,332 | 431 |
| Labour Party | 8,325,260 | 154 |
| Independent Labour Party | 139,517 | 4 |
| Liberal Party (Samuel faction) | 377,962 | 17 |
| Independent Liberal (Lloyd George faction) | 65,150 | 4 |
| Communist | 27,117 | 1 |
| Independent | 274,499 | 4 |
| Total | 9,209,505 | 184 |
| Grand Total | 21,001,837 | 615 |

their appeal especially to workers. One is the Independent Labour Party whose program is of a "left" socialist character. During the debate on postwar policy in Parliament in November 1942, its spokesmen defined the position of the Party as follows:

"We ask for a basic living income for every citizen, including the men and women in the forces and their dependents, workers of every grade and their families, widows' of service men and workers, and those incapacitated by accident, disease, age or infirmity; communal ownership and democratic control of land, industry, transport and finance, in the interests of all the people; the liberation of India and the colonial peoples; and the declaration of peace terms on the basis of social justice, national liberation and the pooling of the world's resources for the good of all peoples."[30]

The other working-class political group is the British Communist Party. The Communists, a negligible factor in England before 1939, have gained considerably in the past two years. Their membership is now estimated at 60,000. Their following in the trade unions has grown despite the ruling of the Trades Union Congress which bars Communists from holding office in the unions.[31] The increasing influence of the Communists is due in part to discontent of some groups of workers with the part the Labour Party has played in the Churchill government but much more to the new popularity of Russia among the British people. The importance of the Communists at the end of the war, as well as of the Independent Labour Party, will lie in their tendency to stimulate demands for more radical measures of economic and social reorganization. Their pressure is bound to be felt first of all by the Labour Party and the Trades Union Congress, and secondarily by the other political parties and the government.

The Liberal Party, weakened by internal disagreement and the growth of the Labour Party, hopes to play a larger part after the war and is evolving a postwar program which would reconcile its traditional ideas with new social demands.[32] On many points the various elements of the Party are united. The Liberal Party Conference held in September 1942 demanded a new drive to overcome "the social evils of ignorance and want," including: the removal of slums, housing at

30. Quoted in *The International Labour Review*, March 1943, p. 352.
31. *Labor Discussion Notes*, published by the Socialist Clarity Group, London, February 23, 1943. See also, *The Economist*, London, September 19, 1942.
32. See Liberal National Party, *A Basis for Britain's Post-War Policy, adopted by the Liberal National Council held in London on September 17th and 18th, 1941; The Liberal Assembly, 1942; Education for All, The Report of the Liberal Education Advisory Committee; Health for the People, Report prepared by a Sub-Committee of the Health Services of the Liberal Party.*

"rents related to incomes," a statutory minimum wage, a system of state-paid family allowances, more generous social insurance and equal educational opportunities.

The main causes of disagreement in the Liberal Party have been rooted in questions of planning and of state intervention in industry. A small group in the Party favors a ministry of national planning to secure full employment. This group is also for nationalizing the banks and basic industries. Other groups of the Liberal Party, however, want a minimum degree of planning under the direction of a committee of ministers. They believe that there is a growing reaction in England against state action in the field of industry and foreign trade, and that the Liberal Party should give voice to this attitude.[33]

The declaration adopted by the Liberals tries to reconcile these differences by stating that the Party "repudiates both the selfishness of unbridled individualism and the tyranny of collectivism," and that "while opposed to bureaucratic regimentation, it advocates vigorous State action in order to equalize opportunity, to prevent exploitation and insure the full use of the Nation's resources." The Party is also on record against a "planned national economy" and in favor of planning for freedom. It advocates the establishment of "an economic general staff" to advise the cabinet on economic policy and the development of industry and trade.

Of greatest importance is the position of the Conservative Party. As the party in power since before 1939, and as the dominant factor in the present national government, it will gain in prestige as a result of a victorious war. It has a long tradition of power, a membership among whom are many persons of large wealth and social position, and a strong party machine.

For some time, even before 1939, there had been a group of "Young Tories" in the Party who were eager to direct it into new channels. Their watchword was "planning" in the sense of greater activity by the state for the promotion of industrial development, export trade and social improvements. Such economic and social planning was regarded as the best way to unify the British people at home and to strengthen the international position of the Empire.

The ideas of these "Young Tories" have gained ground in the Conservative Party as a result of the war. Many of the older and influential leaders of the Party are now agreed that "some sort of plan-

33. *The Economist*, London, September 12, 1942. Also reports of Liberal Party quoted above.

ning" is desirable, that state action and private enterprise are complementary, and that "restricted nationalization" is a necessity.[34]

The most striking expression of these ideas, or what The Times calls "Left Tory Democracy," was given by Prime Minister Winston Churchill in his speech of March 21, 1943 in which he outlined a "Four Year Plan" for Britain. This plan includes an "amalgamation and extension" of the social insurance system, an expansion and improvement of British agriculture so as to grow more food at home, a "vigorous revival of healthy village life," a broad national health service, the encouragement of larger families by state aid, and wider educational opportunities for the people. For these aims, the Prime Minister advocates advance planning by the government and a partnership between the state and private enterprise. It is important to revive as soon as possible a "widespread healthy and vigorous private enterprise," said the Prime Minister, but "there is a broadening field for State ownership and enterprise especially in relation to monopolies of all kinds. The modern State will increasingly concern itself with the well-being of the Nation."[35]

While the three principal political parties have maintained an electoral truce, some new political groups and movements have sprung up and found some support. The group which has attracted the greatest attention is the New Commonwealth Organization formed on July 26, 1942. Its purpose is to place the basic industries, utilities and services of England under public ownership. It advocates a minimum standard of living for all, adequate wages and family allowances, public control of land, the unification of the educational system. Its emphasis is on the application of research and scientific method to economic and social problems.[36] In a number of by-elections during 1942–1943, the New Commonwealth candidates polled 30,000 votes compared with 40,000 for the government candidates.[37]

The programs of the political parties reflect attempts to give expression to the new ideas and attitudes which have spread in all classes of England as a result of the war. They are, therefore, in agreement on many points, especially on such questions as social security, full

---

34. See Edward Hubert Gascoyne Cecil, 4th Marquess of Salisbury, Post-War Conservative Policy, London, 1942.

35. The New York Times, March 22, 1943. See also Educational Aims, A Plan for Youth, and other reports published by the Central Committee on Post-War Reconstruction set up by the Conservative and Unionist Party organizations.

36. The Economist describes the movement as an odd combination of technocracy and socialism.

37. Christian Science Monitor, March 16, 1943. See also Tom Wintringham, "Britain's Political Revival," The Nation, April 17, 1943.

employment, export policy, state action and planning. There remain fundamental differences, more or less theoretical in character, as to long-run questions of social organization. But in so far as immediate postwar tasks are concerned, the differences are largely of emphasis and degree.

The political forces of Great Britain may carry out postwar plans in several ways. The Conservative Party may continue in power and follow its traditional policy of maintaining itself by granting some of the popular economic and social demands. The Labour Party may win the elections and proceed to carry out the more immediate and moderate part of its program. All parties may unite again to form a postwar national government on the basis of the common points of their platforms. Finally, there may be a reshuffling of party lines, and new political groupings may arise with new names but with the same ideas. In any case, the problem will be not so much what should be done for the reconstruction of Great Britain, as how fast it should be done and by whom.

## 5. The Co-operatives

An important factor in the economic and social life of England is the co-operative societies which in December 1944 will celebrate their one hundredth anniversary. The success of the movement in Great Britain has been very great. The co-operatives today claim some nine million members and do a business of about a billion dollars a year. They are now making plans for postwar expansion which are of interest from a national point of view.

Funds are being raised for a million dollar college to train educational and operating personnel for 12,000 co-op shops and 184 factories now operated by co-operatives and to give special training to employees returning from the services. The smaller co-operatives are considering proposals for the formation of "district societies" to consolidate the necessary capital, potential trade, and unused resources to compete more effectively with the trusts and combines in the postwar period.

Co-operative members are also ready to accept new ideas which promise betterment after the war. They are supporting the Beveridge plan, in spite of the fact that it would kill their own industrial insurance program (the largest in Britain) and are backing educational and other social reforms.

## Chapter 6

# PLANNING BY THE GOVERNMENTS-IN-EXILE AND THE OCCUPIED COUNTRIES

THE UNITED NATIONS include the "governments-in-exile" of eight countries occupied by the German armies: Norway, the Netherlands, Belgium, Luxembourg, Czechoslovakia, Poland, Yugoslavia, and Greece.[1] The economic and social systems of these countries have been brought in varying degrees into line with the general pattern of Nazi principles of organization.[2] Their industrial activities have been geared to the military needs of the German army and to the demands of the German market. But the liberation of these countries from Nazi domination and their right to continue their postwar life in freedom are part of the postwar aims of the United Nations.

For these countries, postwar plans are now being formulated by their respective governments-in-exile, established in London. The value of these plans has been questioned on the grounds (1) that some of these governments were not truly representative of their countries even at the time of the Nazi invasion, (2) that they are less representative now in view of their loss of contact with their homelands, and (3) that their likelihood of assuming leadership in the reconstruction of their respective countries after the war is uncertain.

Even granting these assertions, the declarations and programs of the governments-in-exile have real importance. They have been negotiating with the United States, Great Britain, and the Soviet Union and have made commitments which will have to be taken into account in postwar arrangements. Also, these governments are trying to adjust their programs to the changed condition and ideas of the people, in order to influence the postwar development of their countries. Their plans and programs express some of the trends in these countries, and are to be reckoned with in the reconstruction of these European lands after the war.

1. The countries of Europe, outside of the Soviet Union and the United Kingdom, may be arranged as follows: Axis Powers and countries affiliated with them—Germany, Italy, Rumania, Bulgaria, Finland; countries annexed or controlled by Germany—Estonia, Latvia, Lithuania, Denmark; technically neutral countries—Portugal, Spain, Ireland, Sweden, Switzerland; occupied countries having governments-in-exile associated with the United Nations —Norway, the Netherlands, Belgium, Luxembourg, Czechoslovakia, Poland, Yugoslavia, Greece. The position of France is *sui generis*.
2. See Lewis L. Lorwin, *Economic Consequences of the Second World War;* see also Dr. Eugene V. Erdely, *Germany's First European Protectorate*, London, 1942.

In all the occupied countries there is widespread antagonism to the Nazi occupation and to the Nazi-controlled authorities. This opposition takes the form of sabotage, of violent outbreaks, and of individual acts against the Nazi rules and rulers. Some groups of the population are also engaged in organized underground anti-Nazi activities and in preparations for the day when they may again be free to shape the destinies of their own countries.

It is recognized abroad that the experience and thinking of these local groups are of vital importance for the postwar period. Their general ideas, the concrete plans which they are forming and the leadership which they may bring forth, are bound to play a large, if not decisive, part on the morrow of United Nations victory.

The underground struggle against the Nazis has been carried on by liberals, Socialists, trade unionists and Communists. The underground postwar plans are, therefore, of a radical social character and often in disagreement with the plans of the governments-in-exile. Owing to difficulties of communications, only a few of these programs have reached the outside world. But to the extent to which they are known, they are included in this chapter.

## 1. GENERAL ASSUMPTIONS AND PROCEDURES

Soon after their establishment in London, the governments-in-exile, one after another, set up organizations to study the problems of the postwar settlement as they may affect their respective countries and peoples. In view of the differences in the prewar economic development of their countries, the governments-in-exile have emphasized different aspects of the expected postwar reorganization.

They have, however, certain assumptions in common. Most important is the assumption that their countries will be reconstituted after the war—either within their pre-1938 boundaries, or with such changes in frontiers as will make it possible for them to carry on an independent national life. These governments favor, in varying degrees, some form of regional or international federation, but they insist on the value of small states and countries to the economic welfare and political stability of the world.

A second assumption is that these countries will eliminate whatever undemocratic features may have existed before 1939 and that they will reorganize on a truly democratic basis. This is implied in their avowed adherence to the principles of the Four Freedoms and of the Atlantic Charter.

The postwar program procedures of the governments-in-exile are somewhat similar. Most of them also maintain divisions or agencies in the United States for the study of these problems in the light of American economic and political ideas. Nevertheless, the scope and concreteness of their programs differ widely.

## 2. COUNTRIES OF WESTERN EUROPE

The governments-in-exile which represent countries of western Europe, namely, Norway, the Netherlands and Belgium have been more concerned with immediate problems which are expected to arise at the end of hostilities, such as relief. However, they have paid some attention to long-range programs.

### a. THE POSTWAR DEVELOPMENT OF NORWAY

The Norwegian government in London has been primarily, if not entirely, interested in immediate requirements for the relief and rehabilitation of Norway at the end of the war. It is represented on the Inter-Allied Post-War Requirements Committee, entrusted with the tasks of postwar relief, and it has set up special agencies to study the problem and to prepare necessary data.[3] It has not established a special reconstruction agency nor has it formulated any specific programs on the subject.

The postwar problems of Norway will obviously be complicated by the effects of the Nazi occupation, though not more so than those of some other countries. The Germans have developed the use of some of the natural resources of the country, water power, for example, and have expanded some industries, such as aluminum. The social-economic structure which the Nazis tried to force on the country may leave some traces in the form of industrial and commercial combinations and of larger participation of the state in economic life.

But aside from these influences, the effects of the war are such as to intensify the tendency towards state control, at least immediately after the war. According to the spokesmen of the Norwegian govern-

3. The agency is known as the Directorate General of Supplies and is part of the Ministry of Supply and Shipping. The Norwegian government also maintains an agency in New York for the protection of its shipping interests and seamen.

ment, it will be necessary to maintain a rationing system, establish import and exchange controls, and to fix prices in order to avoid inflation and to promote rehabilitation. The government will assume "the role of exclusive importer," will "plan imports and advance the necessary means of payment," and the consumer "will pay for his purchases according to a fixed maximum price."[4]

But it is assumed that even after these immediate steps, a basic change in the economic policy of the country will be necessary. The war, it is claimed, "has made necessary in all countries a national planned economy under the direction of the State."[5] In fact, it will be necessary to have international planning, and the main task of Norway will be to find the proper place in the scheme of the new world economy for its principal industries such as shipping, timber and water power.

Planning, in this connection, means state control and direction, and apparently does not involve any fundamental changes in property relations. This is specifically true as to shipping, the most important industry of Norway. By the decree of May 8, 1940, the Norwegian government requisitioned the merchant fleet for use, and not for ownership. It has since repeated its promise to return all ships that are not lost to their respective owners "as soon as possible after the war," and to turn over newly built ships to Norwegian owners who have lost their ships during the war.

## The Norwegian Labor Party

In contrast with the general and vague official statements quoted above is the reconstruction program of the Norwegian Labor Party as formulated before 1939. While the war may have affected it in some ways, it is still of importance both because it represents the views of the largest single political party in prewar Norway and because it throws light on the social and economic problems of the country.[6]

The central aim of the Labor program is to secure employment by

4. Statement by Mr. Arne Sunde, Norwegian Minister of Shipping and Supply, *The Inter-Allied Review*, March 15, 1942. Also, statement by Prime Minister Johan Nygaardsvold, *The United Nations Review*, July 15, 1943, pp. 301–302.

5. Statement by Mr. Trygoe Lie, Foreign Minister of Norway, *ibid*. The opposite view—that the reconstruction of Norway involves merely ' the restoration of prewar conditions"—is expressed by Alf Sommerfelt, *La France Libre*, London, February 15, 1943.

6. In 1938, the Labor Party had 70 deputies in the Norwegian Parliament (the Storting) as against 36 Conservatives, 23 Liberals, 18 Agrarians, and 3 others. The program summarized here was submitted to Parliament in 1934 as a means of stimulating recovery, and of reorganizing the economic life of Norway.

developing the resources of Norway, extending land settlement and adjusting production to the domestic market. The Labor Party demands that the state assist agriculture in order to create employment and better living conditions for the rural population. From this point of view, one of the principal tasks is to cultivate new land and set up new settlements. In order that land settlement be speeded up, it is necessary that there should be access to cheap land and that roads should be built. Particularly, more land should be made available for the enlargement of existing small farms and for opening new farms.[7]

The Labor Party proposes that a state land commission be set up for buying and supplying land. If land settlement is to lead to a permanent improvement of conditions for the unemployed rural population, the farms must be sufficiently large. Also, the new farms must be as far as possible free of debt. New settlers should be given technical advice so as to obtain as soon as possible an adequate return for their labor. Measures should be taken to ensure that the farmhouses satisfy minimum requirements. According to the Labor Party, about 2,000 new farms should be opened up each year. Small farmers who are mainly dependent on farming should be given an opportunity of enlarging their farms by various measures of state assistance. The state should provide loans at low interest rates (3 per cent) and grants to relieve the farmers from excessive indebtedness.

It is also necessary, according to this program, to aim at a more just distribution of income between country and town. This can be achieved if agriculture is made more profitable through higher productivity and better prices. The purchasing power of the farmers can be increased, however, only by raising living standards of the entire population. Norway imports grains and other food stuffs and exports butter, cheese, eggs and bacon. Such exports, it is claimed, are not an index of the prosperity of the country but of its low purchasing power. The farmers have been forced to export to obtain cash, but in fact the country has had a shortage of agricultural products in proportion to its real needs.

It is Utopian, according to the Labor Party, to believe that the slogan "back to the land" can be applied to industrial workers. The proposed land policy is intended to provide only for the surplus rural

---

7. In 1938, only about 4 per cent of the area of the country was under cultivation and some 24 per cent was in forests. The population dependent on agriculture, forestry and gardening numbered 838,000, or about 30 per cent of the total population (which was about 3 million). It is claimed that a larger part of the land could be cultivated if properly developed.

population on the land. The industrial population must find work in industry. The Labor Party therefore considers it is necessary that the state should do all in its power to develop and reorganize industry in Norway. The working and extension of industrial enterprises is a matter which concerns the entire people. The community cannot allow industrial plants to be closed down or restricted in operation by the arbitrary decision of private individuals and in the absence of absolutely urgent reasons. The Labor Party therefore proposes that concerns which want to close down, or to limit their operations substantially, should obtain permission for such action from the public authorities.

Norway possesses natural resources to become a more industrialized country. Large-scale modern plants exist now mainly in the export industries. The state must help to promote a vigorous growth of other industries, working for the home market.[8] There must also be systematic and energetic promotion by the government of Norway's export trade.

Among the measures advocated by the Labor Party for these ends are public works, lower interest rates to be fixed by a national finance council, and the creation of new credit by the state to finance public enterprise when necessary.

### b. PROBLEMS OF THE NETHERLANDS

Not much more advanced than those of Norway are the postwar plans of the Netherlands government. A Ministerial Committee was set up by this government in London in March 1942, to study social and economic conditions in occupied Holland and to prepare "reconstruction measures."[9] In September 1942 the Dutch government established an Economic, Financial, and Shipping Mission in Washington, D. C., one function of which has been the study of reconstruction problems.[10]

There are some difficulties in making postwar plans for Holland.

8. Norway's principal industries (besides shipping, forestry and fisheries) are mining, pulp and paper, canning, electrochemical and electrometallurgical. In 1930, over 27 per cent of the population (about 775,000 persons) were dependent on industry.

9. This Committee is composed of the Ministers of Foreign Affairs, Economic Affairs, Colonies, Social Affairs, and Public Works. The Committee is presided over by the Prime Minister. Each department was to study its own problems, and these studies were to be co-ordinated by the Ministerial Committee.

10. In addition, the Netherlands government supports directly and indirectly several private study groups in England and the United States such as the Study Group for Reconstruction Problems founded in London in August 1941, and the Netherlands Study Group on Post-War Reconstruction in New York.

One is the Nazi occupation. It has made profound changes in the Dutch economy, which may affect for many years its character and capacity. Before 1939, the Netherlands was, after Denmark, the largest exporter of animal products in Europe[11] and a large exporter of vegetables and vegetable oils. It had some well-established industries, some of which had a long tradition and high reputation, e.g., diamond-cutting, shipbuilding, food processing (chocolate, margarine, beer), tobacco, textiles (especially cotton and rayon), and electrical. It had a large ocean-carrying and transshipment trade which owed its prosperity to the geographic position of the country and to the large and rich colonies of the East and West Indies. It derived considerable income from its overseas investments and from international financial and insurance transactions. This income helped to pay in part for the large imports into the country which generally exceeded exports by a considerable margin. Owing to its highly developed commercial farming, its large trade, its capital resources, and its colonial possessions, the Netherlands could maintain a population of over eight and a half million on a small area on a fairly high level of living.[12]

It is roughly estimated that, as a result of the Nazi occupation, about one third of the cattle of the Netherlands has perished or been slaughtered. Dutch farmers have been made to discontinue some of their growings, e.g., tulip bulbs, and to produce more grains for local and German use. Some of the industrial plants, e.g., textiles, have been closed up and the machinery transferred to Germany. Considerable numbers of farmers and workers have been moved to Germany to work in German factories and to eastern Europe (including the Ukraine) to develop farming and industries for German exploitation. It may thus take years to re-establish the prewar agricultural and industrial capacity of the country—assuming that it will be possible at all.

A second difficulty in planning for postwar Holland lies in its high

11. In 1938, Dutch shipments, chiefly to Great Britain and Germany, included 33,000 tons of bacon, 25,000 tons of other meat products, 96,000 tons of eggs, 240,000 tons of processed milk, 62,000 tons of butter, and 68,000 tons of cheese. For a survey of economic and social conditions in the Netherlands, see *An Economic Survey of the Netherlands*, published by The Economic Intelligence Office of the Ministry of Economic Affairs; G. N. Clark, *Holland and the War*, Oxford, 1941; *The Netherlands, European Conference on Rural Life, 1939*, League of Nations, Geneva; Marinus M. Lourens, *Education in the Netherlands*, Netherlands Information Bureau, New York, 1942; J. Anton de Haas, *Post-War Reconstruction of the Netherlands*, 1942.

12. The population of Holland at the end of 1938 was 8,728,500. The area of the country was 12,712 square miles. The population density—686 persons per square mile.

dependence on international conditions. Many Dutch industries process raw materials which they obtain from the East Indies and other colonies. One of the most important Dutch export markets is Germany. A large part of the national income comes from interest and dividend payments on foreign investments whose disposition depends on the general postwar settlement. What is to happen to the Dutch merchant marine after the war is also still uncertain.

Spokesmen of the Netherlands government, therefore, emphasize the importance to Holland of the international aspects of the postwar settlement. So far the Netherlands government has made a specific declaration only with regard to the colonies. After the war a Netherlands Commonwealth will be created in which the East Indies, Curaçao and Surinam will be autonomous members.

This assumes that the Netherlands will retain its colonies which existed before 1939 and which were such a large factor in its prosperity. The government is pledged to raise the living standards of the Indonesians by improving production and by protecting their place in international trade. Since the East Indies depend on exports of tin, rubber, coffee, sugar, and other foodstuffs and raw materials, the problem is to assure fair prices for these commodities in world markets. While the Netherlands have generally favored as much freedom of trade as possible, there is uncertainty now in the minds of Dutch spokesmen whether the postwar period will not make necessary exchange controls and special price agreements to assure a fair deal for the producers of raw materials.[13]

Finally, thinking about the postwar problems, especially of a domestic character, is affected by resistance to rapid change which is perhaps more pronounced in Holland than in some other European countries. There is a curious dualism in Dutch attitudes toward economic and social reform which springs from the fact that their position as a colonial power binds the people together economically, while their religious and political differences act as a centrifugal force.[14] In general, however, the Dutch may be described as a conserva-

13. See speech of the Netherlands Colonial Minister, Hubertus J. van Mook, to the London Institute of Export, quoted in part in the *Inter-Allied Review*, October 15, 1942, pp. 9–10.

14. Before 1939, there were many political parties in Holland based on confessional and social differences. The largest single party was the Roman Catholic Party. The Dutch Reformed Church was represented by the Christian Historical Party, and nonconforming Protestant sects by the Anti-Revolutionary Party. Some groups of the middle and business classes supported the Liberal Party, while the workers were largely represented by the Social Democratic Party. The trade unions were also divided into Socialist, Syndicalist, Nationalist, Catholic, and several other minor groups.

tive nation and averse to change, especially in matters of property relations.

Domestic issues before 1939 centered around the same problems as in other European countries—land and better housing for agricultural workers,[15] social security and employment for the industrial workers,[16] and more and better housing for the urban population. The attainment of these economic and social reforms was complicated by the struggles of the political parties which were related to the desire for greater control over educational and confessional problems. Greater unity in political life is a prerequisite of a national plan for postwar Holland.[17]

## C. BELGIAN POSTWAR PROPOSALS

The Belgian government-in-exile has been far more active than those of Norway or the Netherlands in its preparations for the postwar period. Early in 1941 it set up in London a Committee for the Study of Post-War Problems which has since carried on extensive studies of the problems with which Belgium will be faced at the end of hostilities. On June 4, 1942, the committee was given official status by an Order of the Council of Ministers and its functions were more clearly defined.

As now constituted, the Belgian Commission for the Study of Post-War Problems is under the authority of the Prime Minister and is directed by a Central Committee of which Dr. Paul Van Zeeland, former Premier of Belgium, is chairman.[18]

15. About half the land in Holland was cultivated by owners and about half was rented by tenant farmers from landlords. Over half the farms were very small, and there was a large class of landless laborers. To satisfy the demands of the latter, it was proposed to reclaim more land from the sea and the lakes, and some efforts in this direction were made by the government.

16. About 40 per cent of the gainful population is engaged in manufacturing industries. The labor and social legislation of Holland was behind that of Great Britain or pre-Hitler Germany. Health insurance was limited and there was no general unemployment insurance. On the other hand, wage rates and the worker's standard of living were relatively high.

17. The need for such unity was recognized in 1937 when the government of Dr. Colijn (a member of the Anti-Revolutionary Party) was succeeded by a coalition of the Catholic, Social Democrat and Christian Historical parties. This coalition forms also the present government-in-exile in London.

18. The Commission is a large one and includes many well-known representatives of Belgian economic, political and social life. Its members are appointed by the Prime Minister on the recommendation of the Central Committee. The five main sections are: The Section on International Policy, concerned with foreign relations, collective security, etc.; The Section on State Reform, which is considering the reform of the Belgian Constitution and governmental reorganization; The Social Section, which deals chiefly with the prevention of unemployment and social security; The Reconstruction Section which covers technical changes, public utilities, public works, housing, and vocational training; and The Economic Section, which is studying postwar relief requirements, monetary policy, customs unions, migration, changes in trade relations, economic planning, and similar topics.

The Belgian Commission has drawn up a list of requirements for feeding the Belgian population, repatriating prisoners of war and Belgian workers deported to Germany, and supplying industry with essential raw materials immediately after the war. The Commission starts from the premise that the large buying and financial operations and the allocation of shipping involved make it necessary to carry out this task of postwar relief and rehabilitation on an international scale and through an international agency. It considers it necessary, however, to reserve for the Belgian authorities an opportunity to protect their interests and to insure their share of the international fund of supplies.[19]

The proposals for long-range economic and social reorganization proceed from the premise that individual freedom and collective action in the national interest can be reconciled by adopting the principles and methods of national planning.[20] The term "planning" is to be understood in the democratic sense of using all free economic and social forces and institutions, under the guidance of the government, to carry out measures for the social security and higher living standards of the people. In such planning, the state exercises supervisory and directive functions only, and bureaucracy is reduced to a minimum. Policies are carried out through a variety of private, public, semi-public and autonomous organizations and institutions. It is important that these organizations work together to carry out a comprehensive and co-ordinated plan of national development.

Three national councils have been proposed to guide and supplement the work of the national Parliament. They are to deal respectively with economic, social and cultural questions and are to be designated as the supreme council of national economy, the council on social policy, and the council of education and culture.

The council of national economy is conceived as a central advisory

19. The Commission has prepared for the Inter-Allied Post-War Requirements Committee elaborate tables showing the normal prewar consumption of the Belgian people, the quantities of imported raw materials used by Belgian industry, and the output of these industries. It has also made estimates of the reduction in agricultural and industrial capacity as a result of the war. On the basis of these computations, estimates are submitted of immediate postwar needs on several assumptions as to the length of the war and the capacity of Belgian production to resume normal operations. Special tables have been prepared showing the needs of Belgium in medical supplies, vitamins, and clothing for a period of six months after the war. See Charles M. Fonck, "Belgian Post-War Planning," *News Letter of American Society of Planning Officials*, Chicago, December 1942.

20. The postwar plans of the Belgian Commission are summarized in an article in *Trade and Engineering*, London, September 1942. See also a summary of a speech by the Belgian Minister of Foreign Affairs, Paul-Henri Spaak, "The United Nations and Their Post-War Policy," *News from Belgium*, June 12, 1943.

body through which the co-operation of private and public agencies may be effected. It would bring together representatives of employers' associations, trade unions, farmers' societies and of middle-class organizations. These private associations were well developed in Belgium before 1939. They are not only to be reconstituted after the war but to be given larger industrial and technical functions with regard to their respective economic groups, and larger opportunities for shaping national economic policy.

The council of national economy is to be an advisory body only, subject to Parliament and to the Ministry of National Economy. The latter is to have powers of decision and execution. It is proposed to create within the Ministry an office of economic co-ordination to centralize the supervisory and directive functions of the government in the economic field. It is to have divisions dealing with monetary and banking policy, price controls, exports and imports, and public works.

The policies of the council and the office of economic co-ordination have been indicated by the Commission so far only in general terms. The trend of thought is towards a more directed economy which would enable Belgium to increase its food supply,[21] to improve its agricultural production,[22] and to strengthen its industrial structure and its position in export markets.[23] In view of the relatively poor

21. Belgium before 1939 depended on trade and imports for a large part of its food supplies. About 50 per cent of the food requirements of the Belgian population were covered by imports. This figure does not give the full measure of Belgium's dependence on foreign trade, since home-produced food was largely of animal origin, and large amounts of fodder had to be imported for its production.

22. Of the total Belgian population of over 8,000,000 some 3,750,000 were gainfully employed (according to the census of 1930) and of these, 635,000, or about 17 per cent, were engaged in agricultural work. About 32 per cent of the total area under cultivation (the total area was 1,832,000 hectares) were under cereals (wheat, barley, oats, rye). The factors which impede agricultural progress are the prevalence of small farms, insufficient mechanization and use of fertilizers, and lack of credit for capital improvements. Out of 1,131,000 farm holdings in 1930, over 48 per cent were freehold and the rest were operated on a lease basis. Over 838,000 holdings were less than a hectare (a hectare equals 2.37 acres), which means that the holders had another additional occupation; 241,000 holdings were under 10 hectares. There has been an increase in small holdings since 1900, partly owing to the financial support of the "Back to the Land" movement by the government. Belgian agriculture could be made more productive by applying modern technical methods, by enlarging holdings, and by easy credit terms to farmers for purposes of improvements. It is considered to be to the advantage of Belgium to restore the cattle and dairy industry. See "Belgium," *European Conference on Rural Life, 1939*, League of Nations, Geneva; also *The Land Tenure Systems in Europe*, League of Nations, Geneva, 1939.

23. The outstanding industries of Belgium are coal mining, iron and steel, textiles, glass. Belgium is a large exporter of steel products, cotton yarns and piece goods, linens, woolen goods, glass products, cement, bricks, and copper products. (Congo copper is refined in Belgium.) The chief Belgian export markets before 1939 were Germany, Great Britain, France, Argentina, the United States, Italy and Switzerland.

natural resources and the density of the population standards of living can be raised in no other way.[24]

The social council is to be composed of fifteen representatives of employers; fifteen representatives of workers' associations and fifteen representatives of the public.[25] It will deal with problems of unemployment, vocational training and rehabilitation, housing, public health and other social services.

The Commission has laid down the principle that no prolonged and widespread unemployment is to be tolerated. The worker must have the right to a job, and this will be guaranteed to him by the "organized national economy." All considerations of profits, taxation, and finance must be subordinated to this basic obligation of the state to assure the worker a chance to earn his living by working. But some unemployment will persist and it is to be met by a system of unemployment insurance. The costs are to be defrayed by contributions from employers, workers and the state.

The housing policy is to be integrated with programs of public works to be undertaken after the war. It will include not merely the improvement of dwellings but also the supplying of house furnishings and equipment. It is also to be co-ordinated with programs of town and country planning.[26] One of the proposals under consideration is to develop on the fringe of large urban agglomerations "new villages" which would provide the worker with a house and a small plot of land on which the worker could raise vegetables, fruits, etc., during periods of unemployment. These "villages" would be semipublic institutions financed by state loans without interest to be repaid in

24. Before 1939 Belgium had an area of 11,775 square miles with a population of about 8,500,000 or about 710 inhabitants per square mile.

25. Occupational organizations were highly developed in Belgium before 1939. Out of some 1,500,000 industrial workers about 1,000,000 were organized in trade unions. Of these, 600,000 belonged to the Socialist unions, about 350,000 to the Catholic unions, and the rest to several other trade union groups. Practically every industry had an employers' association, and there was a central organization of employers known as the *Fédération Patronale Belge*. Some industries, e.g., coal mining and steel, were dominated by monopolistic combinations which also were members of international cartels. The farmers were organized in the "Boerenbond," the Belgian Agricultural Union, the Professional Agricultural Unions (UPA), and many mutual and co-operative associations for purposes of buying, selling and of obtaining cheap credit.

26. Housing conditions in Belgium, both in rural and urban districts, are considered bad. Most of the older rural dwellings are described as being generally too small and not having enough rooms; the ceilings are too low, the floorings defective, the windows too small, the houses are damp and do not have sufficient ventilation or proper plumbing facilities. Out of 2,672 communities in Belgium, about 1,800 lack a water supply. Health conditions are below those in the cities which, in their turn, are below satisfactory standards. About 30,000 slum dwellings in the country were described in 1939 as incapable of reconditioning and some 70,000 dwellings were overcrowded, that is, had more than two persons per room. See *Urban and Rural Housing*, League of Nations, Geneva, 1939, p. 3.

thirty-year installments. The properties would be subject to certain restrictions with regard to sale. During periods of unemployment, no payments would be made and the use of the property would be regarded as part of the unemployment benefits. The improvement of housing will involve an extension of good water supply and of electric power for light and heating.

The council on education and culture is to be composed of a Walloon, a Flemish, and a Brussels autonomous section, and will concern itself with the improvement of schools, the organization of the press, and other cultural problems.

## 3. CENTRAL AND EASTERN EUROPE

Of the countries of central and eastern Europe, Czechoslovakia and Poland call for special consideration in view of their efforts to prepare plans for postwar reorganization.[27]

### a. POSTWAR PLANS FOR CZECHOSLOVAKIA

The government of Czechoslovakia in London was the first to set up a Ministry of Economic Reconstruction.[28] The functions of the Ministry were to prepare plans for a "new economic and social order" for Czechoslovakia and to formulate policies dealing with retribution and war damages. It was also to co-ordinate the reconstruction work of the other Ministries (Finance, Industry and Trade, Education, etc.) and to collaborate with agencies of other United Nations engaged in preparations for the peace settlement. The Ministry was to have the assistance of several research bodies—private and governmental—which were organized in London and in New York.[29]

The spokesmen of the Czechoslovak government feel that their problems of internal postwar reorganization are much simpler than those of other countries of central and eastern Europe. Czechoslovakia, in their opinion, was "one of the best democracies of Europe" and was in the front line of the social-economic reforms which are

27. A large amount of valuable material on conditions in these countries before 1939 and since the Nazi occupation may be found in *Documents and Reports* published by the Central and Eastern European Planning Board in New York; also in the monthly *Survey* published by the same Board in New York.

28. The first Minister was Mr. Jaromir Něcas, Minister of Social Welfare in Prague before 1938, and also at one time Chairman of the Governing Body of the International Labour Office. He was succeeded on November 13, 1942 by Mr. František Němec, who is also Minister of Industry and Trade. See *International Labour Review*, April 1942, and August 1942.

29. Such are the Czechoslovak Research Institute attached to the Ministry of Foreign Affairs in London and the Czechoslovak Economic Council in New York.

now forming an essential element of postwar reorganization. Much of what is to be done after the present war, they say, had been anticipated by them before the war, and all that will be needed is for Czechoslovakia to carry forward previous activities.[30] Such continuity, however, does not mean a return to the past where that past is irrevocably changed and where readjustments are necessary. The effects of the incorporation of Bohemia-Moravia by the Nazis into Germany as a "protectorate," of the setting up of Slovakia as a republic under German control and of social-economic Nazi policies since 1939 must obviously be considered.

Current Czechoslovak declarations stress the need for change in political and administrative organization. Czechoslovakia had a democratic constitution providing for universal suffrage, free elections, and proportional representation before the war. But the practical government of the country was hampered by a multiplicity of political parties and by the discontent of the several minority groups (Germans, Slovaks, Ruthenians)[31] over the alleged predominance of the Czechs in the government and in public service. Czechoslovak leaders do not indicate how they will obviate the first difficulty, but they propose to meet the second by giving more self-government to the minority groups and by a greater decentralization of public administration.[32]

In the field of economic policy and social welfare, the programs of the Czechoslovak government are in the direction of more state intervention and "planned economy." In line with the trend in other countries, it is considered likely that "the whole economic life will be run from a state planning centre in such a way as to correspond with

30. Speech by Dr. Eduard Beneš, President of the Czechoslovak Republic at the National Liberal Club on May 12, 1942. Reprinted in *News Flashes from Czechoslovakia*, July 6, 1942, published by The Czechoslovak National Council of America.

31. The population of about 15 million was composed of some 7 million Czechs, 3 million Slovaks, about 3 million Germans, 600,000 Ruthenians, the rest being Magyars, Jews, and other less numerous groups. The four provinces of the state included Bohemia and Moravia (predominantly Czech), Slovakia, and Ruthenia. For background material see Brackett Lewis, *Democracy in Czechoslovakia*, 3d edition, New York, 1941.

In 1935, the 300 seats in the Lower House of Parliament were divided among 14 parties. The Agrarian Party, which was the largest, had 45 seats; the Sudeten-German—44; the Social Democratic—38; the Communist—30; the Czech Socialist (Dr. Beneš' Party)—28; followed by the Czech Catholic, Slovak Catholic, National Democratic, and several minor ones.

32. These plans refer only to the Slovaks and Ruthenians. The problem of the German minority is regarded as an international one. Its solution depends on the postwar reorganization of Germany. The Czechs claim that the problem can be solved best by making sure that Germany does not misuse her national minorities in other countries for Pan-German aims and also "possibly" by "an organized application of the principle of the transfer of populations" so as to make Czechoslovakia a more homogeneous country.

the interests of the whole and the requirements of the people."[33] The state must assume such extended functions, since "the profit of private capital" can no longer serve as "the sole encouragement for initiative and increased efficiency." But this process of planning is to be democratic by making those who administer it subject to the control of freely elected parliaments.

The program clearly rests on the principle of nationalization on a considerable scale. It is proposed that the state take over the National Bank. Also, all banks and insurance concerns will "go over to the sphere of State and public influence." Only the peoples' financial concerns[34] and provincial banks will be left in their present form. The purpose of this change is to make "money serve the people and not rule them."

The state will also take over the mines and "natural resources of every kind," all "sources of electrical and calorific energy," transport of every kind, and all the heavy and key industries "on which the existence of the nation depends" such as the metallurgical, sugar and cement industries. The nationalization of these industries will put an end to private monopolies and cartels and make possible a "planned and controllable economy in the interests of all, not conducted according to the needs of the private profits of privileged individuals."[35]

In planning the economic development of Czechoslovakia, the government proposes to refrain from overindustrializing the country and from increasing its reliance on exports. On the contrary, it will try to maintain a balance between agriculture and industry and to develop the home market.

In the interests of agriculture, it proposes to carry forward and complete the program of agrarian reform which was begun in 1919-1920.[36] More land will be distributed to the peasants, and measures

33. *Czechoslovakia in Post-War Europe*, Czechoslovak Ministry of Foreign Affairs, London, 1942, p. 65. See also an article by the Minister of Reconstruction, František Němec, in *Čechoslovak*, London, March 5, 1943.

34. That is, mutual and co-operative credit institutions.

35. *Czechoslovakia in Post-War Europe*, p. 69. Before 1939, the Czechoslovak state conducted many enterprises on a commercial basis such as the state railways and airlines, the posts and telegraphs, the state mines and metallurgical works, the state forests and estates, the state tobacco factories, and spas and health resorts.

36. Before the First World War, there were in Bohemia and Moravia-Silesia 401 estates of over 2,500 acres each, while in Slovakia and sub-Carpathian Ruthenia there were 935 estates of over 1,000 acres each. It was estimated that about a thousand individual owners held over 9 million acres of land or 26 per cent of the total area of the Republic. The Land Acts of 1919–1920 limited individual ownership of land to 625 acres, of which no more than 375 acres were to be arable land. All lands above that figure were to be acquired by the state at prewar prices. The government assumed the right to take over some 10 million acres

will be taken to unify the small farms and to promote co-operative cultivation among them.[37] The farmers will be given cheap credit and a more equitable system of taxation. To check the flight from the land, the state will undertake a "more magnanimous housing and settlement policy for agricultural workers and will improve their wages and working conditions." Measures are also projected to give the countryside better schools, better roads, more electrification, more telephones, cheap motorbus transportation to the cities, and more recreational facilities through radios, cinemas, and other cultural entertainments.

Before 1939, some 35 per cent of the population in Czechoslovakia was dependent on agriculture. The farmers, especially in the western parts of the country, carried on their industry efficiently and were on a relatively fair standard of living. The postwar reforms are intended to strengthen the relative position of the farmers, improve agricultural output, and stabilize prices of agricultural products.[38] As a result of these measures, Czechoslovakia will, it is hoped, continue to be self-sufficient in, and even become an exporter of, grain. It will still be dependent, however, on imports for dairy products, feedstuffs, and industrial raw materials such as cotton and wool.

The proposed agricultural measures are part of a program to develop the home market after the war. The other part consists of proposals to develop such new branches of industry as can be geared to an expanding domestic demand. The Czechoslovak Ministry of Reconstruction names artificial textiles, new types of fuel, synthetic petrol, and cellulose, as some of the industries which will need "special atten-

of land, which it intended to sell to small landowners and landless peasants on easy terms. By the end of 1935, the government had distributed over 4,465,000 acres to 639,000 applicants, of whom 235,000 were new farmers. As a general rule, the land was distributed in holdings of 15 to 25 acres, though some larger holdings were allowed. Despite the demand of the Social Democrats to expropriate the land, the government incurred large loans (about £15 million) to pay for it. Still, on the eve of the present war, about 70 per cent of all farms were under 12.5 acres and there was a large number of agricultural laborers practically landless. The subdivision of the land into many small holdings impeded technical progress, and the living conditions of the small peasants and laborers, especially in the eastern parts of the country, were low. See Edgar P. Young, *Czechoslovakia: Keystone of Peace and Democracy*, London, 1938, pp. 137–141.

37. Czechoslovakia before 1939 had a highly developed agricultural co-operative movement including numerous agricultural credit societies, co-operative dairies and breweries, other producers' co-operatives, building co-operatives, buyers' co-operatives, co-operatives for the collective use of machinery, and others. The Federation of Agricultural Cooperative Unions with headquarters in Prague had 11,454 constituent local and regional co-operative societies. Some 335 co-operative exchanges with a membership of 200,000 independent farmers sold over one billion tons of agricultural produce in 1935.

38. In 1934, the Czechoslovak Grain Company was established and was granted exclusive rights to buy grain from farmers at fixed prices and to import and sell foreign grain and fodders. The executive committee of the Company was composed of representatives of agricultural and consumers' co-operatives, millers, and grain merchants.

tion" and government support. Equal attention is to be given also to "home industries" which have a long tradition in Czechoslovakia and which could be an important source of income and employment, especially if developed in connection with seasonal industries and in areas where there is a supply of wholly or seasonally unemployed labor.

However, Czechoslovakia neither wishes to, nor can become wholly self-sufficient. Before 1939 it was a highly industrialized country with a considerable export trade.[39] It had to import many of the raw materials for its industries, e.g., cotton, wool, iron ore, rubber, petroleum, as well as many foodstuffs such as dairy products, coffee, tea, wines, fruits. To pay for these, as well as for other imports, and for services obtained abroad, it exported a large part of its agricultural and industrial output and sought to develop its export markets by means of state credit guarantees, subsidies and other devices. In order to free itself from too great dependence on Germany and on Europe, Czechoslovakia made successful efforts in the decade before the present war to readjust her industries to wider world markets and particularly to the American market.[40] With all due regard to the maintenance of an internal balance between agriculture, industry, and the domestic market, the Czechoslovak government will do its best to develop export markets as far as necessary and possible.

In the field of social legislation, the Ministry of Reconstruction proposes to continue the "advanced social policy of the First Republic." Before the war Czechoslovakia had developed accident, sickness and disability insurance, old-age pensions, provisions for child welfare, maternity and special marriage grants for women, widows' pensions. These services were limited in scope and in amount of benefits. Out of a total of about 4,500,000 employed persons, only about 2,781,000 were covered by sickness insurance. There was no system of unemployment insurance, the state granting only unem-

39. Some 35 per cent of the population, according to the census of 1930, were dependent on industry and handicrafts. Over 2,291,000 workers were industrial workers, of whom over 121,000 were employed in the mining industry and its subsidiaries, about 270,000 in the textile industry, about 150,000 in glass factories. Besides coal, glassware, cotton textiles, Czechoslovakia was an important producer and exporter of agricultural machinery, motorcars, electrical appliances, boots and shoes, chemical products, armaments. Other exports were processed foodstuffs, preserved fruits and vegetables, and beer.

40. In 1929 Czechoslovakia exported to European countries 84.2 per cent of its entire export; in 1936—76.7 per cent. Exports from Czechoslovakia to the United States were valued at $21.3 million in 1935 and rose to $37.1 million in 1937, in which year the United States became Czechoslovakia's second best market. See A. Basch, *Germany's Economic Conquest of Czechoslovakia*, p. 8.

ployment assistance under the so-called Ghent system.[41]   Many of the welfare services were still provided by private and charitable societies and the administration of these services was far from efficient. It is to meet these defects that the Ministry of Reconstruction promises to "intensify and perfect" the social policy of the government and to eliminate the element of charity from the social services.

Czechoslovakia had also developed a system of collective industrial relations[42] before 1939 and a large body of protective labor legislation, including provisions for paid holidays, shop committees, compulsory collective agreements, and labor courts. These and other protective devices are to be further developed after the war.

In brief, the Czechoslovak Ministry of Reconstruction visualizes a postwar Czechoslovakia which will resemble in essentials the pre-1939 Republic but whose trends of development will be more marked and accelerated. The country will exemplify the ideal of a "social republic" in which private profit and private interests exist, but are secondary, and in which the collectivist elements of the economy and of social life are allowed to grow steadily and peacefully.

The experience of 1919–1939 has shown that this ideal is threatened by two dangers—industrial depressions and international conflicts. It is clear that a country like Czechoslovakia, dependent on export markets and situated in the heart of Europe, cannot cope with either problem alone. The Ministry of Reconstruction sketches a program of public works as a means to provide employment, especially during the transition from war to peace, but it has no specific scheme for assuring full employment. On the other hand, the spokesmen of the Czechoslovak government have a number of specific proposals for regional and world organization, which, in their opinion, would guarantee security to all nations.[43]

41. Under the Ghent system, support during unemployment is given by the trade unions to their members out of fees paid by them while employed. The union funds are supplemented by state grants. The system left unorganized workers and especially young workers without relief and caused great hardships. The importance of the problem may be judged from the fact that the number of unemployed ranged from 920,000 in 1933 to 518,000 in January 1938.

42. In 1937, out of the total of 2,325 000 workers employed in industry and trade, over 1,241,000 were members of trade unions. At the end of 1936, some 2,860 collective contracts were in force covering 45,500 establishments and about a million workers. The strength of the unions was greatly undermined because of their division into half a dozen or more rival Socialist, Communist, German, Czech, and other groups. See "Trade Unionism in Czechoslovakia," Czechoslovak Press Bureau, New York, 1943, reprinted from *Acta Victoriana*, Victoria College, University of Toronto, March 1943.

43. See Eduard Beneš, "The Organization of Post-War Europe," *Foreign Affairs*, January 1942; *Speeches by Jan Masaryk in America*, Czechoslovak Information Service in New York, September 1942; *President Beneš' Speech to the Durham Miners*, Czechoslovak Press Bureau, New York, November 27, 1942; also Hubert Ripka, Czechoslovak Minister of State, *The Problem of the Germans*, Czechoslovak Press Bureau, New York, February 5, 1943.

## b. POSTWAR PROBLEMS OF POLAND

The Polish government-in-exile has a less elaborate organization for dealing with postwar reconstruction. The Ministry of Finance, Commerce and Industry is responsible for planning the economic reconstruction of Poland, and has carried out a number of studies on agriculture, housing, and foreign trade. The Ministry of Labor and Social Welfare is entrusted with the task of social reconstruction. It has set up a Social Reconstruction Department to draw up the lines of future policy with regard to population, food distribution, housing and social assistance.[44]

Poland's postwar problems are more complex than those of the other countries so far considered. The Nazi occupation of the country has resulted in great changes in its agricultural production, in the distribution of industrial plants and in the organization of the coal mining and oil industries. The population has been persecuted, subjected to forced removals to Germany, reduced in numbers, weakened in physical strength.[45] Much destruction has been wrought and much more lies ahead if and when the German and Soviet armies begin again to move across the country in the final stages of the war.

Poland is also burdened with a political and social record of 1919–1939 which is a hurdle in its path of reconstruction. Whatever the causes, the fact is that during the twenty years between the two World Wars, Poland did not realize the expectations of those who helped to re-establish her independence. It failed to solve most of the political and economic problems with which it was confronted. On the eve of the present war, political democracy in Poland had become a shadow and the country was ruled by a military clique. The relations between the "minority groups" were strained and permeated with national antagonisms and racial prejudices.[46] The rural population was living on a low standard as a result of low productivity, surplus population, and concentration of landownership, while the land reforms provided for by law were carried out too slowly to meet the situation.[47]

44. *International Labour Review*, November 1942, pp. 580–581; March 1943, pp. 356–357.
45. See Simon Segal, *The New Order in Poland*, New York, 1942.
46. Of the total estimated population of about 35 million in 1939 over one third was composed of "minority groups" including over 3 million Ukrainians, about 2,750,000 Jews, about 1,220,000 Ruthenians, about one million White Russians, some 750,000 Germans, and several other groups. Some of these "minority groups" formed the majority of the population in some of the areas where they were located, e.g., the Ukrainians in eastern Galicia, the White Russians in the northeastern regions. For conditions in Poland before 1939, see Raymond Leslie Buell, *Poland: Key to Europe*, New York, 1939.
47. The Polish agrarian laws of 1920 and 1925 are less radical than similar legislation in other east European countries. The landowners are to be fully compensated for their land, may dispose of their land by private sale, and may appeal to the courts to pass on the valua-

The efforts to develop industry had not made much headway owing to lack of native capital and inadequate international credit,[48] and the cities were filled with large numbers of unemployed and under-employed workers.[49] The social services—such as aid to the un-employed, child welfare, etc.—could be provided by the government only on a small scale owing to budgetary difficulties.[50]

The Polish government-in-exile recognizes that the first step towards postwar reconstruction is to break with the practices of 1919–1939 and to make a fresh start. This has been done, in a measure, by giving representation in the present government in London to the several progressive political parties and to minority groups.[51]

## A Charter for Poland

The other task is to formulate anew the principles on which a demo-cratic Poland may be built. A step in this direction was taken when General Sikorski, the Prime Minister of Poland, in opening the session of the Polish Council[52] on February 24, 1942, laid down, on behalf of the government, the general principles by which the postwar policy of Poland was to be guided, as follows:

1. Poland will stand by Christian principles and culture.
2. The Polish Republic will be a democratic republican state closely con-

---

tion of land. This and the political influence of the landed classes has blunted the edge of the purposes for which the land reform was intended. In 1931, after ten years of the opera-tion of the law, there were in Poland 741,000 "dwarf" farms of less than 2 hectares; 1,136,200 farms of 2 to 5 hectares, and 14,700 farms of 50 hectares or more. The large farms had over 4,606,000 hectares, or about 15 per cent of the land suitable for cultivation. Between 1931 and 1938, some 243,000 new farms were created with a total acreage of about 2 million, or an average of less than 4 acres per farm. It was estimated before the present war that about 65 per cent of the active population was engaged in agriculture, and that from 2 to 3 million peasants could not make a living from agriculture. Also, the application of the land laws aggravated friction with the minority groups, especially the Ukrainians in East Galicia who claimed that the large estates were divided and distributed in such a way as to promote Polish colonization.

48. See Leopold Wellisz, *Foreign Capital in Poland*, London, 1938.

49. See *Workers' Nutrition and Social Policy*, International Labour Office, 1936; and *The Workers' Standard of Living*, International Labour Office, Geneva, 1938, pp. 75–82. Before 1939, Poland's national income was about $4 billion a year, or about $115 per capita. After 1936, the Polish government embarked on a program of industrial development connected in part with rearmament. It is recognized that industrialization must be resumed after the war and that the domestic market must play a large part in taking the products which an expand-ing industry may supply. Still, Polish leaders are concerned a great deal with the problem of foreign markets after the war.

50. See *Workmens' Protection Legisation in Poland*, Preface by Ian Stanczyk, Polish Minister of Labor, Congress of Polish Trade Unions, London, 1941.

51. The parties of the Left before 1939 were the Peasant Party, the Polish Socialist Party, the Democratic Club, the Jewish Socialist Party (the Bund); the parties of the Right were the Polish Labor Party, which is nationalistic, Catholic and anti-Semitic; the National Democrats, who were also anti-Semitic, and the National Radicals, who bordered on fas-cism. The minority groups had parties of their own.

52. See "The Polish Council and the Charter of Poland," *The Inter-Allied Review*, March 15, 1942, pp. 60–62; also *General Sikorski's Speeches during his visit to the United States in December 1942*, Polish Information Center, New York, 1942; also Broadcast by Edward Raczynski, Polish Minister of Foreign Affairs, quoted in *The Inter-Allied Review*, March 15, 1942, pp. 59–60.

forming to the principles of legal government, responsible to a true national assembly fully representative of the common will of the people and elected by the method of general equal and direct secret vote.

3. Poland will guarantee the rights and liberties of all citizens loyal to the Republic, regardless of national, religious or racial differences. Coupled with equality of obligations, equality of rights will be assured to national minorities fulfilling their civic duties towards the state. They will be given the possibility of free political, cultural and social development.

4. Postwar Poland will endeavor to ensure work and a fair livelihood to the whole population, thereby removing once and for all from her territory the scourge of unemployment. Every citizen will possess the right, as well as the duty, to work, while retaining choice of occupation. The national economic policy will be guided by this principle. It will be subordinated to the general principles conforming with the necessity of planned postwar reconstruction and of industrial development and the mobilization of all productive forces vital to the general welfare. Sound agricultural reform, ensuring the just partition of land amongst the peasant population, should, with the exception of a limited number of model and experimental farms, create medium-sized but independent, profitable and productive farms, husbanded as a rule by the farmer's household. On the basis of these legislative, political, economic and social principles, it is proposed to raise the standard of life of the working masses, peasants, workers and intellectual professions and assure to them their rightful co-operation in the development of the national welfare.

5. The Polish nation will make every effort to attain in the shortest possible time the economic level of the western European countries, and it desires to collaborate in this respect with other democratic nations.

6. The spirit of self-sacrifice and of patriotism, as well as sound political judgment . . . demand that the whole public life of Poland be based upon the initiative and activities of the community itself. In particular, the largest possible measure of public affairs should be left to the free administration and decision of local, economic and professional self-governments.

7. Poland will possess a strong and efficient executive power, capable of taking speedy and determined action to frustrate any intentions hostile to Poland, and of rallying in times of danger all the vital forces of the country.

The Polish government is pledged to work out detailed projects for economic and political reconstruction which would apply in a practical way the principles formulated above. So far, however, no concrete proposals have been made public.

## Program for a People's Poland

Whatever projects are developed in London, the Polish government must deal with the currents of thought in Poland itself. Despite Nazi occupation, Polish political groups are continuing their activities underground. The traditions of underground revolutionary movements were not entirely extinct in Poland before 1939, and the Nazi terror merely helped to revive them.

Within recent months, the leaders of this movement smuggled out of the country a plan for postwar reorganization. The plan favors a democratic republic, a redistribution of land and measures for industrial socialization, in line with the policies advocated by the Polish Left parties before 1939. The main points of this "Program for a People's Poland" are as follows:

## (1). *Political*

1. A republican and democratic constitution guaranteeing the necessary stability of the state and assuring the right of all citizens to exercise adequate influence upon the selection of the supreme authorities of the nation and upon their policies. Such influence should be exercised through a parliament, democratically elected and restored to its dignity, as well as through general referendum and the right of popular initiative.

2. A broad local self-government should be supplemented by self-governing professional organizations, and by the autonomous administration of social security agencies and of scientific institutions. Labor unions, both of manual and of professional workers, as well as management organizations and co-operative societies, while retaining a full measure of internal autonomy, will be given their definite place in the general organizational scheme of the Republic.

3. Freedom of expression, and the right to organize political, social, and cultural activities on a democratic and independent basis.

4. Equalization of opportunity for all citizens of the Republic through the establishment of universal free education and unrestricted access to culture and higher education.

5. Equal rights for all loyal citizens of the Republic regardless of religion and national origin.

6. The German population which settled on Polish soil in order to promote the Germanization of Poland, will be returned to Germany. . . . Permission to remain in Poland should be granted only to those citizens of German origin who have given active proof of their devotion and loyalty to the Polish state, particularly during the present war and the Nazi occupation.

7. A thorough reorganization of the social system will eliminate the economic basis for the antagonisms between national groups. This will especially affect the Jewish problem. . . .

8. The Polish Republic will be a member of the Union of Free European Peoples. In that Union, the Polish Republic will strive to promote a maximum of cohesion and a federal authority sufficiently powerful to safeguard the United Peoples from external aggression, and to suppress all attempts to create internal dissension through excessive nationalism.

## (2). *Economic and Social*

1. A just redistribution of national income . . .

2. The realization of the ideal of social justice through the socialization of certain sectors of economic life and through the greatest possible reduction of the inequalities of property and income within those sectors of the economy which remain unsocialized.

3. The establishment of labor as the only title to a share in national income.

4. The new social order will be based essentially on the freedom, independence, and social adjustment of every individual. It will thus be truly democratic, both in its political and economic organization . . . In the process of nationalization, organized groups, such as local communities and co-operative societies, will assume the various functions within the nationalized sector of the economy. Farmers' co-operatives and consumers' co-operatives will be an important component of the future economic order and will enjoy full state support. The collectively owned public utilities will also have an important place in the future economic life of the nation . . .

5. Social security will be expanded both in the cities and in the countryside.

6. Economic development will be planned. The plan will determine the directions and goals of economic activities and define the parts to be played by the various elements of production and distribution. . . .[53]

The "underground plan" was submitted to the Polish Council in London by the representatives of the Polish Socialist Party and the Polish Peasant Party who are members of the Council. Its adoption by the present Council is problematical.

### C. YUGOSLAVIA AND GREECE

The Yugoslav government in London maintains a Post-War Reconstruction Committee. It is composed of five members and is under the joint supervision of the Ministry of Finance and of the Ministry of Food and Supply.[54]

Postwar planning for Yugoslavia is hampered not only by the effects of Nazi occupation but by conflicts in anti-Nazi ranks. The Germans have divided the country politically by incorporating Slovenia into the German Reich, by setting up Croatia as an independent state under Italian auspices, and by subdividing other parts of the country. They have changed agricultural and industrial conditions so as to increase the supply of foodstuffs and minerals to Germany. And they have redirected the trade of Yugoslavia entirely within the orbit of Germany's markets.

The present split of the anti-Nazi forces in Yugoslavia is not only political but social. It must affect all plans for the future reorganization of the country.

*Greece*

The Greek government in London has set up a special agency, under the supervision of the Minister of Labor, to study the economic and social problems which will arise in Greece at the end of hostilities.[55]

53. *Program for a People's Poland*, Polish Labor Group, New York, 1942.
54. *International Labour Review*, April 1942.
55. *Ibid.*, May 1942.

Postwar planning for Greece is entirely overshadowed by the dire condition of the people, large numbers of whom are starving or on the verge of starvation. The problems of supplying food and of rehabilitation immediately after the war will be of first importance.

The Greek government-in-exile considers it has an obligation to resign its present mandate as soon as it returns to Athens after the liberation of Greece, in order that a new government may be formed, representative of all the political and social currents of the nation. All national forces, whether formed into parties or as organizations which have contributed to the liberation of Greece during the occupation and the struggle for freedom, will have a voice in the election of this new government.[56]

The political parties in Greece which were in opposition to the government of King George II before 1939, have their own plans for the immediate postwar period. In May 1942, these parties, with the exception of the Communists, drew up a statement which gave the conditions on which a provisional government is to be formed in Greece at the end of the war. According to this statement, only one member of the present government-in-exile in London will be asked to be a member of such provisional government. The other members will be drawn from the highest nonpolitical officials of the state. The provisional government will call a constitutional convention to determine whether Greece is to be a monarchy or a republic.[57]

The economic and social principles on which domestic policy is to be based in Yugoslavia or Greece are still to be defined.

## 4. Plans for Economic Regionalism

The countries of central and eastern Europe differ from each other in many ways. They are inhabited by some fifteen ethnic groups each of which has its own language, historical traditions, and a sense of distinctiveness.[58] Some of these countries—Hungary, Rumania and Bulgaria—are on the side of the Axis powers, while the others have been occupied by Germany forcibly.

These countries have, however, features in common which have given rise to recurrent proposals for some sort of union among

56. *The United Nations Review*, February 15, 1943, p. 65.
57. The Statement of May 1942 is reported by Colonel Sophokles Venizelos in *Common Sense*, April 1943.
58. Such are the Czechs, Slovaks, Poles, Croats, Serbs, Slovenes, Ruthenians, Magyars, etc. See Joseph Hanč, *Eastern Europe and the United States*, World Peace Foundation, Boston, 1942.

them. One is—that these countries are situated between Germany and Russia. This fact has been the basis of various attempts in the past to use them, singly and jointly, as a buffer against either the East or the West. Suggestions that they play a similar role in the future are not lacking today.

Furthermore these countries are agricultural in character and their social-economic structure is based on the peasantry. With the exception of Czechoslovakia, where the proportion of the working population in agriculture is about 35 per cent, the countries of this region have an active agricultural population which ranges from 50 to 80 per cent of those gainfully occupied.

The conditions of the peasantry in these lands are in many ways alike. With some local modifications, the peasant farmers of these several countries are largely subsistence farmers producing their own food and selling relatively small portions of their output in local and European markets. Farms are generally small, yields relatively low, working capital inadequate. The system of farming is far from modern, and the annual population increase is relatively large. The result is a surplus farm population and low standards of living.

All the countries in this region are trying to remedy the situation by more or less the same methods. They propose to give more land to the peasants, to consolidate peasant holdings, to modernize agricultural techniques, to advance the farmer's credit, and to develop industries to absorb surplus farmers. In pursuing these methods, these countries must become, in large measure, competitors and rivals for foreign capital and foreign markets.

Such a postwar development does not augur well for the peace or welfare of the region. It is claimed that the dangers can be obviated by economic union in one form or another. Taken together, the countries of this entire belt of Europe have a population of about 100 million. Even if limited to the countries on the side of the United Nations, the region had before 1939 from 60 to 70 million people. Here is a large enough area and population, it is claimed, to maintain a program of economic development on a high level—if the policies of the separate countries could only be unified and directed towards a common purpose.

The official effort to solve the problems of central and eastern Europe through greater regional unity is exemplified in the Polish-Czechoslovak Declaration of January 25, 1942 and in the Greek-Yugoslav Agreement of January 15, 1942. The former projected a postwar Confederation of Czechoslovakia and Poland; the latter, a postwar Balkan Union. The purpose of both declarations is to bring about common action of the two federations in matters of defense, foreign affairs, monetary and tariff policies, the development of transportation, and social policies. Both contemplate the creationof a customs union.[59]

While hailed at first as a great step forward, these declarations have lost much of their practical importance in recent months. The ties between the Czechs and the Poles were sundered by the territorial issues raised by Soviet Russia. Serbs and Greeks drifted apart as a result of Balkan political problems.

Unofficial proposals for greater unity in this region are many. One stems from the representatives of the peasant parties in these countries who are now in exile. Before 1939, the peasant parties and farmers' organizations of Europe had an international organization with headquarters in Paris, popularly known as "The Green International." A number of former leaders of this International have put forth what they call a "Peasant Charter for Eastern Europe." This charter contains the agrarian demands made by the peasant parties in the separate countries. These are to be achieved by common action of the countries of the region.[60]

Another type of unofficial proposal for regional unity is based on the assumption that a common effort to raise the living standards of the people is the best approach to the problem. The key to the whole situation is seen in a common program of industrialization. A series of large industrial projects at strategic points is proposed in the region to improve agricultural production and give employment to persons no longer needed on the farms.

The Tennessee Valley Authority (the TVA) is cited as a model for such a procedure. A "TVA on the Danube" is the popular phrase for this type of proposal. It is suggested that hydroelectric power, which is of great importance in many parts of this region, could be made the basis of many large industrial developments based on mineral and other resources.

It is proposed that the economic development of the region be planned as a unit, so that the resources and the labor of the different

59. The text of these declarations is reprinted in "United Nations Agreements and Documents," *Bulletin of the Commission to Study the Organization of Peace*, July 1942.

60. For text of Charter, see L. Feierabend, "Peasant Programme," *The Central European Observer*, July 31, 1942; also, Nicholas Mirkovich., *Yugoslav Postwar Reconstruction Papers*, Vol. 1, No. 1, New York, 1942.

countries could be used more effectively, and that the undertaking be organized by an international agency so that it may obtain the necessary credits abroad. The interest of western Europe and the United States in such a unified development is solicited on the grounds that it offers an outlet for their capital and technical skill and a means of stabilizing the economic and political life of Europe and, indirectly, of the rest of the world.

## Chapter 7

## NATIONAL PLANS IN LATIN AMERICA

OF THE TWENTY republics south of the Rio Grande, nine signed the United Nations Joint Declaration of January 1, 1942, pledging their military and economic resources in the war against the Axis Powers and their support of the Atlantic Charter.[1] These nine countries include the Central American republics—Guatemala, El Salvador, Honduras, Nicaragua, Costa Rica and Panama—and the West Indies nations of Cuba, the Dominican Republic and Haiti. On June 5, 1942, Mexico gave its adherence to the Declaration. Since then, Brazil and Bolivia have declared war on the Axis Powers while seven others—Venezuela, Colombia, Ecuador, Peru, Paraguay, Uruguay and Chile—have broken off diplomatic relations with these Powers. Argentina alone has maintained relations with the Axis Powers, though on a basis of "benevolent neutrality" towards the United Nations.

In a strict sense, only the twelve countries at war with the Axis Powers should come within the purview of the present study. Such a limitation is not justified, however, in view of the special conditions which have affected the actions of the South American republics. Also, there are many common elements in the postwar outlook of all Latin American countries, and it is shaped by closely interacting factors. It is more realistic to consider all Latin American countries, regardless of their position in the war.

In most countries of Latin America the war has accentuated economic trends and ideas which had been developing for some time before 1939. Also, despite the many differences in the economic and social structure of the republics, these trends and ideas have important elements in common which give a unity to all the basic Latin American problems. These general features in the light of the pre-1939 planning in Latin America will give the proper perspective for the postwar plans of these countries.

### 1. NATIONAL PLANNING BEFORE 1939

Despite differences in size, resources, population, and historic backgrounds the Latin American countries centered their attention before

1. For reprint of this document see *Bulletin of the Commission to Study the Organization of Peace,* July 1942, Vol. 11, No. 7.

1939 on certain common problems and objectives and adopted more or less similar methods of action. During the two decades before the present war most, if not all, Latin American countries were trying to reshape their social-economic institutions along new lines. For a century or so before the First World War, most Latin American countries had adjusted their economic structures and social concepts to a system of world economy based on the relatively free movement of goods, capital and people. But, as the heritage of that period was to perpetuate poverty and inequalities between developed and "backward" countries and to keep Latin America in a state of "colonial" economy, the desire for radical social-economic changes became more pronounced and insistent.

### a. NEW OBJECTIVES AND ATTITUDES[2]

Significant changes in policy took place in Latin America in the two decades before 1939, and especially after 1929. In the first place, most of these countries, from the Rio Grande to the Straits of Magellan, set out more definitely and vigorously to develop their natural resources and to increase national income. Many of these countries are in large measure virgin soil. Some of them have wide stretches of fertile land which has not been brought under cultivation or which has been inadequately used. They are also endowed with mineral deposits and with a capacity for producing raw materials of various kinds which are awaiting development.

The exploitation of these resources has been hampered and delayed by the physical difficulties of exploration and utilization due to natural obstacles, lack of means of communication, sparsity of population, inadequacy of technical preparation, and poverty of capital equipment. Even within the long-settled and more or less developed areas, a more rapid development of economic activities could be stimulated by providing a greater supply of facilities for transportation and community living as well as by a better mobilization of available technical and financial resources.

Latin American governments also set themselves to free their economic life from excessive dependence on the exports of a few commodities, coffee or sugar, wheat or cacao, copper or tin. When the present war broke out, Central and South America were producing

2. This section is largely a condensation of part of the study by Lewis L. Lorwin, *National Planning in Selected Countries*, National Resources Planning Board, Washington, August 1941.

about $5 billion worth of goods, over a third of which was exported. Half of these exports were agricultural products.

Even before 1914 some of the Latin American countries had periodic misgivings as to the economic and social effects of their extraordinary reliance on world markets for one or two staple export products. The collapse of agricultural and raw material prices during 1929–1932 brought the situation to a head. Agricultural diversification and greater industrialization began to dominate thinking on this subject. The governments of the Latin American countries began making decided efforts in the agricultural field.

On the one hand, this effort aimed to increase, where possible, the number of exportable commodities. Argentina promoted the cultivation of fruits; Brazil, cotton and oranges; Ecuador, bananas; Paraguay, cotton, and so on. Another aim was to grow locally more of the foodstuffs consumed within a country, such as rice, beans, wheat, vegetables, and fruits, and so to effect a substantial transfer of activity from staple export crops, which were in danger of over-production, to subsidiary crops which could serve local needs.

Agricultural diversification was combined in some of the Latin American countries with agrarian reforms whose purpose was either to develop a landowning farming class or to create a new system of co-operative and collective land tenure. The two policies were not always interrelated. In some countries, e.g., Colombia or Brazil, diversification was not associated with changes in land tenure. In other countries, of which Mexico is the most notable example, the reconstruction of agrarian relations was undertaken for its own sake. As its adverse effects on exports became evident, an effort was also made to free the agrarian economy to some extent from dependence on world markets by giving it greater diversity.

Both agrarian reform and agricultural diversification raised problems of governmental land planning. The governments of several of the countries undertook to study problems of better land use, and adopted measures to aid farmers in the improvement of their land and crops as well as in the extension of the area of cultivable land by irrigation schemes, land surveys, and other means.

Latin American policies were also aimed to promote home industries and to achieve greater industrialization. A number of industries had begun to develop in some Latin American countries about the turn of the century, but it was the World War of 1914–1918 that gave industrialization its first general impulse. The difficulties of obtaining manufactured goods from Europe stimulated the production of many articles at home. By reducing the capacity of Latin America to pay for imports, the great depression of 1929–1932 accentuated this tendency. To these influences were added social motives such as the desire to build up a more stable social system and to increase the purchasing power of the masses.[3]

During 1929–1939 the governments of most Latin American countries set themselves the task of promoting home industries by means of tariffs, import quotas, exchange controls, subsidies to manufacturers, or by direct public financing. The industries encouraged were textiles, leather goods, foods, building materials, toys, pharmaceutical articles, and similar consumption goods industries. In a few cases governments attempted to promote also heavy industry, e.g., the iron and steel industry of Brazil. One of the features of the governmental policy was to stimulate industries based on the use of home-produced raw materials.

In general, the governments of Latin America tried to encourage small-scale private businesses. This was true even of Mexico, where, in accordance with the predominant social outlook, the main effort was to develop co-operative enterprises.[4] Thus, the *Banco National Obrero de Fomento Industrial* was founded in Mexico to finance workers' syndicates, small industrialists, and merchants. A similar institution was created in Venezuela to provide financial aid at low interest rates to small domestic industries.

The results of this process of governmentally stimulated industrialization were considerable. Many manufacturing plants and enterprises were established or further developed with the direct or indirect aid of the governments of the different countries.

Many Latin American countries made an effort to bring economic activities under national control and to give them a more independent national character. Governments tended to require substantial national representation on the boards of foreign concerns, to establish native industries by direct government intervention, and to train national technicians and experts. Some governments tended to take a direct part in business either by setting up their own concerns or by nationalizing existing foreign ones. This policy was exemplified by Mexico, where the law of March 1937 authorized the Federal Pe-

3. Frank E. Williams, "Economic Diversification in Latin America," *Annals of the American Academy of Political and Social Science*, September 1940, p. 150.
4. Uruguay is an exception. It has consistently sponsored the growth of large-scale government-owned or government-controlled monopolies.

troleum Company to develop the petroleum industry "for the benefit of the national economy."

Examples could be found in several other countries. The Argentine government took over the British section of the Trans-Andean Railway.[5] Argentina also developed a government petroleum industry which in 1937 produced nearly half of the total national crude output.[6] Brazil's largest steamship company, the Lloyd Brasiliero, became an integral part of the Ministry of Transport and Public Works.[7] The port works at La Guaira, Venezuela's chief port, formerly owned by a British enterprise, were bought by the Venezuelan government. Chile, Bolivia, and Uruguay took steps to bring under national control, in one way or another, the petroleum and other mining industries, public utilities, and other industries basic to national welfare.

Closely related to this tendency was the new attitude towards foreign capital and foreign investors. In the two or three decades before 1939, much capital had been placed in Latin America by American, British, French, and other investors. On the eve of the present war, American corporations and individual investors had some $4 billion in Latin American countries, and British investments amounted to over $3.5 billion. In the course of the years, the foreign capitalists had done much to develop the countries of Latin America. They had built railroads in Mexico, opened up silver, gold, copper and tin mines in Mexico, Peru, Chile, and Bolivia, constructed big packing plants in Argentina and Uruguay, and developed sugar, coffee, and banana plantations in Cuba, Brazil, Ecuador, and Central America.

Foreign investments undoubtedly helped to increase the wealth of Latin American countries and to improve the living conditions of large numbers of people. But loans were often made to governments on stiff terms and for wasteful purposes, thus burdening the country with debts which it was hard to pay. The governments also often felt helpless before the foreign corporations because the latter could make trouble either by closing down their plants and creating unemployment or by supporting political opposition. Foreign corporations and their local managers had but little interest in the social development of the country in which they lived and industrial and social

5. E. R. Lingeman, *Report on Economic and Commercial Conditions in the Argentine Republic, June 1937*, U. K. Department of Overseas Trade, 1937, p. 17.

6. *Commercial Pan America*, No. 79, December 1938, p. 14.

7. E. M. Harvey and W. G. Bruzuad, *Report on Economic and Commercial Conditions in Brazil, 1937*, U. K. Department of Overseas Trade, 1938, p. 126.

relations between the foreign companies and their workers were often strained. Also, the economic development which resulted from foreign investments was lopsided. Great plantations of sugar, coffee, cacao, etc., were built up which poured their products into a world market which at times expanded and then became glutted. The industries suffered from wide price fluctuations and uncertainty, and were subject to periodic depressions. The system of monoculture—of cultivating one or two special crops for export—made these countries entirely too dependent on world markets and international finance.

Small groups in the Latin American countries shared in the new wealth which was created by foreign investors and some of it trickled down to the middle classes, whose standards of living were improved, though they were far below those of other countries. The laborers on the plantations were sunk in debt and illiteracy. Government revenues fluctuated greatly and when depressions set in, as after 1929, governments as well as private firms found it impossible to pay either interest due on their foreign debts or pay off some of the principal. Shortly before the war, from one half to two thirds of American loans made to governments and corporations in Latin America were in default, creating much bad feeling between debtors and creditors.

In consequence of these developments Latin Americans began to emphasize the need for a rational and planful use of native and foreign capital more independent of foreign corporate dominance and with greater national self-direction. The Latin Americans were willing to let foreign capitalists make reasonable profits in their countries, provided the countries themselves benefited permanently by the process. They did not wish to have the mines exhausted, their soil depleted and their people "exploited." A greater sense of national dignity arose, and a desire to be not only politically but economically free from foreign domination.

The planning movement in Latin America sought also to improve the living conditions of the mass of the people. While conditions differ in these countries, in most of them the mass of the people live at very low levels. The total of the national incomes of all twenty Latin American countries was estimated in recent years at about $15 billion. In other words, though the population of all Latin American countries is about 120 million, or nearly that of the United States, their combined income before 1939 was less than one fourth that of the United States. More than half of the Latin American population, according to estimates before 1939, lived on family incomes of about

$100 a year, and only a very small proportion had as much as $1,000 a year.[8]

Translated into human terms, these figures mean that the vast majority of the population in Latin America is undernourished, that large numbers suffer from deficiency diseases, that housing conditions are primitive, that elementary facilities for a cultural life are lacking in large parts of the area, and that a considerable proportion of the people (estimated from 20 to 60 per cent for the different countries) is illiterate. Conditions are particularly bad among agricultural laborers and small farmers, but even the better paid industrial workers in the cities are below a minimum standard of living as determined by the authorities of their respective countries.[9]

The Latin Americans insist that such low levels are wholly unjustified in view of the natural resources which they possess and of the economic values which they could create by a proper application of labor and capital. Between 1933 and 1939, one country after another passed social legislation on behalf of the industrial and agricultural workers and adopted measures to improve health, nutrition, and housing conditions.

### b. PLANNING METHODS AND AGENCIES

The national planning activities differed considerably in scope and content. In some countries integral plans were formulated for the development of natural resources and for the reconstruction of social-economic life. Such were the First and Second Six-Year Plans of Mexico, the Three-Year Plan of Cuba, the National Industrialization Plan of Colombia, and the Three-Year Plan of Venezuela. In other countries, e.g., Chile, Bolivia, and Ecuador, special agencies called national economic councils or national development corporations were established to consider partial plans for the development of the national economy. Most Latin American countries took emergency measures to combat the effects of the depression of 1929–1932 and to stimulate recovery by controlling output, prices, currency and trade.[10]

Integral planning in Latin America, as in other countries, has found expression in programs of a liberal business, "New Deal"

8. Joseph C. Rovensky and A. W. Patterson, "Problems and Opportunities in Hemisphere Economic Development," *Law and Contemporary Problems*, School of Law, Duke University, Durham, North Carolina.

9. See *Report of the Director of the International Labour Office*, Second Conference of American States Members of the ILO, Geneva, 1939, pp. 37–52.

10. For a more detailed discussion of these developments see Lewis L. Lorwin, *National Planning in Selected Countries*, Part IV.

reformist, corporative, and socialistic character. Mexico exemplifies the more radical type of integral planning. The First Six-Year Plan of Mexico (1934–1940) outlined a new social system for Mexico and indicated a series of legislative measures to establish it. This Six-Year Plan, which attracted world-wide attention, included re-organization of the land system on the basis of co-operative owner-ship and operation (the *Ejido*), the nationalization of natural re-sources other than land (oil and other minerals), and industrial legis-lation which aimed to give organized labor economic equality with employers. In addition to these features, the First Six-Year Plan contained far-reaching proposals for the reorganization of industrial, educational, and health institutions which would transform Mexico into an advanced social-democratic state.

The outstanding proposal for corporative planning was made in Brazil. Article 13 of the new constitution adopted in 1937 provided for the establishment of a National Economic Council which was "to promote the corporative organization of the national economy."

The philosophy underlying these provisions was summarized in Article 135 as follows: "In private initiative, in the power of the individual to create, to organize, and to invent, exercised within the limits of the public welfare, lie the wealth and prosperity of the Nation. The intervention of the State in the economic field is only legitimate when necessary to supply the deficiency of private initia-tive, and to co-ordinate the factors of production in such a manner as to avoid or resolve their conflicts, and to introduce into the play of individual competition the idea of the national interest, repre-sented by the State."

In further elaboration of the corporative idea, Article 140 provided that "production shall be organized into corporations and these, as entities representative of the forces of national labor, placed under the aid and protection of the State, are organs of the State and shall exercise functions delegated by the public power." Though no steps were taken to put the corporative plan into full operation, the idea has lingered in Brazil where it has been re-enforced by the example of corporative planning in Portugal.

What may be called the "New Deal" type of planning was pro-jected on several occasions in Cuba after the change of government in 1933. After the overthrow of Machado, President Grau San Martin took the first step, by sponsoring a series of measures to strengthen the position of labor, spread employment and raise wages, to extend the influence of the government in the economic life of the country, and especially to extend governmental control over public utilities. The adoption of the Three-Year Plan in 1937 was a more decided attempt in this direction. Among other things, this plan provided for a national bank, tax reforms, co-ordination of the sugar industry, protection of farmers and distribution of lands, expansion of the agricultural industry, old-age insurance, and a progressive tax on large uncultivated landholdings, the revenue to be used to finance the distribution of the land among Cubans.[11]

Essentially "New Deal" in character was the economic program adopted by the popular front government of Chile in 1938. The plan called for an "immediate improvement of the standard of living and working conditions of the laboring classes through agrarian reform, minimum wages, state regulation of rents, construction of sanitary workers' dwellings, regulation of hours of work, and strict enforcement of existing social legislation."[12] The Corporation for the Promotion of Industry (the Fomento Corporation) was set up to devise and carry out practical measures with these ends in view.

The Three-Year Plan of Venezuela adopted in 1938 and the National Industrialization Plan of Colombia are examples of liberal business planning. They emphasize the development of the national economy within the existing framework. A large part of the Venezuelan Three-Year "Administrative Plan" is devoted to an enumeration of specific public works whereby the country could improve its system of communications and its sanitary conditions.

Partial and emergency planning developed to cope with a peculiar feature of Latin American economy—the tendency to overproduce one or another export commodity on whose price in the world market the country especially depends. The purpose of this planning was to regulate the output and marketing of these commodities so as to secure a profitable price to producers. Examples are the regulatory boards set up in Argentina, Uruguay and elsewhere to fix prices for wheat, corn, linseed, meat, etc., and the exchange control boards.

Planning procedures in Latin America have been, in general, similar to those in other countries. Chief among these are public works, state aid to agriculture (in the form of relief to farmers, direct payments, reduction of indebtedness, credit at low interest rates, improved marketing facilities), guaranteed minimum prices for specific com-

11. *Economic Review of Foreign Countries*, U. S. Department of Commerce, Bureau of Foreign and Domestic Commerce, Washington, 1937, p. 187.
12. *Economic Review of Foreign Countries*, 1938, p. 152.

modities (wheat, linseed, etc.), state aid to industry (through technical research, direct subsidies, protective tariffs, import quotas, and public financing), exchange controls, and the public financing of social services.

To execute these plans, various agencies were created in the several Latin American countries before 1939. Some have general advisory or co-ordinating powers, while others have more specific administrative, regulatory or developmental functions. These agencies also differ in the degree to which they are based on the principle of representation or of executive appointment. It is impossible to describe here in detail the agencies developed in each country before 1939, but the table on pp. 162–163 gives a summary of their scope and main features.[13]

## 2. WARTIME DEVELOPMENTS AND POSTWAR PLANS

When the war broke out in 1939, most, if not all, Latin American countries had formulated plans and programs which they were endeavoring to carry out. The war has made no basic change in the general direction of these plans and programs. It has, however, affected economic conditions in such a way as to modify certain features and methods, and has brought into being new agencies which supersede or supplement the older organizations.

It is difficult in most cases to draw a line between wartime activities and postwar policy. War activities in Latin America are largely confined to productive and developmental operations to meet the military needs of the United States and other United Nations. Such operations are linked with pre-1939 developments and merge into postwar programs, and must be considered as parts of one process.

The different countries follow the same general pattern of postwar planning but show variation in social-economic policies.

### a. MEXICO

Shortly after the outbreak of the war in Europe, the National Assembly of the Mexican Revolutionary Party[14] meeting in Mexico City adopted a Second Six-Year Plan for the period 1941–1946. President Manuel Avila Camacho, elected in 1940, was pledged to this plan as a basis of and guide to policy.

13. This table is taken from Lewis L. Lorwin, *National Planning in Selected Countries.*
14. The Party of the Mexican Revolution (PRM) was organized in March 1938. It comprises four sections representing the peasants, the workers, the army, and a "popular sector" made up largely of professional men and government employees. This party elected General Manuel Avila Camacho president in 1940. President Camacho assumed office on December 1, 1940.

## PLANNING AGENCIES IN SELECTED LATIN AMERICAN COUNTRIES
### (Established or Proposed—1931–1940)

| Country | General Advisory or Developmental | Concerned with Public Works | Agricultural and Related Boards (Production and Price Control) | Mining, Power, and Industrial Regulation and Development Boards | Public and Semipublic Corporations | Transport Regulating and Co-ordinating Agencies | Financial | Social Improvement Agencies |
|---|---|---|---|---|---|---|---|---|
| Argentina | | Department of Public Works and other Government Departments | Grain Regulating Board National Meat Board Wine Regulating Board Milk Industry Department National Cotton Board | National Petroleum Council Commission for the Standardization of Equipment National Standards Commission | | Commission for Coordination of Transport | Exchange Control Office[a] | |
| Bolivia | National Economic Council | " | National Wool Committee | | | | | |
| Brazil | National Economic Council (proposed) National Foreign Trade Council National Economic Defense Council | " | Cacao Institute of Bahia National Sugar and Alcohol Institute | National Petroleum Council | | | | |
| Chile | Fomento Corporation | Reconstruction and Relief Corporation | Agricultural Export Board | " | Chilean Nitrate and Soda Corporation | | | General Commissariat of Subsistence |
| Colombia | National Economic Council | Department of Public Works and other Government Departments | National Cotton Board Livestock Loan Fund Council | | | | | |

| | | | | | | | |
|---|---|---|---|---|---|---|---|
| **Cuba** | " | Institute for the Stabilization of Sugar<br>Coffee Stabilization Institute | | | National Transportation Commission | | Federal Committee on Subsistence<br>Cinematograph Institute |
| **Ecuador** | National Economic Council | | | | | | |
| **Mexico** | " | National Supreme Council (proposed)<br>Ministry of National Economy | Autonomous Agrarian Bureau | Petroleos de Mexico | Henequen Producers Association<br>Sugar Producers Association<br>Federal Electric Commission | | National Bank of Ejido Credit<br>National Society for Mineral Financing<br>Labor Bank for Industrial Promotion | National Housing Council |
| **Paraguay** | " | Committee for Co-ordination of Government Activities | | | | | | |
| **Peru** | " | | | | Government Monopolies on Tobacco, Salt, etc. | | | Council of Subsistence |
| **Uruguay** | " | National Administrative Council (absorbed by Office of President, 1934) | National Milk Commission | | ANCAP[b]<br>UTE[c]<br>FUNSA[d]<br>CONAPROLE[e] | | | |
| **Venezuela** | " | Council of National Economy (proposed) | Coffee Institute<br>National Cacao Institute | | La Guaira Harbour Corporation | | Industrial Bank<br>Exchange Centralization Office | |

[a] In all the countries listed here, except Mexico and Peru, exchange control is exercised by a special agency or by the National Bank or by both.
[b] National Administration of Fuels, Alcohol and Portland Cement.
[c] State Electric Plant and Telephone Company.
[d] Fabrica Uruguaya de Neumaticos, Sociedad Anonima.
[e] National Co-operative of Milk Producers.

The Second Six-Year Plan follows the main lines of the First, though it softens some of the extreme features of the latter. The Plan gives as the goal of the Mexican Revolution the transformation of the legal structure of the country from a liberal democracy into a workers' democracy, but it also affirms that private initiative will not meet with "hostility or hindrance" provided workers' rights are respected. The Plan provides for further land distribution, for an increasing control of the state over industry, for public works, for labor and social welfare. It places supervision of the Plan in the hands of a National Economic Council on which all the economic, social, political and military forces are to be represented.[15] Various government departments, particularly the Department of National Economy, are to execute the Plan.

The war has had a profound effect on all classes of the Mexican population. The almost complete cessation of trade between Mexico and Europe and Asia cut off a large part of the national income and curtailed the flow of imports on which Mexico's economy is dependent (wool tops, rayon yarn, paints and varnishes, paper, electric wire and cable, tools and machinery). Mexico has had to rely almost entirely on the United States which became its principal customer and supplier. The United States, however, while buying more from Mexico, was unable to supply many of Mexico's requirements. The lack of consumers' goods led to a rise in living costs, while the shortage of raw materials, markets, and shipping facilities caused considerable unemployment.[16] The immediate problems with which Mexico was thus faced were to prevent price inflation, to find new domestic supplies of raw materials and to expand its own industrial production as much as possible.

The United States provided some aid by its efforts to expand agricultural and mineral output in Mexico for military needs. It extended credits to Mexico during 1941-1942 to finance highway construction, mineral production,[17] and also for the purchase of equipment for the erection of a steel plant. It took steps to employ Mexican workers in

15. *The Second Six-Year Plan.* A translation of the main sections of the plan may be found in Lewis L. Lorwin, *National Planning in Selected Countries,* Appendix D.

16. In 1939, Mexico imported about 16 million pesos worth of corn, wheat and beans; about 64 million pesos worth of drugs, yarns and iron and steel products; about 42 million pesos worth of machinery, and 40 million pesos worth of trucks, motorcycles, tires and parts. Of the 630 million pesos of total imports in 1939, about 33 per cent were industrial raw materials.

17. Total investments estimated at $100 million are to be placed in such mining development, highway construction, and new factories. The capital is to be supplied in part from private funds and in part by the Export-Import Bank.

the United States and to train mechanics who would be able to use their skills in Mexican industry.

Closer economic co-operation with the United States, war shortages and financial exigencies[18] modified the application of the Second Six-Year Plan. The distribution of land to peasants decreased;[19] the needs of labor and industry were subordinated to the need for industrial peace and increased production;[20] the government manifested greater readiness to settle outstanding international difficulties, resulting in an adjustment of the dispute with regard to former American oil properties in Mexico.

The war has had a mixed effect on Mexican plans for national development. It has stimulated the movement towards industrial growth, but has hampered the growth of some already established industries such as textiles. It has slowed up agrarian and industrial reform, but has given an impetus to the demand for social insurance legislation. A comprehensive social security bill, along the lines of the most advanced legislation in other countries, has been drafted by the Ministry of Labor and is now awaiting action by the President and the Chamber of Deputies.[21]

Thus, from the Mexican point of view, the war stresses the need for further planning along the lines laid down before 1939. The program is still that of the Second Six-Year Plan. Opportunities for realizing the goals of this Plan are expected to be greater at the end of hostilities, since Mexico will have accumulated credits in the United States and will be stronger financially, provided financial and trade relations with the United States, Great Britain and other countries maintain it in a favorable exchange position.

18. Mexico declared war against the Axis Powers on May 22, 1942.

19. The tempo of land distribution began to slacken as early as 1938 under President Cardenas. The number of acres distributed dropped from 13,139,000 acres for 1937 to about 8 million in 1938. Altogether, some 20 million acres were distributed between 1917 and 1934; during 1934–1940, under President Lazaro Cardenas, over 45 million acres were distributed; about 6,500,000 acres were distributed by President Camacho between December 1940 and January 1942.

20. On June 8, 1942, President Camacho arranged a "unity pact" which was signed by the six rival Mexican labor federations. The pact provided for the suspension of strikes and the submission of industrial disputes to arbitration; submission of interunion disputes for arbitration to the Department of Labor. The unions further agreed to promote efficiency and output. See *International Labour Review*, July 1941 and August 1942.

21. On assuming office on December 1, 1940, President Camacho sent a message to the Chamber of Deputies in which, among other things pertaining to social reforms, he said: "We must make it our aim—for which I myself shall work with all my strength—to have our social insurance laws before long protecting every Mexican in the hours of adversity, in orphanhood, widowhood, sickness, unemployment and old age, in place of the century-old system under which the poverty of the nation has compelled us to live." *International Labour Review*, May 1941, p. 561.

To prepare for this as well as to meet current problems of war economy, the Mexican government has set up several new agencies. These include special agencies such as the Technical Social Welfare Council for the purpose of preventing industrial accidents and occupational diseases, the *Coordinación y Fomento de la Producción* for the promotion of industry, and others for price fixing, exchange control, etc. But the most important new agency is that which was set up by presidential decree on June 30, 1942, under the name of *Comisión Federal de Planificación Económica*—the Federal Commission on Economic Planning, which is to advise the Ministry of National Economy.

The new Commission[22] is composed of regular members who are government officials. They are the Secretary of National Economy, the Undersecretaries of Finance, Labor and the National Marine, and the Chief of the Federal District Department. In addition, the Commission has technical advisers, without the right to vote, who include one representative each of the National Confederation of Workers, the National Federation of Employers, the Mexican National Railways, and the Petroleum Administration.

The tasks of the Commission include the study of concrete economic problems created by the war and of programs for economic mobilization required by inter-American co-operation. The Commission will in particular study and report on problems concerning raw materials, industrial and technical equipment, trend of the postwar direction of production, inter-American economy, and the economic co-ordination of public and private agencies, and will report on the progress of the economic plans put into effect by the government.

The Commission will meet regularly once every ten days, and in addition whenever four members request in writing that a meeting shall be held. The chairman and three members constitute a quorum; decisions are adopted by a majority vote, the chairman having the casting vote. A secretary general and technical and administrative

22. The new agency replaces for the duration of the war the existing National Economic Council, which had been established by an Act of July 31, 1933, as amended by the Act of April 3, 1941, as an advisory body to the Ministry of National Economy. The National Economic Council was composed of twenty members, including representatives from five ministries and from semiofficial and private agencies, such as the National Railways, the Petroleum Administration, the National Cooperative Federation, the public services, the professional organizations, the chambers of commerce and industry, the mining industries, the trade unions, the agricultural organizations, and the Bankers' Association. The new decree states that the diverse membership of the National Economic Council rendered it unsuitable for dealing with the emergency problems of the war; nevertheless the representatives of the private agencies who sat on the Council will on occasion be consulted by the new smaller body.

staff will be at the service of the Commission. The decisions of the Commission will be submitted to the federal executive by the Secretary of National Economy.

The Commission may require both public and private agencies to submit data, to be treated as confidential, when desired. All proposals and programs prepared by the regional economic councils will be submitted to the Federal Commission for study and co-ordination.[23]

## b. COLOMBIA

For several years before 1939, the Republic of Colombia was engaged on a large public works program which had as one of its aims the industrial development of the country. Considerable sums were spent during 1934–1938 on port improvements at Cartagena and Barranquilla, dredging work at the mouth of the Magdalena River, and highway construction throughout the country. The public works program included plans for low-cost dwellings for the municipal employees of the capital, Bogotá. The federal government extended aid to municipalities for the construction of aqueducts, electric light plants, and water supply systems.[24]

Colombia's prosperity depends primarily on the export of coffee, though in recent years oil and other minerals have become increasingly important.[25] The government has tried to develop its mineral resources and to promote industries. In August 1940, the government adopted "a plan to stimulate the development of the country's mineral resources and the encouragement of domestic manufactures." The chemical industry has been the particular object of governmental attention. A Special Institute for Industrial Development was set up in July 1940 to encourage industry. At the same time, the government issued a decree reorganizing the National Economic Council which had been in existence since 1935. The Council was instructed to review the plans submitted by the several ministries and to promote collaboration between private economic groups and the government.

Since 1940, the war has had the same effects in Colombia as in other Latin American countries. Despite shortages of certain raw materials

23. See *International Labour Review*, September 1942, pp. 314–315.
24. *Economic Review of Foreign Countries*, United States Department of Commerce, 1935–1940.
25. Colombia has an area of about 440,000 square miles and a population of about 9 million. It is one of the countries in South America where landholding is more widely distributed and where political conditions have been fairly stable and based on democratic procedures. There is a growing trade union and co-operative movement in the country. See A. Fabra Ribas, "Cooperation in Colombia," *The Cooperative Movement in Latin America*, International Labour Office, Montreal, 1943.

and machinery, industrial activity has broadened. The production of cotton cloth has increased; the output of various native products has expanded; hydroelectric plants have been built by the government; the chemical industry has been enlarged. On the other hand, there has been an accumulation of coffee surpluses and of some raw materials, and certain new developments, e.g., the increased production of rubber, are based on the purchase contracts of United States war agencies.

The situation raises many problems for the postwar period. The government, by an executive order as of April 1, 1942, set up a National Commission for Economic Studies to analyze present and postwar economic problems and to consider the social aspects of proposed economic solutions.[26] It has also established an Institute for Land Credit to study rural housing projects and other improvements.[27]

### C. VENEZUELA

When President Contreras announced his Three-Year Plan for Venezuela on May 6, 1938, he presented it not only as a proposal for immediate improvements but also as preparing "the bases for a renewed and great country." The Three-Year Plan proposed specific public works for the development of transportation, mining, agriculture, and industry as well as large measures for the "hygienization of man" and the "advancement of education" by the construction of hospitals, protective institutions for mothers and children, better housing, and schools.[28]

The war forced new problems on Venezuela, and, with other conditions, made a realization of the Three-Year Plan impossible. Production of oil was curtailed and many oil wells were closed down. Shortages of semifinished products and machinery led to a shutdown of many factories in the textile, boot and shoe, and other industries. The development of iron mining begun in 1939-1940 was retarded. Considerable unemployment of workers in the oil industry, construction and transportation resulted.[29] The impossibility of obtaining food imports caused a shortage of goods and drove up the cost of living already high compared with other South American countries.

26. The Commission is composed of the Ministers of War, Finance, National Economy, and Public Works; it includes also the National Superintendent of Imports, the Head of the Office of Export and Exchange Control, the Manager of the National Association of Coffee Growers, and several other public officials and economic experts.
27. *International Labour Review*, November 1942.
28. For the details of this Plan see Lewis L. Lorwin, *National Planning in Selected Countries*, Appendix C.
29. At the end of June 1942, there were 12,795 unemployed workers in the twenty-one principal towns of the country. *International Labour Review*, October 1942, p. 485.

The measures taken to meet the emergency war situation have long-range implications. A principal one is to promote a return to the land and local production of foodstuffs formerly imported. On July 6, 1942, an agreement was concluded between the government and the oil companies for the transfer of discharged workers to agriculture. The government has undertaken to lease or sell publicly owned land to the workers, particularly land suitable for irrigation and near centers of population. The government estimates that about forty acres for each holding will be sufficient for the support of a family.

The oil workers settling on the land will be paid by the oil companies 15 bolivars per week for thirty consecutive weeks beginning with the seventh week after the discharge. The companies will pay further 90 bolivars per settler for the purchase of agricultural implements, and will lend equipment necessary for clearing the land, etc. The government is to contribute 500 bolivars per settler for the purchase of draught animals.

Another series of measures deal with the development of new industries, on the basis of local materials. Such industries include the production of seed oils and fats for cooking and eating, fertilizers and animal fodder, fish canning, powdered milk and pharmaceutical products.

Supplementing these measures is the new Five-Year Plan of public works which the President of Venezuela announced on January 1, 1942, to run through 1946. The public works will involve an expenditure of 376 million bolivars (about $100 million) and provide for the construction of ports, of about 1,500 kilometers of new roads, the irrigation of some 27,000 acres of land, the construction of workers' homes in Caracas for about 15,000 persons, and other projects.[30]

These plans indicate the direction in which Venezuela intends to move. Its main effort is to overcome the difficulties due to the predominant position of coffee and oil exports in its economic life and to build up a more balanced economy in which agriculture, cattle raising, and industries are properly combined with mining and the production of export crops. With such an economy it might be easier to improve the very low conditions of sanitation and health, housing and education.

### d. BRAZIL

Early in 1939, President Vargas strengthened the national economy of Brazil along the lines followed since 1930 when he issued a decree

30. *International Labour Review*, August 1942.

outlining a "Special Plan for Public Works and Equipment for the National Defense," to be carried out in five years at the cost of 3 billion milreis, or about $150 million at the then existing rate of exchange. The funds, appropriated at the annual rate of about 600 million milreis, were to be applied to diversify agriculture, promote new industries (including an iron and steel industry), to develop natural resources, and to strengthen the military defenses of the country. The funds were to be obtained from national sources such as special taxes, profits from banking and exchange operations and from special issues of Treasury obligations.

During 1939 questionnaires were sent to all municipalities in the country in order to obtain a clearer picture of national economic needs and industrial possibilities. The government continued to foster domestic industry by facilitating the importation of such products as railway materials, tractors, trucks, and agricultural implements.

On the outbreak of war in Europe, several new agencies were established to control production and prices and to secure necessary supplies. Most important of these was the National Economic Defense Council, established on September 29, 1939, whose general function was to protect the national economy in the emergency. The new Council was given power to regulate imports and exports, to make agreements with foreign governments for the barter of merchandise, to assure supplies for domestic consumption and for the basic industries of the country.

The war has helped Brazil considerably in its economic program. Increased trade with the United States has compensated for trade lost in Europe. American capital has been advanced to Brazil through the Export-Import Bank to develop new raw materials, to renew the production of rubber, and to build up an iron and steel plant. Agreements have been concluded with the American government to buy Brazilian coffee, cocoa, vegetable oils, babassu nuts, rubber and other raw materials over a number of years at fixed prices. Sales of merchandise have given Brazil a large trade balance estimated at some $200 million.[31] At the same time, there has been a large development of the domestic market which is served by growing local industries.

The program formulated in the Special Plan of 1939 runs till 1944 but can be extended indefinitely. Its main features remain the same;

31. For the agreements signed by Brazil and the United States providing for credits of about $100 million to Brazil from the Export-Import Bank and other developments see *The New York Times*, March 4, 1942. Also Lewis L. Lorwin, *International Economic Development*, National Resources Planning Board, Washington, 1942, pp. 32–40.

greater diversity in agriculture, greater industrialization, more trade with the United States and Latin America, a social system based on state-approved organizations, a social policy of protection for the farmers and the workers,[32] including provisions for better nutrition and housing and more education.[33]

### e. CHILE

The success of the popular front government in 1938 marked the beginning of a new economic and social period in Chile. The government, which assumed office on December 24, 1938, sponsored a comprehensive plan for the development of the nation's resources and immediate improvement in the social conditions of the mass of the people. It set up two agencies in 1939—the Reconstruction and Relief Corporation and the Corporation for the Promotion of Industry— both for a period of six years. The government was authorized to contract external and internal loans up to two and a half billion pesos (about $100 million) of which one billion was to be allotted to each corporation and half a billion was to be spent for the construction of low-cost housing.

The functions of the Corporation for the Promotion of Industry (Fomento Corporation) are "to develop national production in order to raise the standard of living of the people by taking advantage of the natural conditions of the country and by decreasing costs of production, and to improve the balance of international payments, maintaining due proportion in the development of activities in the fields of

32. As pointed out above, the Constitution of 1937 provides for the organization of all economic groups in corporations and professional associations. The decree of August 31, 1942 requires all occupational organizations to collaborate with the government in developing a "national consciousness," in mobilizing the armed forces (Brazil declared war on the Axis Powers on August 22, 1942) and in studying national economic problems. Employers are not to use the state of war as an excuse for restricting the trade union rights of their employees.

33. The social insurance institutions of Brazil, as of other Latin American countries, are used by the government to carry on some of this work. Thus, the Brazilian government is collaborating with the social insurance institutions in establishing popular restaurants, administered by the Social Insurance Nutrition Service of the Ministry of Labor. The popular restaurants are now supplying some 5,000 meals daily in the cities of Rio de Janeiro and São Paulo. Consideration is now being given to the provision of traveling kitchens which would operate in the neighborhood of big public works so as to enable the workers employed to obtain cheap and wholesome meals.

The insurance institutions have also taken up the problem of housing. The Commercial Workers' Pension Institution has just approved a plan for building a group of 83 houses for its members. These houses can only be allotted to affiliated employees whose earnings are between 430 and 645 milreis a month and who have paid at least six months, contributions to the Institution. Each house consists of five rooms and the usual offices and will be let at 215 milreis a month unfurnished or 235 milreis furnished. See *International Labour Review*, August 1942.

mining, agriculture, industry, and commerce, and satisfying the needs of the different regions of the country." It is administered by a board on which are represented the government, the congress, state credit institutions and enterprises, private individuals, and salaried persons. Its technical and commercial direction is assigned to an executive vice president and to a manager, both elected by the board of the Corporation.

The Corporation is obliged to elaborate a general plan for national production. To carry out its plans, the Corporation encourages both private and public capital to become interested in its projects. To this end it offers loans or contributions of capital, in the case of nationals, and seeks also the aid of foreign capital.

A serious earthquake in 1939 and the outbreak of the war complicated the tasks of the Fomento Corporation. Like other Latin American countries, Chile suffered from loss of markets for some of its exports and from the shortage of imports needed for the industrial development of the country. It obtained only small amounts of credit from the Export-Import Bank in Washington. The cost of living rose and projected social reforms were curtailed.

The new government which was elected in January 1942 holds the same views as its predecessor.[34] The plans of 1938-1939 are to be pursued during 1943–1945. The government created in November 1942 a National Economic Council to prepare specific measures for the realization of these plans:[35] to submit such draft bills, decrees, and regulations to the government as it considers will promote economic activity, to draw attention to the effects that the measures in preparation may have, to suggest amendments to existing legislation, and to propose new measures. The Council is also required to co-ordinate the economic activities of private industry with those of the state in regard to production, finance, distribution, the social organization of labor, and the fiscal system.[36]

34. Juan Antonio Rios was elected to succeed Aguirre Cerda.

35. Chile also has an Agricultural Export Board which fixes prices of wheat and flour. The Chilean Nitrate and Sales Corporation is a state monopoly for the export and sale of nitrates which are produced by private producers.

36. The National Economic Council is composed of the following: (a) the ministers forming the Economic Committee of the government; (b) one member from each of the sections for agriculture, industry, wholesale trade, retail trade, and transport of the Confederation of Production and Commerce; (c) three members of lawfully constituted trade unions of workers; (d) one representative of the national credit institutes and one member of the Chamber of Commerce; (e) one representative of the Institute of Engineers; (f) one representative of the Chilean Agronomic Society. Apart from the ministers, the members of the Council are appointed by the President of the Republic for a term of one year. See *International Labour Review*, December 1942.

## f. URUGUAY

Uruguay is one of the Latin American countries which do not harbor large schemes of industrialization and have no formal national plans. The country is fully aware that its main economic resources are in its agricultural and pastural lands, and it has proceeded consistently for several decades, despite some political and economic ups and downs, to develop democratic institutions and policies of social welfare.[37] Like several other small countries, such as New Zealand and Denmark, it has had considerable success, which is reflected in the fact that Uruguay is often referred to as "a citadel of progress" and as "the social laboratory of the Americas."[38]

While not formally sponsoring any plan, the government of Uruguay undertakes to control and guide the economic development of the country. The characteristic method used for this purpose is the establishment of government monopolies, public corporations and state-owned and state-operated plants. The government of Uruguay owns or controls the railroads, the telegraph and telephone systems, the central bank, packing plants, a number of hotels, casinos, insurance companies, power plants, cement plants, etc. These various enterprises are organized into a series of corporations.[39] General control is exercised through the National Administrative Council.

Although it is essentially an agricultural and pastoral country, Uruguay is attempting to build up local industries. To free its industries from dependence on coal[40] and oil fuel, it began construction of a large hydroelectric plant on the Rio Negro which is to supply power to industry as well as for other purposes. The project has been delayed by the war, but it is expected to be continued with the financial aid of the United States.[41]

37. Uruguay has an area of 72,153 square miles and a population of about 2,500,000. Ninety per cent of the population are of European extraction. It is the smallest republic in South America. About three fourths of the land is used for grazing, and 85 per cent of the country's exports are animal products. The larger industries are those which process foodstuffs, the chemical industries, building materials, textiles, and boots and shoes. Many of the manufacturing plants are small and can maintain themselves chiefly because of tariff protection.

38. See Philip Leonard Green, "Uruguay—Citadel of Progress," *Agriculture in the Americas*, U. S. Department of Agriculture, November 1942.

39. For the most important of these, see Lewis L. Lorwin, *National Planning in Selected Countries*.

40. Imported before 1939 chiefly from Great Britain.

41. The plan provides for the regulation of the Rio Negro to make it navigable for a stretch of 600 kilometers, the creation of an immense artificial lake (eighty-five miles long and from ten to twenty miles wide) on the shores of which a new industrial city is to be built, and finally the construction of a power plant capable of producing annually 500 million kilowatt hours of electric current.

The war has accentuated in Uruguay, as in several other countries, the problems of land use and land tenure. Feeling that a more balanced agriculture depends on the creation either of small farm owners or of co-operative land systems, Uruguay has chosen the former method, modified by the development of farmers' co-operatives. An act passed in September 1941 provides for a new land settlement policy which is to be carried out through "the expropriation, breaking up and exploitation of land."

Under the act, the expropriation by purchase of land for agricultural development or stock raising is considered a matter of public interest. Such land will be duly divided up and allotted by the Mortgage Bank in charge of operations to farmers who satisfy the conditions prescribed in existing land settlement legislation. Priority will be given to farmers who are liable to eviction from their present holdings. The bank may either sell the holding outright, receiving an initial payment, or it may lease it, giving the tenant a first option to purchase and not requiring him to make any cash payment. The size of the holding, which will vary according to circumstances, may not exceed 25 hectares (about 60 acres) if it is in the neighborhood of a marketing center. In exceptional cases a holding of 500 to 1,000 hectares may be granted for purposes of stock raising.

The settlers must live on the holdings allotted to them and work them on a family basis in accordance with guiding principles issued by the bank. The bank will promote the formation of consumers', marketing, and producers' co-operative societies in the settlements.

Before the holdings are allotted, the bank may provide for the construction of dwelling houses and fences, and undertake the necessary preparatory work for operating the holding. Where this is not done, the bank will grant the settler a loan at his request. Such loans may not exceed 500 pesos, unless the purchase price of the holding exceeds 2,500 pesos, in which case the loan may not be more than 20 per cent of the value of the holding, subject to a maximum of 2,000 pesos. The loans, whether granted in cash or in the form of preparation of the holding, are to be redeemed in a period of ten years, and the rate of interest may not exceed 5 per cent per annum.

Any profits earned by the Mortgage Bank in consequence of the application of the act must be restricted to one per cent of the sums invested in the purchase, breaking up, and administration of the land. Deeds of transfer of property will be drawn up free of charge, and will be free of stamp duty. The land allotted to settlers will be free of land tax for ten years. [42]

### 3. NATIONAL PLANS, REGIONALISM AND INTER-AMERICANISM

Looking ahead to the years after the war, most Latin American countries hope that they may be able to carry forward the particular economic plans and programs which they have been advancing for a decade or more. In varying degrees, these plans provide for the building up of industries, for agricultural diversification, for development of transportation and communication, for opening up of new lands, for a better distribution of landownership, and for the extension of social services which would assure to the mass of the people security and opportunities for health, recreation and education.

Latin American countries are prepared to use the powers of government and co-operative and collective forms of organization to the extent necessary for the success of their objectives. An integral part of this outlook is the determination to achieve social-economic aims as much as possible by reliance on local and national resources and effort, and to obtain the help of foreign capital and technical skill only on a basis of respect for their national independence and of democratic international co-operation.

The war, as already pointed out, has promoted the realization of some of these plans. But it has also brought into clearer light some of the difficulties which these countries have always faced in their attempts at economic reorganization, and it has created new problems. The chief difficulties of long standing are the poverty of many of these countries, the backward condition of large groups of the population, the persistence in some countries of semifeudal landholding systems and conditions, the scarcity of organizing talent, the continued dominance of "personalism" in political and social life, and the dependence on exports and foreign markets for a large part of the national income and employment. Most plans based on the development of domestic markets hinge on the capacity to tide a poor people over the period of readjustment, and necessarily the task can be made easier only by making this period longer.

The new problems created by the war are partly a new version of some of the older problems, in part they are the result of the measures taken by the United States to strengthen the military defenses of the

42. *International Labour Review*, March 1942.

Western Hemisphere and to "step up" war production. By the use of long-term agreements, by setting up mixed development corporations,[43] by direct loans and subsidies, and through special technical missions, the United States has stimulated in various Latin American countries the production of tin, copper, iron ore, mercury, manganese, quinine, rubber, vegetable oils, etc. The United States has thus expanded the capacity of some of the mining and agricultural industries, and has brought into being high-cost properties which can operate on the basis of guaranteed prices.

One consequence of this war development is that many countries face a postwar dilemma of either having additional problems of agricultural and mineral surpluses, or of tying their economies more closely to the United States. In view of the fact that the problem of surplus commodities such as wheat and cotton was not resolved before 1939, the prospect of adding to it after the war is disquieting. On the other hand, a preponderant dependence on the markets of one country —even if that country be the United States—is considered undesirable. These are the sharpened horns of the dilemma which the Latin Americans were trying to escape before 1939 through the elaboration of their national plans.

Part of the postwar planning in Latin America is concerned with these new problems. They cannot be settled or prepared for by any country acting alone. One hope for a solution lies in regionalism or closer inter-Latin Americanism. This trend is exemplified by the various bilateral agreements which have been made since 1939 by Bolivia and Chile, Paraguay and Bolivia, Paraguay and Uruguay, Argentina and Brazil for the promotion of trade, building of roads, or for exploration.

Another method of resolving the postwar dilemma is to make inter-Americanism an instrument of democratic economic policy. The organizations through which this aim has so far been promoted are the Inter-American Development Commission, the Inter-American Financial and Economic Advisory Committee, and special technical agencies such as the Inter-American Conference on Agriculture, the Inter-American Committee to Promote Social Security and others.[44]

43. For a description and analysis of these various corporations and their operations in Latin America, see Lewis L. Lorwin, *International Economic Development—Public Works and Other Problems*, Technical Paper No. 7, National Resources Planning Board, Washington, October 1942, pp. 32–41.

44. For the structure and functions of these organizations see *International Labour Review*, September 1942, and November 1942; also *Agriculture in the Americas*, September 1942.

From the point of view of most countries, both inter-Latin Americanism and inter-Americanism would be more effective if woven into a general world economic policy. Many are in favor of the newer schemes for handling agricultural surpluses, for controlling output and for promoting economic stability which rest on international agreements and world co-operation. The International Wheat Agreement embodies these principles in a way which may be applied also to other commodities. The Latin American countries hope that plans of such an international character will be elaborated with their participation and without affecting adversely their own national programs for postwar development.

## Chapter 8

# REHABILITATION AND RECONSTRUCTION IN CANADA

THE DOMINION GOVERNMENT of Canada showed interest in postwar problems soon after the war began. A Cabinet Committee on Demobilization and Reestablishment was constituted in December 1939 to consider the problem of returning the armed forces to civil life at the end of the war.[1] In August 1940, this Cabinet Committee established an interdepartmental committee, known as the General Advisory Committee on Demobilization and Rehabilitation, to study various aspects of the demobilization problem.

## Committee on Reconstruction

The functions of the Cabinet Committee were enlarged in February 1941 to include general questions of postwar reconstruction. Soon after that, the Cabinet Committee created a Committee on Reconstruction to act in an advisory capacity. The Committee on Reconstruction was to report to the Cabinet Committee through the General Advisory Committee on Demobilization and Rehabilitation.[2]

## Advisory Committee on Economic Policy

Government agencies responsible for postwar planning were reorganized in January 1943. The Advisory Committee on Economic Policy, in existence since September 1939, and concerned with wartime economic problems, was reconstituted and given larger functions, including those of postwar planning.[3] Under the new arrangements

1. The Cabinet Committee was composed of the Minister of Labour, the Minister of Agriculture, the Minister of Trade and Commerce, the Minister of National Defense, the Minister of Public Works, with the Minister of Pensions and National Health, the Honorable Ian Mackenzie, as convener.

2. The Committee on Reconstruction consists of six members under the chairmanship of Dr. F. Cyril James, Principal and Vice-Chancellor of McGill University. It has three ex-officio members representing the Department of Pensions and National Health, the Advisory Committee on Demobilization and Rehabilitation, and the Canadian Committee of the Joint United States-Canada Economic Committees. Dr. Leonard C. Marsh, formerly Director of Social Research at McGill University, is research adviser to the Committee. See *International Labour Review*, February 1942, pp. 170–171; also article by A. Brady in *The Canadian Journal of Economics and Political Science*, August 1942.

3. The Advisory Committee on Economic Policy is an interdepartmental committee of government officials responsible directly to the President of the Privy Council (this office is held by the Prime Minister, W. L. Mackenzie King). The chairman of the Committee is the Deputy Minister of Finance; the other members include the Deputy Ministers of Agriculture and of Mines and Resources, the Associate Deputy Minister of Labour, the Chairman of the War Time Prices and Trade Board, and several other high government officials. See *International Labour Review*, March 1943, pp. 354–355.

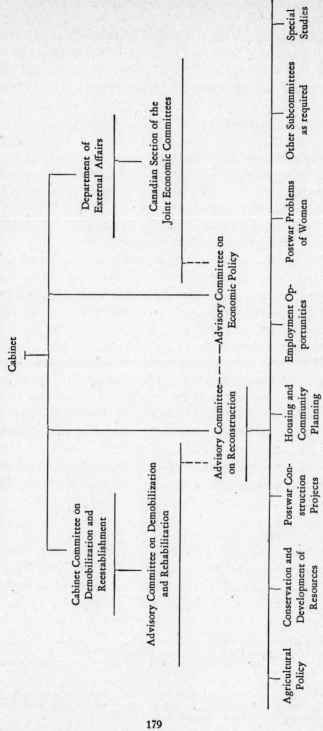

DOMINION GOVERNMENT COMMITTEES CONCERNED WITH POSTWAR RECONSTRUCTION

Cabinet

Cabinet Committee on Demobilization and Reestablishment

Department of External Affairs

Advisory Committee on Demobilization and Rehabilitation

Advisory Committee on Reconstruction — — — Advisory Committee on Economic Policy

Canadian Section of the Joint Economic Committees

Agricultural Policy

Conservation and Development of Resources

Postwar Construction Projects

Housing and Community Planning

Employment Opportunities

Postwar Problems of Women

Other Subcommittees as required

Special Studies

179

the Advisory Committee is charged with the co-ordination of all studies of postwar problems by government departments and agencies. It co-operates with the Committee on Demobilization and Rehabilitation and with the Committee on Reconstruction. The Advisory Committee on Economic Policy has set up a special subcommittee to deal with postwar planning.[4]

### Advisory Committee on Reconstruction

At the same time, the Committee on Reconstruction established in 1941, was replaced by a new Advisory Committee on Reconstruction. The composition of the new committee is the same as that of its predecessor, but it is now responsible directly to the Prime Minister in his capacity as President of the Privy Council.[5]

The Advisory Committee on Reconstruction carries on its work in much the same way as before, in co-operation with the Advisory Committee on Economic Policy. It also makes such investigations as the President of the Privy Council may direct.[6]

### Parliamentary Committees

In March 1942, the Canadian House of Commons appointed a Committee on Reconstruction and Reestablishment to report on the general problems which may be expected to arise at the close of hostilities. In March 1943, the House of Commons Committee was reappointed, while the Senate of Canada also appointed a special committee "to consider and report upon matters arising out of post-war conditions, particularly those relating to problems of reconstruction and reestablishment, and a national scheme of social and health insurance."

### Provincial Agencies

Besides the Dominion government and Parliament, several of the provincial governments have agencies for the consideration of postwar problems.[7] Some of these, e.g., the Economic Advisory Council of Nova Scotia had been in existence before 1939, while others, e.g., the Post-War Rehabilitation Council of British Columbia have been

4. The Chairman of the subcommittee is Dr. W. A. Mackintosh, Professor at Queen's University, and adviser to the Department of Finance in Ottawa.
5. Session 1943, House of Commons, Special Committee on Reconstruction and Reestablishment, *Minutes, March 9-11, 1943*, Ottawa, p. 4.
6. *Ibid.*, p. 16.
7. The Dominion of Canada is composed of nine provinces—Nova Scotia, New Brunswick, Prince Edward Island, Quebec, Ontario, Manitoba, Saskatchewan, Alberta, British Columbia, and the Territory of Yukon and the Northwest Territories.

established since 1939. These provincial bodies are conducting investigations and preparing measures for the solution of postwar problems on the basis of the interests and powers of the respective provinces.

## Unofficial Organizations

In Canada, as in the United States and England, some unofficial bodies and voluntary organizations have also formulated their views on one or another phase of postwar reconstruction. In general, these statements are less specific and comprehensive than those of similar organizations in other countries.

Following the division of functions among the different committees in Canada, it may be convenient to summarize here (1) what has been done with regard to demobilization, (2) what is being proposed by government agencies for purposes of reconstruction, and (3) the ideas and programs of unofficial organizations.

## 1. The Rehabilitation of Ex-Servicemen

The Dominion government has made considerable progress in preparing for the time when the armed forces will have to be demobilized. The legislation which was passed on the subject during 1941–1942 lays down a comprehensive and concrete procedure for the rehabilitation of the veterans of the present war and provides the necessary administrative machinery. The most important provisions of this legislation follow.

### a. TRANSITIONAL BENEFITS

The purpose of transitional benefits is to ease the immediate postwar economic position of men discharged from the Canadian armed forces. A discharged man who has had more than six months' service will be entitled: (1) to retain his army clothing and personal equipment, and, in addition, to receive a civilian clothing allowance of $35; (2) to get transportation free to his home; and (3) to receive a rehabilitation grant of thirty days' pay and dependents' allowances.

### b. POST-DISCHARGE RE-ESTABLISHMENT PROVISIONS

On October 1, 1941, the Post-Discharge Reestablishment Order was approved, which is designed to help ex-soldiers to re-establish themselves in civil life. The emphasis is on employment. Arrangements are made by the Department of Pensions and National Health and by the

Department of Labor to provide vocational training to discharged men so as to fit them for re-employment or for better jobs than they formerly had. The government is to pay the cost of the training and also allowances to the men during training. The period for which training may be given is limited to a period equivalent to the period of service or a maximum of fifty-two weeks.

The Order also provides for the resumption of interrupted education. Discharged men who are able to enter a university within fifteen months after the date of discharge will receive subsistence allowance grants, together with payment of fees to the university throughout the whole period of their university course, provided such students can maintain their university grade and need financial assistance.

Third, discharged men entering private business or farming may obtain allowances while awaiting returns from their enterprise. These provisions are limited to a period of nineteen months from the date of discharge.

Fourth, the Order seeks to establish unemployment insurance parity between those in the armed forces and those now serving in employment covered by the Unemployment Insurance Act.[8] The Order provides that discharged men able and willing to work, but unable to obtain suitable employment, should be paid out-of-work benefits. The benefits are fixed at $13 per week for a married person or $9 per week for a single person and are paid to those seeking employment or taking training courses. The period of such payments is limited to fifty-two weeks. Veterans entering employment covered by unemployment insurance will be credited with having been in such employment since July 1, 1941, and the government will pay to the Unemployment Insurance Fund the contributions which the employer and the employee would have paid. These provisions apply, after fifteen weeks, to discharged men entering insurable employment within a period of twelve months after discharge.

### C. SETTLEMENT ON THE LAND

In planning to re-establish veterans, the Canadian authorities are acting on the assumption that they are obliged to provide for an increased absorption of men into urban life. However, a considerable number of men in the Canadian forces are likely to return to the land. This was made clear by the replies to a questionnaire addressed to the

8. This Act became effective in July 1941.

men in the armed forces in 1942 which showed that 16.6 per cent of those questioned expressed a desire to settle on the land after the war. To provide these men with opportunities to do so, the Veterans' Land Act was passed in the latter part of 1942.

The benefits of the Veterans' Land Act are limited to (1) members of the armed forces of Canada who served in a theater of war; (2) members of the armed forces who did not serve in a theater of war but who served in the armed forces for at least twelve months, and (3) those who are pensioned for disability incurred as a result of service.

Three main types of settlement are contemplated: (1) full-time farming for men with practical experience in farm operation; (2) small holding settlements, which means a rural home and small acreage located close to employment opportunities, and (3) small holding settlements coupled with commercial fishing. Under any of these three programs the veteran must be certified as qualified physically and by experience and training to engage in the type of enterprise planned.

Under the Act, the government purchases for the applicant veteran a piece of land of his own choice (and which has been approved for settlement purposes) which with improvements and building materials shall not cost more than $3,600. The government also provides stock and implements within a maximum of $4,800 for the total establishment. The veteran must make a down payment of 10 per cent of the cost of the land and improvements (a maximum of $360) and assume a debt of two thirds of the cost of the land and improvements (a maximum of $2,400). The debt will bear interest at 3.5 per cent and must be paid in twenty-five years. The monthly payments (principal and interest) are fixed at about $12. No conveyance or transfer of the property shall be made to the veteran within the first ten years and then only if the veteran has complied with the terms of the agreement and is making good in his venture.

To deal with settlers who prove unsuccessful, the director who will administer the Act is given power to rescind the agreement and to retake possession of the property without resort to legal proceedings if the veteran falls down in his payments. The director must, however, refer the case to a provincial advisory board for its consent as to whether the default warrants cancellation of the veteran's agreement. The object of this repossession feature is to prevent a veteran from continuing a doomed enterprise beyond the point at which his failure is indicated, and to give him an opportunity to try some other enterprise before he is too old to make the change. Any surplus proceeds from the sale of repossessed property, over the government's outstanding costs, are paid to the veteran.

Provisions with identical terms are made for establishing veterans on small holdings (one to three acres is the size suggested) where they may live while engaged in industrial, commercial or other employment for which they are suited by training and experience, or in commercial fishing (under which section it is possible for the veteran to obtain a grant for purchase of boat, nets and gear as well as a home).

The Act provides a further type of assistance for the veteran who owns farm land and who may desire to pay off a mortgage, make improvements or purchase livestock or equipment. Advances up to $3,200 may be obtained for such purposes provided they do not exceed 60 per cent of the value of the land. Repayment may be made over a period of twenty-five years with interest at the rate of 3.5 per cent.

The administration of the Act will be decentralized, with several local or regional offices in each province. In addition there will be regional advisory committees to advise the director as to the qualifications of applicants and the selection of lands for settlement. For veterans who have been out of touch with farm practice for several years, "brusher-up" courses with selected farm operators will be arranged.

In the preparation of the Act, all the provinces of Canada were consulted, and they indicated their desire to co-operate by way of surveys and otherwise in making the scheme a success. Sufficient land for the purpose is believed to be available in various parts of Canada.

## 2. GOVERNMENT PLANNING FOR RECONSTRUCTION

The measures for dealing with demobilization and re-establishment are already in force. On the other hand, reconstruction measures are largely in the stage of study, though some practical steps have been taken.

### a. THE BACKGROUND OF RECONSTRUCTION

Postwar policies in Canada are being considered against the background of economic and social changes which had become evident before the war. In 1937, a Royal Commission on Dominion-Provincial Relations was established to analyze these changes, to study the problems which they had created and to make recommendations for their solution. While its terms of reference were largely fiscal, the Commission extended its inquiry to practically all phases of economic and social life. The work of the Commission resulted in a number of special studies and in a general report in several volumes which is remarkable for richness of content, breadth of view, keen analysis, and clarity of exposition.[9] Those concerned with postwar problems accept this report as part of their data and regard its recommendations as pertinent to their own task.

*Prewar Problems*

The main conclusions of the Royal Commission on Dominion-Provincial Relations were that the Canadian economy in 1939 had reached a critical point when its further direction had to be reconsidered.[10] The question was whether Canada could continue to rely on exports and world markets for a large part of its national income or should develop a more balanced economy on a national basis. The answer to this question, according to the Commission, did not depend entirely on Canada but on the decisions of other countries with regard to their foreign commercial and investment policies. As Canada's economic relations are overwhelmingly with the United States and the United Kingdom, the policies of the latter two countries are of decisive importance in this connection.

The Commission pointed out that Canada had achieved a high national income per capita and relatively high living standards owing to the part it had played in world economy. Although containing less than one per cent of the world's population, Canada in 1937 was sixth among the leading trading nations of the world, first among debtors, fifth among creditors, third or fourth among security dealers, and first in the tourist trade. Industrially, Canada ranked eighth in the world; Canadian railways were the fourth largest in the world, and the volume of shipping from Canadian ports was the fourth largest.[11] In other words, Canada on the eve of the war was one of the least self-sufficient countries in the world, and its prosperity depended on making the most of its specialized resources and on exchanging them

9. The first chairman of the Commission was Newton W. Rowell, Chief Justice of Ontario. After his death, Mr. Joseph Sirois, of the city of Quebec, became chairman. The report is thus currently referred to as the Rowell-Sirois Report.

10. *Report of the Royal Commission on Dominion-Provincial Relations, Book I, Canada: 1867–1939*, pp. 178–201.

11. The population of Canada in 1941 was about 11.5 million. The per capita income in 1937 was $377 as compared with $536 for the United States—Canada's exports in 1937 were $1,110 million and its imports $809 million. In 1937, British and foreign capital invested in Canada amounted to $6,765 million of which about $4 billion were invested by residents of the United States. Canada's investments abroad amounted to about $1,750 million. See *The Canada Year Book, 1941*, Ottawa, p. 797.

as advantageously as possible for the goods and services of other countries.

Canada's chief economic and financial problems, according to the Commission, arise from the fact that it is a large producer and exporter of bulky, relatively low-value articles (wheat, forest products, minerals), and one of the world's largest importers of coal, oil and steel products. It depends on cheap transportation and on the free movement of goods and capital, and is particularly vulnerable to the ups and downs of business in other countries, to price fluctuations and to restrictive trade policies. The breakdown of the international economy and the rise of economic nationalism after 1929 made it increasingly difficult for Canada to play the part in world economy on which its entire economic and social edifice had been built up over a period of half a century.[12]

*Effects of the War*

Canada has greatly expanded its industrial plant and productive equipment since 1939 as a result of war requirements. Large iron and steel plants have been erected and airplane construction and shipbuilding have been enormously developed.[13] Canada now has the largest aluminum plant in the world, and is a large producer of magnesium. Many new industries have been established, especially for the production of chemicals and electrical supplies. Guns, tanks, explosives, etc., are manufactured on a large scale, and many plants used for these war materials are expected to be capable of conversion to peacetime purposes. There has also been a further development of mineral resources and of hydroelectric power.

The war has had a marked effect on Canadian agriculture. To meet the demands of Great Britain, Canadian farmers have been called upon to increase their production of hogs, cheese, butter, eggs and milk. By subsidies and other means, the Canadian government induced the farmers in the prairies to shift from wheat to barley, oats and other crops. As a result, Canadian agriculture has become more diversified, while Canadian farmers have profited from high prices.[14]

12. The Report of the Commission contains interesting surveys of the changes in the economies of the separate provinces which have made it necessary for the several sections of Canada to adopt new policies of internal development.

13. The output of steel ingots and castings rose from 351,000 short tons in the first four months of 1939 to 755,000 in the same period of 1941. The gross value of commodity production was estimated at $8,970 million, in 1941, compared with $7,261 million in 1940. See *Canada Year Book, 1941*, p. XLVI, and *Canada Year Book, 1942*, p. XLIII; also "Canada Speeds Activities in Fourth War Year," *Foreign Commerce Weekly*, U. S. Department of Commerce, December 26, 1942.

14. *Canada Year Book, 1942*, p. XLIV.

The war has thus stimulated to some extent the trend towards a more balanced economy. But it has not changed the essential problem of the Canadian economy as stated by the Royal Commission. On the contrary, at the end of the war Canada will not only be faced with the problem of world markets for its foodstuffs and raw materials but will also need an outlet for its increased industrial capacity which will be far beyond its own needs.

### b. AIMS AND METHODS OF RECONSTRUCTION

It is against the background sketched above that the several committees of the Dominion government have formulated the aims and methods of reconstruction. These may be presented by summarizing some of the statements on the subject by representatives of the government and by the committees.

### (1). *Statements by the Prime Minister*

The Canadian government has at various times since 1941 endorsed President Roosevelt's Four Freedoms and the principles laid down in the Atlantic Charter. What these mean for Canada has been outlined by the Prime Minister of Canada, W. L. Mackenzie King, on several occasions, but perhaps most clearly in his speech to the annual convention of the American Federation of Labor, on October 9, 1942.

Speaking of the new order which the United Nations will develop after the war, the Prime Minister said:

The new order must be based on human rights; not on the rights of property, privilege or position. . . . In estimating human values, the new order will be concerned with men's character and personality, not with their power and position, nor with the extent of their possessions. . . .

The era of freedom will be achieved only as social security and human welfare become the main concern of men and nations. It is necessary that social security and human welfare should be expressed in definite terms. It is, however, not my purpose to attempt to give a blueprint of the new order. Of the kind of objectives I have in mind, I would merely mention the following as a national minimum: useful employment for all who are willing to work; standards of nutrition and housing, adequate to ensure the health of the whole population; social insurance against privations resulting from unemployment, from accident, from the death of the breadwinner, from ill health, and from old age.

Monopoly of control must give way to joint control in all that pertains to just relations. I should like to see labour-management committees in every industry in our country, and in agriculture. Happily, the principle of the partnership of management and of workers in the community is making steady progress. Where it is tried it is proving its worth. It is only by fully realizing and accepting this partnership that the necessities of industry can be harmonized with the hope of humanity.[15]

## (2). *Statements by the Committee of the House of Commons*

The Committee on Reconstruction and Reestablishment appointed by the Canadian House of Commons on March 24, 1942, held sixteen meetings, at which it heard statements by members of the Cabinet, by government officials, by representatives of special groups and associations, as well as by independent individuals and experts. On July 20, 1942, the Committee submitted its report to the House of Commons. The report formulated the central postwar problem as that of "full employment." The text of the report is as follows:

Your Committee feels strongly that the most immediate reconstruction problem confronting Canada today is the creation of employment for and the settlement of returned soldiers and workers from war industry. Your Committee therefore has commended an intensive study of Canada's natural resources for the purpose of being in position to make recommendations designed to bring about their proper utilization in such manner as will make it possible for the government of Canada, in cooperation with provinces and municipalities, to avail itself of every opportunity to create employment for, and arrange the permanent and satisfactory settlement of, men and women discharged from our armed forces and from the merchant navy and workers released from industry.

Your Committee hopes to continue this study when the House meets again following the adjournment. Convinced, however, that it will be unable to complete its enquiry during the present session, your Committee recommends that a Reconstruction and Reestablishment Committee be set up during the next session of Parliament.[16]

The recommendation of the 1942 committee was carried out, and a new committee was appointed by the House of Commons in March 1943. The Parliamentary Committee of 1943 has held a number of hearings, but has so far made no report.

## (3). *Statements by the Advisory Committee on Reconstruction*

The most detailed analysis of reconstruction aims and policies has been made made by the Committee on Reconstruction, which was organized in March 1941, and reorganized in January 1943. The Committee has been conducting through special subcommittees a large number of inquiries dealing with one or another phase of Canadian economic and social life.

15. *International Labour Review*, December 1942, p. 719.
16. Session 1942, House of Commons, Special Committee on Reconstruction and Reestablishment, *Minutes, July 20, 1942*, Ottawa.

The central issue of this program of research has been formulated by the chairman of the Committee, Dr. F. Cyril James, as "the attainment of full employment within the Dominion of Canada," coupled with an increase in the standard of living. The Committee assumes that, as far as compatible with the attainment of full employment, the attempt should be made to preserve "the basic Canadian tradition of free enterprise and personal initiative in both political and economic life."[17]

The Committee has divided its problems into three broad classes: (1) the problems that are purely domestic, in regard to which Canada can go ahead and do practically what it wants without consulting anybody else; (2) the problems which are domestic in the sense that they have to be decided by the Dominion government (or at least are dependent on Dominion policy), but which are conditioned by events and activities in other parts of the world; and (3) the group of problems of vital importance to Canada, in regard to which Canada alone can do nothing at all because their solution depends upon international action.

Classifying the various problems in accordance with this division, the Committee presents what it designates *The Framework of the Reconstruction Problem* as follows:

I. Problems that are entirely domestic in the sense that Canada can proceed entirely on its own initiative:
  1. Employment opportunities within the Dominion.
  2. The conservation and utilization of natural resources.
  3. The development of plans for publicly financed construction projects.
II. Problems that lie within the field of domestic action, although the effectiveness of the solutions will be greatly affected by developments in other parts of the world:
  4. The relaxation of wartime controls.
  5. The rehabilitation of agriculture.
  6. The rehabilitation of industry.
III. Problems that affect vitally the future prosperity of Canada, but depend for their solution, in large measure, upon international discussion and co-operation:
  7. The structure of the world economy.
  8. Monetary and fiscal policies.
  9. Canada's foreign trade.[18]

17. Session 1942, House of Commons, Special Committee on Reconstruction and Reestablishment, *Minutes, May 14, 1942*, "Statement by Dr. F. Cyril James," p. 36. Also, Session 1943, House of Commons, Special Committee on Reconstruction and Reestablishment, *Minutes, March 9–11, 1943*, pp. 15–18.

18. Session 1942, House of Commons, Special Committee on Reconstruction and Reestablishment, *Minutes*, p. 43.

### C. PROPOSALS FOR SOCIAL SECURITY

In the two years of its existence, the Committee on Reconstruction has prepared a number of reports dealing with agriculture, population, public works and other problems. Most of these reports are, however, of an interim and preliminary character and have not resulted so far in specific proposals of policy.

The main exception is the work of the Committee in the field of social insurance and the social services. Early in 1943, the Committee completed a *Report on Social Security for Canada*[19] which surveyed the present status of social security legislation in Canada and outlined a program for its extension and improvement. This report was submitted on March 11, 1943, to the Special Committee of the House of Commons on Reconstruction and Rehabilitation.

*Existing Legislation*

The report and the proposals based on it, like parallel schemes in England and in the United States, aim to enlarge and to unify the partial and disconnected provisions already in existence. Canada has developed since 1927 a considerable body of legislation on social insurance and the social services. The several provinces, which under the Canadian federal system of government, have jurisdiction over the social services, have introduced workmen's compensation acts and various forms of public assistance such as old-age pensions, pensions for the blind, mother's allowances, and unemployment relief. The provincial laws vary greatly with regard to the amounts of assistance given, qualifications of eligibility, standards for relief, and the extent of grants by the Dominion government.[20] In general, the provisions are regarded as inadequate to meet the needs for which they are designed, except in the case of ex-servicemen.[21]

Dominion legislation covers old-age pensions and unemployment insurance. Under the Old-Age Pensions Act passed in 1927, the Dominion government offers grants to any province that establishes old-age pensions. The Dominion Parliament began by paying 50 per cent of the cost of such noncontributory pensions, but later increased its share to 75 per cent of the cost. The average pension paid by the

---

19. The Report was prepared by Dr. Leonard C. Marsh, Research Adviser to the Committee and formerly Director of Social Research at McGill University. It is entitled, *Report on Social Security for Canada: The Requirements for Post-War Planning.*

20. A. E. Grauer, *Public Assistance and Social Insurance, A Study Prepared for the Royal Commission on Dominion-Provincial Relations*, Ottawa, 1939.

21. *Report on Social Security for Canada*, pp. 21-22.

provinces at present is $18 a month, and most of the provinces apply a means test in paying pensions.

The Unemployment Insurance Act passed in 1940 and in operation since July 1, 1941, is under the exclusive jurisdiction of the Dominion government. The Act applies to all persons employed under a contract of service or apprenticeship, who are earning less than $2,000 a year. Excepted from the Act are workers in agriculture, lumbering, transportation by air and water, domestic service, and in charitable institutions. Contributions and benefits are in proportion to earnings. Contributions are paid by workers and employers, and one fifth of such contributions is added by the Dominion government. Weekly contributions of employees range from 12 to 36 cents a week, and benefits for persons with dependents vary from $4.80 to $14.40 a week. There are many qualifications and conditions for benefiting under the scheme, a waiting period of nine days is required, and total benefits are limited by the amount of contributions made.[22]

*A New Social Insurance System*

While recognizing the value of partial improvements in existing legislation, the Advisory Committee on Reconstruction strikes out for a complete overhauling of the system of social insurance and of the social services in Canada. It wants a social security structure which would lay the foundation of a "social minimum" and eliminate poverty. That can be achieved, the Committee believes, if provisions are made against all the contingencies which threaten to undermine the economic and social position of the individual and the family.

The contingencies are arranged in the report of the Committee in three groups: (1) those which result in interruptions of earning power and of income, that is, unemployment, sickness, disability, old age and premature death of the breadwinner; (2) those which require special expenditure, births, major illnesses and death; and (3) those which result from the fact that the normal income does not provide for the continuous budgetary needs of the family. Some of these contingencies concern the entire population, some affect all gainfully employed, while still others are limited to special groups.

The report stresses the merits of social insurance for dealing with the most important of these contingencies. Social insurance, according to the Committee, is an application on a much larger scale of the

22. *Canada Year Book, 1941*, pp. 665–667.

principle of pooling risks on which commercial insurance is based, but it also has the advantage of using the resources of the entire community for meeting risks. It is a "pooling of individual risks by collective means along with state control and participation." It derives added value from the fact that it "avoids the evils of pauperization and the undemocratic influence of excessive State philanthropy." However, to provide for all situations, it is necessary to combine the principle of social insurance with that of social assistance. Also, the method of income maintenance in the form of cash payments must be combined with that of services (in such form as medical care, national rehabilitation, etc.)

If a social security system is to fulfill its role, the Committee report states, it must have some yardstick for determining the level of family income which is to be maintained. There must be, in other words, a "desirable minimum" to which the "social security fabric" is to be geared. That depends, on the one hand, on the share of the national income which is to be devoted to the purpose; and, on the other hand, on the requirements for a minimum of health and decency.

On the basis of family living studies made in Canada, the report estimates the cost of a minimum family budget for 1939 as $122.85 a month for a family of five of which food expenditure would be $34.66. This computation produces a figure of $16 per week as the living wage minimum for both adults in the family and an average for each child of $4.10 weekly. A more economical budget would provide $10.30 per week for the adults and an average of $3.40 for each child. The first budget is the one recommended by the Committee as a "desirable living minimum." At the present time many families, urban as well as rural, are below this minimum. The second budget, referred to as a "restricted assistance minimum," is offered merely as a second best in case the first is not feasible.

The Canadian situation with respect to the relationship of social security expenditures and national income is described as midway between the British and American conditions. Under the Beveridge plan about 10 per cent of the national income will be spent on social security for the first year on the assumption that the postwar national income of Britain would be about £7 billion and that later on the percentage would rise. If the British social security budget were translated into Canadian terms and for Canadian population figures the social security sum would be $800 million to $900 million. The report states:

If social security for Canada involves something approaching a billion-dollar programme, it must be remembered that not all of this amount of collection and disbursement would be tax-financed or state funds; and it must be measured also against the wholly new levels of national production and Dominion budgeting that a war economy has brought into existence. The national income, which averaged around $3.8 billion in the twenties and thirties, is nearer $8 billion today. Even if some temporary reduction is to be anticipated on the grounds that unit-costs of war goods are higher than those of peace goods, it would be reasonable to assume levels of post-war national income which are more than twice as high as those of the years of depression: 10–12½ per cent of these levels for social security disbursements would be a reasonable commitment.[23]

## Specific Proposals

On the basis of these general principles, the report of the Committee makes a detailed analysis of the various aspects of social security in Canada, and offers specific suggestions with regard to each. Briefly summarized, the recommendations of the Committee are as follows:

1. The coverage of the present Unemployment Insurance Act should be extended and the benefits under the act for workers with dependents should be raised to a figure about 50 per cent above the benefits to single persons. (Benefits now range from $4.08 to $12.24 a week for single persons and from $4.80 to $14.40 a week for married persons.)
2. Unemployment assistance is to be paid to uninsured persons at rates about 10 per cent below the benefits paid under unemployment insurance.
3. A new compulsory contributory old-age insurance system (retirement insurance) should be established, payable to all persons reaching the age of retirement, regardless of income. The retiring age is to be lowered to sixty-five for men and sixty for women. The old-age pension is to be fixed at $30 a month for a man and $15 more for his wife.
4. Permanent disability pensions are to be provided at the same rates of $30 and $15 a month as in the case of old-age pensions.
5. Survivors' pensions are to be paid to widows on the same scale as old-age pensions.
6. Children's allowances are to be established in respect of every child regardless of family income. The allowances would range from $5 a month for a child under four years of age to $12.50 for children fifteen and sixteen years old. Present income tax exemptions for dependent children are to be abolished.
7. Maternity benefits are to be provided for employed women.
8. A national compulsory contributory health insurance system is to be established for all citizens.
9. Funeral benefits are to be paid in the amount of $100 for adults, $65 for juveniles and $25 for children.

The cost of the proposed social insurance system is estimated at 75 to 90 cents a week for farmers and rural workers and from 75 cents to $1.80 a week for industrial wage earners. Employers are to pay 90

23. *Ibid.*, p. 121.

cents a week for each employee. The total cost is placed at about $1 billion a year of which half is to be provided by contributions of the insured and the other half by the government from public funds.

### Health Insurance Bills

The report of the Advisory Committee on Reconstruction on social security is to be used as a basis for further studies, but health insurance has been made the object of immediate legislative proposals. Three draft bills have been submitted to the Social Security Committee of the House of Commons by Ian Mackenzie, Minister of Pensions and National Health, as follows:

1. A Dominion health bill, under which the Dominion government would make grants to the provinces for health insurance and other health measures.
2. A draft provincial bill, containing the machinery under which each province could set up health insurance.
3. A physical fitness bill, authorizing the establishment of a Dominion fund from which grants would be made to the provinces carrying on approved programs.

If the proposed bills become law, every Canadian will receive medical and dental services, hospital care and drugs as necessary. The annual premium for adults earning incomes will be not more than $26 a year. Those with very low incomes will contribute not more than 3 per cent of their income if single and 3.7 per cent if they have dependents. The total cost is estimated at $260 million of which about $131,436,000 a year would be paid from public funds.

The health insurance plan obligates the provinces to assist actively in the general health program by providing free treatment and care for persons suffering from tuberculosis and mental disease and by carrying on a program for the prevention and cure of venereal disease.

The provinces will also be required to train doctors, nurses, engineers and other health experts, make special investigations into public health matters and promote the physical fitness of young people.

In return, the Dominion government will provide grants for this work and for the construction of additional hospital buildings.[24]

The health insurance bills are in the form of "enabling" bills. The constitutional difficulty will thus be avoided, and there will be no necessity of amending the British North America Act to give the Dominion Parliament jurisdiction over health insurance. The prov-

24. *Christian Science Monitor*, March 16, 1943; also *The New York Times*, March 17, 1943; also "Social Security Planning in Canada," *International Labour Review*, May 1943, pp. 591–616.

inces will pass laws based on federal legislation and administer the schemes when adopted.

The bills also provide for the creation of a National Council on Health Insurance. The members of the Council will be the Director of National Insurance of the Department of Pensions, the Deputy Minister of Health of each province, representatives of each of the professional groups, doctors, dentists, etc., directly concerned in the administration of health insurance, of labor, industry, agriculture and of women's organizations. The Council will advise the Minister of Pensions and National Health.

*Unemployment Insurance and Employment Security*

While the Committee on Reconstruction proposes to improve the Unemployment Insurance Act, as indicated above, it stresses the point that the "only basic answer to unemployment is employment." To insure "full employment," especially during the period of "economic demobilization" at the end of the war, it suggests: (1) an "employment reserve" of construction projects of at least $1 billion for the first year after the war; and (2) a system of occupational readjustment including placement, guidance, and the provision of training facilities.

### d. FISCAL, MONETARY AND TRADE POLICIES

The Committee on Reconstruction has made it clear that all proposals for social betterment after the war depend on the capacity of Canada to maintain its foreign trade and to provide employment for its people.[25] This involves also problems of fiscal and monetary policy.

The lines along which the government is considering these problems have been indicated by F. Cyril James, the chairman of the

25. The Canadian government is exploring the possibilities of closer economic co-operation after the war with the United States as well as the problems of general world organization. Some work along these lines is being done by the United States-Canada Economic Committee. There are also projects for closer regional collaboration, e.g., those under investigation by the State of Minnesota and the Province of Manitoba. According to the *Foreign Commerce Weekly*, the Joint Economic Committees of Canada and the United States and the Joint War Production Committee of Canada and the United States are collaborating on postwar planning. The Committees are giving consideration to: measures that would cushion social and economic hardships and provide full employment upon demobilization; utilization of additional wartime productive manufacturing facilities and agricultural resources; avoidance of postwar inflation by orderly release of blocked purchasing power and consumption needs; legislative and administrative barriers, including tariff and trade barriers, with a view to eliminating all forms of discriminatory treatment in international commerce by appropriate international and domestic measures. See *Foreign Commerce Weekly*, U. S. Department of Commerce, December 19, 1942, p. 20.

Advisory Committee on Reconstruction. A statement which he made to the House of Commons Committee on Reconstruction and Re-establishment, contains the following points:

1. The creation in Canada of something corresponding to the Public Works Reserve in the United States may be necessary.
2. The recognition that the ideal for the future structure of the world is an organization that is world-embracing in its scope—either because the whole world is treated as a unit or because provision is made for the close co-ordination of the several regions. The center or nucleus of such an organization would necessarily be some broad economic affiliation between the British Commonwealth of Nations and the United States.
3. If there is to be a world economy, it is essential that there should be throughout the area of that world economy a co-ordination of monetary policies. That does not imply, in any sense, a restoration of the pre-1939, and still less of a pre-1914, gold standard.
4. It is recognized by a very large number of monetary theorists that monetary policy is the handmaiden of commerce, industry and agriculture, and not itself the governing factor by which those basic economic activities should be regulated. There is in this country, in the United States and in Great Britain, a widespread recognition of the idea that the postwar aim of monetary policy must be the attainment of full employment.
5. The attainment of full employment implies at certain periods an unbalanced budget. It implies that when a program of publicly financed construction projects is put into operation, the government will be spending more money than it will be collecting in the form of taxes. Furthermore, the whole reconstruction program implies that at the end of this war taxation probably will continue to be heavy for some years.
6. If Canada is going to sell goods abroad, either it must take payment in goods or services produced in other countries, or it must frankly express its willingness to supply such goods as a long-term capital investment to be paid either by principal and interest in traditional fashion or to be repaid intangibly by better relations and a better ordered world.
7. Tariffs and export markets depend very largely on the structure of the world, either as a unit or regionally, and upon the extent to which Canada is lending capital or buying goods. If the first stage of the problem is satisfactorily solved, a study of tariffs and market opportunities may be very much more easily attempted.

### 3. The Position of Unofficial Organizations

The Advisory Committee on Reconstruction and other Canadian government agencies are encouraging private groups and organizations to consider postwar problems and plans. Though there has been considerable discussion, few organizations have formulated plans or taken a definite stand on the questions at issue.

#### a. employers' associations

In Canada, as in the United States, there are many trade associations and several national employers' organizations such as the Canadian Chamber of Commerce and the Canadian Manufacturers' Association. The latter is somewhat parallel in composition and character to the National Association of Manufacturers in the United States.

At its annual general meeting in July 1942, in Toronto, the Canadian Manufacturers' Association held a one-day "Post-War Planning Conference."[26] The members of the Association heard a report on the activities of the Advisory Committee on Reconstruction. Since then the Association has appointed a committee on postwar problems.

Similar committees have been established by the Chamber of Commerce, by the Association of the Pulp and Paper Industry, the Cotton Textile Institute, the life insurance companies and several other trade associations. The Heavy Industries Post-War Planning Committee set up by the Canadian Institute of Steel Construction has set forth a program of nineteen points, the most important of which are:

1. Transference of established firms from "slum" plants to new war plants and demolition of the old ones;
2. Development of new materials which have made great strides during the war;
3. Government control of orderly marketing of salvageable material from demolished temporary buildings, or of donations to devastated foreign countries, so as not to undermine new manufacture and employment;
4. Surveys by heating and ventilating engineers of existing plants in Canadian industries, with a view to postwar modernization;
5. Installation of underground transit in the bigger cities to relieve traffic;
6. Elimination of level crossings;
7. Solution of sewage and water problems which many cities have deferred during wartime;
8. Demolition of municipal areas with low sanitary and moral standards;
9. Provision of two weeks' holiday a year for all workmen.[27]

## b. LABOR ORGANIZATIONS

Trade union membership in Canada, as in other countries, has increased since 1939. At the end of 1942, there were some 500,000 members in Canadian labor unions. The largest numbers of organized workers are in railroad transportation, the building trades, the metal trades, mining, and the public and amusement services.[28]

Organized labor in Canada is divided among four national labor

26. "Post-War Planning Conference, held at the 71st Annual General Meeting, Canadian Manufacturers' Association," reprinted from *Industrial Canada*, July 1942.

27. The Senate of Canada, Session 1943, *Proceedings of the Special Committee on Economic Reestablishment and Social Security*, Ottawa, 1943, p. 16; also C. S. Kane in *Engineering and Contract Record*, Toronto, February 10, 1943; also *The Monetary Times*, Toronto, May 1943.

28. The *Canada Year Book, 1942* reports 365,544 members in trade unions in Canada at the end of 1940. According to the Department of Labour, the total membership of Canadian labor unions at the end of 1941 was over 461,000. The total number of workers and employees in Canada is about 3 million.

organizations. The oldest and strongest is The Trades and Labour Congress of Canada with a membership of about 184,000 in 1940. It is the Canadian parallel of the American Federation of Labor. The Trades and Labour Congress has a number of unions which are affiliated with the AF of L.

The Canadian Congress of Labour, organized in 1939, had about 77,000 members in 1940. It is the Canadian counterpart of the Congress of Industrial Organizations in the United States. A number of the unions of the Canadian Congress of Labour are affiliated with the CIO.

The Confederation of Catholic Workers of Canada, organized in 1921, had in 1940 about 45,000 members.[29] It is similar to the Catholic labor unions which were in existence in Belgium and Holland before 1939.

The Canadian Federation of Labour is a small organization with 4,319 members in 1940.

Of the four national trade union organizations, the first two described above are of greatest importance, and their pronouncements on postwar problems are of interest here.

### Trades and Labour Congress of Canada

This organization, like the American Federation of Labor, emphasizes particularly the need for social insurance legislation. At its annual convention in August 1942, it passed resolutions urging the early enactment of a national health scheme, improvement of the present Unemployment Insurance Act, the lowering of the age limit for pensions from seventy to sixty-five and increasing the rates under the present Old-Age Pensions Act.[30]

### The Canadian Congress of Labour

At its convention in September 1942, the Canadian Congress of Labour passed a resolution on postwar problems which stressed the need of formulating plans to assure "the common people the Four Freedoms," "full employment" and "decent standards of living all over the world."

The convention also went on record in favor of public ownership and control of financial institutions, various improvements in the Unemployment Insurance Act and the Old-Age Pensions Act, the introduction of a system of national sickness insurance, the adoption

29. *International Labour Review*, February 1943, p. 254.
30. *Ibid.*, November 1942, p. 622.

of a nation-wide housing plan, and closer co-operation between the workers of the American, British and Soviet trade unions.[31]

### C. OTHER ORGANIZATIONS

Various university and professional groups have organized public discussions of the problems which Canada may face after the war. The publications of these groups cover a wide range of subjects— from conservation of natural resources to foreign trade, housing and education.[32]

Among the organizations which have formulated definite proposals is the National Council of Women of Canada.[33] In July 1942, it issued a program which covers all phases of Canadian life as well as problems of international relations.

The section of the program of the Council dealing with national problems includes demands for improved health and other social services, for an extension of the unemployment insurance systems, and for a revision of the National Housing Act "to make the building of houses more easily available to persons of low and moderate incomes."[34] The Council wants "a rigorous policy of immigration after the war," on a selective or quota basis, combined with land settlement and with an organized employment service to place immigrants in suitable employment.

The program of the Council favors a large role for women in the industrial and public life of Canada after the war, and the "appointment of well-qualified women on bodies concerned with peace terms and postwar reconstruction."

31. *Ibid.*, p. 624.
32. See for instance *Reconstruction in Canada*, Lectures given in the University of Toronto, edited by C. A. Ashley, Toronto, 1943; also *Radio Talk Series on Post-War Reconstruction*, given under the auspices of the Extension Department of the University of Alberta (available only in manuscript form); also *Journal, Royal Architectural Institute of Canada*, Toronto, September 1942; Vol. 19, No. 9.
33. National Council of Women of Canada, *Preliminary Program for Post-War Planning*, July 1942 (mimeographed). This organization carries on educational work on public problems. It has provincial and local branches, and a considerable following among various groups of the population. Catholic women's organizations are not affiliated with the Council.
34. Surveys made since 1932 have shown that housing conditions in Canada are "generally bad" in urban and rural areas, that there is much overcrowding, and that there are many "slum areas" in the larger cities. The Dominion Housing Act of 1935, and the National Housing Act of 1938, and the provincial legislation on the subject have not materially relieved the situation. The Royal Commission on Dominion-Provincial Relations summed up the situation before the war as follows:
"There is an absolute shortage of houses in Canada. This shortage presses hardest on the low-income groups and leads to overcrowding. Overcrowding means that large numbers of people live under insanitary and undesirable conditions, a condition tending to the physical and moral deterioration of whole districts, that is, slums." See A. E. Grauer, *Housing, A Study Prepared for the Royal Commission on Dominion-Provincial Relations*, Ottawa, 1939, p. 49.

The National Council of Women of Canada emphasizes that the approach to the problems of reconstruction "must lie in the strengthening of the moral and spiritual foundations" of democracy. According to the Council, "emphasis" is needed "on the brotherhood of man and the social responsibilities of the individual," the eradication of poverty and of social injustices, "re-affirmation of our faith in democracy," and acceptance of "the implications of the democratic way of life and of the responsibilities which accompany its privileges."

## 4. POSTWAR RECONSTRUCTION AND POLITICAL PARTIES

The fate of Canadian postwar proposals hangs on the relative strength of different political groups after the war. The Dominion government has been under the control of the Liberal Party since 1940.[35] While there is considerable agreement in the country on some of its proposals, there are also wide differences of opinion on general policy which are partly sectional and occupational in origin, partly traditional and nationalistic. The middle-of-the-road progressive Liberal Party is flanked on the right by the Conservatives who are lukewarm to social reform and strongly protectionist. On the left of the Liberals are the radical agrarians of the West and the Cooperative Commonwealth Federation which advocates government ownership of essential industries and financial institutions and more far-reaching programs of social insurance and "industrial democracy."

35. In the elections of March 1940, the Liberal Party gained 177 seats out of a total of 245. The Conservative Party won 40 seats. The Cooperative Commonwealth Federation, known as the CCF which has a socialist program, won only 8 seats. Gallup polls indicate, however, that the CCF has been gaining in strength since 1939. See Frank Underhill, "Canada's Rising Socialists," *The Nation*, March 27, 1943; also William Henry Chamberlin, *Canada—Today and Tomorrow*, 1942, pp. 174–200.

## Chapter 9

# STATUS QUO OR CHANGE IN AUSTRALIA?

AUSTRALIA BEGAN considering problems of postwar reorganization about the same time as Canada. Early in 1941, a Commonwealth Inter-Departmental Advisory Committee on Reconstruction was created.[1] In February 1941, a Division of Reconstruction Research was established in the Department of Labour and National Service, and Dr. H. V. Evatt was appointed Director.

The functions of the Division were to carry on research, to coordinate the research work of the universities and of private technical institutions working on reconstruction problems, to encourage and assist the study and discussion of reconstruction problems by non-official groups; and to act as secretariat for the Commonwealth Inter-Departmental Advisory Committee on Reconstruction, for the Premiers' Conferences and for other conferences which might be called to further reconstruction studies by the Commonwealth and by the several states.

In the course of the year, New South Wales, Queensland, and several other states[2] established postwar reconstruction committees to consider state problems and to co-operate with the Commonwealth Advisory Committee in the study of general national problems.

While these committees were appointed by the executive authorities, the legislative branch of the government took steps in the same direction. In July 1941, the Commonwealth Parliament appointed a Joint Parliamentary Committee to report on ways and means of improving the social conditions of Australia.

1. The Inter-Departmental Advisory Committee on Reconstruction was appointed by the Minister of Labour and National Service. The Committee consists of representatives of all the departments directly concerned with reconstruction problems. Its functions have been defined as including the allocation to appropriate departments of interdepartmental investigations requiring co-operative action, exchange of views, and information on interdepartmental reconstruction problems, and review of current policy from the point of view of its implications for the postwar period. A number of subcommittees have been set up by the Inter-Departmental Committee to study specific problems.

2. The Commonwealth of Australia is composed of the states of New South Wales, Victoria, Queensland, South Australia, Western Australia and Tasmania and of two Territories—the Northern Territory and the Australian Capital Territory. The population of Australia in 1939 was estimated at about 7 million, of which New South Wales had 2,770,-000; Victoria—1,887,000; Queensland over a million; South Australia about 600,000. Western Australia with an area of nearly a million square miles had about half a million people, and the Northern Territory with an area of over half a million square miles had a population of some seven thousand.

The official committees have made use of the universities and of private research institutions. Organized groups such as employers' associations and the trade unions have also made contributions to the discussion.

As the preparatory studies proceeded, it became evident that the problems of postwar reorganization cut across the lines dividing the powers of the state and Commonwealth governments. To overcome this difficulty, a bill was introduced in the Australian Parliament on October 1, 1942, to amend the Constitution so as to enable the Commonwealth Parliament to deal with postwar reconstruction on a national basis. The bill specified that in order "to achieve economic security and social justice in the post-war world and for the purpose of post-war reconstruction generally," it would be necessary to legislate on the following subjects: (1) the reinstatement and advancement of soldiers and dependents of those killed or disabled; (2) employment, including the transfer of workers from wartime industries; (3) development of the country and expansion of production and markets; (4) prices of goods, including their regulation and control; (5) encouragement of population; (6) carrying into effect the guarantee of the "Four Freedoms"; (7) national works and services, including water conservation, irrigation, afforestation, and protection of the soil; (8) transport, including air transport; (9) national health and fitness; (10) housing of the people; (11) child welfare.[3]

The Constitutional Convention held in Canberra during the last week of November 1942, unanimously carried a motion transferring to the Commonwealth the powers of the states for postwar reconstruction. At the end of the war, or earlier, a referendum is to be held to determine permanent amendments to the Constitution. On December 2, 1942, the Constitutional Convention approved a draft bill specifying the powers to be transferred to the Commonwealth Parliament, and limited the period of such transfer to five years. Provisions were inserted to insure that certain powers will be exercised only with the approval of and in co-operation with the state authorities, officers and agencies. The Premiers of the several states agreed to introduce this bill in their state parliaments before the end of January 1943, and to do their utmost to secure its passage promptly. It has not been ratified as yet.

Following the decision of the Canberra Convention, a subcommittee of members of the Cabinet assumed responsibility for postwar

3. *International Labour Review*, November 1942, p. 58.

planning. J. B. Chifley, Treasurer of the Commonwealth of Australia, became also Minister for Post-War Reconstruction. A Department of Post-War Reconstruction was established under the direction of Herbert C. Coombs, which will operate through a number of committees consisting of representatives of different groups of the population.

The subjects included in the program of postwar planning cover a wide range. Australia, like Canada and New Zealand, has taken definite action on the rehabilitation of demobilized soldiers which is regarded as of primary importance. Much attention has also been given to the reconversion of war industries, possibilities of land settlement and population policies, the prospects of further industrialization, and of trade outlets for old and new industries, social security and employment, the relations of Australia to the British Empire and to the United States.

### 1. TRAINING AND PLACEMENT OF DEMOBILIZED MEN

In accordance with a decision of the Cabinet on January 17, 1941, a subcommittee of the Inter-Departmental Advisory Committee on Reconstruction prepared a program for the peacetime retraining and placement of men from the armed forces of Australia.[4] The report of the subcommittee became the basis of a bill which was introduced in Parliament early in 1943.

By 1943 there were over 700,000 men in the Australian armed forces. The problems which these men will face at the end of the war, according to the subcommittee which studied the subject, will vary in accordance with the physical and psychological injuries which they may have suffered. But apart from injury or loss of health, the men will also have to face the loss of opportunities for advancement due to changes in Australian industry and to the fact that those who remained at home will have had the advantage in adapting to changes. Furthermore, the return of the men from the army will coincide with the discharge of workers from war industries.

The Australian program for dealing with this problem is based on the principle that the government must provide for the returned soldiers comprehensive educational and vocational training to fit them for re-entry into civil life.[5] The limiting conditions are that the

4. The subcommittee consists of representatives of the Department of Labour and National Service, the Repatriation Commission, the Education Service of the Army, and the Royal Australian Air Force Rehabilitation Service.

5. After the First World War, returned soldiers were accorded preferential appointments to positions in the Civil Service. Such a provision is not likely to affect a large number of persons; the total number of returned soldiers appointed to permanent positions in the public services between 1918 and 1939 was 7,099.

applicant must seriously wish to be trained in some specified profession or trade, that he have aptitude for it, that three months after discharge he reach the recognized standards for entry into the occupation, and that he will be able to find employment in the occupation. The training is to be given free by the government except that in the case of professional courses the applicant must undertake to repay, with interest, the maintenance paid to him after the first year, which is to be regarded as a loan.

Payments for maintenance during the period of vocational training are to be adjusted in such a way that the total amounts received from such payments and from other public or private sources of income shall not exceed £2.2s.0d. a week for a man, 18s. for the wife of the man or his dependent mother, and 7s. 6d. for each child under sixteen years of age. After the training period is over and while he is awaiting placement, the returned soldier is to be paid maintenance, not to exceed £4.2s.6d. a week for a maximum period of six months. To administer this program, a Commonwealth Co-ordinator of Training will be appointed—a civilian educator who has knowledge of industrial and commercial organization.

The proposals of the subcommittee were embodied with some changes in the Australian Soldiers' Repatriation Act passed in April 1943.[6]

## 2. Re-employment and Public Works

The training program for demobilized soldiers may relieve to some extent the competition for jobs immediately after the war. Still, there is some doubt in Australia whether even under favorable conditions it will be possible to carry out the reconversion of industry to a peacetime basis quickly enough to absorb workers as fast as they will be released from wartime occupations. The government has built and financed in the last few years a number of plant extensions and new plants for the production of munitions and other war materials. The number of workers employed by the government in munitions, aircraft and shipbuilding is about 125,000, or, 22 per cent of all workers in arms factories. The transfer of soldiers and war workers to peacetime industries, it is estimated, will affect 1,300,000 persons.[7] The danger of widespread unemployment, a source of industrial and

6. The Act is in the form of amendments to the Australian Soldiers Repatriation Act, 1920–1941.
7. See Lloyd Ross, "Australian Labor and the War," *Far Eastern Survey*, January 25, 1943.

social unrest, looms at the end of the war. Public opinion, it is claimed, will not tolerate such conditions, especially since the people have become used, during the war, to large public expenditures and to the idea that such expenditures can reduce unemployment to a minimum.

It is therefore proposed that the government prepare to secure temporary employment to released war workers until they can be absorbed in peacetime industries. The government is to take steps now to establish a "reservoir" of planned public works with the aid and co-operation of the state governments. The states of the Australian Commonwealth have been the chief promoters of public works in the past and they have the personnel for mapping out projects which accord with their needs and resources.

The public works considered include projects of afforestation, irrigation, and soil protection.[8] It is also proposed that some of these works be woven into long-range plans for the agricultural and industrial development of the country. Although no program has as yet been definitely prepared, the proposal to use public works for these purposes is widely approved. The Department of Reconstruction of the Ministry of Post-War Reconstruction is now studying the subject.

## 3. Social Security and Housing

Australian standards of living are among the highest in the world and provisions for social security are more advanced there than in many countries. Nevertheless, large numbers of the population are ill-nourished, ill-clothed, and poorly housed. Social services have developed piecemeal and vary considerably from state to state. The Commonwealth legislation covers only old-age and invalidism pensions, maternity benefits, and child endowment provisions. There is no unemployment insurance on a Commonwealth basis[9] or in any of the states.

8. At the first meeting of the Post-War Reconstruction Committee of New South Wales, the Prime Minister of the state included in the list of proposed public works water conservation, housing, hospitals, land settlements, forest conservation, water supply and sewerage, railways and schools. *International Labour Review*, February 1942, p. 168.

9. The Commonwealth Invalid and Old-Age Pensions Act came into effect in July 1909, and has since been often amended. The law now provides old-age pensions to persons over sixty-five who have lived in Australia twenty years (in some cases to persons over sixty), and invalidism pensions to incapacitated persons who have been in the country five years. The rates of payment vary, but they must not exceed £52 a year, and the pensioner's income £84.10s. a year. In 1940, there were over 270,000 old-age pensioners and over 58,000 invalid pensioners. War pensioners are provided for under a separate system. Under the Commonwealth Maternity Act, a special payment is made for every newborn child to mothers of families with an income below £247 a year. On April 7, 1941, the Commonwealth Child Endowment Act came into force, which provides payment under certain conditions in sup-

As pointed out above, the Commonwealth Parliament in July 1941 appointed a Joint Parliamentary Committee to report on ways of improving the social insurance system in Australia. The publication of the Beveridge Report in England further stimulated this movement. Spokesmen of the Australian government, which is a labor government, claim that Australia intends to go further than the Beveridge Report. The new social insurance system of Australia is to provide "security from the cradle to the grave," including maternity allowances, child endowment, widows' pensions, health insurance, free hospital and medical services irrespective of income, much larger old-age pensions without a "means test," and a living allowance during unemployment on a family basis about equal to the present basic wage of £4.10s. a week (about $20). The cost of these provisions is estimated at £50 to £60 million a year.[10]

Plans to improve the health of the Australian people will involve the zoning of Australia into medical districts and the employment of 2,000 doctors, thousands of nurses, and salaried staffs of hospitals and health centers. Doctors demobilized from the fighting forces may be absorbed into this scheme.

The Commonwealth may take over public hospitals, now a responsibility of the states. Doctors' salaries will range from £800 for junior general practitioners to £1,650 for senior physicians and surgeons. There will be more than 450 new one-man health centers throughout the Commonwealth.

Cities also will be zoned, Sydney having thirty-five health centers, Melbourne twenty-five. Infant health centers and convalescent and rest centers form part of the scheme.[11]

The National Health and Medical Research Council has submitted to the Joint Parliamentary Committee a plan for full community control of medical practice on the principle that "care of personal health is a social duty and no longer entirely an individual responsibility."

In February 1943, the government announced that a system of unemployment benefits would be established in six months, and of sickness benefits in nine months. At the same time, the Treasurer of the Commonwealth introduced a bill establishing a National Welfare

port of children, in excess of one, under sixteen years of age. This is similar to the family allowance system in other countries and was intended to stimulate the natural increase of the population. The number of children benefiting from this Act runs into hundreds of thousands.

10. See speech by Australian Prime Minister, John Curtin, The New York Times, November 25, 1942.

11. The New York Times, November 25, 1942 and December 7, 1942.

Fund of (A.)£30 million a year to be financed from increased income taxes, and to be used to increase payments for children's allowances, maternity benefits, old-age pensions and funeral benefits.[12] The bill became law in April 1943.

The Joint Parliamentary Committee has advanced the proposal to establish a commonwealth housing planning authority. The prewar period has left many slum areas in its trail. The war will have created a housing shortage, to meet which some 250,000 houses will have to be built, giving employment to 60,000 workers for ten years. The government will also improve dwellings in rural areas by an extension of electric power projects, and by increased provisions for communal services and facilities.

## 4. INDUSTRIALIZATION, LAND SETTLEMENT, AND POPULATION POLICY

In considering postwar economic development, Australians generally look outside their own borders for a large part of their future income and prosperity. Perhaps a majority of the Australian people, and especially the labor groups, seek economic and social security on the basis of the international economic position which Australia held before 1939. This means that Australia would continue to develop its resources slowly, would maintain its limitations on immigration, would allow for only a small annual increase in population and labor supply, would remain essentially a producer and exporter of primary products such as wheat and wool,[13] and would develop secondary industries slowly and on a moderate scale.

12. *The Times*, London, February 12, 1943.

13. Despite the growth of manufacturing, agriculture remains the basic industry of Australia, if pastoral and dairying activities are included with agriculture. For the decade 1930–1939, about 20 per cent of Australia's gross value of output was derived from field cultivation, about 21 per cent from pastoral activity, about 12 per cent from dairying, making 53 per cent from farm life as compared to 38 per cent from manufacturing activity. Only about 6 per cent of the gross value of output was derived from mining and but 3 per cent from forestry and fisheries.

Among the farm crops wheat is foremost both in terms of acreage and value of output. In terms of acreage under cultivation in 1938–1939, about 61 per cent of the land used was devoted to wheat with hay the second most important Australian crop far behind with only about 14 per cent. Oats and green forage crops each utilized about 7.5 per cent of the total acreage and the cultivation. For the same period the value of wheat production amounted to about 22 million Australian pounds as compared to £13 million for hay and about £9 million each for sugar cane and orchard production. The volume of wheat produced fluctuates between 150 and 210 million bushels a year.

Australia is noted for its large livestock population, particularly of sheep, which produce its most famous "crop"—wool. In 1938 sheep numbers aggregated 111 million. This amounted to about 16 sheep to every Australian. The average annual wool output is about 1 billion lbs. Other animals living off the green pastures of Australia include 13 million cattle, which produce large quantities of meat, milk, butter and cheese for the domestic and export markets and about 1,700,000 horses and about 1,150,000 hogs. See *Commonwealth Year Book, 1940;* also "Australia's Agricultural Resources," *Foreign Agriculture,* U. S. Department of Agriculture, January 1943; also *Foreign Commerce Weekly,* December 19, 1942, p. 33.

However, there is a growing opinion among some groups—especially among businessmen and the middle class—that to maintain Australia in such a position may be neither possible nor desirable. From the point of view of national security, it is questionable whether a population of some 7 million can protect a continent of nearly 3 million square miles. From the point of view of national prosperity it is argued that changes in world markets make Australia's former position less tenable and her outlook less secure. The main market for Australian primary products, namely, the British, was beginning to contract even before 1939. Japan's purchases of Australian wool eased the situation only for a short time, and, as a result, Australia faced a problem of surpluses difficult to solve.[14]

If Australia accelerated the development of its secondary industries and increased its population more rapidly, it would be possible for it to consume a larger portion of its own agricultural and pastural products, to supply more of the manufactured articles which the country now imports, and thus to achieve greater balance in the national economy as well as to create a more solid basis for national security.

Australia has already been tending in this direction. Australian industries had been growing rapidly before 1939,[15] and the war has accentuated this trend in a marked degree. While detailed statistics

14. See Samuel McMahon Wadham and G. L. Wood, *Land Utilization in Australia*, Melbourne, 1939, pp. 343–355; also David M. Dow, *Australia Advances*, 1938, pp. 251–253.
15. The value of output of the manufacturing industries in Australia increased from some 320 million Australian pounds in 1921–1922 to 500 million pounds in 1938–1939. The labor force in manufacturing industries rose from 378,540 to 565,106 during the same period. According to the census of 1933, slightly more than 32 per cent of the breadwinners in Australia were employed in the industrial groups (factories, construction, etc.) while only 20.3 per cent were engaged in agricultural, pastoral and dairying industries. In 1934–1935, there were 671 industrial workers for every 10,000 of the population, while in 1938–1939 there were 816 such workers. According to the official yearbook, out of 3,155,600 gainfully employed, nearly 600,000 were employed in primary agricultural production, about 70,000 in mining, about 870,000 in manufacturing, construction and other industrial occupations, about 925,000 in transportation, trade, public administration, and finance, and some 242,000 in personal and domestic service. According to latest figures, on March 31, 1943 about 1,878,000 persons were employed in shops and factories.
The steel industry illustrates the extent of the advance of Australian industrialization. In 1930 about 300,000 tons of pig iron were produced in Australia, but in 1939 the volume of production mounted to 1,105,000 tons. The production of steel ingots rose from 315,000 tons in 1930 to 1,170,000 tons in 1939. The production of steel rails, bars, and sections rose from 257,000 tons at the beginning of the decade to 988,000 tons in the last year of the last decade. Australian industry is heavily committed to two types of goods: (1) industrial metals and machines, and (2) food processing. In 1938–1939, the first group produced to the extent of 140 million Australian pounds and the second about 152 million Australian pounds. After these two groups of industries there followed in about equal order the chemical industry, the textile industry, the apparel industry, and the paper products industry to the extent of about 25 to 35 million Australian pounds. In terms of labor, the metals and machines group led all the other Australian industries, as it employed in 1938–1939, 178,000 people, compared to about 85,000 each for the food processing industries and the clothing industries. *Commonwealth Year Book, 1940.*

are not available, there has been a considerable wartime expansion of many industries, including iron and steel, food processing, and vehicles, especially aircraft. Provided this process continues after the war Australia could become a highly industrialized country, developing not only its iron and steel industry,[16] but such industries as high-speed tools, constructional materials, motor cars for domestic use, glass, optical instruments, and aircraft.

The advocates of such a postwar industrial development realize that it depends on two factors—capital investment and a larger labor supply. In the past, Australia depended for its capital needs, in addition to local savings, almost entirely on the British capital market.[17] In view of the declining position of Great Britain as a creditor country, it is hoped that American businessmen might be induced to expand their investments and operations in Australia after the war.

The war has accentuated the feeling that Australia's labor force is too small to support a large long-range industrial program and that a larger labor supply involves a change in immigration policy. Whether justified or not, the "White Australia" policy which has held for half a century has become "an article of national faith,"[18] and precludes drawing labor from the nearby overpopulated areas of the Pacific. The Australians prefer immigrants from Great Britain and northwestern Europe but are not entirely unwilling to accept immigrants also from southern and eastern Europe.

Opinions differ widely on how large an annual immigration would be possible and what the maximum or optimum population might be. The absorptive capacity has been estimated at from 30,000 to 50,000 immigrants a year, and the maximum population which the country might support from 15 to 30 million. These estimates were made without considering industrialization. They might be subject to revision

16. The iron and steel industry of Australia is already highly developed. It is organized along monopolistic lines in a corporation known as Broken Hill Proprietary, which owns iron and coal mines, controls all steel production, has a plant for making alloys, produces many by-products, owns shipping facilities, and since 1937 has been also a large builder of aircraft. Broken Hill Proprietary is allied with Imperial Chemical Industries and with other large international corporations. It has been called "the apotheosis of Australian capitalism," and though its policies are of the benevolent type, they are subject to political attack, as representing the "monopolistic stranglehold" upon Australian industry. However, monopoly is not so important an issue in Australia as in England or America, and it is argued that the industrialization of Australia depends upon a sympathetic environment for private enterprise. The Labour Party has not raised the issue of nationalization of the Broken Hill Proprietary.

17. The total of British investments and loans in Australia are estimated at £600 million. American investments are about $75 million.

18. It is claimed that this policy is not due to any "negative prejudice against the people of the Orient" but rather to "a positive prejudice in favor of preserving Australia's racial uniformity." Jack Shepherd, *Australia's Interests and Policies in the Far East*, Allen & Unwin, London, 1940, p. 195.

upward if a large industrial development were undertaken and capital funds obtained.[19] The Australians, however, are against unorganized mass migration and would only accept immigrants under controls which would protect prevailing standards of living.

Along with industrialization, there might be a change in agricultural methods, new settlements on the land, and a greater decentralization of the population, now so overwhelmingly urban.[20] The settlement of immigrants on the land—the traditional form of developing a new country—is not regarded favorably in Australia because the good lands are presumably already occupied[21] and further expansion of agricultural production would aggravate the already serious problem of surpluses. Furthermore, the war has increased the mechanization of agriculture which is likely to continue and which reduces the demand for agricultural labor. Further industrialization of the country and an increased industrial population are needed to make more land settlement profitable.

### 5. TRADE POLICIES AND EXTERNAL RELATIONS

Even with accelerated development of secondary industries, Australia for some time to come can maintain high prosperity and full employment, only by finding markets for its large exports of agricultural products.[22] The opinion is growing that trade policies and ex-

19. The rate of natural increase of the Australian population was steadily declining for several decades. In recent years, the net reproduction rate has increased, but this increase is expected to be short-lived. The increase of population through net immigration was 136,862 during 1911–1915 and 312,970 during 1921–1930. During 1931–1935, there was a net emigration. From 1936 to 1939, there was a small net immigration of about 30,000. It is estimated that on the basis of present rates of natural increase and immigration, the maximum population in 1981 would be about 9 million.

20. According to the census of 1933, over 3,100,000 persons were living in cities. The largest cities were situated on the southeastern coasts.

21. Australia is one of the most sparsely populated regions in the world. It has only 2.2 persons to the square mile. This compares with 3.0 for Canada, 41.3 for the United States, 75.0 for Indo-China, 104.3 for China, 349.4 for Japan, and 678.0 for Java. However, the largest part of Australia is desert land. The area suitable for occupation and settlement has been estimated at 600,000 square miles. This is land with a rainfall of over ten inches in the temperate zone and twenty inches in the tropics. Of this area, some 200,000 square miles are arable, and 60,000 square miles of the best land are already farmed.

22. Compared with most countries, Australia has one of the highest per capita volumes of imports and exports. During most years Australia has an export surplus. The average annual value of exports in the five years from 1934–1935 to 1938–1939 was about (A.) £102 million. Imports in the same period were about (A.) £90 million. The growth of the export balance is due not only to the development of wool and wheat, but also of butter, meat, cheese and some mineral ores and minor industrial products. If gold is included among recent exports the balance is larger.

Of the total exports in the decade of the thirties about as much as 48 per cent derived from pastoral activities and 23 per cent from field crops with 13 per cent from mining, 10 per cent from dairying and only 5 per cent from manufacturing. The dependence of the major economic sectors of Australian life upon the export market is shown by the fact that about 71 per cent of the gross value of pastoral output is derived from the export market, about 37 per cent in

ternal relations must change to obtain secure and adequate markets after the war. Doubt increases as to the value of the Empire preference system and "Ottawa" is said to be on the dissecting table. The large dependence of Australian exports on the British market has caused economic instability and is likely to cause more after the war in view of the decline of population growth in England and changes in British economic policy.[23]

The discussion of postwar trade policy in Australia is a complicated tangle[24] from which we may pull the following main threads:

1. Markets must be secure. Security can be achieved by having more and wider markets. Australia could develop a mutually profitable trade with the Pacific countries (China, Indo-China, the Dutch East Indies, the Philippines) and with the United States.

2. Trade must be competitive. However, the doctrine of comparative advantage and lower costs must not be followed at the expense of living standards. This may call for international co-operation in adjusting prices, especially those of primary commodities.

3. Markets should be widened and made more secure by raising the levels of living in the less developed countries.

4. Surpluses must be controlled by international management. The International Wheat Agreement, to which Australia is a party, adjusts output and supply to anticipated market demand. Another method might be guaranteed purchases at fixed prices, along the lines of the agreement by which the United Kingdom has been taking Australia's entire exportable surplus of wool, butter and cheese during the war and has agreed to take the entire wool export for one year after the war.

5. "Protectionist excesses" must be avoided, but developing industries will require some form of state aid. The need of wider outside markets for agriculture must be reconciled with protection of domestic industries. This might be accomplished through trade agreements and common trade policies, subject to constant revision, and through periodic trade conferences. A country could be allowed to develop a particularly important industry under

---

the case of field cultivation and about 25 per cent in dairy activities. In the case of mining, about 71 per cent of total income is derived from sale abroad. In the case of manufacturing only 4 per cent of the gross value of output is derived from foreign sales. For statistical data, see *Commonwealth Year Book, 1940.*

23. The Australian export market is largely a British market. In 1938–1939 about 54 per cent of the value of all exports was gained from United Kingdom purchases, and including all British countries, as much as 70 per cent. Britain has been nearly the sole outlet for butter, meat, eggs, sugar and wine and has absorbed 60 per cent of the wheat and dried fruits, and 40 per cent of the wool of Australia. The United States took only 2 per cent of Australian exports in that year.

The Australian suppliers are also largely British. In 1938–1939 about 42 per cent of the value of total imports was derived from the United Kingdom, and about 60 per cent from all the British countries. The United States is more important as a supplier than as a purchaser; in the same year it supplied 15 per cent of the Australian import market. Australian imports are dominated first by metals and metal manufactures and secondly by apparel and textiles. Paper imports and chemicals are also important.

24. For a discussion of these problems, see G. L. Wood, W. D. Forsyth, P. D. Phillips *et al.*, *Australia and the Pacific, a collection of papers submitted to the Eighth Conference of the Institute of Pacific Relations*, December 1942.

a tariff shelter for a fixed period of time after which the shelter would be removed. An industry which became expensive and obsolete would be liquidated as the tariff was reduced.

6. Trade policy must be associated with other economic policies to create employment. Economic welfare, national and international, needs private and public investment as well as tariff reductions.

The search for new trade outlets and connections is strengthening Australia's conception of itself as a Pacific country. Japanese bombers also intensify this conception. Australia thinks much today of its part in the reconstruction of the Far East, especially China. There is much ambition in Australia to build up China, not only as a bulwark against Japanese aggression, but also as a market for export goods. This increased consciousness of China's importance has taken form in a sympathetic desire to participate with other countries in rebuilding its devastated areas and in developing and expanding its economic life. Australia further shows increased appreciation of its place in the Pacific by the desire for greater participation in the life of Malaya and other far eastern countries.

There is also a growing interest in Australia to associate more closely with the United States.[25] One reason for this is the military partnership on the same Pacific battlefields. Another is the fact that America today is taking the place of old customers. The war has seen an increasing shift of world leadership from Europe to America. As a large part of Europe will be impoverished after the war, the United States will be in a position to buy what Europe formerly imported and to supply the capital needed for Australian industrial development.

Australia thus sees America as having a bigger place in its future external relations, although it does not consciously wish to weaken ties with Britain. It looks to the United States not to fill Britain's former place, but to help enlarge the sphere of Australian world relations. However, there are groups—the so-called "conservatives"— who doubt America's capacity for world economic leadership, and who oppose too much dependence on the United States.

## 6. Group Opinions and National Policy

New theories of industrialization, immigration, trade, and external relations are shared in essence by various groups in Australia,[26] with differences of opinion on method, extent and ultimate changes.

25. See Fred Alexander, *Australia and the United States*, World Peace Foundation, Boston, 1941.
26. See Harold Lark Harris, *Australia's National Interests and National Policy*, 1938, p 85.

The differences of opinion are reflected in the attitudes of the several political parties.[27] The Labour Party, which is now in power, stands for nationalization of industry and for socialism as an ultimate end, but in practice this means merely that the Party is in favor of larger social insurance provisions, and of public works, and is not averse to applying nationalization in some cases, especially banking and finance. The critics of the government say that, if re-elected, it will introduce socialism, and business groups stress the need of more moderate taxation and less governmental interference.[28] The extent to which these group differences will affect Australian postwar policy will be determined by the new elections to be held this year.

27. In the elections to the Commonwealth Lower House in September 1940, the Federal Labour Party obtained thirty-two seats, the United Australia Party twenty-three, the Country Party fourteen, and all others five.

28. The programs of the different groups in Australia are not considered here partly owing to limitations of space, partly because they are not specific enough to add much to the discussion of this chapter. For some of these programs, see C. Hartley Grattan, *Introducing Australia*, 1941.

## Chapter 10

# SOCIAL-ECONOMIC PLANNING IN NEW ZEALAND

IN NEW ZEALAND, postwar planning is largely a continuation of plans inaugurated in the prewar period. The starting line is 1935, when the New Zealand Labour Party came into power. Suffering from the depression of 1929–1932 which was particularly severe because of the dependence of the country on world prices for agricultural products,[1] the people of New Zealand voted into power the Labour Party on a program of specific reforms directed towards expanding the role of the state in maintaining adequate material and cultural standards for all citizens.[2]

### 1. SOCIAL-ECONOMIC REFORMS, 1935–1939

The Labour government was quick to carry out its economic and social program. Its major economic measures during 1936 were an amendment of the Reserve Bank Act and the passage of the Primary Products Marketing Act. The first measure was intended to bring the Central Bank of New Zealand under direct government control. The government bought out the private shareholders, paying the market

1. New Zealand is a small country with an area of some 103,000 square miles and a population of 1.6 million. Standards of living are among the highest in the world. The economic strength of the country lies in its dairying and pastoral industries—in the production of butter, cheese, meat, and wool. These industries are organized in relation to export markets, especially to the British market. Of the 19,721,000 acres of cultivated land in 1938–1939, over 16,783,000 were devoted to pasture. In 1938, New Zealand produced 2,614,549 cwt. of butter; 1,610,523 cwt. of cheese; 5,373,308 cwt. of frozen and chilled meats; and over 271 million lbs. of wool. From 70 to 80 per cent of the agricultural and pastural output is exported. Meat, butter and cheese go almost entirely to the United Kingdom; wool has to compete in world markets. New Zealand's prosperity is thus highly sensitive to fluctuations in business and in world prices. Between 1928–1929 and 1931–1932, gross income from pastural produce fell from (N. Z.) £31.4 million to 14.6 million; and gross income from dairying, poultry and bees fell from (N. Z.) £25.5 million to 17.4 million. The effects of these fluctuations were insolvency and bankruptcy for farmers and unemployment throughout the country. It was this situation which led to the triumph of the Labour Party which obtained 392,972 votes and 53 seats in Parliament. In 1938, the Party obtained 530,000 votes (more than half the votes cast) and 53 seats in the Lower House (out of a total of 80 seats). See *The New Zealand Official Year Book, 1942;* also H. Belshaw, *Recovery Measures in New Zealand,* Institute of Pacific Affairs, Wellington, 1936.

2. The main points of the program were: (1) state control of the central banking and credit system; (2) guaranteed prices to farmers; (3) a living minimum wage and higher earnings for industrial workers; (4) a comprehensive scheme of social insurance including a national health insurance system; (5) a more balanced national economy through the development of secondary industries; (6) public works for the maintenance of employment and for the stimulation of new industries; (7) support of the League of Nations and of the International Labour Organization. See W. B. Sutch, *New Zealand's Labor Government at Work,* League for Industrial Democracy, New York, 1940.

price for their shares, and thus obtained the right and power to appoint the directors. The powers of the Bank were altered so that it could make loans to the government to finance its marketing schemes, public works, and other public projects.

The purpose of the Marketing Act was to ensure a "fair and reasonable income" to the dairy farmer by enabling him to sell his products at guaranteed prices. A Marketing Department was set up, under the control of the Minister of Marketing, which bought all butter and cheese for export. Under the Act, the government fixed an arbitrary and highly favorable price for the farmer, in accordance with the grade of quality of the product. The price was fixed so that the average efficient farmer could cover costs of production and have a sufficient net income to maintain a comfortable standard of living.

To pay for the butter and cheese, the government drew checks on the dairy industry account, which it opened at the Reserve Bank. The sale of the dairy products in the London market became the government's task, which the Marketing Department performed through its office in London. The government supervises the shipments of the dairy products to England so as to adjust supply to anticipated demand and to eliminate serious fluctuations in price. The receipts from these sales are expected to cover the outlay for the purchase of the products in New Zealand. If there is a surplus, the government maintains it to the credit of its account in the New Zealand Bank. If there is a deficit, it is either charged against a previous surplus or to the government's account at the New Zealand Reserve Bank.

The scheme was favored by the preference given Empire products under the Ottawa agreements. In the first year of the operation of the scheme there was a deficit of £272,000. In the second year there was a surplus of about £500,000. In the third year, after the guaranteed price was raised a second time, there was a deficit of some £2 million. The outbreak of the war affected the operation of the scheme so as to make it impossible to judge its results.

While trying to stabilize the agricultural and pastoral industries, the Labour government embarked on a policy of developing secondary industries and of directing foreign trade. The Labour Party believes that the New Zealand economy could be better balanced by the promotion of industries which can use local raw materials and employ local labor. The government therefore undertook public works to develop water power and other resources, and used the mechanism of exchange control to dovetail imports with a policy of protecting domestic industry.[3]

Parallel with these aids to agriculture and industry, the Labour government sponsored a series of measures to strengthen the position of labor and to widen the system of social insurance. The arbitration system for settling industrial disputes was again made compulsory.[4] The Arbitration Court fixed a basic minimum wage securing a decent living standard for all adult wage earners. Furthermore, the Industrial Conciliation and Arbitration Amendment Act of 1936 restricted the formation of new unions in districts and industries where unions already existed, and provided for the registration of national unions covering all workers in an industry, if the majority of the district unions concurred. This legislation, which made unionism almost compulsory, resulted in a large increase in union membership.[5]

The government set up a Housing Department under the control of a Ministry of Housing, which provides houses owned by the state and rented by citizens. The Department buys the land, and the towns plan the development and draw the contracts, which are let to private builders. The housing is financed by the Reserve Bank at low rates of interest.

After some amendments to existing social insurance legislation,[6] the Labour government passed the New Zealand Social Security Act of 1938. This is probably the most advanced act of its kind in the world. It brought into a single system and under unified administration provisions for protection against all hazards and risks (invalidism, sickness, old age, widowhood, orphanhood, unemployment) and provided also for a system of universal medical and hospital benefits. It went into effect on April 1, 1939.

3. Exchange control was established by the New Zealand government for other reasons as well, namely, to improve the unfavorable position of the New Zealand currency after 1938. The government ascribed this situation to a flight of capital which it was determined to stop. Under this system, goods can be imported only by first obtaining a license.

4. The New Zealand Arbitration Court for settling industrial disputes has been in existence for nearly half a century. The Court consists of a Judge of the Supreme Court and one representative each from employers and workers. Trade unions may or may not choose to come under the jurisdiction of the Court. If they do, they must accept its decisions as binding and give up the right to strike. If they do not register with the Court, the unions retain the right to strike. The awards of the Arbitration Court are important in so far as they fix wages and other conditions of employment. During 1931–1935, the compulsory feature of the arbitration awards was abolished.

5. The number of trade union members, which had dropped from 104,000 to 72,000 between 1928 and 1933, rose from 81,000 in 1935 to 233,000 in 1937 and to over 250,000 in 1938. The proportion of trade unionists to total number of wage earners is over 50 per cent.

6. New Zealand introduced old-age pensions in 1898. Between 1898 and 1936, several other forms of social insurance were added, such as pensions for blind persons, widows' and minors' pensions, family allowances, and unemployment payments.

The Act establishes a universal superannuation benefit system for every person over the age of 65 irrespective of income or property. Benefits begin at £10 a year and will increase until a maximum of £78 a year is reached in 1968–1969.[7] The law also establishes a system of benefits for widows with dependent children. The basic rate is £1 a week for widows without children and £1.5s.0d. a week for those with dependent children, and 10 shillings a week for each dependent child under sixteen. It further establishes a system of benefits for orphans, both of whose parents are dead, with a benefit range up to 15 shillings a week.

The system includes allowances for families of limited income, which are paid for each child under sixteen years of age at the rate of 6 shillings a week for each child, if the income of the family is £5 a week.

The law includes a system of unemployment benefits. Every person, except the seasonal worker, who has been unemployed for more than seven days is eligible. The benefits are 10 shillings a week for persons over sixteen and under twenty years of age and £1 a week for all other persons. Additions are also allowed for a dependent wife and dependent children, with a maximum rate of £4 a week.

The Act provides a complete system of medical, hospital, and related benefits without cost to the citizens. These benefits include medicines, drugs, and also free obstetrical care in state hospitals or at home.

The social security and health benefits are financed by a special Social Security Tax of 5 per cent on salaries, wages and all other income, with some exceptions. The tax is deducted at source in the case of incomes derived from wages and salaries; in the case of other incomes, including those of corporations, it is paid quarterly on the basis of an annual declaration of income received. A subsidy from general tax revenues is also paid each year into the Social Security Fund. For the present financial year (1943) the Social Security expendi-

---

7. The universal superannuation benefit system is thus to be introduced gradually and to supplant the old-age benefits system now in operation. Under the present system of old-age benefits, unmarried persons at the age of sixty receive £1.1s. 0d. a week; married couples, if both eligible, receive £3 a week; if wife is ineligible, the husband receives £2 a week; for each child under sixteen years of age a benefit of 10s. a week is paid. To be eligible for the maximum benefit, a person cannot receive income from other sources exceeding £1 per week. An applicant may, however, own his own home, have an interest in an annuity or life insurance policy, and possess, in addition, up to £500 in cash or in securities. Information supplied by the Hon. Walter Nash, former Minister of Social Security in New Zealand. See also Walter Nash, "Down Under—and Up," *Survey Graphic*, May 1943.

tures are expected to reach a total of £16,198,000 of which about £11,150,000 will come from the Social Security Tax. [8]

## 2. WAR AND POSTWAR PLANNING

The war introduced no new long-range problems in New Zealand. The important new problems are connected with demobilization and the re-establishment of ex-servicemen in civil life. As far as postwar economic development is concerned, the war merely accentuated the determination of the government to carry forward its social-economic program. To deal with both immediate and long-range questions, the government established machinery under the National Rehabilitation Act passed on October 17, 1941.

### a. THE NATIONAL REHABILITATION COUNCIL AND BOARD

The New Zealand Rehabilitation Act provides for the establishment of a National Rehabilitation Council to consist of the Minister responsible for administering this part of the Act, as chairman, and "such other persons as the Governor-General from time to time appoints to be members of the Council either by name or as the holder for the time being of any office."

The function of the Council is to recommend to the Minister measures relating to the re-establishment of ex-servicemen in civil life, including in particular:

1. The reinstatement of discharged servicemen in civil employment;
2. The training of ex-servicemen for entry into such employment and the provision of financial assistance during training;
3. The modification of qualifications or requirements of certain kinds for the entry of ex-servicemen into any employment or occupation;
4. The granting of financial assistance to ex-servicemen or to the widows of servicemen so that they may obtain homes, furniture, tools, stock, land or other things necessary for commencing their employment or occupation.

In addition to advising the Minister on these matters, the Council may be charged with administrative responsibility for questions referred to it by the Minister. [9]

The National Rehabilitation Council was set up in January 1942. It consists of twenty members, with the Minister of Rehabilitation as chairman and the National Secretary of the New Zealand Labour Party as deputy chairman. The members of the Council were not appointed as direct representatives of any particular organizations, but,

8. Information supplied by the Hon. Walter Nash.
9. *International Labour Review*, February 1942.

before making the appointments, the government invited nominations from associations representative of discharged servicemen and of employers and employees in the primary and secondary industries.

In addition to the Council, which is an advisory body, the Act of October 17, 1941, also set up a Rehabilitation Board, to consist of the deputy chairman of the Council, as chairman of the Board, and not more than five other members of the Council appointed by the Governor-General to serve on the Board. The functions of the Board are to promote and to make all the necessary arrangements for the establishment in civil life of ex-servicemen and of the widows of servicemen.

The Board is subject to the control of the Minister and is responsible for co-ordinating and using the services of other government departments and of other agencies. Specifically, the Board is authorized:

1. To set aside suitable unoccupied land to be used by or for the benefit of discharged soldiers;

2. To purchase furniture, tools, stock or other things and to dispose of them to or for the benefit of discharged soldiers or the widows of soldiers;

3. To grant financial assistance, in the form of loans, to discharged soldiers or to widows of soldiers;

4. To make grants to servicemen during any period in which they are unemployed or in which they are undergoing a course of training or study to fit themselves for civil employment;

5. To establish or promote or carry on schemes for the training (industrial, educational or vocational) of discharged soldiers and for caring for the disabled.[10]

### b. PROVISIONS FOR EX-SERVICEMEN

The government has announced the following plans. Experienced and competent farmers suitable for immediate establishment on existing farms will be granted loans up to (N.Z.) £3,000 at 4.5 per cent. Applicants may get a loan of (N.Z.) £1,250 at 5 per cent to purchase stock and implements. Loans for homes will range up to 100 per cent of the cost of the dwelling, with a maximum of (N.Z.) £1,500. Interest on these loans will be $4\frac{1}{8}$ per cent, and the loans are to be repayable in installments. Loans to ex-servicemen who establish themselves in business will bear interest at $4\frac{1}{8}$ per cent, reducible to $2\frac{1}{8}$ per cent in the first year. The maximum for such loans is fixed at (N.Z.) £500.

The deputy chairman of the Rehabilitation Council has estimated that after the war 150,000 men will be demobilized in New Zealand. It will be necessary to provide homes for these men, and although the

10. *International Labour Review*, July 1942.

state housing program has made efforts to fill the gap between demand and supply, there is already a demand for every house built and no indication of a surplus to meet the postwar rush. Furthermore, the number of New Zealanders just married before their departure overseas or who would marry upon their return will be about 30,000, and housing must be provided for each of these.[11]

### C. ECONOMIC RECONSTRUCTION

During the debate on the National Rehabilitation Act, Walter Nash, Minister of Finance, explained that, in the view of the government, there were two main postwar problems. One was the demobilization and re-establishment of ex-servicemen in civil life. The other was that of "building a new economic structure." A "new economic structure" did not mean a complete reorganization of New Zealand on socialistic lines, though the New Zealand Labour Party regards socialism as the ultimate goal of social evolution. This goal, however, is far off and for the time being no basic changes in property relations are contemplated. All that is planned is to carry forward the program begun in 1935.

In addition to projects for land settlement, public works, including the building of schools and hospitals, railway improvements, irrigation, afforestation, housing and electrification, the government is determined to promote the expansion of existing industries and the development of some new industries.

According to Mr. Nash, probably half a dozen major new industries could be started in New Zealand, and they are imperatively needed for a decent postwar economic and social life. There is not enough room to put men on the land nor enough markets for their products. Overseas markets for New Zealand's primary products will exist only for a short time after the war. It is therefore desirable to expand industries to a maximum, especially those which the war has already stimulated. These include the linen and flax industry, clothing, synthetic motor spirit, sugar beet, the manufacture of motor tires, iron and steel, and some of the engineering trades.[12]

11. *New Zealand National Review*, February 1942, p. 11.
12. The growth of the motor-assembling and allied industries has been an outstanding example of industrial expansion, while, more recently, notable advances have been made in a number of industries—e.g., hosiery, radio, confectionery, tobacco, and cigarettes. It has become quite evident that the expansion of industries is no longer limited to those lines where ready access to raw materials is the deciding factor. Local manufactures now cater for the Dominion's needs in many products which were formerly almost exclusively imported. This trend has been accelerated by the closing of certain sources of supply of manufactured com-

To facilitate reconversion of war industries to a peacetime basis and to develop new industries, the Rehabilitation Act provides for the setting up of a special Reconstruction Account. The Minister of Finance, on the recommendation of the appropriate Minister, may terminate war contracts at any time after the close of the war. A contractor or subcontractor damaged by contract termination may receive compensation, the amount to be determined by special procedure.

To assist in converting war industries to the needs of peace, in establishing new industries, or in extending existing ones, the Minister of Finance, on the recommendation of the Minister of Industries and Commerce, may make grants or lend money or guarantee loans; acquire and hold shares in any company; arrange to supply raw materials, machinery or other equipment; or purchase part or all of the output.

Finally, the Act authorizes the Minister of Labour to require any employer in a war industry to continue to employ all the workers employed by him at the time when this obligation is notified to him or to continue to employ specified numbers or classes of workers. On the recommendation of the Minister of Labour, the Minister of Finance may grant a subsidy to any employer on whom such an obligation has been placed. An individual employer who fails to comply is liable, on summary conviction, to a fine of £20 for every day during which the offence continues, a corporation to a fine of £100 per day of offence.

The plans for postwar industrialization in New Zealand raise problems of trade and foreign policy similar to those of Australia.[13] New Zealand's reliance on the British market will continue to be great. But New Zealand like Australia may develop closer economic relations with the United States.

---

modities consequent upon the outbreak of the war. Evidence is also provided by recent statistics that the vast supplies of hydroelectric power now available are being used in industry to an increasing extent, the reticulation of the Dominion (now almost completed) offering a ready solution of one of the major problems of industrial expansion—the provision of ample supplies of cheap power.

The growth of industrialization is shown by the fact that the number of manufacturing establishments increased from 5,536 in 1935–1936 to 6,146 in 1938–1939 and to 6,342 in 1939–1940. The number of workers was 86,588 in 1935–1936; 102,535 in 1938–1939 and 108,722 in 1939–1940. At the end of March 1941, the number of factory workers had risen to 132,907, of whom 82,316 were men and 34,291 women. The total value of output in 1939–1940 was £129,061,000. The industries contributing chiefly to the increase in the number of establishments reporting operations in 1939–1940 were—engineering, iron and brass founding, furniture, sawmilling, electrical engineering. The principal decreases were—printing and publishing, butter and cheese. See New Zealand Official Yearbook, 1941, pp. 395–396. Also, International Labour Review, March 1942, pp. 329–330.

13. Contemporary New Zealand, New Zealand Institute of International Affairs, 1938; also Ian Frank George Milner, New Zealand's Interest and Policies in the Far East, New York, 1940.

The war also draws New Zealand into closer relations with Australia. New Zealand may seek a revision of the Ottawa trade agreement and of imperial preference policy. Nevertheless, New Zealand's strongest economic ties remain with Great Britain and with the British Commonwealth of Nations. The Labour government believes that its program of industrial development after the war can be fitted into a scheme of close economic relations with the mother country.[14]

### 3. Views of Other Parties and Groups

Owing to war conditions, no elections were held in 1941, and the Labour government is continuing in power. The opposition to the government is of several shades of opinion. There is a small "leftist" group in the trade unions and the Labour Party which would move more rapidly in the direction of nationalizing industry and of socialism. At the other extreme are business groups, especially among importers, exporters and related financial elements, which are strongly opposed to the whole program of the government.

The middle-of-the-road groups accept what the government has done but are anxious that it does not go much further either in the field of social insurance or of "economic planning." The New Zealand Farmers' Union, for instance, stresses the fact that New Zealand is poor in industrial raw materials and that it would be absurd to try to make it into a great industrial country. The Farmers' Union wants some industries, but stresses the importance of the "production of grass and trees." The farmers' associations are anxious that New Zealand should keep its position in the British market, and emphasize that New Zealand's future depends on world reconstruction and that her contribution consists in creating as large a surplus of agricultural products as possible. Manufacturers' associations are clearly interested in more protection for industry, but they, too, feel that the ties with Britain are of paramount importance.

In line with these criticisms from the "right" and from the "left" proposals have been made for setting up both a ministry of reconstruction and an Empire council of reconstruction. However, the government proceeds on the assumption that what lies ahead is a continuation of what was being done before 1939 and that there is no need for more machinery at present.

14. H. Belshaw, W. T. G. Airey *et al.*, *A New Zealand View of the War and Peace Aims in the Pacific*, Eighth Conference of the Institute of Pacific Relations, December 1942. These problems are also examined in a series of pamphlets published by the New Zealand Institute of International Affairs under the general title: *New Zealand Looks Ahead*.

## Chapter 11

# RECONSTRUCTION IN SOUTH AFRICA

AMONG THE DOMINIONS of the British Commonwealth of Nations, the Union of South Africa faces some of the most difficult social and economic problems. Their roots lie in the historical traditions of the country, in the character of its natural resources, in the predominant place of gold mining in its national economy, and in the heterogeneous composition of its population, divided into Dutch- and English-speaking groups, into white and colored races, and the colored races into Asiatics and natives.[1] The main task of internal policy, especially since 1933, has been to hold these elements together and to prevent their conflicting viewpoints from bursting the bonds of representative government and peaceful administration.[2]

1. The situation may be summed up in a few salient facts and figures. The Union, with an area of 472,550 square miles, consists of the four provinces of the Cape of Good Hope, Natal, the Transvaal and the Orange Free State, under a unitary and centralized government. The estimated population in 1941 was 10,521,000 of whom 2,188,200 were whites of European descent and over 8,300,000 were natives, "colored" (that is, persons of mixed blood), and Asiatics. Of the European population, about 800,000 are English-speaking and 1,200,000 form the Dutch- or Afrikaans-speaking group. The country is poor in arable land; the area of maximum cultivability is estimated at 15 per cent of the total area of the country and about 6 per cent is now under cultivation; the area of maximum irrigability is about 2 million acres. The country has to import foodstuffs and its livestock and dairy industries are dependent on the import of feed. The Union has mineral resources, including coal and iron (though no oil), but the economy of the country is based on gold mining. The prosperity of the people and the revenue of the government depend on the large output of gold from the Rand mines and on the gold policy of the United States which buys all gold at the fixed price of $35 an ounce. Secondary industries have developed considerably owing to tariffs and state subsidies since the First World War, but the country still depends in large measure on imports for manufactured goods. The people of the country are highly stratified both occupationally and socially. The British are predominant in industry, business and finance. The Afrikaners (Dutch-speaking) are largely farmers and skilled or semiskilled wage-earners. All unskilled labor is done by nonwhites who are strictly segregated. The native Negroes, still close to their tribal past and institutions, earn in a week what the white man earns in a day. Mining and industry are largely concentrated in Southern Transvaal, which with its adjacent farming districts contains about half of the European population. Large numbers of the white population also live in the coastal towns and cities. The white population is united on the issue of white supremacy in South Africa, though a growing number of whites are opposed to the policy of segregation. For detailed statistical data, see *Official Year Book of the Union of South Africa, 1941*, Pretoria.

2. Such has been the guiding idea of General Jan Christian Smuts who has been Premier since 1938. The government of which he is head is a coalition of the United Party, the Labour Party and the Dominion Party. General Smuts is the leader of the United Party which, in the elections to the Lower House in May 1938, won 111 seats out of a total of 150. General Smuts is an ardent advocate of the League of Nations and of full association with the British Commonwealth of Nations. As a result of the war, the United Party lost the support of some of its former followers, and General Smuts now has 88 votes in the House. His political strength is due to his own personality, his international reputation, and to dissensions in the ranks of his opponents. The political opponents of General Smuts, all of them Afrikaners, are divided into three groups which disagree on many points but which are united in their opposition to

223

The outbreak of the war brought South Africa increased prosperity, chiefly as a result of Great Britain's need for gold to pay for purchases in the United States. Mining and industrial activities increased greatly, government revenues became larger, the budget was balanced, and the government was able to repatriate large quantities of its securities held in London.

But as the war went on the anomalous conditions of the South African economy became more evident. The excessive dependence of the national economy on gold mining aroused profound apprehensions. The drop in imports due to the lack of shipping facilities caused serious shortages in foodstuffs, raw materials, and manufactured goods.[3] These economic difficulties added fuel to the smoldering fires of political and social discontent, and brought the problem of the social-economic future of the Union to the fore.

The government took the first steps to solve this problem shortly after the outbreak of the war. The Governor-General of the Union appointed an Industrial and Agricultural Requirements Commission to study the issues. In 1941, a Cabinet Committee was appointed by the Prime Minister, General Smuts, to consider and recommend plans for future development. A Social and Economic Planning Council was established in March 1942, to provide machinery for dealing with problems of reconstruction. These government measures aroused wide discussion and various groups of the population came forward with proposals of social-economic policy.

The result has been clarification of the postwar problems of the country and a series of specific recommendations.

### 1. GOVERNMENT DECLARATIONS OF POSTWAR AIMS

The leaders of the government of the Union of South Africa have repeatedly stated that postwar reconstruction must mean a new and better economic and social life for the people.

---

British influence and to the Union's participation in the war. The three groups are: (1) The New Order Party, under the leadership of Oswald Pirow, which follows Nazi Doctrines; (2) The Reunited National or People's Party, led by D. F. Malan, a Dutch Reformed clergyman, who advocates an independent Dutch Republic on the model of the old Boer Republics; and (3) The Afrikaner Party, under N. C. Havenga, which broke away from the party formerly led by General Hertzog who advocated separation from the British Commonwealth of Nations. General Smuts, an Afrikaner himself by origin, has the support of the English-speaking group in South Africa and of those Afrikaners who believe in the necessity of unity of the two European groups and who hope to develop it by maintaining the Union of South Africa as a self-governing Dominion in the British Commonwealth of Nations. General Smuts' strongest support comes from the province of the Cape of Good Hope.

3. See "Commercial History of 1942," *The Economist*, London, March 13, 1942, p. 10.

### a. STATEMENTS OF PRIME MINISTER SMUTS

Speaking before the annual congress of the United Party of the Union of South Africa of which he is the leader, General Smuts defined the ultimate aim of postwar policy as providing, as far as possible, fruitful employment, housing and the necessities of life for the whole community of all races. Large social reforms will become possible, in his opinion, as a result of industrial expansion stimulated by the war.

We are now taking the longest stride ever taken towards the greater industrial future that surely awaits this country. At last we are learning to exploit the vast resources of this country as never before. Our war effort has compelled us to embark on a manufacturing venture almost beyond our power, one which in normal circumstances might have taken at least a generation to carry through. At last our full man-power of all races, colours, and of both sexes is fully employed in a great constructive task. And in this war-work the foundations of the peace-work to follow the war are being laid. Much—very much—of the plant we are laying down, of the industries now being developed, of the factories now being established, will endure beyond the war and form the starting point of future peace industries. The buildings now being built will be useful for peace purposes of all kinds. The vast war hospitals will form the basis of our larger public health policy of the future.[4]

In another more recent statement, General Smuts outlined his views of the larger meaning of the war:

. . . What is the sort of world which we envisage as our objective after the war? What sort of social and international order are we aiming at? . . .
. . . Certain points of great importance have already emerged. Thus we have accepted the name of the *United Nations*. This is a new conception much in advance of the old concept of a League of Nations. We do not want a mere League, but something more definite and organic, even if, to begin with, more limited and less ambitious than the League. The United Nations is itself a fruitful conception, and on the basis of that conception practical machinery for the functioning of an international order could be explored.
Then again, we have the Atlantic Charter, in which certain large principles of international policy in the social and economic sphere have been accepted. That, too, marks a great step forward which only requires more careful definition and elaboration to become a real Magna Carta of the Nations.
Again, we have agreed on certain large principles of social policy, involving social security for the citizen in matters which have lain at the roots of much social unrest and suffering in the past. We cannot hope to establish a new heaven and a new earth in the bleak world which will follow after this most destructive conflict in history. But certain patent social and economic evils could be tackled on modest practical lines on an international scale almost at once.

4. *Cape Times*, October 22, 1941, quoted in the *International Labour Review*, March 1942.

. . . I feel that in this vast suffering through which our race is passing we are being carried to a deeper sense of social realities. We are passing beyond the ordinary politics and political shibboleths. It is no longer a case of socialism or communism or any of the other isms of the market place, but of achieving common justice and fair play for all.[5]

General Smuts also emphasizes the need of a new policy with regard to the natives. Addressing a meeting of the South African Institute of Race Relations on January 21, 1941, he criticized the doctrine of race supremacy and the idea of a *Herrenvolk*. In South Africa, he said, public attitudes had been complicated by fear, and by the belief that the European minority would be in physical danger if it did not retain complete mastery over the natives. We have tried to get round this fear, he said, by a policy of segregation, by keeping whites and natives apart. The results have been disappointing.

General Smuts commended the principle of trusteeship with regard to the natives, especially in matters of social policy. Sickness rates, housing conditions and nutritional standards which should not be tolerated exist among the native population. In the big towns, the wages are too low for the natives to support families. Unless this maladjustment is dealt with drastically, the results may be most lamentable. General Smuts appealed for an adjustment of race relations in a spirit of co-operation.[6]

### b. THE CABINET COMMITTEE ON RECONSTRUCTION

Early in 1941, Prime Minister Smuts appointed a Cabinet Committee to consider and recommend plans for the development of South Africa.[7] The chairman of the Committee, Jan H. Hofmeyr, who is also Minister of Finance, has described the objectives of the postwar policy of the government as follows:

. . . For some time now we have been giving thought to the reabsorption of our soldiers in civil life. That is, or course, one of our primary obligations. . . .
But the reemployment of discharged soldiers is only part of the process of repairing the dislocation caused by war. . . . So, then, we pass on to the conception of post-war reconstruction . . . as a process which at least holds out the promise of building a new and better world, a new and better South Africa. . . . The plain ordinary citizen should have an overwhelmingly predominant claim to whatever fruits of peace there may be.[8]

5. *International Labour Review*, December 1942.
6. *Ibid.*, June 1941.
7. The Committee consists of the Minister of Finance, who is the chairman, the Minister of Agriculture, the Minister of Railways and Harbours, the Minister of Mines, the Minister of Labour, and the Chairman of the Civil Reemployment Board.
8. Quoted in *International Labour Review*, March 1942, p. 304.

On another occasion, Mr. Hofmeyr referred more specifically to the industrial and trade policies which South Africa would pursue after the war. After describing the wartime development of industry in South Africa, he said that the new industries were not all munition factories and that after the war even the munition factories could be put to other uses. Although fostered by war conditions, the new industries were not necessarily dependent on them. After the war there would be increased competition and a reduction in purchasing power. The government would not fail to deal with the scourge of dumping by countries which relied on sweated labor. The factories and plants, coupled with the technical skill gained, would provide the starting point for further industrial progress. The relations between the Union and the rest of the continent were being developed. South Africa would be more closely linked with the African continent as a whole, which was an important factor in industrial development.

Mr. Hofmeyr stated further that industry would have to play a new part, promoting cost reduction, a higher degree of mechanization, and the elimination of waste. Democracy must learn and apply the lesson that the continued justification for its existence is the welfare of the many and not of the few. The tempo of social advancement would have to speed up, and he had no doubt that industry would give its full support to such policy.[9]

## 2. Recommendations of the Industrial and Agricultural Requirements Commission

Shortly after the outbreak of the war the Governor-General of the Union of South Africa appointed a commission to survey the Union's industrial and agricultural situation and to inquire into the development of South Africa's resources. The Commission[10] made several reports on immediate problems of supply and production, but in order to deal with these issues, it also had to consider long-run interests and possibilities. It submitted late in 1941 a comprehensive report which is a remarkably thorough analysis of the economic position of South Africa and which outlines a series of specific recommendations for the postwar development of the country.[11]

The Commission's study starts with two ideas, namely, that the

9. *Ibid.*, p. 305.
10. The Commission consisted of six men under the chairmanship of Dr. H. J. Van Eck, a well-known engineer.
11. *Third Interim Report of the Industrial and Agricultural Requirements Commission—Fundamentals of Economic Policy in the Union*, published by Authority, Pretoria, 1941.

social well-being of the community is determined by its capacity to produce, and that the individual's share in the productive process and in the national income is determined by the general structure of society. According to the Commission, both maximum production and the greatest individual welfare and freedom can be obtained by continuing the economic system of private enterprise. But as individuals are prone to act on temporary monetary considerations, it is the responsibility of the state to prevent the misuse of natural resources and to ensure stability of employment. Also, in order to prevent an inequitable distribution of income and the abuse of individual freedom, the economic and social system must be subject to collective control. The dynamic character of modern life makes it essential that the state should give some guidance to economic development and that social aims and economic needs be harmonized by means of careful planning.

The Commission analyzes in detail the present weaknesses of the Union's economy,[12] and the resources on which a stronger and larger structure may be built. The Commission wants the transition to the new economy after the war to be gradual, and recommends a series of modifications of the present economic policy. Its most important recommendations are seven.

1. The Commission recommends that gold production in the Union be maintained for the longest period possible on a stable basis. The Commission accepts the generally held view that cost-price relations in the gold mining industry and the known reserves of payable ore are such as to make a rapid decline of the industry inevitable within ten years. But since the gold mines are of such great importance to the national economy—both for the maintenance of the national income and for overseas payments[13]—it is desirable to postpone the inevitable exhaustion of the industry as long as possible. The Commission recommends that the government should aid in exploring the possibilities of ultradeep mining and in stimulating new mining developments.

2. In view of the inevitable decline of gold mining and of the in-

---

12. *Ibid.*, pp. 10–11.

13. The importance of the gold mining industry to the Union of South Africa is shown by the fact that it yields almost 20 per cent of the nation's net income, contributes over 40 per cent of the revenue of the state, and accounts for over £110 million of the Union's annual exports which are between £140 and £150 million. It was estimated in 1941 that about 38 per cent of the spending power of the Union is on the Rand, that 39 per cent of industrial activity is concentrated on the Rand and that 41,000 of the Union's 76,000 income tax payers live on the Rand and pay £11,882,000 of the £13,270,000 *total* yield of the income tax on individual and corporate incomes.

herent weaknesses of farming,[14] the Commission recommends wide and rapid industrialization of the Union. South African manufacturing industry developed steadily after the First World War, especially with the expansion of gold mining after 1933. A further and accelerated increase began with the outbreak of the Second World War.[15] But the industrial structure of South Africa has suffered from high costs, insufficient mechanization, lack of trained workers, low efficiency, and the so-called "civilized" labor policy.[16] South African industry is dependent in large measure on tariffs and subsidies.

The members of the Commission believe that the Union of South Africa has large industrial potentialities. It has labor, coal, iron, a number of other minerals (copper, tin, manganese, corundum, mica, tungsten, lead, etc.), and a diversity of agricultural raw materials. To develop these resources the Commission recommends that indiscriminate protective policies be discontinued; that protected industries be periodically examined to make sure that they are operated efficiently; that sound rationalization schemes formulated by industries be encouraged and enforced by the state, if necessary; that wage and labor policies be revised so as to provide better trained workers, and encourage a larger use of unskilled and semiskilled and native workers,[17] and that no general increases in the wages of skilled workers be allowed until the position of the lower income groups is improved and the competitive position of the manufacturing industries is strengthened.

The Commission finds that it will take time for South African industry to attain a high level of industrial technique. It recommends as

14. See below, p. 230.
15. The rapid development of secondary industries is shown by the following figures. Between 1925-1926 and 1937-1938, the number of establishments increased from 7,085 to 10,224; the fixed capital from £54.3 to £106.6 million; the value of gross output from £91.5 to £187.5 million; the number of workers of all races from 193,400 to 348,500. See Year Book, p. 853.
16. The "civilized" labor policy promulgated by the government in 1924 requires that a certain ratio be maintained in industry between European and non-European workers. As applied to wages under the wage regulation system inaugurated in 1926, it requires that wages of European workers be in excess of those of non-European workers. In the Transvaal gold mines, the regulations under the Mines and Work Act exclude natives from certain occupations. On the other hand, in farming and in domestic service no legal or de facto color bar applies. As a result of this policy, about eight non-Europeans are employed to one European in mining, about four to one in farming, and less than two to one in manufacturing industry. Year Book, 1941, pp. 216–231.
17. In 1936, there were 5,305,000 gainfully employed persons in the Union. Of these, 741,500 were Europeans; 276,700 were colored; 64,400 were Asiatics; and 4,222,400 were natives. The natives were distributed as follows: 3,096,500 in agriculture, forestry and fishing; 213,800 in manufacturing; 393,000 in mining; 356,300 in domestic service; and the rest were in the professions, etc. Of the Europeans, 181,400 were in farming and forestry; 132,600 in manufacturing; 46,900 in mining; 119,600 in commerce and finance; 124,500 in public service and the professions; and 77,800 in transport.

a first step that the Union concentrate on the production of the simpler and less refined products which could be sold in large quantities to the natives on their present low level of living. It would be possible to find markets for such products in other South African territories. The Union could benefit by an increased interchange of its products with those of the tropical regions of Africa.

3. The Commission emphasizes the need to protect and build up grazing and arable land, to make grain production auxiliary to animal husbandry, and to grow more fruits and vegetables. It favors assistance to farmers to enable them to check further erosion, and to readjust farming methods. The Commission finds, however, that the position of farming cannot be permanently improved, that rural income is very low compared with urban, and that it is necessary to reduce the proportion of the population engaged in agriculture by transferring farmers to other industries as they develop. The Commission also recommends that every inducement be given to the extension of both private and government afforestation in order to make possible the production of large-sized timber, a local sawmill industry, and a larger plywood industry.

4. The Commission endorses a long-range mining policy to develop the rich mineral resources of the country in connection with heavy industries and for export.

5. The Commission urges measures to improve the position of low-income groups, both because low incomes are a cause of "serious social degeneration" and because they limit the local market for industrial and agricultural products. Specifically, the Commission recommends that unskilled industrial wages be gradually increased,[18] that lower-paid workers be provided with better housing and with free medical services, and that the state subsidize food consumption of the low-income groups in order to combat malnutrition.[19]

6. The Commission recommends that the government combat industrial fluctuations and try to maintain a reasonably stable rate of

18. As a general rule, the remuneration of urban native employees is from 20*s.* to 30*s.* a week as against the basic skilled wage rate of 22*s.* a day.

19. These proposals are far behind the provisions for social services in other countries. The fact is, social security legislation in South Africa is a recent growth. In 1928, old-age pensions were granted to men over sixty-five and to women over sixty, who could not show means above a certain prescribed amount. Under this plan, 62,000 persons are receiving £2 million annually. A scheme of workmen's compensation applying to whites and non-whites, dates from 1934. In 1937, the Union government passed permissive legislation which permits an industry to set up an unemployment fund, to which contributions are made by employers, workers, and the state. The Minister of Labour has power to compel the establishment of an unemployment "fund" in a particular industry, but the power is very sparingly used. The engineering and gold mining industries have established "funds." The Union of South Africa has, however, an extensive code of labor legislation including accident compensation, minimum wage fixing, etc.

economic development by regulating public investment, by controlling interest rates and by an appropriate foreign exchange policy. Capital expenditures of various public authorities should be timed and co-ordinated so as to exercise a stabilizing effect on the economy. The Commission favors both the accumulation of budgetary surpluses and short-term loans to finance public works programs prepared in advance for use when a trade recession sets in.

7. In order to implement the policies recommended, as well as to co-ordinate the work of various government authorities, the Commission recommends the establishment of a permanent economic advisory and planning council. The Commission proposes that the council consist of a judge of the Supreme Court as chairman and six other members selected for their wide knowledge of the general social and economic structure. The council is to have power to appoint part-time members to serve as a consultative committee.

## 3. The Social and Economic Planning Council

Following the suggestions of the Industrial and Agricultural Requirements Commission, Prime Minister Smuts announced in the House of the Assembly of the Union of South Africa, on March 7, 1942, that the government was considering the establishment of a Social and Economic Planning Council. The Prime Minister stated that there had never been any proper planning or co-ordination of policies in South Africa and that "the result had been a certain amount of chaos." The time had come to correct the situation. The idea of the government was to establish an agency, independent of government departments, which would co-ordinate government activities, plan policies, and advise the government on the administrative and legislative steps to create national welfare along more harmonious lines.[20]

On March 25, 1942, the government established a Social and Economic Planning Council, which consists of eight men and two women, and includes engineers, businessmen and officials, but no representatives of labor.[21]

20. *Cape Times,* March 7, 1942, quoted in *International Labour Review,* May 1942, p. 537.
21. The Council is composed of the chairman of the Industrial and Agricultural Requirements Commission (who is also the government nominee and managing director of the Industrial Development Corporation of South Africa); a member of the Industrial and Agricultural Requirements Commission (a mining engineer); the resident director of the Victoria Falls and the Transvaal Power Company; the former head of the Division of Plant Industry of the Department of Agriculture; a businessman; a senator (representing the Natives); two farmers; a director of the South African Board of Barclays Bank (formerly Secretary for Finance); and two women who are members of the Cape Provincial Council.

The Planning Council is to act as an advisory body only and is directly responsible to the Prime Minister. Its functions are as follows:

1. To investigate, and make representations for promoting, the planned development of the resources of the Union and its internal and external trade, as well as the prosperity and well-being of the population as a whole;
2. To examine and make recommendations on schemes and suggestions made from time to time to improve the social and economic standards of the various sections of the community;
3. To review the policies and programs of the various departments and boards which have an economic or social bearing, with a view to advising the government on steps to secure their better co-ordination;
4. From time to time to nominate, with the concurrence of the government, consultative subcommittees for special investigations and enquiries;
5. Generally to advise the government on social and economic policy.

In an address to the Council on June 13, 1942, General Smuts emphasized two of its tasks as of particular importance. One is to harmonize and co-ordinate the activities of the different government departments. The other is to survey the resources of the country and to explore the possibilities of their postwar development.

The Social and Economic Planning Council submitted its first report to Parliament on January 25, 1943. The report estimated the number of soldiers and "displaced workers" who would have to find new employment at the end of the war and made a number of recommendations with regard to a housing program, agricultural production, the improvement of nutrition, and further investigations into the living conditions of the natives.

The Council also recommended that it be placed on a statutory basis. The government did not think the time ripe for that. The Prime Minister thought that the Council was in an experimental stage and that for a few years at least, it should remain "a social and economic adjunct to Parliament" and should provide advice and guidance when needed.

## 4. Proposals of Organized Groups

The postwar proposals of the government and of the Industrial and Agricultural Requirements Commission, if carried out, would change considerably the present position of the several economic groups in the Union. These groups, recognizing the need for far-reaching changes after the war, are concerned with the particular policies which may be adopted, and have formulated their own ideas.

## a. STATEMENTS BY EMPLOYERS

In general, the employers' groups in the Union[22] are in favor of further industrialization. Many industrialists and businessmen claim that the Union of South Africa can become the workshop of Africa and that the whole African continent, with its 150 million people, should become the outlet for the expanding manufacturing industries of the Union.

Different opinions arise as to how this should be achieved[23] and what part the government should play in the process. In general, businessmen want a closer partnership between the commercial community and the state in postwar reconstruction, without turning over their interests "to the tender mercies of an army of civil servants." They favor a system of self-government or "self-discipline" by the business community, sanctioned by the state.[24]

The South African Federated Chamber of Industries wants the government "to give the utmost encouragement to the industrial development of the natural resources of Southern Africa." It favors "a long-term, liberal but controlled, immigration policy." The Chamber of Industries suggests that "when the war ends all Governments stores of consumer goods (e.g., canned foods, clothing, footwear) should be liquidated through the Department of Social Welfare and/or shipped to countries in need of them as a result of war devastation." This is proposed in order "to preserve the local market for secondary industry, which, as the largest employment avenue, would be required to absorb many men returning from active service, and as such should be placed in the most favourable position to discharge its obligations in the interests of the country."[25]

## b. LABOR'S PROGRAM FOR FULL EMPLOYMENT

The Union's labor organizations emphasize full employment. This is one of the main demands of the South African Trades and Labour

22. In 1939, there were in the Union 105 registered employers' associations with a membership of over 7,600. Over half of these associations were in the engineering, metal working and building trades. In addition, there are the local Chambers of Commerce affiliated in a central Chamber of Commerce.

23. The report of the Industrial and Agricultural Requirements Commission, according to some, shows a strong bias in favor of "big business." The chairman of the Commission is said to be "a convinced and able propagandist" of "Iscor"—the South African Iron and Steel Corporation at Pretoria—which is a large and highly integrated corporation, with expanding activities in various fields. Most of the Union's factories, however, are rather small. See "Problems of Industry," *The Star*, Johannesburg, August 7, 1942.

24. See Statement by W. B. Collier, President of the Association of Chambers of Commerce, quoted in the *International Labour Review*, March 1942.

25. *International Labour Review*, February 1943, pp. 221–222.

Council which is composed of white or European skilled workers.[26] At its annual conference in April 1942, the Council considered a proposal to establish a National Planning Board whose main task would be to prevent industrial depressions and unemployment. The proposed Board is to consist of an equal number of employers and workers. The proposal is inspired by a fear that returned soldiers and the "dilutees"[27] will increase the labor supply out of proportion to the demand.

The National Planning Board would plan industrial expansion in such a way as to make employment secure. The specific measures suggested for the attainment of this purpose are as follows:

1. Establishment of a state fund to embark on public works schemes;
2. Introduction of a maximum working week of forty hours;
3. Introduction of compulsory annual leave for all workers and increase of existing annual leave where it is enjoyed;
4. Introduction of a national housing scheme;
5. Extension and development of our base metal industry;
6. Development of state shipping services and the establishment of a shipbuilding industry;
7. Building of motorcar chassis in this country;
8. Building of more rolling stock by the Railway Administration;
9. Introduction of numerous other schemes which may be relatively unimportant in themselves, but in the aggregate will make a considerable contribution towards postwar employment.[28]

The Conference of the Council also passed a resolution to establish a committee representing all industries and labor organizations in order "to draw up a workers' charter providing a more equitable economic system after the war." This Committee has not yet made its report.

### C. THE FUTURE OF NATIVE WORKERS

Some of the statements quoted above show growing recognition of the need to improve the economic condition and status of native

26. Trade unions have grown in the Union as a result of the Industrial Conciliation Act of 1924 which was intended to promote collective bargaining between employers and workers and the peaceful adjustment of industrial disputes. The Conciliation Act applies to European workers only and provides for the registration of employers' and workers' organizations in all trades, except public service, farming, domestic service. Under the Conciliation Act employers and workers may form joint industrial councils which fix wages and working conditions. Between 1934 and 1938, the membership of registered trade unions increased from 77,737 to 215,822 but fell to 179,412 in 1939; it has grown since. The membership of registered trade unions and other employees' associations in 1940 was 235,051. The strongest unions are in the mining and building trades. The unions are divided on the national level. The South African Trades and Labour Council, more liberal in its outlook, has about 28,000 members. A movement is now under way to unite the South African Trades and Labour Council, the Cape Federation of Labour Unions and The Western Province Trades Council into a South African Federation of Trade Unions. See *Year Book, 1941*, pp. 222–228; also, *The International Labour Review*, February 1943, p. 255.

27. The "dilutees" are unskilled workers who have been allowed to enter skilled occupations during the war.

28. *International Labour Review*, May 1942, p. 54.

workers who form the overwhelming majority of the working population. The specific problems are numerous and complex. The natives
are in many cases too poor, and have not the means of transportation,
to look for jobs, are untrained in elementary habits of industrial
work, suffer from malnutrition and disease, are prone to accidents
owing to their unfamiliarity with technical appliances, are unwilling to leave their native homes and tribal living, are suspicious
and afraid of their employers and white superiors, and are accustomed
to primitive living conditions. For generations they have been held
down by European farmers, and businessmen who wanted cheap and
docile (even if inefficient) labor, and by white workers who were
afraid of the competition of low-standard labor.

Efforts to improve the conditions of native labor have been made
from time to time. The government has applied the provisions of the
Industrial Conciliation Act so as to give some protection to native
workers.[29] The natives have also made some advance in self-help.
A number of trade unions composed entirely of native workers are
now in existence, and though they are not registered under the Conciliation Act, they exercise some influence in protecting wages and
working conditions of their members.

The war has caused a large influx of native workers not only from
the provinces of the Union, but from the adjoining protectorates and
regions.[30] All plans for further industrial expansion imply the use of
more native workers. A larger domestic market depends in a measure
on raising their living standards. General Smuts and the Industrial
and Agricultural Requirements Commission point to the necessity
for lifting the status of native labor. The position of a growing portion of European labor is evident from the report to the 1942 conference of the South African Trades and Labour Council which reads
in part as follows:

It would appear that our urbanised Natives are becoming more and more
conscious concerning the advantages offered in being organised into trade
unions of their own. Most of these unions are now led exclusively by experienced African negotiators. Whatever advice they need from European trade
unionists is at all times promptly given—a gesture much appreciated by both.
The growth of Native trade unions is perhaps not as rapid as could reasonably be expected, but that is not in any way due to the lack of interest dis-
played either by the Africans themselves or their European collaborators.

29. When agreements are made by industrial councils, inspectors of the Labour Department may attend the meetings and take part in the discussion whenever matters affecting
the interests of native workers are concerned.
30. The Union of South Africa holds a mandate from the League of Nations for the
former German colony of Southwest Africa. It draws labor also from British Northern
Rhodesia and from Portuguese East Africa.

The average Native who enters industry as a newcomer is usually 'raw' and not sufficiently intelligent or schooled to appreciate the value of collectivity. Coming from areas where wages are mere pittances, they are, at first impressed with the wages paid to them in the big towns. Soon they realise that their earnings do not permit them to buy much clothes and good food, which, according to their observations, the European has in abundance, and presently they hear about a group of fellow-workers who have succeeded in obtaining small increases in their wages. It dawns on them that as individuals they have little chance of getting a few shillings more, for their employer can easily get others. Briefly, the task of African unionists is to inculcate into the minds of simple, honest people the doctrine of collective representation for better wages and conditions, and that contributions are necessary to enable the carrying out of such essential representation. But it is pleasing to note the increasing progress in that direction.[31]

## 5. RECONSTRUCTION AND NATIONAL UNITY

Underlying all plans for reconstruction in the Union of South Africa are the problems of national unity and of the international position of the country. Those who see a large development for South Africa after the war believe that the problem of national unity can be solved by giving larger economic opportunities and greater social security to all.

This point of view is clearly expressed in the resolution adopted by the United Party, which is the government party, at its Congress in October 1942. The resolution states:[32]

1. That one of the basic causes of racial strife in the Union is poverty and the menace of want;
2. That a fuller measure of national unity, happiness and contentment can best be achieved by the overcoming of these evils;
3. That it is the legitimate hope and aspiration of the citizens of this country that one of the outcomes of the sacrifices of the war will be the evolution of a planned economy based on the co-operative use and control of the nation's resources for the social security and upliftment of its citizens;
4. That a declaration by the government that such a plan forms part of its war aims would reassure the nation and lend added purpose and direction to our fighting forces;
5. That it has become an urgent national necessity to prove that the problems of poverty and unemployment and the evils that flow therefrom can be overcome by a democratic form of government.

It is on this platform that General Smuts and his party hope to unite the majority of the South African people after the war.[33]

31. *International Labour Review*, August 1942.
32. *Ibid.*, March 1942.
33. For a summary of the political situation in the Union of South Africa, see J. P. Cope, "Dynamite in South Africa," *The New Republic*, December 19, 1942.

## Chapter 12

## THE POSTWAR DEVELOPMENT OF INDIA

IN CURRENT DISCUSSIONS of India, the problem that overshadows all others is its future political status: whether India will be a self-governing part of the British Empire or will become an entirely independent country whose relations with Great Britain will be shaped freely by its own representative government.

Settlement of the question hinges on whether one or another of the current proposals will prevail or some new compromise will be evolved. The main political formulas today are: (1) the offer of the British government to create "a new Indian Union which shall constitute a Dominion, associated with the United Kingdom and the other Dominions by a common allegiance to the Crown, but equal to them in every respect, in no way subordinate in any aspect of its domestic or external affairs";[1] (2) the demand of the Congress Party[2] for "complete independence," for complete national unity[3] and for the right of India to determine through a constituent assembly what

1. This proposal was made by Sir Stafford Cripps during his "Indian Mission." Sir Stafford emphasized that the proposal was meant to be applied after the war, but that it gave the Indian people the right to decide ultimately whether they wished to remain in the British Commonwealth of Nations, or not. See Sir Frederick Whyte, *India, A Bird's Eye View*, and *Documents on the Indian Situation*, Papers Submitted to the Eighth Conference of the Institute of Pacific Relations, December 1942.

2. The Indian National Congress, or Congress Party, was inaugurated in 1885, and is today the most influential political movement in India. It aims to unite all elements of the Indian people into a national whole regardless of race or creed. It is composed of various economic groups which differ considerably in their views on social policy. The membership of the Congress Party is predominantly, though not exclusively, Hindu. In 1937–1938, it was claimed, the Congress had a membership of about 3 million, including some 200,000–300,000 Moslems. Its President, Dr. Maulana Abul Kalam Azad, is a Moslem. Its leaders are Gandhi and Jawaharlal Nehru. See W. E. Duffet *et al.*, *India To-day*, New York, 1942, pp. 62–66; also Kate L. Mitchell, *India Without Fable*, 1942.

3. British India and the "independent" Indian states have a total area of 1,575,187 square miles, and a total population of 388 million. British India includes about three fourths of the total. Under the Government of India Act of 1935, British India is divided into eleven provinces which have local self-government in a considerable degree.

The "independent" Indian states number 562 and have a population of some 92 million. These states vary greatly in area, population, resources, etc. Some are large, e.g., Hyderabad which has a population of over 16 million. Others are small and have a population of a few thousand. The states generally have autocratic rulers, some of whom, however, have recently introduced some democratic reforms. The rulers of the Indian states are "independent" in their internal affairs, except for their treaty obligations to the British government and special powers reserved by the British government. The Indian states have a central organization for the discussion of common problems—*The Narendra Mandal* (Chamber of Princes).

its relations to other countries of the world shall be;[4] (3) the demand
of the All-India Moslem League[5] for "Pakistan," i.e., the division of
India into autonomous Hindu and Moslem states; and (4) the compromise proposals of various groups which would accept some
amicable arrangement with Great Britain, preferably that of Dominion status.[6]

The economic and social future of India will depend in large measure
on the settlement of the political issue. Nevertheless, economic and
social policies are being pursued today and plans are being considered
for the postwar period which are likely to have important effects,
regardless of political adjustments. These policies and plans are proposed partly to meet the long-standing problems of India, partly to
adjust to the changes of war.

## 1. THE COMMITTEE ON RECONSTRUCTION AND POLICIES OF THE GOVERNMENT OF INDIA

In the spring of 1941 the government of India established an Inter-
departmental Committee on Reconstruction. Included in its membership are the ministers for Finance, Commerce, Defense, Supply,
Labour, Education, Health, and Lands; the Chief Commissioner for
Railways, and the Economic Adviser to the Government of India.
Subordinate to this group is a consultative committee of economists
appointed from various Indian universities to advise on long-range
planning and the retention in peacetime of certain war controls.[7]

4. The resolution adopted by the Indian National Congress on March 20, 1940, contains
the following declarations:
"The Congress hereby declares again that nothing short of complete independence can
be accepted by the people of India. . . . India's constitution must be based on independence,
democracy and national unity, and the Congress repudiates attempts to divide India or to
split up her nationhood. . . . The Congress cannot admit the right of the rulers of Indian
States or of foreign vested interests to come in the way of Indian freedom." Quoted in *India
and the War, Presented by the Secretary of State for India to Parliament by Command of His Majesty,
April 1940,* London.
5. The Moslem League was founded in 1905 to represent the interests of the Moslem
population of India which is estimated at some 80 million. The Moslem League is opposed
to the Congress Party and aims to unite all Moslems of India under its leadership. It is led by
Mohammed Ali Jinnah. See *Muslim Demand for Pakistan*; also Mehr Chand Khanna, *Pakistan,
A Hindu View,* Eighth Conference of the Institute of Pacific Relations, 1942.
6. Among these are the Mahasabha, the Orthodox Hindu Party, which stresses Hindu
tradition and is socially conservative; the Azad (Free) Moslem Conference which is a combination of Moslem organizations opposed to the extreme political views of the Moslem
League; the National Liberal Federation under the influence of Indian banking and industrial
groups, the small India Socialist Party, and others.
7. The Government of India Act, 1935, approved by the British Parliament aims to organize India as a federation of autonomous provinces and of the Indian native states. On the
basis of this Act, British India is divided into eleven major and some minor provinces with
provincial legislatures and a governor appointed by the British Crown. But the main provisions of the 1935 Constitution have not been put into effect. India is governed now under
the Government of India Act, 1919. There is an Indian Legislature consisting of an Upper and

The committee is subdivided into six subcommittees to deal with various aspects of postwar planning such as labor placement and demobilization, disposals and war contracts, public works and government purchasing policies, postwar trade policy, industry, agriculture, and finance. Some of these subcommittees have held meetings to consider their respective problems, but have not as yet formulated policies.[8]

## 2. GOVERNMENT MEASURES

Meanwhile, the government of India has adopted measures to deal with the effects of the war on Indian economy and to prepare for the postwar period.

### a. AGRICULTURAL POLICY AND LAND REFORM

The central government of India has for a number of years tried to improve agriculture. Following the report of the Royal Commission on Agriculture in India of 1926–1928, the government established the Imperial Council of Agricultural Research which has carried on extensive studies for developing the production and marketing of agricultural products throughout the whole of India.

The government emphasizes the problem of increasing the food supply of the country. Despite the great volume of some of its products,[9] India has to import rice from Burma and Indo-China, and wheat from Australia. The agricultural output is insufficient to meet the needs of the Indian population either in calories or vitamins. The diet of the bulk of the population is deficient in calories, in animal proteins, A and B vitamins, calcium and iron, milk and sugar.[10]

Lower House. The former consists of 58 members of whom 26 are nominated by the government. The Lower House has 141 members of whom 102 are elected. This Legislature can make laws, subject to certain limitations and to the veto power of the Governor General. Real power is exercised by the central government which consists of the Viceroy and Governor General and of an Executive Council appointed by the Crown. Each member of the Executive Council is a minister and responsible for some department of government. As a concession to public opinion, the British government enlarged the Council in 1941, and it now includes a majority of nine Indian members out of a total of fourteen.

8. *International Labour Review*, March 1942, p. 309; May 1942; February 1943, p. 218.

9. In 1937–1938, some 152 million acres were devoted to the cultivation of staple food grains (rice, wheat, jowar, cajra, barley, maize, gram) and their total output was over 47 million tons. Some 45 million acres were devoted to other food crops. In addition, large quantities of fruits and vegetables were grown. The most important staple crop is rice, and India produces about 40 per cent of the world's rice crop. Practically all of India's grown rice is consumed in the country.

10. India possesses some 30 million cows, 15 million female buffaloes and large numbers of she-goats, all of which are used for milking purposes. The total milk production has been estimated at over 10 billion gallons a year, but the milk consumption per person per day is only 8 ounces. The consumption of sugar is 7.3 lbs. per capita per year. See Sam Higginbottom, *India's Agricultural Problems*, Paper submitted to the Eighth Conference of the Institute of Pacific Relations, December 1942.

Productivity is also low in nonfood cash crops such as cotton, jute, oilseeds, groundnuts, fodder, etc., which play an important part in supplying Indian industries with raw materials and in the export trade of the country.[11]

The government of India has encouraged the introduction of better varieties of staple crops and livestock, irrigation, the use of more and better farm implements, the control of pests, easier and cheaper credit, greater marketing facilities, and agricultural education in high schools and colleges. Efforts have also been made to improve the quantity and quality of cotton and other non-food crops.

Government efforts, however, have had only modest results. Indian agriculture is still backward, and, on the eve of the war, the majority of the Indian peasants were on very low levels of existence, often on the verge of starvation. Many students of the problem feel there is little opportunity for improving Indian agriculture unless and until its root evils are eradicated. These evils are not only technical but economic and social in character—an exploitative system of land tenure, high land rents, usurious rates of interest, an inequitable tax system which falls heavily on cultivators of the land,[12] and a rapid increase in population which creates an excessive rural population. Under prevailing conditions of small holdings, rents, interest rates, taxation, and population pressure, the Indian peasant cannot afford to use selected seeds, or introduce modern tools, or manure his land adequately, or improve his cattle.

The war has affected Indian agriculture in several ways which modify the postwar outlook. On the one hand, it has caused a serious shortage of food, partly by cutting off imports and partly by causing transportation difficulties within the country. On the other hand, the loss of European and far eastern markets have made it necessary to reduce production of cotton, jute, and several other crops. This shift

11. India is next to the U.S.A. and the USSR in cotton production; has a monopoly in the production of jute; and is second only to China in the output of oilseeds.

12. The land systems of India are complex, but in broad outline, the systems which are widely prevalent are: (1) the "ryotwari" system under which the "ryots" have the right to cultivate the land and pay directly to the state a share of the produce; (2) the system under which the state collects its land revenue through intermediaries. It is estimated that of the 250 million people who derive their livelihood from the land, about half a million families are large landlords ("Zamindars" and others), and a million or so families have thirty acres or more. Of the remainder, two thirds cultivate their own land or are tenants on small holdings, while about one third are landless agricultural laborers. Rents are often out of proportion to the average yield of the land, and the peasants have other payments to make for the use of water, etc. The indebtedness of the Indian peasantry has been estimated at £1,200 millions, and interest rates on this debt are high. See Vera Anstey, *The Economic Development of India*, 1931. It is claimed that rising agricultural prices as a result of the war "have diminished the real burden of agricultural indebtedness." *International Labour Review*, June 1943, p. 754.

in the production is further accentuated by the increased demand for foodstuffs due to military requirements and the expansion of industrial activities.

The problem of the food supply became of paramount urgency in 1941-1942, and the government took a number of steps to ease the situation. Public funds were appropriated for a "Grow More Food Campaign." Intensified efforts were made to assist the cultivators not only by special personal loans, seeds, manure, and irrigation facilities, but also by reducing rents or taxes on land reclaimed and employed in the cultivation of food crops.[13] A Department of Food was established in the latter part of 1942 to control prices and distribution.[14]

The postwar outlook is for greater concentration in India on increasing production of foodstuffs. The government plans to extend and intensify aid to the cultivators of land, especially to improve water supply, transport and marketing facilities. The plans of the government also include changes in size of land holdings, but no indications have been given as to the nature of these changes and whether they will affect the systems of land tenure.

## b. INDUSTRIALIZATION AND TRADE POLICY

One of the important postwar problems of India is the degree and character of further industrialization. A great quickening in the industrial life of the country took place during the First World War. It was accelerated after 1920 by the policy of "discriminating protection," which helped to build up the iron and steel industry[15] and the

13. See B. D. Adarkan, *War Time Economic Trends and Post War Policy*, Indian Paper No. 3, submitted to Eighth Conference of the Institute of Pacific Relations, December 1942. Also, *International Labour Review*, December 1942, pp. 724–726.

14. *International Labour Review*, March 1943, pp. 360–362.

15. India is an agricultural country and four fifths of the population derive a livelihood from the land. Also, the bulk of domestic needs for manufactured goods is still supplied by the handicraft village industries whose products are produced and consumed locally. But modern manufacturing industries and mining have grown greatly since 1919 and have assumed increasing importance in the economic life of the country. India is rich in many mineral resources such as coal, iron, manganese, chromite, mica, petroleum, bauxite, etc. It is the second largest coal producing country in the British Empire with an annual output of about 25 million tons. Among the modern large-scale industries are the cotton and wool industries, the iron and steel industry, chemicals, the leather and sugar industries. There are 390 cotton mills in India with about 10,000,000 spindles and 200,000 looms. India is the second largest producer of iron ore in the Empire, and its output of steel is about a million tons a year. The Tata Iron and Steel Company is the most important iron and steel plant in India and the second largest in the British Empire. It turns out a variety of products and has been greatly expanded as a result of the war. According to the Census of 1931, some 30 million people were engaged in industry, transport and trade. The number of workers in factories in 1939 was about 2,725,000; about 700,000 were employed on the railroads and about 300,000 in mines. In 1938, over 512,000 workers were employees in the cotton mills, and about 210,000 in engineering works. The industries are concentrated in Calcutta, Bombay, Ahmedabad, Madras, Cawnpor, Magpur and a few other cities.

giant cotton industry. Indian industry was being developed in increasing measure even before 1939 by indigenous capital and by Indian entrepreneurs.[16]

The present war has greatly stimulated the productive capacities of India, and is making it one of the great industrial countries of the world. There has been a rapid development of the iron and steel industry; by the middle of 1942, the production of steel had reached the rate of 1,250,000 tons a year. An expansion has taken place in the facilities for repairing and building ships, in the machine tool industry, munitions and small arms, cotton, wool and silk production, the clothing industry, leather manufactures, and the production of chemicals.[17]

The government of India is committed to protect these industries after the war from foreign competition, as far as their capacity for further development warrants. In an address to the Associated Chambers of Commerce at Calcutta on December 15, 1941, the Viceroy made the following statement on the subject:

That important question has been constantly before me and before my advisers; and in the budget session of 1940 the Government of India formally stated that they (the Government) were prepared, in the case of specific industries started in war conditions, to give assurances that such industries, after peace was restored, would be given some form of protection against competition from abroad. That assurance was inevitably confined to specific industries, since in each case the scope of the industry, its needs, and the part that it will play in the general economy of the country, have to be considered.[18]

The Indian government has proposed to contribute one tenth of the net excess profits tax paid by industry for postwar rehabilitation and re-equipment of plants, provided that the assessee deposits a sum equal to double this amount. The contribution is placed in reserve by the assessee and will be repaid within twelve months of the end of the war. The proportion contributed by the government will be paid out after the war at such time and subject to such conditions as may hereafter be determined. The government is also considering a proposal to

16. Indian capital and management are dominant in the cotton textile industry, iron and steel, rice milling, manufacture of cement, flour milling, chemicals, brewing, and in banking. Bombay is the center of Indian capital, while Calcutta is the center of foreign capital. The total amount of British investment in India has been variously estimated, but on the eve of the war it included holdings of about £250 million of Indian government loans, and about £250 of privately issued securities. The government securities have been largely repatriated since the beginning of the war. British investments predominate in the tea, coal, rubber and petroleum industries. See *Indian Finance*, Regional Planning Supplement, December 1939.

17. See Kate L. Mitchell, *op. cit.*, pp. 219–225.

18. *International Labour Review*, May 1934, p. 543.

use the surplus of sterling balances accruing in India for a reconstruction fund to be used to re-equip and expand industrial plants.[19]

### C. LABOR STANDARDS AND SOCIAL SERVICES

Industrial expansion in India is bringing more workers into industry and into the cities,[20] and thus giving greater importance to problems of wages, labor conditions, and industrial relations. The government of India has adopted measures to offset the effects of rising food prices and higher living costs by giving the workers temporary expense allowances and war bonuses.

Less temporary are the steps the government has taken to enlarge factory legislation and to improve the machinery for settling industrial disputes. The Factories Act of 1934 has been amended so as to permit provincial governments to apply their labor regulations to all industrial establishments employing ten or more persons. Under this amendment, several provincial governments, e.g., those of Madras, Mysore, and Bengal have recently passed laws to provide weekly rest days and paid annual holidays for certain groups of employees. In 1941 the Central Legislative Assembly of India passed a law prohibiting the employment of women in mines during the four weeks following the day of delivery of a child, and providing maternity benefits.[21]

The most important step the government has taken to regulate industrial relations is the establishment of a Tripartite Labour Organization (on the model of the International Labour Organization) with an annual plenary conference, standing committees and so forth. This organization will consist of representatives of the central government, employers and workers' organizations. Not only the provinces of British India, but also representatives of the Indian princes and independent states, take part in this organization. The functions of the organization are to promote uniformity in labor legislation, to provide procedure for the peaceful settlement of disputes, and to

19. *Ibid.*, August 1942, p. 184.
20. The number of industrial workers increased from 1,737,000 in 1938 to 2,727,000 in 1940.
21. See *International Labour Review*, November 1942, p. 604. Labor legislation in India applies to workers in many specific industries. It covers such matters as methods of recruiting and living, minimum age of admission to industry, sanitation and safety, protection of the payment of wages, limitation of working hours to nine a day with certain exceptions, etc. Conditions of labor are better in the large modern factories but leave much to be desired in the smaller factories and shops, and especially in the unregulated industries in which millions of workers are employed. Labor legislation is, in large measure, a prerogative of the provincial governments.

arrange for discussion between employers and employees of "all matters of all-India importance."[22]

No special measures or plans have been reported with regard to the improvement of social conditions such as health, housing and illiteracy.

### d. DEMOBILIZATION, RE-EMPLOYMENT AND PUBLIC WORKS

With a view to the reabsorption of demobilized men,[23] and the placement of war workers in peacetime production, the Reconstruction Committee is making a survey to determine the previous occupation and training of members of the Indian army. It is preparing plans for gradual demobilization. Studies are also being made to determine the probable postwar volume of industrial employment, and the extent to which the training and experience received in war industries can be utilized for peacetime production. Proposals for the retraining of war workers and demobilized men in accordance with postwar needs are under consideration. Employment exchanges are to be established throughout India to facilitate labor placement. Consideration is also being given to problems of work relief and to the conditions of work and rates of pay which should obtain if work relief becomes necessary.[24]

The Reconstruction Committee also aims to aid in an orderly transition to peacetime production by providing for a gradual tapering off of war production proportionate to the expansion of commercial demands. The disposal of stocks on hand or accruing under war contracts and the "demobilization" of war industry are to be carried out in such a way as to prevent a sudden collapse of prices and unemployment.

Private employment may not increase sufficiently, when war demands decline, to absorb all workers seeking employment. Public works are therefore being considered. Extensive public improvements are needed in India. The war has proved the present transportation

22. *International Labour Review*, January 1943, pp. 1–21.
23. India has from about two million men in her Army, Air Force, and in the Royal Indian Navy.
24. Welfare plans are under consideration for the benefit of the soldiers who will be demobilized. The government of India has allowed deferment of pay which is to be paid to the soldiers in a lump sum at the end of war. This deduction since April 1942 has been increased to 2 rupees per person per month in the case of soldiers and to 1 rupee per month in the case of enrolled noncombatants. A special fund is also to be established which will be used after the war to finance special schemes for the welfare of demobilized soldiers. The sums to be allocated and the nature of the "schemes" are to be worked out by the Reconstruction Committee in consultation with the provincial governments. See *International Labour Review*, February 1943, p. 218.

system inadequate:[25] there is need for more roads and highways, and for the development of inland waterways and marine transport. There is a demand also for drainage works and irrigation, canals, reforestation and land reclamation, hydroelectric works and other public improvements.

## 3. Programs of Social-Economic Organizations

The government of India has aimed to obtain the co-operation of the various organized economic groups in its policies and programs. These groups have on various occasions expressed their own views on postwar problems, often for the consideration of the government, but also as a means of clarifying issues and policies. Their declarations are not always in accord with governmental policies and some of them definitely presuppose a change in the political structure.

### a. RURAL CO-OPERATIVES AND PEASANT UNIONS

The land cultivators of India have made an effort at self-help through the organization of co-operative societies. Of special importance are the rural credit co-operatives which have assisted the farmers in obtaining loans at reasonable rates. In 1937-1938, there were over 105,000 co-operative societies in India with a membership of over 4.3 million. Some 90 per cent of these co-operatives were concerned with financing agriculture.[26]

Peasant leagues (Kisan Sabhas) and agricultural laborers' unions have arisen during the last few years in various parts of India to protect the interests of the small peasantry and landless workers and to press for reforms in the system of land tenure. The All-India Kisan Sabha which was formed to federate local and provincial organizations, and which claimed to represent 750,500 members, held its first session in 1939. The immediate aims of the leagues are to improve the irrigation system and local forest privileges, and to reduce rents and taxes. Their methods include meetings, demonstrations, rent strikes, and mass refusals to pay taxes. They are followers of Gandhi and of his nonviolence doctrines.[27]

One program for the relief and reorganization of Indian agriculture

25. India has 39,712 miles of railways and 307,000 miles of road.
26. *The Indian Year Book & Who's Who*, 1937–1938, Times of India Press, Bombay, p. 299.
27. *Labour Discussion Notes*, issued by the Socialist Clarity Groups, London, March 1941. For earlier development of rural co-operatives, see B. B. Mukherjee, *Cooperation and Rural Welfare in India*, Calcutta, 1929. The convention of the Kisan Sabha held early in 1943 was attended by 231 delegates claiming to represent 300,000 members.

by peasants' associations is that advocated by the South Indian
Agricultural Workers' Union whose secretary and leader is a member
of the Servants of India Society[28] and a lifelong student of Indian
agricultural conditions.[29] The proposals of the Union for settling the
land problem of India peaceably are as follows:

1. Creation of corporations under special statutes with reservation of adequate state control in essential general matters for utilization of state
   lands and for organizing rural industries.
2. Abolition of Zamindaris with compensation.
3. Abolition of private property in land in the case of noncultivators with
   provision for compensation, or fixation of the maximum cultivable area
   in the case of a single holder, with provision for occupancy rights at
   fair rents for cultivating tenants in the remaining lands.
4. Prohibition of habitual subletting except for legitimate purposes, on
   penalty of transferring all rights in land from the lessor to the lessee.
5. Fixation of a minimum wage for agricultural labor.
6. Restriction of sales of land and mortgages with possession only to
   cultivators.
7. Right of the state to appropriate private land which is not properly used.
8. Fair rent and minimum agricultural wage which will ensure a living
   wage for families of agricultural tenants or laborers, taking due account
   of the fact that every earner has to support at least one nonworking
   dependent.
9. Prevention of subdivision of holdings of cultivators (owners and tenants)
   below a size which is economic.
10. Cancellation of past debts in the case of holders of minimum holdings
    yielding a net income of RS. 150 and below; exemption of a minimum
    holding from attachment for debts.
11. Financial assistance by the state for purchase of lands for the conversion
    of uneconomic to economic holdings.
12. Reduction in land revenue for economic holdings, and a graded tax on
    larger holdings.
13. Development of irrigation facilities by the state.
14. Cheap supply of electric power by the state for agriculture.
15. Provision of free house sites for the agricultural population.
16. Promotion of an agricultural collective economy among cultivating
    small holders on the following lines:
    (a). Formation of co-operative societies at market centers for pro-
    moting group cultivation of crops, for introducing new processes and
    improvements, for sale of agricultural requisites and domestic require-

28. The Servants of India Society is a missionary organization of persons who pledge
themselves to give their best for the service of India. The members of the Society "accept
the British connections as ordained, in the inscrutable dispensation of Providence, for India's
good." Their goal is self-government of India within the Empire. The Society runs schools,
farming institutes, co-operatives, and carries on many other activities. See The Servants of
India Society, *Report for 1940–1941*, Poona; also The Servindia Rural Centre, Mayanoor,
*Reports and Accounts, 1939–1941*, Madras.
29. The program is printed in leaflet form by the South Indian Agricultural Union at
Mayanoor, S. I. and is dated 10-5-1941. It is signed by the Secretary of the Union, Mr. K. G.
Sivaswamy.

ments and for marketing produce, and developing livestock breeding, poultry keeping, and the like.

(b). Enforcement of compulsion among members towards group action in production where necessary, and by prohibiting outside dealings for purposes mentioned in (a).

(c). Formation of branches of the Provincial Co-operative Bank where co-operative societies cannot be formed.

(d). Formation of central societies subject to state control for issue of credit, supplies, and sale.

(e). Creation of a whole-time rural development service and its regulation and control on a provincial basis by a body comprising representatives of societies and paid workers in the movement.

(f). Development of distributive co-operative societies in towns either as branches of village agricultural co-operatives or as consumer's societies; co-ordination of these societies with agricultural co-operatives and their central societies.

17. Formation of central bodies by the state for regulating agricultural production, ensuring a price, finding markets, and regulating imports.

## b. EMPLOYERS' ASSOCIATIONS

There are several All-India organizations of businessmen, the most important of which are the All-India Organization of Industrial Employers, the Associated Chambers of Commerce of India, and the Employers' Federation of India.[30] Besides these, some provincial and local employers' organizations have more than local influence. During 1941-1942, the three All-India associations held conferences which dealt largely with war problems, but which discussed also questions of postwar policy.

The employers' associations are concerned particularly with postwar industrialization and labor policy. At the meeting of the All-India Organization of Industrial Employers in 1941, the president of the Organization expressed the view that "to develop industry one must first develop its workers and that the workers' well-being is an industrial insurance, an industrial investment." He stated further that "the theory that the worker's place in the employer's production scheme is that of a producing machine combining cheapest possible cost with the highest possible efficiency is happily out of date."[31]

The Employers' Federation emphasized the need to develop the basic industries of engineering, machine tools, power and transport, if India is to become a really important industrial country. The president of the Federation welcomed the appointment of postwar recon-

30. Some of India's industries are dominated by international cartels, e.g., The Association of Indian Cement Industries, The Jute Mill Owners' Association, etc.
31. *International Labour Review*, September 1942, p. 362.

struction committees by the government though he found them too "officialized." He called for more assurance from the government that protection will be accorded not only to war industries, but to "all deserving industries."[32]

More far-reaching are the recommendations formulated at the 1942 convention of the Federation of Indian Chambers of Commerce and Industry. The object of economic planning was described by spokesmen of the Federation as: (1) "to give employment to the population of the country which will enable it to maintain a reasonable and decent standard of living; and (2) to keep the economy of the country balanced with regard to agriculture and manufacturing industries."

The convention laid much stress on desirable agricultural changes. It called for a diversion of land from commercial to food crops, for the development of long-staple cotton to replace the unmarketable surpluses of short-staple cotton, and for relief to jute growers. The Chambers of Commerce Federation recommends: (1) proper planning of crops with a view to increasing internal consumption; (2) the establishment of new industries to absorb a large part of accumulated stocks of raw materials; (3) search for new markets for agricultural products; and (4) the appointment of trade delegations to neighboring countries.

Many recommendations were also made by the Federation of Chambers of Commerce for the establishment or expansion of particular industries with government aid. Particular emphasis is laid on the development of the power alcohol industry in view of fuel shortages. It is also urged that India's rapidly growing sterling balances be used to strengthen the position of Indian capital in industry, especially in the jute, rubber and oil industries.

Although they favor an expansion of export trade, the several groups of Indian industrialists believe that the postwar industrial development of India depends primarily on the home market. Higher living standards and greater agricultural prosperity are necessary, in their opinion, to create a larger internal market for industrial products.[33]

### C. THE POSITION OF THE TRADE UNIONS

The growth of industrialism since the First World War has been accompanied, in India as elsewhere, by the emergence of a trade union

32. *Ibid.*, p. 363.
33. See Gilbert E. Hubbard, *Eastern Industrialization and Its Effects on the West*, London, 1938, p. 317.

movement. The peculiar geographic, economic and social conditions, however, have hampered the growth of labor organization, and the Indian trade unions are still, with a few exceptions, small and weak.[34] Nevertheless, their membership has increased from about 400,000 in 1938-1939 to 511,000 in 1939-1940.[35]

Indian trade unions are weakened by internal divisions. The largest organization is the All-India Trade Union Congress which was organized in 1920-1921 and which has generally been closely connected with the Indian National Congress. The Trade Union Congress split because some of its leaders and members disapproved the negative attitude of the Congress Party towards the war. The discontented elements broke away in 1941 and formed a new organization known as the Federation of Indian Labour which is under the influence of more radical and "leftist" leaders.[36]

Neither of the two labor organizations has formulated any specific postwar policies. The All-India Trade Union Congress follows to a large extent the lead of the Congress Party. The new Federation of Indian Labour is primarily interested in stimulating the war effort of Indian workers. Its first conference in 1941 advocated the development of large-scale industries with government aid.[37]

### 4. Economic and Social Plans of the Congress Party

Although it devotes its energies almost entirely to political reform, the Congress Party has formulated an economic and social program to guide its postwar activities.

The Party is far from homogeneous. Its membership includes landlords, peasants, employers, workers, and middle-class people. Its financial support comes from some of the big industrialists, e.g., the Birla and the Tata firms. Its leadership includes men, like Nehru, who are socialists and others who are very far from socialism, and the groupings within the Party range from the conservative Right to the radical Left.

The Congress Party has tried to conciliate different views in a program which would be acceptable to all its groups. As far back as May 1929, the Working Committee of the National Congress declared that,

---

34. The larger unions include the All-India Railwaymen's Federation and the Textile Labor Association of Ahmedabad.

35. *International Labour Review*, August 1942, p. 226.

36. See M. N. Roy, "Indian Labor at War," *Far Eastern Survey*, New York, January 25, 1943.

37. *International Labour Review*, May 1942 and July 1942.

"the great poverty of the Indian people is due not only to foreign exploitation, but also to the structure of society, which the alien rulers support so that their exploitation may continue. In order to end the exploitation of the masses, political freedom must include real economic freedom of the starving millions." Since then, the Party has on several occasions formulated a series of specific demands and policies which may be summarized as follows:[38]

*Agriculture*

1. Freedom of organization of agricultural labor and peasants.
2. Standard provisions for living wages and suitable working conditions for agricultural labor.
3. Just and fair relief of agricultural indebtedness; a moratorium on agricultural debts and the establishment of tribunals for inquiry into those debts.
4. Fixity of land tenure and a reduction in rent and revenue demands.
5. Just allotment of state expenditures for the social, economic, and cultural amenities of villages.
6. The establishment of common pasture land.
7. The development of co-operative farming.
8. A fostering of industry for the rural unemployed.

*Industry and Labor*

1. State ownership of key industries and services, mineral resources, railways, waterways, shipping, and other forms of public transport.
2. Regulation of currency and exchange in the national interest, control of interest rates and elimination of usury.
3. The protection of indigenous cloth and the exclusion of foreign cloth and yarn.
4. The protection of labor from serfdom and conditions bordering on serfdom. (Indenture and the jobber system of recruitment.)
5. The right of workers to form unions and to protect their interests.
6. Protection of women workers and the abolition of child labor.

*Taxation and Public Expenditures*

1. Reform of the system of land tenure and rent, and an equitable adjustment of the burdens upon agricultural land to give relief to the smaller peasantry.
2. Progressive income taxes.

38. The discussion of this section is based on notes taken from the report of the Congress National Planning Committee proceedings by Mr. John Gunther. A photostat copy of the resolutions of the Committee is in the Library of Congress. It is believed that it is the only copy of the resolutions to have reached the United States. While the material relates to the period before 1939, the programs outlined are indicative of the postwar India envisioned by the Congress Party.

3. The reduction of expenditures and salaries in civil departments.
4. The abolition of duties on salt manufacture.

*Social*

1. Free and compulsory primary education.
2. Prohibition of the use of intoxicating drinks and drugs.

This program contains some seemingly contradictory items, but the Party regards them as capable of reconciliation. As is well known, Gandhi and the Congress Party as a whole have long advocated the Swadeshi policy—the development of cottage goods industries. A resolution of the Working Committee of the Party of July 1934 committed Congress members to use, and to encourage the use of, hand-spun and hand-woven *khadi* to the exclusion of other types of cloth. In October 1934, the All-India Village Industries Association was constituted, to promote "the revival and encouragement of small village industries and the moral and physical advance of such villages."

Efforts have since been made to encourage consumption of goods produced by cottage and small industries. The latter must accept "the guidance of Congress on any items in the regulation of prices and in the matter of the wages and welfare of the labor under their control." The development of these industries, it is claimed, will serve to relieve the problem of chronic agricultural unemployment, and aid in raising the living standards and self-sufficiency of the villages.

Congress Party leaders minimize the conflict between this policy and the development of large-scale industries in urban centers. Jawaharlal Nehru has stated that certain industries must by their very nature be large, but that there must be a demarcation of the domains of large-scale and cottage industries for an orderly and far-reaching improvement of living standards of the mass of the Indian people. A resolution passed by the Congress Party in 1938 claimed that the economic regeneration of India is impossible without industrialization, and that industrialization implies national planning for large-scale heavy industries, medium-scale industries, and cottage industries. The resolution recommended specifically the establishment of large-scale industries for the production of machinery, tools, automobiles and accessories; of all equipment for transportation, communication, and electric plants; of heavy chemicals, fertilizers, and metals.

The resolutions of the Working Committee of the Congress contain several references to public ownership of basic industries. In 1929 the Working Committee stated that "to remove poverty and misery and to ameliorate the condition of the Indian masses it is essential to make revolutionary changes in the present economic and social structure of society, and to remove gross inequalities." Mr. Nehru explained this statement as follows: "The resolution indicates an approval of socialistic theories, but apart from this general approval and some further advance in subsequent resolutions the Congress has not in any way accepted socialism." It was also impractical, in Mr. Nehru's opinion, to insist on state management of those industries which are already in private hands. Nehru urged, however, that the state "take necessary steps to assure uniformity among enterprises with a view to basic policy and objectives." Such action by the state was necessary in all instances where state aid or protection is granted to private industries, in the case of monopolies, and of industries whose policies conflict with national measures for the protection of labor and consumers.

At the time these programs were being elaborated, the Congress Party appointed an All-India Planning Committee to determine the most suitable location of particular industries, methods of finance and management, and whether an enterprise should be public or private. The Planning Committee defined the objectives of national planning in India as follows:

The object of comprehensive national planning is to enforce the well-being of the community, principally by intensifying the economic development of that community on an all-around basis in an ordered, systematic manner so as to observe a due proportion between the various forms of producing new wealth; to secure its equitable distribution among the members of the community, and to ensure adjustment between the interests of producers and consumers individually and the community collectively.

## 5. POSTWAR INDIA AND EXTERNAL RELATIONS

India thus will develop chiefly its home market after the war. Indian manufacturers and businessmen, regardless of political parties, want protective policies and government aid for this purpose. The various political groups have no quarrel on this issue.

However, there is no question that India must also develop its economic relations with the rest of the world. Such Indian products as tea, jute, cotton, hides, etc., must be sold in foreign markets. And though the war has stimulated the growth of industry and savings in

India, expansion after the war will depend in large measure on foreign capital and technical aid.

Various suggestions have been made by Indian spokesmen as to the place which India may and should have in the postwar world economy. These suggestions will not be considered here, first because they are rather vague, and second, because they are bound up with problems of India's political status and of international political organization which are outside the scope of this study.

*Chapter 13*

# THE RECONSTRUCTION OF CHINA

In china, as in the Soviet Union and some countries of Latin America, the movement towards national reconstruction antedates the war. It derives its inspiration from a national revolution which has been in progress for over two decades. In order to make postwar programs more understandable, it is necessary to present them against the background of prewar plans and developments.

## 1. Sun Yat-sen's Principles and Program

The basis for planning in China today was laid down by Dr. Sun Yat-sen, Father of the Chinese Republic, in his various writings, especially in his books, *Three Principles of the People* and *International Development of China*.[1] After two decades of internal upheaval and war, the Chinese government still proclaims itself to be a revolutionary government whose aim is the realization of the ideas of Sun Yat-sen. In a recent statement which had a world-wide hearing, Generalissimo Chiang K'ai-shek reaffirmed this basis in the following words:

What we mean by revolution is the attainment of all three of Dr. Sun's basic principles of national revolution: national independence, progressive realization of democracy, and a rising level of living conditions for the masses. When victory comes at the end of this war, we shall have fully achieved national independence but will have far to go to attain our other two objectives. Hence our claim that ours is still a revolutionary government, which means no more or less than it is a government dedicated to attaining these other two objectives.[2]

Sun Yat-sen went beyond general principles and outlined a specific program for the development of China which has since served as a sort of basic blueprint. The main points are:

1. Development of a communications system:
   100,000 miles of railways;
   1,000,000 miles of macadam highways;
   Improvement of existing canals;
   Construction of new canals;
   River conservancy;
   Construction of more telegraph and telephone lines and systems.

1. *Three Principles of the People* was published in 1921.
2. Generalissimo Chiang K'ai-shek's speech read before the New York Herald Tribune Forum, November 17, 1942. For text see *Contemporary China*, November 30, 1942, Vol. II, No. 14.

2. Development of commercial harbors in North, East and South China.
3. Development of modern cities in all railway centers and alongside harbors.
4. Water power development.
5. Building of iron, steel and cement works on a large scale to supply the above needs.
6. Mineral development.
7. Agricultural development.
8. Irrigation work on a large scale in Mongolia and Sinkiang.
9. Reforestation in Central and North China.
10. Colonization and development of Manchuria, Sinkiang, Chinghai (Kokonor), and Tibet.[3]

For the advancement of the general welfare and livelihood of the people, Dr. Sun further outlined various projects concerning the food industry, the clothing industry, the housing industry, the motor industry and the printing industry.

This economic blueprint, according to Sun Yat-sen, could be put into effect only by private and public enterprise working together. Above all, Dr. Sun emphasized the need for international co-operation in this huge undertaking. He visioned China as an "economic ocean" capable of absorbing most of the surplus capital of the advanced industrial countries. In order to carry out the project successfully, Dr. Sun suggested that the various governments of the capital-supplying powers agree to joint action and a unified policy, and that they form an international organization "with their war work organizers, administrators and experts of various lines to formulate plans and to standardize materials in order to prevent waste and to facilitate work." Dr. Sun further emphasized the importance of gaining the confidence and co-operation of the Chinese people for such a reconstruction program. Dr. Sun left the details of the proposed international organization to be elaborated, and he also allowed for changes in the program as studies and surveys brought more data to light.

## 2. Prewar and War Developments, 1928–1943

After the National Government of Chiang K'ai-shek was established in Nanking in 1927, attempts were begun to put some of Sun Yat-sen's ideas into practice. A six-year plan for highway-railway construction and for industrial development was prepared in 1931,

3. For further details, see W. K. Chen, "The Postwar Reconstruction of China: Its Program and Proper Machinery," *National Reconstruction*, August 1942, Vol. I, pp. 54–63; also *Contemporary China*, January 11, 1943.

and a National Economic Council was established in the same year to aid and direct the work. After the disastrous floods of the Yangtze and Hwai rivers in 1931 and the Japanese occupation of Manchuria and Inner Mongolia, attention was turned largely to hydraulic works and to land reclamation projects. Between 1933 and 1937, considerable progress was made in extending the railway system, building new roads, in the development of aviation, the reform of the monetary and tax systems, and in increasing agricultural and mineral output.[4]

The outbreak of the war with Japan in July 1937, and the transfer of the capital to Chungking changed the activities of the Chinese government in several ways. Military needs became of paramount concern and most of the industrial and economic plans were geared to these needs. The field of operations was restricted to the area of Free China and emphasis was shifted to the development of the western and southwestern regions of the country. The government directed its energies towards building up new industrial and mining enterprises in these regions and towards the expansion of agricultural output not only for domestic use but also for export.

To carry out these immediate and practical programs, the planning machinery of the government was reorganized and enlarged. The Ministry of Economic Affairs became the most important agency for promoting the industrialization of China and absorbed the National Economic Council and other pre-existing planning agencies. The National Resources Commission was incorporated into the Ministry of Economic Affairs, but continued to play a leading part in developing and operating mining, electric power, and other basic industrial public enterprises. A Central Planning Board was established to consider the problems of over-all planning for economic reconstruction.[5]

### 3. Postwar Economic and Social Objectives

Six years of war have had their effect on Chinese programs of economic and social development. While the general aims of national development remain the same, official statements of government spokesmen now place more emphasis than before on national security and on regional development.

The shift in outlook is reflected in the "Program of Armed Resist-

4. For details, see Lewis L. Lorwin, *International Economic Development*, pp. 42–45.
5. For the organization of national planning agencies, *ibid.*, pp. 45–50; also, "China's Wartime Economy," in *Contemporary China*, August 24, 1942; and *The Economist*, London, October 17, 1942.

ance and National Reconstruction" adopted by the Kuomintang National Congress[6] on March 29, 1938. The "Program" laid down the principle that during the war "economic reconstruction shall concern itself mainly with matters of military importance and only incidentally with matters which contribute to the improvement of the livelihood of the people."[7] Since this statement was made, the change in emphasis has made itself felt also in current thinking about the postwar period.

The main features of the planned postwar development are a rapid industrialization of China, with emphasis on heavy industries, power plants, chemicals, railway and highway transportation, aviation and port facilities. Light industries will be of secondary importance. Industrial development will proceed under state guidance and to a large extent under state ownership and direction. The shortage of private industrial capital in China, the absence of a vigorous industrial class, and the large financial problems involved are presumed to necessitate state action and control.[8] The Chinese scientists estimate that the natural resources of China allow for a substantial degree of industrialization. Besides, Chinese leaders claim that under proper conditions China could use large amounts of imported raw materials in combination with her own man power.

## 4. NATIONAL AND REGIONAL PLANS

Specific plans for national and regional development are now being prepared by various departments of the National Government, especially by the National Resources Commission,[9] and by the People's Political Council.[10]

6. The Kuomintang Party, reorganized in 1924, is the only legal political party in Free China. It regards itself as the source from which the government derives its real power. It is strongly organized locally, and on the provincial level, and is highly centralized. It is an elaborate organism with many divisions and subdivisions which examine in advance the questions of public interest and formulate the policies on which the government is to act. It also has a number of affiliated organizations such as the Central Political Institute, the Youth Corps, the National Spiritual Mobilization and the Mass Mobilization—by means of which it aims to influence the mass of the people. See Paul M. A. Linebarger, *The China of Chiang K'ai-shek*, World Peace Foundation, Boston, 1941, pp. 124–158.

7. *Contemporary China*, January 25, 1942.

8. See Robert W. Barnett, *Factors in Chinese Economic Reconstruction*, Institute of Pacific Relations (mimeographed). Also, Guenther Stein, "Chungking Considers the Future," *Far Eastern Survey*, September 7, 1942.

9. According to recent reports, a general official organization has been established to study postwar problems and planning.

10. The People's Political Council was first organized in July 1938, and was reorganized in 1941 and 1942. It has no legislative powers, but acts as an advisory and supervisory organ of the National Government. It makes recommendations to the government and reviews reports of the government on national problems and policies. The Council which was in

### a. FIVE- AND TEN-YEAR NATIONAL PLANS

Economic thinking in China runs in terms of three-, five-, and ten-year industrial plans. In 1936, the National Resources Commission prepared a three-year industrial program which had to be dropped when war with Japan began in 1937. Dr. Wong, Minister of Economic Affairs, outlined some time ago a ten-year program which, in his opinion, would be "big enough to be of real value to the country but modest enough to be within the means of the people." While this program is not known to have been formally adopted, it is indicative of government thinking on the subject. Some of the goals of this plan are stated as follows:

| Commodity | Ten-Year Output | Tenth Year Output |
|---|---|---|
| Steel | 14,000,000 tons | 5,000,000 tons |
| Coal | 500,000,000 tons | 100,000,000 tons |
| Gold | 12,000,000 oz. | 2,500,000 oz. |
| Cement | 85,000,000 barrels | 20,000,000 barrels |
| Steel Plates | 5,000,000 tons | 1,000,000 tons |
| Cotton Yarn | 29,000,000 bales | 5,000,000 bales |
| Railways | 48,000 kil. | |
| Rails | 3,360,000 tons | |
| Locomotives | 2,400 | |
| Steamships | 3,000,000 tons | |

The National Resources Commission is reported to be studying a more modest postwar five-year plan. The plan will require at least 30,000 engineers and 800,000 skilled workers. The Commission has now only 9,534 engineers and 170,000 skilled workers. A program to train engineers and technicians has been started.[11]

### b. PLANS FOR REGIONAL DEVELOPMENT

In outlining his program for the economic development of China, Sun Yat-sen projected schemes for the development of the various regions of the country, especially of the Northwest. The war with Japan has given a strong impetus to the idea of regional planning. In all current plans, emphasis is placed on the need for regional plan-

---

session in October 1942, consisted of 240 members. Of these, 160 were elected by the provincial and municipal peoples' councils; the rest represented economic and cultural institutions or were appointed by the government. The Council passed over fifty resolutions and recommendations bearing on various economic, political and administrative problems. The Council is a war substitute for a National Assembly which cannot meet as a result of the military situation. See Guenther Stein, "Wartime Government in China," *Far Eastern Survey*, December 14, 1942.

11. *Contemporary China*, September 7, 1942.

ning agencies under central direction to accelerate the use of regional resources. Regional planning under national guidance is advocated in order to make Chinese industry less vulnerable to future aggression, to relieve population pressure in central and eastern China by the colonization and development of the Northwest and Southwest,[12] and to develop a balanced national economy.

Planning commissions and "development corporations" have been organized in fourteen provinces with the aid of the National Government.[13] Many factories have been established by these authorities, and several provinces have mapped out three-year or five-year plans. Chekiang Province is an example of provincial reconstruction, in co-operation with the central government. Although fighting has reduced its sphere of activities, the Reconstruction Department of the provincial government continues its work. Agriculture, industry, co-operatives, shipping, and public utility enterprises are included in a comprehensive plan.

Under the Department are twenty different units, each of which handles its own particular province-wide functions. The Agricultural Improvement Institute, one of the most important of the twenty, is responsible for experiment and training work in the agricultural field, for the increase of food production, propagation of selected seeds, and the development of Chekiang's special products. The Handicraft Promotion Bureau has as its main work the production of articles of daily use through the promotion of rural and small industries and handicrafts. Model and experimental plants have been established to train skilled labor. An oil, tea, cotton and silk administration has been established by the provincial authorities jointly with the Foreign Trade Commission and the Agricultural Credit Administration of the National Government to promote the output of these four commodities.

The Cooperative Enterprises Administration supplies funds to co-operative enterprises in the province and promotes the organization of co-operative societies and banks. The Reconstruction Department is operating iron and chemical works, a spinning and weaving plant and an electric supply shop, each of which is capitalized at between one and two million Chinese dollars. In the field of communications,

12 "China's Postwar Economic Reconstruction," *Contemporary China*, January 25, 1943.
13. Such are the Shensi Development Corporation, the Yunnan Enterprise Bureau, the Szechwan-Sinkiang Development Corporation.

the Department is operating a highway transportation company, a shipping administration and a telephone company.[14]

Increased efforts to draw the "Great Northwest"—the area formed by the provinces of Sinkiang (Chinese Turkestan), Kansu, Chinghai (Kokonor), Ningsia and Shensi—closer to the central government have taken form in a number of specific measures. The war has accelerated industrial progress in this area and Lanchow in Kansu province has become not only the administrative center of the Northwest, but also one of the main eight or ten centers of Free China's war effort.[15]

In September 1942, the Executive Yuan announced its decision to appropriate CNC $100 million at the rate of $10 million a year for irrigation projects among the seventeen districts in the Kansu corridor. A large portion of Kansu's population of 6 million will benefit directly or indirectly. The plans for the irrigation of the Northwest will affect several districts known at one time as the granary of the Northwest, but which have become almost barren since the ancient irrigation canals became dry more than a century ago.

In addition to the large irrigation project, afforestation is under way. Means for increasing the number of sheep and improving their wool are being studied, together with means for expanding the modern spinning and weaving industries which the Chinese industrial co-operatives introduced into Kansu. The small engineering shops which the war brought to Lanchow and a few other cities of the Northwest are gradually being developed into a solid industry deriving its raw material from insufficiently exploited or as yet untapped resources of the local region. Power plants to make use of rapid streams are being projected. Transportation is one of the most acute problems. None of the northwestern provinces, with the sole exception of Shensi, possesses a single mile of railway and the international Sino-Russian route which goes from Szechwan through Shensi, Kansu and Sinkiang is the only major highway of the territory.

Settlement on the land is also to be started soon. The Southwest is regarded as a future center of heavy industries. It is proposed to establish heavy industries immediately after the war in Hsiantan and

14. *China at War*, October 1942. For further details, see Lorwin, *International Economic Development*, pp. 47–48. For developments in another province see "Reconstruction in Szechwan," *China at War*, March 1943.
15. See Guenther Stein, *Christian Science Monitor*, September 16, 1942.

Chuchow in Hunan; Chungking and Chikiang in Szechwan; and Kiating, Wutungchiao, and Tzeliuching in Szechwan. Four other potential industrial centers in the interior provinces are: the Chungking area, based upon the Kialing and Nanchuan coal fields and the Chikiang iron deposits; the Kiating-Loshan industrial area, around Kunming, which produces tin and copper and is abundantly provided with coal; the Lancho-Sian industrial area which has reserves of coal and petroleum and produces raw cotton and wool.[16]

The consensus of opinion in China is that the main regions of the country can and should be developed in accordance with their local resources as parts of an integrated and balanced national economic plan.

### C. THE FUTURE OF PRIVATE ENTERPRISE

While national economic plans emphasize large projects of a public character, they provide a place also for private enterprise. The National Government has been encouraging private enterprise since 1938 as a war measure,[17] and it is expected to continue this policy after the war in order to accelerate the utilization of all economic and human resources.

Government aid is now granted to Chinese-owned private industrial enterprises in the following groups: (1) those engaged in the manufacture of goods that compete with imported goods in the domestic market or goods in foreign markets; (2) those first adopting the latest foreign methods of production; and (3) those employing new patents granted by the Chinese government. The forms of assistance are reductions of, or exemptions from, export duties or taxes on raw materials; reduction of freight charges on government-owned transportation systems; the granting of subsidies; and the granting of exclusive manufacturing rights in a specified locality for a period of not more than five years.

The government also encourages the development by private interests of specially important industries. It provides aid to enterprises owned and operated by Chinese that have a paid-up capital of more than a million dollars and which manufacture motors, dynamos, electrical equipment, tools, machines, or transportation equipment, or

16. See H. D. Fong, *Post-War Industrialization of China*, National Planning Association, Washington, 1942.
17. This is being done under the Industrial Encouragement Act of June 7, 1938, the Regulations Governing Government Aid to Special Industries of the same date, and the Regulations Governing the Encouragement of War-Time Industry of November 25, 1938.

engage in various forms of metallurgical work or in the refining of liquid fuel. To these industries the government guarantees profits limited to 5 per cent per annum on paid-up capital and 6 per cent per annum on bonds issued within a period of seven years and grants cash subsidies on the basis of production costs and of the market price of industrial commodities during the year.

The Ministry of Economic Affairs also provides government assistance to small industries with a capital investment of $10,000 to $50,-000, half of which must be paid up. In order to qualify for obtaining such aid, the industries concerned must (1) be able to produce commodities that can be used for military purposes or for improving the welfare of the people; (2) use native raw materials solely or largely; (3) use modern methods or improved native methods of manufacturing; (4) be able to fulfill their own schedules of production; (5) have real prospects of development; (6) have made new inventions or devised new methods of production.

It is generally agreed that similar measures on behalf of private industry are to be continued after the war, and that private initiative may be combined with government direction in the development of various industries. The official position of the government on this question has been stated by Dr. Wong Wen-hao, Minister of Economic Affairs and Chairman of the National Resources Commission:

The purpose of government enterprise is to create wealth for the State and not to compete with the people; it should be confined, therefore, to the following types of enterprises: (1) enterprises urgently needed by the government and requiring specialized management; (2) enterprises requiring large-scale planning or control; (3) enterprises too large or difficult to be undertaken by private entrepreneurs; (4) enterprises urgently needed for national defense but offering no prospect of profit to the private entrepreneur; (5) enterprises supplying power and fuel to private industries. . . .

Only enterprises that can be classified in any of the above categories will be undertaken by the government. If private investors wish to put their money in government enterprises, agreement should be reached for joint operation. The government will allow private entrepreneurs complete freedom to engage in fields of enterprise in which it also is engaged, except in cases where restrictive action is justifiable for special reasons. Even in cases where certain fields of economic activity are reserved by law to government enterprise, the government can set up companies jointly with private interests or lease concessions to private entrepreneurs. . . . Our most urgent need at present is to increase production enormously in order to meet the demands of the front and the rear. If we define the scope of government enterprise too broadly, and if the resources of the government are not sufficient to develop to the fullest extent the enterprises assigned to it, there is danger that the country's productive power will be needlessly curtailed. Thus, while we are trying our best to establish government enterprises, we are also paying close attention to the encouragement and promotion of private enterprise.[18]

## d. THE INDUSTRIAL CO-OPERATIVES (CIC)

The National Government is also lending its support to the development of industrial co-operation which is expected to be important in the postwar economy of China. The plan for the industrial co-operatives came into being in the difficult days of 1938. It called for development of a widespread system of small-scale, co-operative workshops scattered throughout the interior of Free China. These "vest pocket" industries were to have three functions: (1) to provide productive jobs for refugees; (2) to create new supplies of consumer, medical and military goods; and (3) to erect an economic wall against the traffic in smuggled Japanese goods.

With the financial and moral aid of the government and of sympathizers outside China, the Chinese Industrial Cooperatives have grown to an industrial organization comprising over 1,700 co-operative workshops throughout eighteen provinces of Free China. They give employment to many thousands of workers, and indirectly provide a livelihood for large numbers of formerly destitute refugees. They produce about 500 different commodities, and are an important factor in supplying the country with some of its elementary needs. Among items produced are clothing, shoes, army blankets, soap, porcelain, leather goods, chemical products, medical goods, machinery, power equipment, minerals, transport facilities and military material.

The CIC are sponsored by the Executive Yuan, and Dr. H. H. K'ung, the Minister of Finance and Vice President of the Yuan, is president of the organization. Dr. K'ung has supported the movement from its early days because he believes that "through this movement not only China's economic resources will be mobilized to offset the loss of the occupied areas, but also a foundation will be laid for the new economic order of the future, more consonant with Chinese life and free from the evils which inevitably accompany industrialization of the accepted pattern."[19]

In organization, procedure, and methods of financing, the Chinese Industrial Cooperatives differ markedly from familiar types of consumer or productive co-operation. They are a product of war condi-

18. Quoted by Pi Ming, "The Relation Between Government Enterprise and Private Industry," *Hsin Chin Chi*, July 16, 1939, Vol. II, No. 3, pp. 55–56. From unpublished manuscript on the Economic Development of China submitted to the Institute of Pacific Relations.
19. Delbert Johnson, *China's Industrial Cooperatives* (Leaflet).

tions. Their role after the war will depend on their capacity to find a place for themselves between private industry and government enterprise. Those who sponsor the industrial co-operatives believe that they are peculiarly fitted to meet China's postwar needs for low-priced goods and to gratify the desire of Chinese artisans and workers for collective self-employment.

### e. LAND REFORM AND RESETTLEMENT

The reform of land tenure in China has been both one of the main goals of the National Revolution and one of its main stumbling blocks. The position of the National Government and of the Kuomintang on this issue was formulated in the Draft Constitution of 1936[20] as follows:

Article 117. The land within the territorial limits of the Republic of China belongs to the people as a whole. Any part thereof the ownership of which has been lawfully acquired by an individual or individuals shall be protected by, and subject to, the restrictions of law.
The State may, in accordance with law, tax or expropriate private land on the basis of the value declared by the owner or assessed by the government.
Every landowner is amenable to the duty of utilizing his land to the fullest extent.
Article 118. All subterranean minerals and natural forces which are economically utilizable for public benefit belong to the State and shall not be affected by private ownership of land.
Article 119. The unearned increment shall be fixed by means of a land-value increment tax and devoted to public benefit.
Article 120. In readjusting the distribution of land, the State shall be guided by the principle of aiding and protecting the land-owning farmers and the land-utilizing owners.

The aims of the government are thus to create a landowning farming class which would be free from the exactions of a moneylending and officeholding class of landlords. So far the government has made only the first steps in this direction. The Ministry of Agriculture, created in 1939, the Agricultural Credit Administration, the National Agricultural Production Commission, and the Joint Office of the Four Government Banks have extended loans to farmers and given them subsidies and technical aid with a view to increasing agricultural output. The Farmers Bank of China issued in 1942 land bonds worth 100 million yuan for the purchase and distribution of land to small

20. On May 5, 1936, the Legislative Yuan promulgated the Draft Permanent Constitution which still is the official proposal for a permanent constitution to be ratified by the National Constituent Congress which is to meet after the war. For a translation of articles 117–120 which bear on land reform, see Paul M. A. Linebarger, *op. cit.*, p. 296.

farmers.[21] Many of the provincial governments have done much to establish agricultural experiment stations, to promote scientific farming, to improve horticulture, sericulture, and animal husbandry, and to expand the cultivation of tobacco, sugar, cotton and other agricultural products. However, "readjusting the distribution of land" remains one of the basic postwar tasks.

The National Government has also encouraged land reclamation and settlement of war refugees on the land. The Ministry of Economic Affairs, in co-operation with the National Relief Commission and the provincial governments, has made extensive surveys of the possibilities and conditions for settlement in the Northwest, Southwest, Kiangsi and Fukien. It is expected that after the war it will be possible to settle several million farmers on reclaimed land in Shensi, Szechwan, Yunnan, and Kwangsi. A program of organized colonization is proposed for Manchuria where, according to some, the present population of some 30 million could be increased to 100 million within the next thirty years.

### f. FINANCIAL REORGANIZATION

China's current inflationary problem due to war conditions must be met if the economic plans are to be carried out.[22] The government of China will also have to unify the diverse monetary systems set up in different parts of the country as a result of Japanese occupation, puppet governments, and local isolation, and to adjust the external value of the national currency to its internal purchasing power.

The efforts of the National Government towards currency and banking reform since 1935 have been thwarted by war and internal difficulties. The nature of these efforts, however, has been fairly consistent. They aim to secure a uniform issue of notes throughout the country, a restriction of the amount of notes in circulation, the nationalization of gold and silver to replenish the reserves for the notes and the placing of the Central Bank under government control.[23]

### 5. SOCIAL RECONSTRUCTION

The plans of the National Government envisage what may be called a "mixed economic system" in which the basic industries will

21. "Land Reforms Increase Farm Owners," *China at War*, February 1943.

22. The shortage of goods, the printing of money by the government to cover the largest part of the huge military expenditures, the inadequate income from taxation, etc., have resulted in an extremely serious inflationary situation in China. See Lawrence K. Rosinger, *China's War Economy*, Foreign Policy Reports, New York, November 15, 1942.

23. See Frank Tamagna, "China's Post-War Financial Problems," *Pacific Affairs*, September 1942.

be managed by the state, while the light industries, agriculture and trade will be left to private enterprise and to co-operative associations. This system is often described as state capitalism because of the predominant part which the state will play in operating or controlling the industrial activities of the country.

The purposes which the postwar economy of China is to serve are strategic and social. In accordance with the principles of Sun Yat-sen, as peace becomes more secure, social aims must be accorded increasing importance. The economic development of the country is to become more and more a means of improving the "livelihood of the people."

The Draft Constitution of 1936 contains a number of articles dealing with the measures which the state is to carry out for such social purposes. The state is to improve rural living conditions and to enforce protective labor policies. Special protection is to be accorded women and children. The state is to accord "suitable relief to the aged, feeble or disabled who are incapable of earning a living." Free education is to be provided for all children between the ages of six and twelve. Equal opportunities are to be given to the people of different sections of the country to receive higher education. All this is in line with the social legislation of the western world. The scope of the proposed provisions is, however, still rather limited.

The social changes aimed at by the National Government affect every phase of China's life. Reforms are to be made in local and provincial administration to break down the old provincial divisions by increasing the number of political units directly responsible to the central government. Illiteracy is to be wiped out among the large masses of the people[24] and especially in the rural areas through the Mass Education Movement[25] and the National Institute of Rural Reconstruction.

While the best traditions of the Chinese family system are to be retained, new social customs are to be encouraged through the New Life Movement embodying the four basic virtues of *li, i, lien, ch'ih:* reasonableness, propriety (in accordance with social order, natural

24. Of the 450 million people of China, only about 90 million are literate. Of the 360 million illiterates, 45 million are between the ages of six and twelve and about 30 million between twelve and fifteen years of age. About 80 million are over forty-five years of age. See Linebarger, *op. cit.,* p. 215.
25. The Mass Education Movement was started in 1923 and has done much, under the leadership of Dr. James Y. C. Yen, to educate the rural masses and to improve social and cultural conditions in the villages. It is one of the important factors in rural reconstruction.

law and national discipline), clearness (that which is right agrees with *li* and *i*), and consciousness (being ashamed of contravening the other principles). The leaders of this movement stress simplicity of clothing, short hair, personal cleanliness, obedience to the government and the importance of education.[26]

## 6. INTERNATIONAL CAPITAL REQUIREMENTS

China clearly realizes that the success of national policies will be closely bound up with postwar international conditions. The manner in which and the degree to which Chinese postwar aims are carried out will depend on four factors: (1) the complete abolition of extraterritoriality; (2) the re-unification of China; (3) the terms of the peace settlement; and (4) the supply of foreign capital.

As far as extraterritoriality is concerned, the United States and Great Britain signed treaties with the Chinese Republic on January 11, 1943, by which they relinquished all extraterritorial rights.[27] The end of the war will presumably create the conditions necessary for the re-unification of all Chinese lands under the central government. Some of the terms of peace which the Chinese have outlined, e.g., the complete disarmament of Japan, are part of the United Nations program, though others, e.g., those relating to the status of Korea and Indo-China as well as certain economic demands, depend on the general settlement following the war.

Following Sun Yat-sen, the spokesmen of China would welcome the co-operation of foreign capital in the postwar development of China. The Third People's Political Council at its sessions in October 1942 adopted a resolution requesting the government to "draft a program for inviting Allied capital and technical cooperation so as to accelerate the materialization of Dr. Sun Yat-sen's industrial plan for China." The amount of credits that China can use has been estimated in billions of dollars.[28] China hopes that the largest part of such credits may be supplied by the United States, and lesser portions by other "friendly powers."

There is, however, much emphasis in China on the need for such relations with foreign investors as would not jeopardize national plans or limit the powers of the National Government. It is proposed

26. The movement was started by Generalissimo and Mme. Chiang K'ai-shek in 1934.
27. For main provisions of these new treaties, see *Contemporary China*, February 8, 1943.
28. T. V. Soong, Minister of Foreign Affairs, told a closed session of the People's Political Council in October 1942, that China will need from $5 to $10 billion in foreign credits for postwar reconstruction. *The New York Times*, October 31, 1942.

to allow private investors to place their funds in state-controlled basic industries provided control remains in the hands of the government. There are also wide opportunities for private foreign capital in consumer goods industries. The returns to foreign investors, it is claimed, will be reasonable but secure.[29] It is assumed that, under postwar conditions, more use will be made of intergovernmental loans, especially for projects of reconstruction which normally involve public investment and enterprise.

## 7. Plans of Non-Government Groups

The government position finds support increasing among private groups formerly less in accord with it. The views formulated in the *Draft Outline of the Principles For China's Post-War Economic Reconstruction*, published by the Chinese Economic Reconstruction Society exemplify this.[30]

The Society is a private organization of influential bankers, manufacturers, university professors, research workers, and engineers, and has existed since April 1939. The *Outline* was completed only after a year of conferences and discussions, when common agreement on policy was reached. It thus is said to represent "probably the best informed opinion of the leaders" in Free China during wartime.

In terms almost identical with those of the Kuomintang resolution of 1938, the *Outline* lays down the principle that "economic reconstruction shall aim primarily at strengthening national defense and secondarily at raising the standard of living."[31]

The Economic Reconstruction Society looks towards the establishment of a more directed economy under which defense industries, embracing "heavy industries" as well as "principal railway, highway, shipping, tele-communication, and air transport facilities," shall

29. See Robert W. Barnett, *op. cit.*; also Lorwin, *International Economic Development*, pp. 52–55.

30. The *Outline* was compiled and published in the Chinese language by the Chinese Economic Reconstruction Society in October 1940. References to it were made in *Contemporary China*, January 25, 1942. It was first presented in more complete form in this country at the Institute of Pacific Relations, Eighth International Conference, held at Mont Tremblant, Quebec, in December 1942, and constitutes Part I [of *China Council Paper No. 2*. A translation of the Outline was made by Mr. K. Y. Lin, with an introduction and summary by H. D. Fong, Chinese economist, now at Harvard University.

31. The *Outline* covers both principles and explanatory notes on those principles. The condensed English translation is confined to the principles only, divided into ten sections as follows: General Principles, Communications, Water Conservancy, Agriculture, Mining, Manufacturing, Municipalities and Construction, Public Finance, Money and Banking, and Foreign Trade. The text here follows the introduction, in which Dr. Fong summarizes the underlying trends of thought presented in the *Outline*, particularly with regard to the objectives of reconstruction and the system of economy envisaged.

be developed as quickly as possible, as state enterprises. The Society further advocates that "for the execution of a planned economy a supreme national economic planning bureau shall be established." Such a bureau "shall be separated from the executive agencies of the government and shall be independent." State enterprises shall include heavy industries such as power and fuel, metallurgy, machine industry including armaments and shipbuilding, and basic chemicals.

The Society suggests that domestic capital for industrial development be obtained from voluntary savings and idle capital. It also favors a decrease in consumption, a gradual reduction of government expenditures for direct military purposes and loan services so as to make possible larger expenditures in building a defense economy. It recommends an increase in export surplus in order to meet the passive balance of payments after the war. It proposes that restrictions on foreign capital be relaxed in order to encourage its inflow into China.

## 8. Postwar Plans and Political Parties

The National Government of China assumes that it will be able to command the support of all groups of the people in the postwar period. The Kuomintang Party, on which the political strength of the government rests, expects to remain the dominant, if not the only, political organization.

Threats to this needed unity are three. In the first place, the Kuomintang is not entirely homogeneous and several groups contend for its control. Second, there are a few minor political groups outside the Kuomintang which may increase their influence at the end of the war. The third is the Communist Party of China which is admittedly the most serious potential factor for internal struggle.

From 1927, when the Kuomintang broke with the Communists, to 1935, the Chinese Communists were in control of the Chinese Soviet Republic in Kiangsi and adjoining areas. As a result of the Long March of 1934–1935 during which they marched some 6,000 miles north, they transferred their army, followers, schools and other belongings to Shensi and Shansi. They have been established in this frontier area since then and exercise control over the government and social-economic life of this part of China.

In 1937, the National Government and the Communists concluded a truce to carry on the common struggle against Japan. The National Government and the Kuomintang maintain that they are willing to recognize the Communist Party after the war and to co-operate with it, provided the Communists cease to form a state within the state and accept the status of a recognized opposition party. The Communists are not entirely convinced that their position would be safe if they disbanded their armed forces—the Eighth Route Army—and their political stronghold in the Northwest.

As far as economic and social programs are concerned, the differences between the Kuomintang and the Communist Party center chiefly around land and bank reform.[32] The Communist Party wants to expropriate the landlords at once, organize farming on a co-operative basis, and break the economic power of the "money-lenders" and "tax-gatherers." The Chinese Communists admit that communism, in its theoretical sense, is not applicable under Chinese conditions. They demand land reform and nationalization of basic industries and the banking system, with a fierce insistence that these reforms be carried out now. The National Government, in their opinion, is too much under the influence of the wealthy classes, and, therefore, too opportunistic and dilatory. Some of the Communist criticisms find a responsive chord among the "left" elements of the Kuomintang itself.

The situation in China in this respect, does not differ much from that in many other countries. But China is in a revolution, and the struggle of political groups is therefore carried on with particular vehemence.

32. For program of Chinese Communists see Anna Louise Strong, *China Fights for Feedom*, 1939, pp. 201–203; also Edgar Snow, *Red Star Over China*, London, 1937.

## Chapter 14

## POSTWAR PROBLEMS OF THE UNION OF SOVIET SOCIALIST REPUBLICS

On november 7, 1942, the Union of Soviet Socialist Republics marked, in the midst of war, the twenty-fifth anniversary of the revolution to which it owes its existence. In the course of these twenty-five years, the Soviet Union fought some minor and undeclared wars—with Poland, Japan and Finland. It went through several internal economic and political upheavals such as the famine of 1921–1922, the struggle for the collectivization of agriculture in 1930–1932, and the political "purges" of 1936–1937. It was finally engulfed in the Second World War which its leaders had regarded as inevitable but which they had tried to escape.

Under the pressure of internal and external difficulties, the Soviet Union often followed a zigzag course in its domestic and foreign policies. It veered from "war communism" to NEP,[1] experimented with various forms of industrial organization and tried to compromise with individual peasant farming. It co-operated for a time with foreign "capitalists" and investors and swung repeatedly from economic and political isolationism to internationalism and back again.

However, in the decade before 1939, the economic and social program of the Soviet Union became clearly defined. It centered around four ideas: (1) that the Soviet Union was building a socialist system and was preparing the ground for a "gradual transition to a communist society;"[2] (2) that it could achieve its social-economic aims only by the method of "socialist planning" and specifically through a series of Five-Year Plans; (3) that the Soviet Union could construct a socialist system within its own borders, without regard to the continuance of "capitalism" in other countries; and (4) that the Soviet Union had to develop its resources and economy as fully as possible so as to be able to defend itself by its own efforts against external

1. The New Economic Policy, or NEP, was introduced by Lenin in 1921 to meet the economic difficulties which Russia faced at the time. Under the NEP considerable scope was given to private industry and trade and to individual peasant farming, though the large industries and foreign trade remained under state ownership and control.

2. The socialists of Western Europe and of the United States regard the Soviet economic system as a form of "state capitalism."

attacks, but that in the interests of peace and economic growth it was desirable to support a system of "collective security" in co-operation with the democratic nations of the West.

In February 1941, the Communist Party of the USSR held its 18th All-Union Conference in Moscow, at which these ideas were re-affirmed. The Conference spent considerable time severely criticizing the defects of the Soviet economy and the shortcomings of Soviet planning. But the question was how to improve methods of planning and increase output during 1941–1942, the last year of the Third Five-Year Plan.[3] The new Central Committee of the Communist Party elected at the Conference directed the State Planning Commission to draw up a fifteen-year plan intended "to surpass the most advanced capitalist countries in per capita production of iron, steel, fuel, electric machines and consumer goods."[4]

Thus, four months before the Nazi invasion of Russia, the Communist Party and the Soviet government looked ahead to a program of internal development which, in their opinion, would take fifteen years.[5] There has since been no indication of any change in the outlook either of the Communist Party or of the Soviet government. Their social-economic aims and methods for the postwar period remain as outlined by the 18th Conference of the All-Union Communist Party held in Moscow, February 15–20, 1941.

The problem of postwar reconstruction in the Soviet Union, as in some other countries, is thus not one of determining new aims and methods. The social-economic course is mapped out in accordance with revolutionary developments since 1917. The problems are the capacity of the Soviet Union to rebuild itself after the war by its own means, the pace at which its industrial development may proceed, the degree to which the aid of other countries may be needed, and the methods by which such aid may be given.

Information from the Soviet Union to answer these questions is limited. However, since no break with the pre-1939 period is intended in Russia, the available data are adequate.

3. The First Five-Year Plan covered the period 1928–1932; the Second Five-Year Plan was for the period 1933–1937; the Third Five-Year Plan was prepared for the years 1938–1942.
4. *The New York Times*, February 22, 1941.
5. The Communist Party, is the only legal political party in Russia. It formulates policies and gives directives to the Soviet government. The party organization and the government apparatus are separate and distinct in their forms and functions. But the Party is the dominant force upon whose support the government depends and whose program it is supposed to put into practice.

## 1. PREWAR PLANS AND PROBLEMS

The aim of the Soviet Union is to build a socialist society and to "lay the foundation for" a transition to communism. It is the official doctrine of the Communist Party, proclaimed and vigorously maintained by Joseph Stalin, that the USSR "has all the necessary prerequisites for the realization of socialism," and can develop along socialist lines independently of other countries.

The industrial and economic plans of the Soviet government, especially since 1932, have been based on this doctrine. When the Second Five-Year Plan was projected for 1932–1937, its task was defined as follows: "to liquidate completely all exploiting classes, to destroy forever the causes which breed the exploitation of man by man and the division of Society into exploiters and the exploited, i.e. to liquidate private ownership of the means of production."[6] The aim of the Third Five-Year Plan adopted for 1938–1942 was to "complete the establishment of a classless Socialist Society" and to begin the gradual transition from socialism to communism.[7]

Soviet spokesmen claim that the objectives of the Second and Third Five-Year Plans were being fulfilled when the war broke out. On the eve of the present war, the Soviet Union had removed most traces of the private economy which had lingered on before 1932. All natural resources, factories, shops, mines, banks, transportation, stores had become part of a nationally organized state-owned and centrally planned economy. The individualistic system of peasant farming had been practically eliminated, and its place taken by collective farms based on national ownership of land and on co-operative methods of agricultural work. While private property remained in the form of personal belongings, home equipment, family-owned houses, individual savings, some individual peasant holdings and some private trading, there were no "classes" of factory owners, bankers, landlords, stock exchange brokers, or persons deriving their main income from private property. The population of the Soviet Union, estimated at about 175 million in 1937, was composed almost entirely of collective farmers, industrial workers, technical and professional workers, and state officials and employees.

The activities of this economic system were carried on in accordance with plans worked out in advance by the State Planning Commission

6. A. Yugow, *Russia's Economic Front For War and Peace*, Harper, New York, 1941, p. 11.

7. *Ibid.*, p. 12; also "Soviet Planning in War-Time," *Planning*, PEP (Political and Economic Planning), London, November 17, 1942.

(the Gosplan). The Commission laid down a Production Plan for each year of the five-year period, assigning output programs for all the main branches of industry and their products. The Plan determined how much labor, materials and plant equipment should be used to make consumer goods, how much to expand the capital goods industries, what industries should be developed in the different regions of the country, what was to be imported and exported. These decisions were made on the basis of plans and programs which were elaborated by the different individual plants, industries and industrial combinations throughout the country and which were submitted to the State Planning Commission for examination and co-ordination.[8]

The Production Plan was supplemented by a Financial Plan. Each plant or enterprise in the Soviet system was assigned a definite amount of funds for the year (in cash and in credit at the State Bank) with which to buy materials and equipment and pay for labor. The amount of money assigned to each plant or industry was supposed to cover the expenses of the physical goods allotted to the plant or industry by the Production Plan. The buying and selling between plants was thus carried on in terms of money. The prices of all goods, however, were not determined by supply and demand or by market operations. They were fixed by the State Planning Commission in such a way as to check the carrying out of the production plans and to balance all the transactions of industry.

The final prices of the goods produced by each plant were also fixed in advance by the Planning Commission. These prices were based on the costs of production ("planned costs"), including allowances for depreciation, a profit for the enterprise ("planned profit"), certain taxes to be paid, and a "turnover tax" which was the main source of the state budget.[9] The "planned profit" of each enterprise was divided into three parts: one part went to pay a profits tax, another part was reserved for capital expansion, and a third was left at the disposal of the enterprise.

In these financial operations, money was used largely as a means

8. The State Planning Commission (the Gosplan) is a large body of economists, statisticians and technical experts under the direction of a Board of eleven persons. The Board is responsible to the Council of the Peoples' Commissars (which is equivalent to a Cabinet of Ministers), and the President of the Board is a member of the Council. The Gosplan has four main departments which deal respectively with (1) the general economic plan, (2) capital construction, (3) finance, and (4) regional distribution of production. See Maurice Dobb, *Soviet Planning and Labour in Peace and War*, London, 1942, p. 27.

9. See below, pp. 284-285.

of accounting and of checking the execution of production plans. But in the daily life of the country, money played a more important role. It distributed the consumable income of the people. All persons at work were paid money wages or salaries with which they bought what they needed, paid rent, etc. Wages and salaries varied in accordance with skill, responsibility, and individual productivity. The inequalities of wages and earnings made for considerable differences in standards of living of individuals, families, and groups. Such inequalities, according to Soviet economic doctrine, are a feature of socialism which is based on the principle of rewarding each individual according to his work and productive merits.

That, in addition to the use of money, is the main feature which, according to the Bolsheviks, distinguishes socialism from communism. A communistic society would distribute the national output in accordance with the principle: "to each according to his needs, from each according to his capacity." Communism would be possible, according to Soviet theory, only in a highly developed economic society in which goods are produced in abundance with relatively little effort. Socialism, according to the same theory, is a transitory stage during which the people are trained to work efficiently, are habituated to discipline, and are educated in the co-operative spirit needed for communist living. The present socialist regime in Russia, according to this Soviet interpretation, will give way to communism gradually as the people are prepared for it, and as technical means are developed for more productive work and higher standards of living.

The key to the further development of socialism and to the realization of communism in Russia, according to Soviet spokesmen, is the technical progress of the country. The development of mechanical, chemical and electric power and of technical proficiency in industry, agriculture, transportation, is the sine qua non of the Soviet socialist system, of its capacity to make socialism acceptable to the Russian people, of defending the country against enemy attacks from without, and of preparing the ground for the future communist society.

The problems which arose on the eve of the war, were partly technical and partly social. They were concerned with the pace and character of the further industrialization of the country, the development of collectivized agriculture, the rebuilding of cities, changes in the methods and machinery of planning, and the means of raising the living standards of the people.

## a. EXTENT AND CHARACTER OF INDUSTRIALIZATION

The 18th Conference of the Communist Party set as the goal of the Soviet Union for the next fifteen years surpassing the "most advanced capitalist countries" in the per capita output of basic producer and consumer goods. Such a goal was justified by the Party on the basis of the experience of the three Five-Year Plans and on the assumption that the industrial progress of the Soviet Union could be continued at the high rates achieved between 1928 and 1940.

Allowing for the limitations of statistical data, it is no longer questioned, even by the most critical students of Soviet economics, that the Soviet Union made enormous strides between 1928 and 1940 in building up a large and powerful industry. Old industries were expanded and modernized, and many new industries such as electrical equipment, machinery, precision machine tools, automobiles, and chemicals were introduced and developed on a large scale. Thousands of large and well-equipped plants, mines and power plants were opened up in different parts of the country. During the period of the First Five-Year Plan (1928–1932), 1,500 new industrial establishments were put into operation with an aggregate fixed capital of 15.7 billion roubles. In the period of the Second Five-Year Plan (1932–1938), 2,100 new plants valued at about 60 billion roubles were begun. The Third Five-Year Plan (1938–1940), saw some 2,900 new establishments capitalized at over 90 billion roubles started. The total fixed capital of Soviet industry increased from 10.5 billion roubles in 1928 to over 75 billion roubles in 1937.[10] The number of workers in industry increased from some 12 million in 1929 to 26 million in 1937 and to over 30 million in 1940, or over 30 per cent of all gainfully employed.[11]

As a result of this growth, Russia has today "huge mines, plants and factories with the latest equipment. It has created its own machine and tool making industry, has developed or newly created the most important branches of industry. . . Industries which never existed before in Russia have sprung up and taken root, such as the production of steel alloys, electric machinery and apparatus, manufacture of motors, automobiles, machine tools, aniline dyes, artificial silk, heavy chemicals. . . Year by year Russia learned to make more

10. Soviet Russia is a country of large-scale production. Of the 574,000 industrial enterprises on January 1, 1936, over 61,000 were large-scale enterprises. In 1935, the large plants employing over 1,000 workers each employed 50.4 per cent of all the workers, used 68.8 per cent of all the horsepower, and accounted for 56.8 per cent of the total output.

11. Yugow, *op. cit.*, pp. 17–19, 20, 32, 160.

and more complex machinery and during the past few years her dependence on foreign importations has been greatly reduced. . . In the last few years, Russia has almost ceased to import non-ferrous metals, has greatly reduced the importation of rubber, having established the manufacture of synthetic rubber and greatly expanded the planting of rubber-bearing plants; and has completely stopped the importation of cotton, having greatly increased the planting of cotton within her own boundaries."[12]

The Soviet program of accelerated industrialization has laid special stress on the development of producers' goods and heavy industries. Between 1928 and 1940, the output of these industries increased fourteenfold, while the production of consumers' goods during the same period increased 4.3 times. In 1928, producers' goods formed 32.8 per cent of total industrial output, and consumers' goods 67.2 per cent. In 1940, the ratio was reversed: producers' goods formed 61 per cent of total output, and consumers' goods 39 per cent. The rate of growth of heavy industries in Russia during these years exceeded that of the United States, Germany, Great Britain, Japan and other countries even in the periods of their greatest industrial progress.[13]

The government carried out this program of industrial development by putting to use its large natural resources and labor supply, and by applying a larger share of the national income for purposes of long-term investment than had ever been attempted in any other country in times of peace. In 1932, long-term investments absorbed 26.9 per cent of the national income, and in 1937 about 26.5 per cent.[14] More than two thirds of this investment during 1933–1937 continued to be devoted to the capital goods industries.[15] The Soviet government was able to maintain such a high rate of investment owing to its complete control over resources, labor and capital accumulation, and to its planned direction of all the economic activities of the country.

12. *Ibid.*, pp. 33–34. A few figures on the output of some of the most important industries are illustrative of the progress made. Thus, between 1928 and 1940 the output of coal increased from 35.5 million tons to 164 million tons. The output of electric power from 5 billion kwh to 40 billion; the production of pig iron from 3.3 million to about 15 million tons; the output of steel from 4.3 million to 18.4 million tons; the manufacture of automobiles from 700 to 211,000 (in 1938); the output of copper from 35,500 tons in 1929 to 166,000 tons in 1940; the output of cotton textiles from 2.8 billion meters in 1928 to 3.5 billion meters in 1938; of footwear from 24.6 million pair in 1928 to 213 million pair in 1938. See Yugow, *op. cit.*, p. 16; also, *Statistical Year-Book of the League of Nations*, 1940–1941.

13. *Ibid.*, pp. 16–17.

14. In the United States investment during 1922–1932 averaged 9 per cent of the national income.

15. See Maurice Dobb, *Soviet Economy and the War*, London, 1942, p. 23. During 1929–1940, total investments in the reconditioning of plant and in new building was 152.6 billion roubles.

Soviet leaders take pride in pointing out that in less than fifteen years Russia became one of the leading industrial countries of the world. In 1939, it held fourth place in the output of coal, second in the production of iron ore, third in the production of pig iron and ferroalloys, third in the output of steel, second in copper smelting and it is among the largest producers of aluminum, electric power and machinery.[16] They are aware, however, that in proportion to its population, Russia is still far behind the leading industrial nations of the world in the output of both producers' and consumers' goods. In submitting the Third Five-Year Plan to the Communist Congress in 1939, Molotov said: "We are greatly behind in per capita production of electricity, pig iron, cement, steel, coal. . . The U.S.S.R. is greatly behind in per capita production even of such products as cotton and woolen fabrics, footwear, sugar, paper, soap, etc."[17] In 1937, the Soviet Union produced *per head of population* only 215 kwh of electric power as against 1,160 kwh in the United States; about 105 kilograms of steel against 397 in the United States; only 16 square meters of cotton cloth against 58 in the United States; and only one pair of footwear against 2.6 pair in the United States.[18]

This then is the road which the Soviet Union has to travel to "overtake and surpass" the United States. To attain the goal set by the Communist Conference in February 1941, it would have to increase its output of electric power about five times, of pig iron and steel over three times, of coal fivefold, of cotton cloth three and a half times, and of footwear two and a half times, assuming that the population of the USSR remains the same. But as the population was increasing at the rate of over a million a year in the decade before 1939, the task given the Soviet government by the Communist Conference of 1941 is of still greater magnitude.

### b. PRODUCTIVITY AND QUALITY OF OUTPUT

The industrial goals of the Soviet Union call for an increase in labor productivity and for an improvement in the quality of the output. The rapid pace of Russian industrialization has meant that large numbers of workers had to be recruited for the new factories from the

16. In 1937, the output of coal was 451 million tons in the United States, 244 million in the United Kingdom, 184 million in Germany and 122 million in the USSR in round figures; the output of steel in 1937 was 51 million metric tons in the United States, 19 million in Germany and 17 million in the USSR.   For these and other figures of output of principal commodities, see *Statistical Year-Book of the League of Nations*, 1940–1941, pp. 134–145.

17. Quoted by Yugow, *op. cit.*, p. 35.

18. *Ibid.*, p 36.

peasantry, from the ranks of unskilled laborers, and from among women[19] unfamiliar with machines and with industrial processes. Also, large numbers of young people had to be trained hurriedly as mechanics, foremen, engineers and superintendents. The price for this rapid tempo has been paid in the waste of materials, spoilage, poor work, inefficient plant management, and personnel difficulties.

Each Five-Year Plan has aimed at increasing production and quality of work. The Third Five-Year Plan called for an increase in labor productivity of 65 per cent. Such a large increase was to be achieved partly by further mechanization and better organization of work, and partly by stimulating the workers to greater individual and group efficiency. The incentives which Soviet industry offers the workers include various systems of piece rates and bonuses, special food rations, priorities in housing and clothing, "socialist competition" and "Stakhanovism."[20] The most important are piece work and the opportunities for larger earnings due to higher efficiency.[21]

### C. PROBLEMS OF THE COLLECTIVE FARMS

Despite industrialization, agriculture remains of basic importance in the Soviet Union. Over half of the gainfully occupied population is engaged in agricultural pursuits. Soviet agriculture supplies most of the food for the urban population and raw materials for Soviet industry.

As a result of the rapid and forcible collectivization of agriculture carried out during 1930–1933, private ownership of land and individualist peasant farming in the Soviet Union have been reduced to insignificance. There are still about 1.3 million individual peasant farmers in the Soviet Union, but their holdings and output are very small.

Of far greater importance are the state farms (*sovkhoz*) of which there were some 4,000 in 1939. These are large-scale farms owned and operated by the state with hired managers and workers. They are

19. The total number of women wage earners and salaried employees increased from 3,300,-000 in 1929 to about 9,350,000 in 1937. In November 1939, women formed 43.4 per cent of all manual workers in large-scale industries.

20. "The idea of socialist competition is that the more advanced workshops or plants should assist the more backward by friendly rivalry, example and actual help, to catch up so that a general advance is secured. Contracts are entered into by various units to reach certain targets of productive efficiency by restricting absenteeism, eliminating waste and raising technical standards." See "Soviet Planning in War-Time," *loc. cit.* Stakhanovism attempts to raise output by a more rational subdivision of labor and by setting standards based on the performance of the best workers.

21. It was estimated that in 1937 about three fourths of the work done in industry was on a piece work basis.

highly mechanized and well equipped with machinery, selected seeds and fertilizers, and special livestock breeds. The government has invested large sums of money in their equipment, in living quarters for the workers, and in educational and recreational facilities.

The state farms supply considerable amounts of grain, meat, lard, dairy products, wool, and vegetables to the government. They are the chief source of supply of raw materials for industry. They act also as agricultural experiment stations and as training centers for agricultural specialists. Nevertheless, they form but a small part of the agricultural industry of the country. Their total holdings are some 68 million hectares of which about 12.4 million are under cultivation. They gave employment to about 1.5 million persons in 1938. While their output and productivity have been increasing, they are far from being well-managed and profitable enterprises.[22]

The backbone of Soviet agriculture is the collective farms (*kolkhoz*) which determine the new social structure of the Soviet village. A kolkhoz is a sort of producers' co-operative association of peasants usually living in the same village. The collective farms vary in size (containing from a dozen to several hundred peasant families) and in the amount of land which they use and cultivate. The members of a farm own collectively the farm buildings, machines, working animals and all other forms of farm capital. They work the land in common, but share the results of their work in accordance with the amount and grade of work done individually. The unit of computation is the "working day" which is a norm of production based on the quality and character of work done, e.g., ploughing so many acres or threshing so many bushels of grain. A peasant may do two or three "working days" in a day on some work or may take two or three days to finish a "working day" as computed by the regulations. The affairs of a collective farm are managed by the general assembly of members and by an elected council and officials.[23]

In 1939, the millions of Soviet peasants were organized in some 242,000 collective farms. About 290 million acres of arable land and over 99 per cent of all land under cultivation were in these kolkhoz.

A peasant member of a collective farm is permitted to have a garden or allotment of between half an acre and two acres for his own use and

22. Yugow, *op. cit.*, pp. 57–62.
23. See Lewis L. Lorwin and A. Abramson, "The Present Phase of Economic and Social Development in the USSR," *International Labour Review*, January 1936, pp. 7–10; also Lazar Volin, "The New Agrarian Order in Nazi-Invaded Russia," *Foreign Agricultu e*, U. S. Department of Agriculture, April 1943.

private cultivation. He is also allowed to retain in his own possession and for his own use a certain number of dairy cattle, sheep and goats, pigs and fowl.

The net produce of a kolkhoz is determined after certain obligatory payments are made. In the first place, each kolkhoz has to pay a certain share of its crop to the local machine tractor station which does the ploughing and harvesting for the farm.[24] This share may be as high as 20 per cent of the crop. Secondly, the kolkhoz is under obligation to deliver each year to the government a specified quota of its produce at fixed prices. The quota is fixed by the government in advance on the basis of the area cultivated, estimated fertility of the soil and probable yields. The government prices are low, much below the level of prices in the market. The obligatory deliveries in kind at low prices are in the nature of a tax on the produce of the farms. Thirdly, the kolkhoz have to assign part of their crop to the Sowing Fund and to the Social Fund (for invalids and children's nurseries).

The remainder is the net produce which is distributed to members of the kolkhoz in proportion to their "working days." A kolkhoz may sell part of this net produce to various government buying agencies at higher prices than those fixed for obligatory deliveries, or to co-operatives or in the "free" market. It distributes its net produce among its members partly in kind and partly in cash.

The income of the individual peasant consists of earnings from his work on the collective farm and of what he obtains from selling the produce of his own garden and animals. A peasant may sell his surplus grain, milk or vegetables in the special "kolkhoz" market in the neighboring town or to co-operatives at free market prices.

From the point of view of the government, the system of collectivized farming has several advantages. It provides a fairly simple way of collecting the foodstuffs and raw materials needed by the urban population and by industry.[25] It gives the government control over agriculture through the machine tractor stations. It is said to make for greater stability of output and yield per acre and increases the capacity of agriculture to feed the Soviet population. Mechanization

24. A machine tractor station is a government agency which owns and operates plows, tractors, combines, threshers and other agricultural machinery. It hires out its machinery and employees to the kolkhoz for a fee. There were in the USSR, 6,480 machine tractor stations in 1939. They had about 484,000 tractors in 1941 with over 9 million horsepower and 125,000 combines in 1939. In 1938, they cultivated over 91 per cent of all the land in collective farms.

25. The kolkhoz supply 86 per cent of the market demand for grain, while the sovkhoz supply 12.5 per cent. Yugow, *op. cit.*, p. 53.

reduces the demand for agricultural workers, and thus increases the supply of labor for manufacturing industries. It enables the government to calculate more accurately the agricultural supplies on which the general economic plans of the country must be based. Last, but by far not least, it eliminates the individual peasant proprietor whom the Soviet government regards as a threat to its entire social and economic program.

The Soviet government faces problems regarding the kolkhoz because of conflict between government programs and the self-interest of the individual peasant. The collective farm offers the peasant only indirect incentives to bring more land under cultivation, to increase the number of his "working days" or to work more effectively. There is a tendency on the part of collectivized peasants to do the minimum number of "working days" required by statute (eighty a year) and to devote more time to their individual plots of land, whose produce they can sell freely and at higher prices, or to other paid work. The result is a slackening of agricultural progress both with regard to area under cultivation, efficiency of work, yield per acre (which is low in Russia) and quality of produce. Considerable friction arises within the collective farms with regard to methods of computing "working days," dividing the net output, use of funds, and methods of management. There is jealousy between the more prosperous and the poorer kolkhoz.

Spokesmen of the Soviet government affirm that the collectivization of agriculture, costly and painful as its introduction may have been, has fully justified itself. They point, as proof of this, to the increase in acreage under cultivation before 1939, to the larger total crops, to the rise in yields per acre, to the improvement in the livestock situation, and to the increase in the total income of the collective farms. In 1940 the government issued a decree changing the method of assessing obligatory deliveries according to the number of acres in each collective farm, and allowing additional payments for increased yields of agricultural and livestock produce. This was intended to give the kolkhoz a greater interest in increasing productivity and output. This step is cited as an illustration of the possibility of reconciling the interests of the government and of the peasants.[26]

The program of the Soviet government and of the Communist Party is to "consolidate" further the system of collective farming and to use

26. *Economic Conditions in the U.S.S.R. in 1940*, International Reference Service, U. S. Department of Commerce, May 1941.

it as an instrument of further agricultural development.[27] It plans to help the kolkhoz to become more mechanized and better equipped,[28] to use more fertilizers and better farming methods, and to make farm labor more remunerative. The growth and importance of agriculture depend in large measure on the success of the government program for greater industrialization, higher productivity and lower prices of manufactured goods.

### d. THE NATIONAL BUDGET AND LIVING STANDARDS

National defense and the improvement of standards of living are posited in the new Constitution of the USSR adopted in 1936 as the guiding purposes of the national economy.[29]

In contrast to other industrial countries, the Soviet Union is not concerned with "full employment." There has been no unemployment in the USSR since the adoption of the First Five-Year Plan. In fact, during the five years before the present war Soviet industry was faced with increasingly serious labor shortages. Soviet economists assume that there can be no unemployment in a Socialist economy since steadily rising standards of living will cause demand to outrun supply. In 1930, the Soviet government repealed the legislation providing for unemployment insurance. Instead of promising the "right to work," which has been a traditional socialist principle, the Soviet Constitution makes work the duty of every able-bodied citizen.[30]

Most students of Soviet economic and social life agree that a steady though slow improvement in the material conditions of living of the Soviet Union took place after 1933. There was an increase in the per capita consumption of bread, meat, milk, and other foodstuffs; a slight improvement in the consumption of manufactured goods, and in housing.[31] The greatest advance was made in the provision of educational, cultural and recreational facilities.

Despite these improvements, it is also an undeniable fact that living

27. *The U. S. S. R. Speaks for Itself*, London, 1941, pp. 7–12.

28. The government has invested considerable sums of money since 1932 in improving the capital equipment of the collective farms, in teaching the peasants methods of crop rotation, giving them better seeds, and in other improvements.

29. Article 11, Chapter I of the Constitution reads as follows: "The economic life of the U.S.S.R. is determined and directed by a state plan of national economy in the interests of increasing the public wealth, of steadily raising the material and cultural standard of the working people, and of strengthening the independence of the U.S.S.R. and its capacity for defense." For a translation of the Constitution, see Sidney and Beatrice Webb, *The Truth About Soviet Russia*, 1942, pp. 86–122.

30. Article 12, Chapter I of the Constitution of 1936 reads: "Work in the U.S.S.R. is a duty and a matter of honor for every able-bodied citizen, on the principle: He who does not work shall not eat."

31. See Yugow, *op. cit.*, pp. 198–219; also Lorwin and Abramson, *op. cit.*

standards in the Soviet Union are low compared with other countries of Europe and with America. This applies to industrial workers in the cities[32] as well as to peasants on collective farms.[33]

Further improvement in Soviet living standards depends in part on the wage policies of the government. Under the five-year plans, an annual wage-fund is set aside for each industry as a whole and for the individual enterprises in the industry. This wage-fund determines how much the industry and each plant will pay out in wages and salaries during the year. Within each plant and within the industry as a whole, the wage rates of particular groups of workers are fixed by collective agreements, and total earnings are determined by wage rates, bonuses, and overtime payments. An increase in the total wage fund and in wage rates would give the workers higher money incomes.[34]

Higher money wages, however, may result not in more real wages but in inflation. The living standards of the workers depend on the policies of the government which determine the relation of money incomes to the supply of consumers' goods. These policies, like the amount of the wage fund, are laid down in the annual and five-year plans which allocate the amounts of raw materials and labor for different industries and fix the total amount of goods each industry is to produce, and the prices at which the goods are to be sold. The budget in the USSR is of decisive importance, as it centralizes in the hands of the government the financial means whereby part of the net annual income is distributed among the people for their use while part is retained for capital accumulation.

32. "In 1938 the Soviet workman was not only more poorly fed than the French or German workman, but more poorly even than the Bulgarian. Compared with the Swedish workman, the Soviet worker, though he ate much more bread, had one-third the meat, two-fifths the fats, one-third the milk, one-tenth the sugar, and one-fifth the eggs, not to speak of vegetables, fruit, and so on. Naturally, the engineer who drew a salary 8 times as high ate much better. But . . . the less skilled workman, with wages half those of the skilled worker, was much more poorly nourished." Yugow, *op. cit.*, p. 212.

33. The Soviet village "has undoubtedly advanced toward greater material and cultural well-being, but it is only taking its first steps. Its standard of living is still rather low Its food, its housing, its supply of clothing are all better than they were before the Revolution, and growing year by year, but a comparison with conditions typical not only of American or Danish farmers, but even among the peasants of Latvia or Finland, would show how long a road they must still travel to reach a state of well-ordered, civilized life." Yugow, *op. cit.*, p. 218.

34. The wage fund was 32.7 billion roubles in 1932; 82.2 billion roubles in 1937, and 123.7 billion roubles in 1940. The average annual wage for the entire country was 1,427 roubles in 1932; 3,093 roubles in 1937; and 4,020 roubles in 1940. In the determination of the total wage fund, the government consults the trade unions which take part in the discussion of the five-year plans. The collective agreements fixing wage rates are made between the unions and the management, usually on an industry-wide basis. The majority of Soviet workers are organized in 160 industrial unions.

Reference to the operations of a prewar year, say 1938, may clarify the subject. In that year, total government receipts amounted to 127.5 billion roubles. Over 80 billion roubles, or over 63 per cent, was obtained from the turnover tax. This is an indirect tax which is levied on most articles produced by state industries through a "mark up" in the final prices of the taxable commodities. The government determines the prices of the commodities by computing the costs of production, then the profit of the producing or trading organization, then any excise taxes which may be due, and finally a "markup" which goes to the government treasury. This tax is fixed at a certain percentage of the total turnover of the operating firm, and is imposed only once, either on the producing or on the wholesale selling organization.[35] The tax ranges from 1 to 20 per cent of the turnover, and is paid by all operating firms whether they are working at a profit or at a loss.[36]

The other main receipt item of the national budget, namely the profits tax, yielded to the government in 1938 some 10.6 billion roubles, or 8.3 per cent of total receipts. The profits tax is collected by the government only from operating and selling organizations which are making a profit. The most profitable industries in the USSR have been railway transportation, municipal enterprises, and the "light industries" producing consumption goods, e.g., textiles.

The turnover and the profit taxes together produced about 72 per cent of the receipts of the national budget in 1938. The remainder was obtained from the social insurance tax, from direct and indirect taxes on individuals, and from public loans. The social insurance tax is paid by all industrial and trading firms in proportion to the number of their employees and wages paid; it provides the funds which the government uses to pay disability, old-age, maternity, and other benefits and for medical and other social services. In 1938, the social insurance tax amounted to 3.7 billion roubles or about 3 per cent of total receipts.

Receipts in 1938 from taxes on individuals were 5 billion roubles or 4 per cent of the total. The important direct taxes on individuals are the income tax which is paid largely by the urban population, and the agricultural tax which is paid either by the collective farm on its profits or by individual peasants.

35. Agricultural products of the peasants sold in the free market are not subject to the tax.
36. The Soviet turnover tax thus differs from sales taxes in the United States. It is imposed in advance on the final price of an article; it is not added to the retail price at the time of sale.

Public loans in 1938 produced 5.1 billion dollars or 4 per cent of total receipts. The Soviet government issues internal interest-bearing bonds in which the savings of the population are invested.[37]

The national budget expenditures in 1938 amounted to 124 billion roubles. Of this total, 51.7 billion roubles, or 41.7 per cent, was devoted to the national economy. The largest part of this item went for new machinery and other capital outlays.[38] Over 35 billion roubles were spent for cultural purposes, which include education, health, and the social services. Over 23 billion roubles, or 18.7 per cent went for national defense. Service on the public debt cost 2 billion roubles.

Analysis of these financial operations shows that the real purchasing power of the workers could be increased and standards of living improved in one of several ways. The government might decrease the rate of the turnover tax and thus reduce prices. It might appropriate a larger proportion of its budget for the development of the consumers' goods industries and thus increase the output of consumable goods. It could spend a smaller proportion of the budget on national defense and use the money for industrial and cultural purposes. As far as the peasants are concerned, it could pay them a higher price for obligatory deliveries of grain and sell them manufactured goods at lower prices.

Such government measures for the improvement of living conditions depend, in their turn, on other more basic factors. A lowering of turnover taxes and prices hinges on increased labor productivity and lower costs of production. A larger output of consumable goods implies a slowing up of the pace of industrialization. To some extent, it also depends on the capacity of the Soviet Union to sell its export goods at more favorable prices and to obtain foreign credit for economic development. A reduction in defense expenditures implies an international situation which would promise reasonable national security.

For a few years after 1933, the Soviet government took some steps to raise living standards through such budgetary policies. The total wage fund was increased and wage rates were raised. Efforts were made to stimulate labor productivity.Large sums were invested in training technical staffs for industry and agriculture. Special attempts

37. The total outstanding internal public debt of the Soviet government in 1941 was 46.9 billion roubles. See Yugow, *op. cit.*, p. 135. The Soviet government has practically no external public debt.

38. Of the 51.7 billion roubles, some 20 billion were spent for industry, over 11 billion roubles for agriculture, and 7 billion roubles for transportation and communications.

were made to expand the production of consumers' goods and to stimulate regional and local consumer goods industries.

However, all efforts to improve living conditions were subordinated, especially after 1937, to the program of industrialization and to national defense. In 1938, over 22 per cent of the national budget expenditures were for national defense as against less than 9 per cent in 1933. In 1940, national defense accounted for 32.4 per cent of total expenditures. Increased sums were also allotted to the heavy industries for armaments.

The economic system of the Soviet Union, it is clear, has not done away with inequalities in the distribution of income or in living standards. The emphasis in the USSR has been not so much on more equal distribution as on more goods for all. The road to plenty was declared to lie in greater individual output, better organization and management, a more balanced development of producers' and consumers' industries, lower taxes and lower prices.[39]

## 2. EFFECTS OF THE WAR

At its meeting in February 1941, the Communist Conference approved plans for the year 1942 which were to enlarge total production, increase the output of individual industries and improve living conditions.[40] The year 1942 was the last year of the Third Five-Year Plan and Soviet leaders hoped that the task mapped out would be largely fulfilled.

The Nazi invasion of Russia on June 22, 1941, not only shattered the 1942 plan, but destroyed a large part of what the Russians had built up with so much pain and at the cost of great privations since 1928. It is impossible at present to assess the destruction by the Germans in the occupied areas of Russia. It is certain that much more havoc will have been wrought in these areas before they are freed from the Nazi armies.

The costs of the war to the USSR will be great not only in terms of factories and buildings destroyed, of ruined towns and vil-

39. Thus, the paradox that the criteria of economic policy so dear to the disciples of the classical economists and to the protagonists of laissez faire should be particularly emphasized in the Soviet economy.

40. According to the plan for 1942, total gross production of industry was to amount to 180 billion roubles of which 112 billion were for investment goods and 68 for consumption goods; the output of coal was to be increased to 243 million tons; 2,340 locomotives were to be built; 4 900 million meters of cotton textiles were to be produced, etc.   See Dobb, *op. cit.*, p. 28.

lages, of depleted agricultural crops and loss of livestock. The loss of human life not only on the battle fronts but as a result of enemy action, forced evacuations and lack of food and shelter is enormous. At the end of the war, a large part of the gains of more than a decade of hard work will have been wiped out. In the European part of Russia, at least, the situation may be comparable to that of 1922–1923 when Russia, as a result of war and revolution, was at the lowest depths of economic exhaustion.

The accelerated economic growth of the Asiatic regions of the Soviet Union has compensated to some extent for the destruction in European Russia. The Soviet government, even before 1939, adopted the policy of developing the resources of these regions and of building up their industries on a decentralized basis. The Soviet Union was, in fact, developing a series of industrial regions which had a large degree of self-sufficiency in resources and which could be used as supply bases for the national economy in war or peace. These regions, including the Ural district, the Kuznetsk district in Western Siberia, the Kazakh Socialist Soviet Republic in Central Asia, and the Far East, have expanded their industrial activities and capacity[41] since 1939.

The war has caused a serious deterioration of Soviet living standards. The output of consumers' goods industries has been greatly reduced. Agricultural output, especially of foodstuffs, has suffered from labor shortages and lack of tractors and other machinery. As construction has been devoted to war needs, housing and municipal improvements have had to suffer. Hours of labor have been lengthened, shop discipline made more severe, and the social services less effective.

On the other hand, the Soviet government has made strenuous efforts to increase efficiency in the factories, to train new technical staff, and to enlist science in the development of resources. Boys and girls between the ages of fifteen and eighteen, have been forcibly drawn into industry and agriculture for short periods of training and work. Thousands of students in the technical schools and universities have been given accelerated courses and graduated so as to enter industry.

41. For details, see E. S. Bates, *Soviet Asia*, London, 1943; Raymond A. Davies and Andrew J. Steiger, *Soviet Asia*, New York, 1942; William Mandel, *The Soviet Far East*, International Secretariat of the Institute of Pacific Relations, New York, October 1942; also a series of articles by E. C. Ropes, "The Chief Industrial Areas of the U.S.S.R.," in *Foreign Commerce Weekly*, U. S. Department of Commerce, July 26, October 4, 1942, and "Commercial History and Review of 1942," *The Economist*, London, March 13, and May 8, 1943.

Many technical processes have been rationalized so as to make possible the employment of unskilled workers, women and young people.

The economic and social structure has not been affected by the war in any of its essential features. The changes which have taken place affect chiefly administrative procedures. War conditions and regional development have decentralized some of the processes of planning and economic management. The handicraft trades and producers' co-operatives have had a chance to become more important sources of supply. Collective farmers have been stimulated to increase output by some concessions with regard to prices and sales in the "free" (kolkhoz) market.[42]

In brief, the effects of the war have so far been not to change the institutions or methods of the Soviet Union, but to aggravate the difficulties of reconstruction after the war. But even assuming that the situation at the end of the war in some parts of Russia may be as bad as it was in 1921–1923, there will be this difference: the Soviet government and industrial leaders have technical facilities, economic mechanisms and administrative experience which they did not possess in 1921–1922.

### 3. METHODS OF POSTWAR RECONSTRUCTION

Restoration of the economic life of the Soviet Union at the end of the war will begin with a problem of demobilization and immediate relief. Millions of soldiers will return to the villages and cities and will need places in agriculture and industry. Industry, which has concentrated in such large measure on the making of armaments, will have to reconvert to produce civilian goods. Stocks of food for the people and of raw materials for industry will have to be replenished.

This problem, though complex, may be eased by several factors. Russian industries were established with a view to their militarization at some time or other. Their demilitarization may, for that reason, be somewhat easier. The industrial expansion of Asiatic Russia may help. The population which moved eastward during the war may be kept there, at least for some time,[43] and industries in the Asiatic regions may develop further with local resources and

42. "Soviet Planning in War-Time," *loc. cit.* Also, *The Economist*, July 3, 1943, p. 17.
43. A decree preventing the return of those evacuated to the eastern areas was promulgated in 1942.

labor. The Soviet government may obtain some relief also through compensation claims which it proposes to make on Germany as well as from rehabilitation programs of the United Nations.

Rebuilding the Soviet economy on a long-range basis, especially in European Russia involves more difficult tasks. The industries of the Ukraine, White Russia, the North Caucasus and parts of Russia proper will need repairs, new buildings, and other equipment and machinery. Cities and villages in the same areas will urgently demand housing, improvements and public utilities. The destroyed working capital in agriculture and livestock will have to be replaced. Large numbers of skilled workers and technical staff will be required to put factories, mines and transport into operation on the scale attained before 1941.

The Soviet social-economic structure has three methods for meeting these tasks. One is to repeat the industrial procedures and experience of the First and Second Five-Year Plans. That would mean trying to rebuild the destruction of the war by diverting as much labor and resources as possible to construction and to the capital goods industries. It would mean large compulsory collections of foodstuffs and materials from the collective farms, high taxation, and privations for the consumers. If the Soviet government should at the same time have to maintain a large military establishment, the economic strain would be far greater than it was after the last war and during 1928–1932. It could be relieved to some extent only if the output of consumers' and producers' goods in the Urals, Kazakhstan, and Siberia were large and rapid enough to supply a substantial surplus for the rest of the country.

The second method is a modification of the first. Russia might try to rebuild her economy with her own resources and yet with less strain on the people, by spreading the process over a longer period of time, and by reducing military expenditures to a minimum. This method presupposes that Soviet Russia would have adequate assurance of security against external danger.

The third method is to rebuild and develop the Soviet economy with the aid of the United Nations, particularly of the United States, Great Britain and Canada. The governments of Great Britain and Soviet Russia have approved this method in general terms. The Anglo-Soviet Agreement of June 11, 1942, in article 6, states that "the high contracting parties agree to render one another all possible economic assistance after the war."[44] While it has not been expressly accepted

44. For text of Agreement, see *Bulletin of the Commission to Study the Organization of Peace*, July 1942, Vol. II, No. 7, p. 7.

by the United States, this method is implied in the general principles
of Lend-Lease "to expand trade and employment by appropriate
international and domestic measures."

Financial and technical aid to the Soviet Union by Great Britain,
the United States and other nations raises many questions as to the
form of credit, the means of repayment, and the conditions on which
goods and services are to be exchanged. These questions affect largely
the lending countries or involve international arrangements which are
outside the scope of this study.

## Chapter 15

## POSTWAR PATTERNS AND PROBLEMS

THE POSTWAR PLANS of the members of the United Nations have many elements in common, but differ in some essential features. Their aims and purposes are similar. Their differences appear chiefly in the social-economic institutions through which the aims are to be realized.

Neither the similarities nor the differences of the plans can be classified systematically, nor can the countries themselves be arranged in any order based on their postwar plans. However, the survey reveals several patterns which are interwoven in different ways in the postwar proposals of the different countries.

### 1. THE PATTERN OF SOCIAL AIMS

Practically all the countries aim to improve the economic and social condition of the mass of the people. In the advanced industrial countries, especially in the United States, the British Commonwealth of Nations and western Europe, where the memories of 1929–1932 are still fresh, emphasis is on "full employment" and "social security." The USSR and the industrially less developed countries, e.g., Latin America, India and China stress the idea of "higher living standards" through more production and greater productivity. The concrete objectives, however, are alike—an increase in the material goods of life, better nutrition, housing, health and education, as a means for a larger spiritual and cultural life of all people. Most plans also imply that bettering the condition of the people will bring about a greater economic and social equality among all groups and classes.

To attain these social aims, most postwar proposals lean heavily on social insurance and expansion of the social services. The proposals cover all phases of life, "from the cradle to the grave," as the now famous phrase goes. Men, women and children are to be protected against all the hazards of work and life, to be assisted in getting an education or a vocation, to be helped in providing themselves with better nutrition, decent homes and good health, and to be assured of the means of maintaining themselves in old age. The "Beveridge plan" in England is the prototype of similar proposals in Canada, Australia and other countries. It is paralleled by the proposals of the

National Resources Planning Board in the United States and by the social legislation of New Zealand. Latin American countries are advancing along the same path. China and India accept the principle, though their concrete programs on the subject are limited and meager.

Current proposals are only in part a result of the desire for stability and security which became keen in most countries after 1929. In part, they reflect a growing demand for a basic "social minimum" as a "right" of the individual or family in return for productive and other services rendered to the community. The "social minimum" is thought of as a sort of "social floor" for the individual and the family and at the same time as a claim for a share in the total national income. In contrast to such economic or social reforms as the minimum wage or shorter hours of work, social insurance and particularly some of the social services call for free payments to particular groups of people from general public funds. They are meant to redistribute the national income in favor of the lower income groups just as "parity prices" and "tariff subsidies" presumably do in favor of farmers and manufacturers respectively.

Most plans make provision for "rebuilding" their respective countries, for creating a new and better physical environment for social life after the war. The Scott Report in England and the program of the Rural Reconstruction Movement in China, have the same aims, though the variations in methods are great in view of differences in economic structure. Cities and towns are to be more spacious, have more public utilities, easier and better transportation and larger facilities for neighborhood and community life.

A theme which runs through most plans is that of bettering the conditions of economic and social life in villages, especially for rural workers. The urban-rural gap in physical comforts and in social opportunities is to be greatly reduced. Agricultural workers and small farmers are to be included in the various systems of social insurance or of the social services, and the village is to be given facilities for a larger and more varied economic and social life.

There is strong emphasis in most plans also on the need for widening the access of the people to education and to a larger cultural life. In some countries, e.g., England, this emphasis is based on a feeling that differences in educational opportunities are responsible for existing economic and social inequalities and for the waste of human and intellectual resources. In Latin America, in India, and in some other countries, the question is one of doing away with illiteracy and of laying the elementary educational foundations of a modern community. In most countries, there is also the notion that education and recreation, like the social services, offer a growing field for the use of resources and labor and for employment directed not so much to the material needs as to the comforts and amenities of an advancing civilization.

## 2. PATTERNS OF ECONOMIC POLICY

Most postwar plans not only have similar social aims, but agree to a large extent on the economic policies which they propose. In general terms, postwar national plans in the different countries stress the need to develop national resources, to increase and to diversify agricultural production, to expand manufacturing industries, to enlarge the domestic market, and to find export markets for agricultural and manufactured goods.

The plans vary, however, with regard to the specific methods by which these policies are to be carried out, and especially with regard to the role of private and public enterprise in the postwar economy. The countries of the United Nations fall into three broad groups. The first group includes the United States, Great Britain, Canada, Australia, and some countries of western Europe. Most official and unofficial plans of these countries assume that private enterprise will remain the dominant form of economic activity. Their proposals are intended to strengthen private enterprise by imparting to it a larger social purpose and by extending to it governmental aid.

The second group includes some countries in central Europe, a number of Latin American countries and China. The plans of these countries assign a large and permanent place to state enterprise and to other forms of collective organization, e.g., industrial co-operatives, in the tasks of reconstruction and postwar development. These countries contemplate nationalization of many basic resources as well as a large part of the heavy industries. The tendency in these countries, some of which are in the early stages of industrialization, is towards an economic system which may be described either as "state capitalism" or a "mixed economy," depending on the degree to which government ownership and operation will be combined with other forms of public and semi-public enterprise.

The third group consists of the Union of Soviet Socialist Republics with its complete nationalization of economic life and centralized planning methods.

In the case of a number of countries, it is difficult to decide whether they belong in the first or second group. New Zealand might be cited as an illustration. But even in such countries as England, government and private plans indicate a tendency towards reorganizing some industries on the basis of national ownership or of "industrial self-government" under state control.

There is almost complete agreement in all plans on one point, namely, that the government assume the task of providing employment, if and when private enterprise fails to do so. For this purpose, all plans outline schemes of public works ranging from the usual road construction to the building of low-cost houses, schools, hospitals and recreational facilities. So far as they advocate such public works, all plans provide for a larger participation of the government in economic life after the war.

### 3. Group Interests and National Planning

In most of the United Nations there is a cleavage on essential policies between the postwar plans of different economic, social and political groups. In some countries, e.g., the United States and Great Britain, the differences center around such questions as social security and public works; in other countries, e.g., South Africa and New Zealand, the disagreements concern such problems as the degree of postwar industrialization and government control.

The war has stimulated in all countries the growth of the idea of economic and social planning. Employers' associations call for more "planning" in order to provide employment, develop market demand, and improve standards of living. In many of the countries, planning committees and agencies have been set up by private groups and by the governments. In all cases, it is proposed to maintain or develop these planning agencies after the war.

Private groups in most countries view the problems of "national planning" from the angle of their particular group interests. Some governments have made efforts to reconcile group differences in a common "national" program, but not always with satisfactory results.

The problem which faces most of the United Nations is how to concentrate the various economic and social groups around a national postwar program. The disagreements loom large when general social philosophies and long-range objectives are stressed. The area of disagreement is narrowed down where more immediate needs and specific policies for the postwar period are considered. In most countries, the various programs contain elements which form what may be called a "minimum program" on which there is "majority agreement." The question is whether such a "minimum program" offers a basis for a policy of "national concentration" which would make possible a smooth transition to peace and gradual readjustments after the war.

### 4. NATIONAL PLANS AND INTERNATIONAL POLICY

The postwar plans of the different members of the United Nations are being worked out independently, without regard to their mutual relations. This raises the question of their compatibility with the international commitments which have already been accepted by the United Nations under the Atlantic Charter, and the Lend-Lease Agreements or which may be made in the near future for international economic co-operation.

There is no doubt that most nations, especially the larger and stronger ones, can put into effect many of their postwar proposals without regard to what is done elsewhere. That applies to policies of social security, to changes in land distribution and ownership, to town and country planning, and in some measure even to public works. But most of the proposals for the development of national resources, industrialization, and economic expansion can not be realized in any one country to any considerable extent without affecting economic and social conditions in other countries.

From the point of view of international economic relations, the proposals of practically all countries of the United Nations to maintain their war-created industries and to develop new industries after the war are of particular importance. Most, if not all, plans state explicitly or imply that "full employment" and higher living standards depend, to a large extent, on the capacity of the respective countries to reserve as much of the home market as possible for domestic industries. At the same time, they stress the need of foreign markets. Added to this is the idea that a balance must be maintained between agriculture and industry even if that should mean an enlargement of the domestic output of some agricultural commodities, formerly obtained through imports.

Many specific measures proposed for postwar industrial expansion can not but aggravate the international issues raised. These measures include, on the national level, large public expenditures for public works, subsidized housing and government subsidies to industry, which affect fiscal and monetary policies. On the foreign policy level, the measures proposed in many countries include protective tariffs, exchange controls, export subsidies, import control, and government supervision or direction of foreign trade.

The question is whether these national policies and methods can be woven into a system of international economic co-operation, and, if so, how. Many plans assume that national policies must be devised first and that they may be reconciled afterwards with measures for international collaboration. In other words, international economic policy is to be adjusted to national plans, and not vice versa.

On the other hand, many members of the United Nations realize that the success of their national economic plans depends on the financial and technical aid of the industrially and financially stronger countries. The problem, as they see it, is to obtain such aid without having to give up their programs of national development.

The terms of the problem are affected in large measure by what may be called the postwar economic outlook. The sponsors of most plans are in the throes of an economic dualism. They see an opening ahead for a new upsurge of industrial energy and of economic growth. But this outlook is darkened by the lingering memories of the aftermath of the First World War and the great depression. Most postwar plans seek to resolve this dualism by recourse to more national control and self-direction. On the other hand, a few governments and some employers' groups, would release the future by reviving the past. They seek a way out of their dualism by proposing to remove both national and international controls in order to allow free play to individual and group interests.

Another way out of this economic dualism is suggested by some of the plans, e.g., those of Latin America. It is to make the fulfillment of the national aims and purposes of some countries the specific tasks of international organizations set up for the purpose. The program for the postwar development of China is based on such an assumption. If this method could be adopted, it would necessitate building up a new international framework which would adjust the aims and policies of different groups and nations.

The national plans of the United Nations point clearly to a postwar world in which social aims are to be the chief guide to economic policy. Those who have drawn up these plans evidently look forward to an industrial expansion which will derive its driving power from the conscious effort to give every man, woman and child a better place in the world. They place their hope of national fulfillment in the willingness of all groups within each nation to adjust their differences in a common program of "national concentration." They seek a surer method of national balanced development in the co-operative planning of public and private agencies. The chief limitations of current postwar plans are the conflicting elements in the proposals of the different countries and their lack of co-ordination with plans for international economic and social organization. The capacity of the United Nations to reconcile these conflicts in their domestic postwar plans will determine the degree of their success in building a better postwar world for all.

# INDEX